The Scandal of the State

Women, Law, and Citizenship in Postcolonial India

Rajeswari Sunder Rajan

DUKE UNIVERSITY PRESS   Durham and London 2003

© 2003 Duke University Press   All rights reserved
Printed in the United States of America on acid-free paper ∞
Typeset in Monotype Garamond by Keystone Typesetting, Inc.
Library of Congress Cataloging-in-Publication Data appear
on the last printed page of this book.

In memory of my father
P. B. Sreenivasan
(1924–1993)

Contents

III   Killing Women

Preface

The state has grown to be a particularly pressing concern for Indian feminism in recent years, especially following the Shahbano issue in the 1980s. This controversy over a legal case, in which a Muslim woman claimed maintenance under the Criminal Procedure Code and was opposed by proponents of Muslim personal law, definitively altered the Indian political scene as no previous post-Independence event had. It also presented Indian feminists with a dilemma about their own political choices: whether to support a uniform egalitarian civil code for women of all communities or throw their weight behind minority communities' identity crisis in a climate of increasing majoritarian resurgence.

While the state has always been an important locus for any feminism, as a significant site of the construction of gender and citizenship, it was the Shahbano case that brought it sharply into focus as an issue, theoretical as well as political, for the Indian women's movement. Three major developments in the years since then, all similarly related to policies of the state, have been similarly "critical" for feminism, as Maitreyi Krishnaraj describes it: the new economic program of liberalization and globalization, the uniform civil code debates (sparked off by Shahbano), and the proposal for women's reservation. Economic liberalization's "vociferous clamour for doing away with big government" has forced feminists and left-liberals into a position where they are now seen as "defenders of the state"—even though earlier they had been "harsh critics" of its "inadequate guarantees for minorities, the poor and women" (Krishnaraj 1998, 392). But though they may wish to retain the state as a bulwark against the market, they need to examine the past record of *this* state: "We have to pause to ask the question what kind of socialist, secular, democratic republic we had whose loss we bemoan" (391).

The Indian state's dismal failures in these respects are all too apparent in the poor indices of women's status, as reflected in sex ratios, literacy rates, employment and wages, infant mortality, life expectancy; in the widespread violence against women that goes unchecked; in discriminatory laws; in low representation in political bodies—the standards of all of which have systematically worsened over the past decades. But at the same time it is a state that constitutionally guarantees women's equality and that has even responded—sometimes inadvertently, sometimes as a result of pressures from outside (including those from women's groups), and sometimes with deliberate benign or progressive intent—in a "positive" way to women's issues, by which I mean by setting aside its own (putatively patriarchal) interests. The Indian state has sponsored reports, set up commissions, involved women's groups in the drafting of laws, participated in international forums, and subscribed to international norms of gender equality. This book goes to press in the suspenseful interregnum before the Women's Reservation Bill is passed in Parliament, a proposal that seeks to propel women into political visibility at one stroke. These are aspects of the inherently contradictory and uneven functioning of the postcolonial democratic state in response to the social and political considerations of gender that need to be taken into account for both a theory and a praxis of feminism.

If Indian feminism is deeply divided about the state today, it is a division that reflects a renewed and energetic rethinking of the women's movement's trajectory, politically as well as theoretically, rather than a disengagement from the state. The women's movement has not in any case been a monolith, at any time. There have always been a range of ideological positions, differences in organizational structures and agendas, and a variety of strategies for mobilization and action. Conflicts have admittedly become more distinctly visible in recent years, and the divide is indeed centered on the question of how women, and feminism, must relate to the state. This is a matter of historical shifts and changes in the Indian state as well, some of which have been identified above.

Feminists' rethinking of the state and the women's movement's attitude toward it and, concomitantly, toward questions of rights, equality, legal justice, minority/group rights, and civil society have been prompted by reflection on the perceived failure of the efforts of the past two decades of activism in the women's movement. There is the evidence of the nonimpact of a slew of new laws passed in the 1980s (Agnes 1997) and the continuing, even worsening, situation of women, especially under the regime of liberalization; the impact of communalism, visible in the growing phenomenon of women members' prominence in Hindutva organizations and in many women's insistence on maintaining their separate religious identities (significant to them but divisive for the movement); the urgent questions of caste and minority rights, which make an exclusive focus on gender untenable; the backlash, expressed as popular hostility to feminism's "Western" bias and in fundamentalist calls for "traditional Indian" womanhood in the wake of the Bharatiya Janata Party (BJP; also known as the Indian People's Party) government's coming to power; and co-optation, the price of succeeding too well.

It is in this climate of contention, even crisis, that this book has been produced. Each chapter is an examination of a specific issue or event of the recent past that reveals a facet of the constant and close transactions between women and the nation-state. In this sense the book is an examination of women, in India. The question it poses to both Indian women and nation is that of a "better state": meant not so much to offer an explicit agenda of reformism as to inquire whether the limits of such reform have been reached—by asking how women in India have engaged with the state in their lives, and by identifying the contradictions that gender issues consequently reveal in the state.

The "state" is not an abstraction. It has to be understood in both institutional and historical ways. The existential realities of our everyday lives—the "nation" as a space of habitation, our interpellation as citizens, law as that which "rules" us (a fact we come up against all the time) and that to which we take recourse some of the time, the transactions with state bureaucracy—are all produced within the context of the nation-state, which has also, therefore, become the inescapable problematic within which to locate our understanding of issues of gender.

Though I envisage this book as a departure in terms of its explicit focus on the state, my earlier work did presage some of the issues I grapple with more frontally here. The theoretical concern with representation in my book *Real and Imagined Women* (1993) framed the inquiry as cultural analysis. In talking predominantly about religion, media, popular culture, and literary texts as the forms of culture, I kept the state, as such, in the margins. But even with such a different emphasis, the discussions of the law, especially as it related to various forms of violence against women—law is never not a "cultural" fact—meant that the state was implicitly present in my thinking even then.

While the "political" therefore is rarely absent from feminist theorizing,[1] recognizing and naming the problem explicitly as the "state" in these essays has required my entry into the disciplinary and theoretical fields of legal studies and political theory—unfamiliar territory to me, hence risky but also exciting. If I have learned much in writing this book, I have also had to learn much in order to write it. What I have to say here about women in relation to the state, like all feminist theorizing, is the product of my grappling with issues "on the ground," applying and stretching the cognitive frames available for their understanding, and entering into dialogue with other feminists in the field.

One last point of clarification apropos the question of theory. It cannot have escaped observation that in this preface (and this is true of the rest of the book) my discussion oscillates between "this" (the postcolonial Indian) state and "the" state, reflecting the predicament of wishing simultaneously to hew closely to the context and history of contemporary India and to make claims for a larger generalization and offer a more "theoretical" argument about women and the state. While I have been confronted by this as a methodological predicament, its source lies equally in the disciplinary classification of studies of/from regions or nation-states in the non-West as "area studies." There is a case, nonetheless, to be made for recognizing postcolonial studies as not simply case studies of this kind but increasingly representative modes of a critical and theoretical understanding of democracy in the modern nation-state. Such an understanding has relevance beyond the immediate context of the region, but also, more crucially, it ought to unsettle the paradigmatic status of Western political theory. It is a case I advance in these writings about women, in India.

Acknowledgments

The major part of this book was written while I was Senior Fellow at the Center for Contemporary Studies, Nehru Memorial Museum and Library, Teen Murti, New Delhi. I am grateful for the award of the fellowship and all the institutional support that it made available to me, especially for the library facilities at Teen Murti. Dr. Ravinder Kumar, then director of the NMML, was unfailingly generous in his support of my travels and research. I remember him with affection and gratitude.

I had the support of a Visiting Fellowship at the Center for Women's Development Studies, New Delhi, during the last year of the writing of this book. I am particularly grateful for the cheerful and expert assistance of the librarians at the Center.

I have been helped by the example, encouragement, and active involvement in this project of three people without whom my life would have been impoverished in many ways, and not just intellectually. I take this opportunity to offer fervent thanks to Daniel Moshenberg, You-me Park, and Anupama Rao, especially for sustaining me through the "U. S. years." Kaushik Sunder Rajan joined this community in 1998, beginning to teach me as fast as he learned himself. All of them read endless drafts of each chapter and offered me the benefit of their scholarship (daunting enough individually, but formidable collectively!), their fierce and exhilarating criticism, and, not least in the difficult circumstances of living away from home, love and sustenance. Mary John's involvement began as referee of an early draft of the manuscript of this book and has remained constant and steady in the long period of the book's completion. Usha Ramanathan read the entire manuscript and guided me through the legal terrain. All have helped to make this book a better one than it would have been without their ideas, suggestions, and corrections.

Audiences at various forums where I presented chapters from this book over the years have been my most stimulating respondents. My students at the George Washington University who explored postcolonial theory with me—and never seemed to think that my work on India was irrelevant to their concerns—made my teaching years there worthwhile and memorable.

To the many friends who have been steady sources of support, inspiration, criticism, and affection over the years, this book is offered as a modest return for their friendship. It is a pleasure to name and thank here Homi Bhabha, Chungmoo Choi, Alison Donnell, Judith Plotz, Arvind Rajagopal, Sumathi Ramaswamy, Bruce Robbins, Gayatri Spivak, and Robert Young.

Ken Wissoker and Christine Habermaas at Duke University Press and Rukun Advani at Permanent Black have been the best of editors. The two anonymous readers of the manuscript offered encouragement and advice in inspirational ways. I was moved by their generosity to a colleague from afar and deeply honored by the standards they set for my work. To all of them, heartfelt thanks.

My larger family have given me support in ways large and small. Their love and faith sustain me, as always.

Finally, but most of all, my unbounded gratitude to my husband who, in his steadfast support and faith, has been the rock in my itinerant and turbulent life. He and our son Kaushik have lived long with this book in its making, with cheerful patience and understanding.

This book is dedicated to my father.

The following chapters have been previously published, though most of them have been substantially revised for inclusion in this book. Permission to include them in this volume is gratefully acknowledged.

Chapter 2, as "Ameena: Gender, Crisis, and National Identity," *Oxford Literary Review* (special issue "On India," ed. Ania Loomba and Suvir Kaul), 16, nos. 1–2 (1994): 147–76.

Chapter 4, as "The Prostitution Question(s): (Female) Agency, Sexuality, and Work," in *Feminist Terrains in Legal Domains: Interdisciplinary Essays on Women and Law in India,* ed. Ratna Kapur (originally published, New Delhi: Kali for Women, 1996), pp. 122–49.

Chapter 3, as "Beyond the Hysterectomies Scandal: the Family, the Institution, and the State," in *The Pre-Occupation of Postcolonial Studies,* ed. Fawzia Afzal-Khan and Kalpana Seshadri-Crooks (Durham: Duke University Press, 2000), pp. 200–233.

Chapter 5, as "Women Between Community and State: Some Implications of the Uniform Civil Code Debates in India," *Social Text* 65 (Winter 2000): 55–82.

1 Introduction:
Women, Citizenship, Law,
and the Indian State

The subject of this book is the relationship between women and the state in India. More accurately, the argument of the book *posits* such a relationship—in the belief that it is central to our understanding of both Indian women's identity and the Indian state's role and functioning. The issues that arise from this relationship, though fraught, have remained largely unresolved, chiefly because they have not yet been interrogated in any sustained way. In the essays that constitute this book I undertake, therefore, an exposition and exploration of the relationship as it operates in different contexts and under varied circumstances, focusing on events in the recent past, hoping to address the lacuna in this way.

Living *in* the nation today involves, also, living *with* the state. This is a matter of our being inescapably constituted as citizens—a fact which, in addition to the familiar duties and obligations of civic citizenship, entails everyday, existential negotiation with bureaucratic regulations, welfare institutions, and the functionaries of the state; and entails being regulated by and having recourse to the laws of the land. As a recent collection of essays on women and citizenship argues, it is necessary to move beyond an earlier "liberal and political science" understanding of the "formal relationship" between the individual and the state. Citizenship is instead "a more total relationship, inflected by identity, social positioning, cultural assumptions, institutional practices and a sense of belonging" (Yuval-Davis and Werbner 1999, 4).

But because citizenship has been for so long exclusively viewed as the domain of men (of property), women's identities and lives have been either excluded from or subsumed within a purview of state-citizen relations. Their concerns have been examined instead primarily in relation to cultural institutions in the realms of family and community. Not only does this overlook the impact on women of political institutions of law and citizenship, it also fails to acknowledge how closely these institutions are themselves regulated by state mechanisms. Thus, for instance, as Jacqueline Stevens has shown (in an important essay invoking an "anthropological theory" that goes beyond liberal social contract theories or Marxist theory), it is the state that defines marriage, by distinguishing between "sacred and profane forms of sexuality and reproduction" (Stevens 1997, 62).

Nation-state formation too is only now beginning to be considered in acknowledgment of the identitarian differences among its citizens rather than in a unitary way, but even this occurs within a frame of "multiculturalism," that is, in relation to ethnic, religious, racial, and other cultural minorities, rather than with reference to questions of gender. "Women's issues" have tended to remain a mere item on the developmental agendas of postcolonial nations. If women and the state are seen in relation to each other, a corrective to the partial views of each can be provided.

The gendering of citizenship draws attention to the way the state constructs "women"—primarily in their difference *from* men by formulating laws and policies specific to them, but also by differentiating *among* them: thus, women may be "different" in law and in policy according to their different religious identities, or in terms of categories of "good" and "bad" (housewives and prostitutes), normal and deviant (the "deviant" consisting of the destitute, insane, mentally retarded, or "criminal" populations), working and nonworking, child and adult. The construction of "women" in these ways—both as a unitary category and as a differentiated one—is primarily the work of the state in its governmental function. But equally, though within a different schema of political identity, the rights of "citizenship" propel women into an equal and "same" identity with men and with other women, which is necessarily contradictory in its effects.

Conversely, "women" have served to describe the state, primarily via the index of their status. The "status of women" has served as a crucial signifier in different contexts. For the colonial state, for instance, it indicated the degree of a colonized people's civilizational backwardness or progress. The British colonial government's (selective) measures to improve the condition of Indian women were therefore pressed into service to legitimize its rule, while at the same time these interventions, carefully planned in relation to different sections of indigenous patriarchy, left large parts of it untouched as the domain of the "private."[1] The question of "women" is also central to nationalism, especially to postcolonial nationalism at the inception of independent nationhood. For example, recent feminist researches on Partition reveal how fraught the problem of abducted Hindu and Muslim women became to the self-representation of the new Indian and Pakistani nations (Das 1995; Menon and Bhasin 1998).

The status of women index has moved to a different context and gained a different significance and meaning today. If in the early years the Indian state had deployed its role on behalf of women primarily to initiate "social reforms" in continuation of the colonial state's perceived mission of establishing civilizational modernity, or otherwise to rescue, reclaim, and rehabilitate them in the fervor of a nationalist identity politics, it is now called on to attend to the status of women as a matter of its accountability as a state, in the internationalist arena. The new international standards and indices of women's welfare and status sponsored by the United Nations and its agencies, which reflect each nation-state's priorities in the health, welfare, development, enforcement of legal rights, and protection of women and thereby indicate its unequivocal responsibilities in these areas, have become influential "universal" indicators of "human development" levels.[2] As early as 1975, the report of the Committee on the Status of Women in India (cswi) commissioned by the government of India— now regarded by widespread Indian feminist consensus as a landmark document—had exposed the independent Indian state's dismal record in these areas and spurred on the third wave of the women's movement to address these issues.[3] Together, these consensual standards and the demands of women's groups (including those set up by the state itself, like the National Commission for Women) have positioned women's status prominently on the state's agenda.[4] The demands on the state have shaped its responsiveness and thereby shaped its self-representation in noticeable ways.

The chapters in this book therefore set out to ask: How do women inhabit the nation-state? How do the names "citizen" and "woman" inflect each other? How does citizenship function as identity and existential reality for women, beyond the traditional questions of its privileges and obligations? How does the law function in relation to women, with the contradictions of its obligations to observe both equality and difference? How does the state identify or, more accurately, name "women's issues"? What kinds of commitments or pressures operate in determining its address to women as citizens, to women's issues, and to gender equality?

In the context of contemporary India in which these chapters are placed, the relationship between women and the state sheds light on both the issues of gender that the women's movement has brought to prominence and the crises of the state that these issues have provoked. Each of the chapters in this book, following this introductory chapter, is an examination of a specific issue or event of the past decade that exemplifies this double focus.

As a prelude to the discussion of these specific issues and topics, I offer in the first part of this chapter a discussion of the key terms "state," "women," "citizenship," and "law," and their interconnections. In the second part of the chapter, I describe and explore the transactions between women and the state, "transactions" being a particular way of designating but also of constructing this relationship.

Terms of Discourse: State, Women, Citizenship, and Law

The Indian State

It is useful to talk of the "state" as an institution possessing certain common attributes of sovereignty, constitutionality, and laws of governance. But since states are inevitably linked to and inhere in geographical territories, it is also necessary to identify them in terms of *nations* in our analyses.[5] Hence, the specificity of the Indian nation-state is a matter of its particular national history and of a "national" symbolic order or "culture."[6] The disjuncture between the two, between the modular forms of the nation-state, its constitutionality, its apparatuses of government, on the one hand, and the presumed differences of national history and culture, on the other, is often made the grounds of the inauthenticity (or the derivativeness, or the catachresis) of concepts like nationalism itself, democracy, secularism, equality, liberalism, and human rights in postcolonial nations coming "after" Europe.[7] The difficulties posed by this dispute for, among other things, justifying *women's* rights and equality as citizen-subjects are obvious and emerge most clearly in the conflicts around personal law. The idea of the nation is also the powerful legitimization of the state institution; and different ideologies of nationalism have determined the projects and trajectories of the postcolonial nation-state differently.[8] I explore the connections between gender and nation in this way in chapter 2, through the specific contours of the Ameena case in 1992, a moment caught between two fraught communal incidents in India, the controversy over the Shahbano case and the destruction of the Babri Masjid.

The Indian nation-state is a democratic republic, with a new constitution that "the people" gave themselves at the time of independence. It follows a parliamentary form of government, whose representatives are chosen through periodic national elections. The Indian nation is a federation of regional states formed on linguistic lines, with a strongly centrist government. Like most decolonized nations, its government has clear continuities with colonial government, above all a powerful central administrative bureaucracy, and an independent judiciary. Franchise is universal. In addition to these textbook characteristics, there are the other well-known aspects of the Indian state: as a "developing" nation (the most populous in the world, and among the poorest), it is motivated by strong developmental imperatives; it is multireligious and officially "secular" but has a powerful and politically influential Hindu majority; it is a nuclear power; its economy has been newly liberalized, overturning four decades of "planned" controls and socialism. Electoral democracy has had mixed effects: populism, majoritarianism, electoral expediency, interest groups and identity politics, and relative political stability, each of which also works to produce both harm and (dubious) benefit.

The state, clearly, is not a unitary or monolithic structure: it consists of different arms that do not necessarily work in tandem and are indeed intended to provide checks and balances (the Indian judiciary, for instance, has often taken progressive positions and acted to thwart excessive or undemocratic executive power). The ideologies of political leaders and regimes, the different styles and attributes of individual bureaucrats and officials, and the climate of the times are contingent factors influencing policy and praxis; and these are frequently marked by contradiction, cross-purposes, and confusion. Any understanding of state-citizen relations requires, therefore, attention to the microlevel workings of the state regimes, as much as to the terms of liberal democratic principles in the constitutional provisions; nor is the distance and disjuncture between the two always reducible to the (inevitable) gap between practice and promise. (My discussion of Phoolan Devi's surrender to the police, which is examined in chapter 7, is based on such an understanding of the state's meanings and workings in gendered terms.)

The traditional Marxist view of the state as an organ of ruling-class interests—primarily those of class and capital, but also extendable to patriarchal, racial, and other hegemonic interests—is in more recent political left theory usefully inflected with a Foucauldian understanding of "governmentality." Thus Philip Corrigan and Derek Sayer argue that the state is not only a *totalizing* project that unifies the "people" as a national community (as well as marks and excludes its "others," both within and outside national territories); it is also, following Foucault, an *individualizing* project that produces citizens in specific ways and in specific roles: "as citizens, voters, taxpayers, ratepayers, jurors, parents, consumers, homeowners—individuals" (1985, 4–5). This makes state formation a cultural as much as a political and economic process, "concerting wider forms of regulation and modes of social discipline through which capitalist relations of production and patriarchal relations of reproduction are organized" (ibid).

The state is therefore significantly defined in relation to "society," a relationship that in India is both oppositional to and continuous with it. The newly decolonized Indian state embarked on a journey of rapid modernization that included, apart from infrastructural material development, major social reform missions: literacy, the eradication of social "evils," the propagation of secularism and a "national" spirit to override regionalism and faction. Very soon, however, it began to invoke the diagnosis of "social evils" as an alibi: if the real impetus for change did not come from society, the axiom went, then the state's laws and policy measures could hope to have little impact.[9] Since a great many social reforms were related to the status of women, the state-society conceptual divide served as not only a convenient division of responsibility but also a cover to hide the patriarchal continuities and complicities between the two. I will be examining the state-society negotiations over the woman question in more detail in a later section of this chapter, and particularly in chapter 6, in relation to the phenomenon of female infanticide in Tamilnadu. In all such matters, "society" defined as recalcitrant, backward, poor, illiterate, and narrowly parochial is the burden of the state, a perception that further creates divisions within society itself, between the "masses" and a superior "elite" that is none of these.

The state-society opposition plays into a variety of corresponding oppositions in much recent anti-state rhetoric, so that the state is pitted against communities; government against people; modernity against tradition; science against religion; the abstract against the concrete; structure against process/history; Nehru against Gandhi; theory against practice; monolith against fragments. Any discussion of the Indian state today feeds into this "great divide" of political thought, as it has been called, between the "left-liberalists"[10] and the "anarcho-communitarians" (Bardhan 1997, 184–95). Their disagreement is not indeed over the record of the Indian state (of which the completion of fifty years of Independence in 1997 provoked a number of assessments)—which all are agreed on as being meager, disappointing, and failure-ridden—but on the constitutive nature of the state itself. The issues I discuss are located within the contours of this debate, offering a critique of the state that is also and at the same time grounded in the belief that the state in India continues to have a central directive role in social and economic issues and that, consequently, political struggle is most usefully directed at the state to make it accountable in these matters. This is a belief, as many in the women's movement will attest, compounded of faith, political principle, pragmatism, and, sometimes, despair over the lack of viable alternatives.

My understanding of the state, though broadly left-liberal in the context of this polarization of positions in Indian political discourse, draws considerably on radical feminist critiques of the state; I will shortly engage with these at greater length. As I have indicated, it is also based on a broadly poststructuralist understanding of its workings. Such an eclectic mix of positions, while perhaps theoretically inconsistent, is nonetheless necessitated and I hope legitimated by the contingent nature of the issues of gender that constitute my material.

My left-liberal leanings toward a reformist position on the question of the Indian state (reflected in an alternative title to this collection that I had envisaged, "Of Women/In India: Towards a Better State?") require perhaps some further justification. I draw support for them from my understanding of feminism itself as a reformist, as opposed to revolutionary, movement.[11] There is no equivalent in "sisterhood" to "Workers of the world, unite!" Radical feminist theory has undeniably powerful intellectual energies and imaginative reach—consider the work of Catharine MacKinnon, Donna Haraway, Judith Butler—but the alternative social arrangements that these writers envisage do not include a takeover of political power structures (except playfully, in fantasies like Rokeya Shekawat Hossain's fable "Sultana's Dream"). Liberal feminist demands for equality, justice, inclusion, and nondiscrimination are met by means of negotiations with and through existing institutions of rule. This form of politics has been sharply criticized and its limits have been astutely marked by radical feminists, but without, as far as I can see, any implications for the existence itself of the institutions of nation-state, law, and citizenship, beyond their reform. In what follows I review some recent influential feminist political theories, originating in and relating for the most part to the Western liberal democracies, as a way of charting something of the range of views reflecting the divisions on the question of the state.

"Feminism has no theory of the state," Catharine MacKinnon famously declared in 1983, as a prelude to her critique of feminism's abject confinement to either liberal or Marxist views of the state, both of which serve women ill: "Liberal strategies entrust women to the state. Left theory abandons us to the rapists and batterers" (643).[12] MacKinnon insists on the need for feminism's autonomous inquiry into "what is the state, from women's point of view?" Her answer, in brief, is that the state is "masculine," and the burden of her essay is the demonstration of the male interests that underpin the ways in which the state constitutes the social order and its laws perceive women.

As feminist political theory, MacKinnon's diagnosis of the state as patriarchal and sexist is monolithic and, finally, monotonous. (Equally, her construction of women solely as sexualized subjects, and of female sexuality solely as the site of male violence and victimization, turns out to be partial and inadequate.) Nevertheless, MacKinnon's radical feminism—feminism "unmodified" in her formulation—has been pioneering and vastly influential for U.S. feminism, especially in the area of law reform relating to women's sexuality, on issues such as rape, pornography, wife-battering, incest.[13] Other feminist theoretical attempts to go beyond liberal and left positions on the state to arrive at an "unmodified" radical position of their own have also been richly productive, particularly in the work of Carole Pateman, also beginning in the early 1980s. Pateman's critique of the social contract, so vital a fiction in the Lockean philosophy of liberalism, is built on the assertion that "the original contract is a sexual-social pact, but the story of the sexual contract has been repressed" (1988, 1). This sexual contract is both "patriarchal—that is, it establishes men's political right over women," as well as "sexual—in the sense of establishing orderly access by men to women's bodies" (2). Pateman in her turn creates a powerful fiction of patriarchy as no longer paternal rule but a "fraternal" social contract. In the same way that MacKinnon's theory of the state leads to a focus on the sexism of rape and pornography laws, Pateman's critique of contract theory leads to an interrogation of the institution and conceptual basis of prostitution in law and society.

The most radical recent critique of the masculinist state is to be found in Wendy Brown's book *States of Injury* (1995). Brown identifies four modalities of contemporary U.S. state power: the *juridical-legislative* or *liberal* dimension of state power, which refers to its "formal, constitutional aspects," including law; the *capitalist* dimension of the state, its "provision of capitalism's moorings in private property rights as well as active involvement in capitalist production, distribution, consumption and legitimation"; the *prerogative* dimension of state power, its "legitimate arbitrary power in policy making and legitimate monopolies of internal and external violence in the police and military"; and the *bureaucratic* dimension, one of the "voices" of "the organizational structure of state processes and activities" (1995, 175–77). In this description Brown is drawing widely on familiar Marxist, radical feminist, Weberian, and Foucauldian ideas of the state's functions. But she takes radical feminist political theory to its contemporary aporia in a "post-political" United States by questioning the implications for feminist politics of negotiating with a state viewed as so constitutively masculinist, thus going beyond and interrogating MacKinnon's struggles for law reform. She expresses concern over the "potential dilution of emancipatory political aims" in feminism's turn to the state to adjudicate or redress practices of male domination, as part of a larger theoretical/political argument about the futility of an identity politics grounded in *ressentiment,* the cruel hoax of rights for the disempowered, and the compromised politics of redressal from state institutions that are "repressive, regulatory, and depoliticizing" (ix), which, she argues (following Foucault), actually *produce* their subjects as powerless victims.

In contrast to Brown's position, Jacqueline Stevens's work, also focusing on the United States (because, in Marx's words, it is the most "completely developed political state"), insists on the state's fundamental and constitutive role in defining American society via its influence on marriage, and hence on family, racial identity, gender relations, and citizenship (1997, 62–83).

Susan Franzway, R. W. Connell, and Diane Court have extended the inquiry into the "patriarchal" state by insisting on two developments in state theory influenced by poststructuralist insights as well as the specific case of the Australian state: the state as not merely a set of rules or institutions but a social *process;* and the state as not just an instrument of dominant interests but a social force that initiates *change.* This allows them to offer a more dialectical version of state-society dynamics and of the state's contradictory imperatives. Their idea of the "patriarchal" state remains a radically feminist one: they insist that the state's relationship to gender is *more* intimate and fundamental than to class since, whereas it only supports class relations, it actually *constitutes* gender relations (Franzway et al. 1989, 6–7).

In Britain in the early 1980s, feminists interrogated the state from a Marxist-feminist standpoint, seeking to extend and modify Marxist theory by identifying the class *as well as* gendered interests of the state. As Mary McIntosh (1978) argued in "The State and the Oppression of Women," the state did this in the interests of capital, in two ways: by sustaining the patriarchal family and its arrangements, especially the sexual division of labor; and by using women to regulate capitalism's supply of wage-labor. To this end the state pushes a variety of measures, from control of fertility to wages, taxes, and welfare that regulate women's activities. Understood thus, the state was the enemy, and feminist politics in relation to it could only be oppositional.[14]

But since then, and largely as a result of Thatcherite politics of the 1980s, liberalism has begun to resemble a progressive politics in Britain, not least for feminism. The most reasoned expression of faith in the liberal democratic state's potential to deliver women's equality is to be found in the work of Anne Phillips. Her proposal rests on the argument that the opposition of the neoliberals and neoconservatives to its politics is itself an indication that liberal democracy has moved far from its founding moments (1993, 105). She points to the advances it has made in three areas (chiefly in the Western democracies): "Partly under the impact of labour and social democratic parties, liberal democracies have extended the legitimate scope of government interference to include extensive regulation of the workings of the market. And partly under the impact of feminism, they have entered more decisively into the regulation of sexual violence. . . . Meanwhile the work of Scandinavian feminists suggests the scope for a new 'social citizenship' that builds care work into the responsibilities of the state" (109). Phillips stands staunch against the radical critique that liberalism is constitutively, that is, "in its very logic," inegalitarian. According to her, "this case is not yet established, and remains an important, but open, question" (ibid.).

Rosemary Pringle and Sophie Watson (1992) in an important recent essay, " 'Women's Interests' and the Post-Structuralist State," trace the shift from the early "against the state" agenda of British feminism to contemporary engagements with it, particularly in local politics. Their task is to retain the state as a focus of feminist strategies while reconceptualizing it in poststructuralist Foucauldian ways as a "bureaucratic/legal/coercive order" (53) that is complex, nonunitary, and incoherent (63). This view of the state corresponds to the antiessentialist critique of "women" that enables a recognition of differences and different priorities among women.

A collection of essays edited by Shirin Rai and Geraldine Lievesley, *Women and the State: International Perspectives,* similarly takes as its starting point the premise that the state is "an uneven terrain with dangers as well as resources for women's movements" (1996, i). Rai's essay,

"Women and the State in the Third World," also seeks to introduce postcolonial issues to a Western feminist state theory that has hitherto overlooked them. Nira Yuval-Davis and Prina Werbner's recent collection (1999) is also written from a similar location, that of Britain and the "new discourse of citizenship" that its contemporary politics have generated: multiculturalism, race politics, immigration issues, the European Union. Feminist studies of Islamic nations in West Asia have been at the forefront of analysis of gender in the context of the politics of religion, anti-imperialism, and modernization programs in this region (Mernissi 1991; Anthias and Yuval-Davis 1989; Kandiyoti 1991; Badran 1994; Hale 1997); and feminists writing about other regions in East and Southeast Asia, under repressive military regimes spurred by rapidly transformative economic "miracles," provide a different perspective on the state and women (Heng 1997; Kim and Choi 1998). I draw on these, and on the contributions of other South Asian feminists, wherever their insights are applicable to gender issues in India, as they clearly are in the debates over issues like tradition and modernity, religious laws, nationalism, development, population control, and women's work.

If I have privileged feminist theory of the state emerging from and relating to the West, that is because it both offers a more substantial and developed body of work and has somewhat closer relevance for understanding the liberal democratic political structure of the Indian state. The positions outlined here, and in the discussion that follows, both reflect and actively inform the emerging political differences among feminist theorists and activists in India—pointing to not just the disseminatory powers of Western feminist theory but also, I wish to suggest, its uses.

"Women"

Many feminists writing about the state assume that "the state" is the category to be interrogated, while the terms "gender" and "women" are relatively stable. But how correct or even useful is it to talk of "women" in relation to the state (or to anything else) when the identity "women" is itself riddled with difficulties at all levels, conceptual, empirical, and political? Different kinds of problems of definition are immediately apparent. There is the problem of women defined in binary opposition to men, a definition phrased in terms either of lack, the negative (not-man), or of an essentialized alterity. These definitions feminists have refused, both because they overlook the social construction of gender identities and because they are built on a fixed and unchanging oppositionality between "women" and "men." The identity "woman" has also been problematized by lines of thought from poststructuralist theories that have set out to destabilize the unitary and fixed "man" at the center of Western metaphysics and history, viewing him instead as an ensemble of subject-effects produced by language and its discursive effects. But women and minorities are suspicious of this theoretical move, produced when subjecthood is now being claimed by those categories of human beings previously denied it. How can a subjectivity thus decentered ground the agency of an oppositional praxis? In response to these difficulties, some kind of essentialism must be strategically invoked to ground a feminist politics, as we will see, but one that at the same time remains alert to differences among women.[15]

For "women" has been a problematic category also because of the differences *among* women. Gender is recognized as being not a sole defining quality but one that exists along with other constituents of identity that intersect with it, such as class, race, sexuality, age, nationalism, and ethnicity, which constitute women as social beings, equally with men. This has been a major problem confronted by a women's movement that initially sought to stress the commonality of (women's female) sex over other differences, but only at the cost of homogenizing and essentializing the category of women and also implicitly norming some women (middle-class, heterosexual, white, Hindu, brahmin, as the case may be) and excluding others (working-class, homosexual, black, minority communities, lower-caste). In a recent article, Meena Dhanda has usefully discussed the problem of the identity "women" (in the context of political quotas), which seeks to explain how "women" may be seen to possess a "group identity" without our necessarily essentializing the category "women." She distinguishes between, on the one hand, the "serial collectivity" of women, where they are defined by "their respective *passive* situation in a world constructed as heterosexual and defined by a sexual division of labour," but without any "self-consciousness" about a shared project; and, on the other hand, a "group" identity that, in contrast, is achieved by "sharing some project or other aimed at removing such constraints on their activity" (2000, 2972–73).

Empirically, where are "women" to be found? For the most part "women are not congregated in localized constituencies but are dispersed in households separated by class, ethnic, or religious distinctions" (Jeffery 1999, 237). Actual collectivities of women may be discovered, no doubt, in some historical and social contexts such as the household (zenanas and harems), religious institutions (nunneries), communes, brothels, and similar environments. Elsewhere I have discussed the political efficacy of all-women panchayats in Maharashtra (Sunder Rajan 1993, chap. 5). I will argue in chapter 5 that women's coming together in workplaces or work-based struggles may be similarly regarded as constituting a significant political grouping within civil society as it is presently constituted in India. But beyond such contingent situations, it is not clear whether women have associational tendencies with other women in any social setting, belonging instead more "naturally" to mixed-gender (and hierarchical) families and communities, an important fact (though not the only one) that makes any kind of separating out and mobilization of women acutely difficult (in contrast to, say, male workers' association).

The move that is discernible in recent feminist thinking in response to the predicaments posed by invoking "women" is to make analytically clear the distinction between the different ways we use the term: women as an empirical group (sexed individuals constituting half the human population), women as an identifiable interest group, and "women" as a category. Questions of representation become acute in the first, while questions of equality and democratic politics predominate in the second (with inevitable overlaps between the two). Women's struggle for parity, for example, as Etienne Balibar explains, is not an attempt to "win particular rights for a 'community,' which would be a 'community of women.'" For "from an emancipatory standpoint, *gender is not a community*"[16] (1995, 67; emphasis in original). (Balibar points out that "the only gender which is a community is the masculine, inasmuch as males establish institutions and develop practices to protect old privileges.") He echoes, uncannily, a point made in the CSWI report in 1975: "Women are not a community, they are a category" (Government of India, CSWI report 1975, 304).[17]

It is this understanding that informs the French feminist movement for parity, as Joan Scott explains. *Paritaires,* she says, "are not seeking to represent women as a distinct social category; they are not claiming that women's fundamental differences from men require separate representation; they are not denying the notion that the individual must be the basic unit of political representation. Rather, they insist that the abstract individual must be conceived as having two sexes" (1997, 11).

An understanding of the state and of women that is aided by poststructuralism has potential for contemporary feminist political struggles that are necessarily more heterogeneous and contradictory than the single-issue agendas of earlier phases of the movement; for example, the agenda in the work of Chantal Mouffe promotes an anti-essentialist critique and an "articulatory" politics of radical democracy (1993, chap. 5). "Women," then, are not defined solely by sexual difference, as in MacKinnon's and Pateman's arguments; on the contrary, Mouffe suggests, "in the domain of politics, and as far as citizenship is concerned, sexual difference should not be a valid distinction" (82). A radical democratic politics requires the replacement of communitarianism (a group defined by a single identity) by pluralism (the individual defined by multiple identities) as the subject of politics, and an articulatory principle that would entail the "construction of multiple points of unity and common action" (87). Feminist politics would then cease to be a form of separate interest-group demands; "the pursuit of feminist goals and aims" would instead take place within "the context of a wider articulation of demands" (87). In not viewing "women" as primarily a group/class/community with a common interest to pursue, Mouffe sidesteps the questions of identity, differences, and representation that so bedevil feminist thinking and practice as well as the social structures they inhabit.

We recognize, however, that we do need to retain "women" as political subjects in feminism for some projects, even while deconstructing the category "woman" or refusing the idea of "women's interests." Teresa de Lauretis quotes Kristeva as saying,

> Believing oneself "a woman" is as obscurantist as believing oneself "a man." I say almost because there are still things to be got for women: freedom of abortion and contraception, childcare facilities, recognition of work etc. Therefore "we are women" should still be kept as a slogan, for demands and publicity. (1984, 95).

Two things are operative here beyond theoretical contradiction and political doublespeak: one, the identification of a historical common oppression, or more correctly an oppression both inflicted on women and experienced by them *as women;* and two, the politicization of this oppression as it becomes the grounds of solidarity and collective struggle in that name. The ascribed identity "women" may be (selectively) both embraced and repudiated by female subjects in waging their struggle against patriarchy.

Indian feminism contends with the problem of naming "women" as political subjects at various levels and in different contexts. The problem of religious and community differences among women is, for instance, at the center of the conflict over introducing a uniform civil code in India. The existing personal law system gives primary recognition to the religious community identity of the Indian people, even at the cost of supporting differential laws and discrimination against women; but neither is the politics of minority identity something to be easily dismissed in the present Indian context. Differences among Indian feminists themselves about the recognition and weight to be given to women's community identities, in addition of course to other significant considerations, makes this proposed reform a fraught issue. Similarly, in the opposition to the pending bill to secure quotas for women's representation in Parliament, the problem of "women" as a unitary category looms large. The demand by backward caste parties that dalit and Other Backward Castes (OBC) women be given a quota within the quota is a response to the heterogeneity of, and the feared privileging of upper-caste women within, that category.

Like much feminist rationalization of the term and concept "women," mine too acknowledges a foundational contradiction and is a matter of negotiation at every point of its use. Joan Scott (1996) has described the contradiction as the inescapable "paradox" of a feminism that demands formal equality for women while emphasizing their difference precisely as the grounds for substantializing the equality, speaking in the name of "women." The negotiation lies in shifting between a strategically singular and a "multiple" concept of female identity in different contexts. It is in these circumscribed but nonetheless unequivocal senses that I speak of "women" in relation to the "state" in this book.

Citizenship

Citizenship is a status conferred on the people of a nation-state, which, within a parliamentary democratic framework, establishes a relationship of equality among them in legal and political terms by constitutional fiat and allows them to participate in government. Its most visible political manifestation is the universal right to vote. How significant is citizenship as an identity and as a right in this sense? The question is a fraught and contested one in feminist and other political debates. Though suffrage and other forms of political representation and participation were relatively easily won for women in India in the course of the struggle for freedom, the acceptance of women's equality in actual political and socioeconomic structures comes up against resistance and opposition in powerfully entrenched patriarchal structures; hence the continuing valence of the concept and the struggles around it in various spheres.

The belief that the one-person-one-vote democratic norm implies both universal equality and (equal) participation in government is a cherished myth of citizenship but one that is contested by the disillusioned view that elections are at best an empty ritual and the vote an impoverished expression of the power of citizenship rights. Nevertheless, in a polity that is as highly nonegalitarian and hierarchical as that of India, equality of citizenship must be viewed as a major prerogative, compensating for and contesting social inequality by granting political power to individuals belonging to the various religious, regional, and linguistic minorities, to backward castes and dalits, and to women—equally with majoritarian upper-caste men, traditionally the ruling class. Electoral constituencies in India are significantly made up of precisely such groups from the disadvantaged sections of the population who constitute "vote-banks." By voting *en bloc,* they have been able to influence political outcomes.

This would still leave the question of women hanging, however: what if any is the specificity of women as a constituency? Can any electorate be viewed as made up significantly of women? How useful and progressive is political parties' appeal to the "women's vote"? Patricia Jeffery, for instance, writes, "In such politics of expediency, a consistently prowoman orientation is unlikely, unless governments become convinced that enhancing women's interests is a vote winner" (1999, 233). When such perceptions do take hold, governments have in the past addressed matters like prices, the provision of water and fuel, primary education, or prohibition as "women's issues," with more or less sincerity and success.

Other questions around citizenship have to do with its practice: with what these rights imply, their limits, dangers, and possibilities, and with the ways they are (or not) translated into an actual exercise of powers and privileges for women and other disadvantaged groups. I identify some of these issues in what follows.

There is, first of all, the problem of the *insufficiency* of the political rights granted by citizenship to achieve women's full equality and autonomy, a realization that French women, for example, woke up to very soon after they won the right to vote in 1946. Simone de Beauvoir expressed their disillusionment: " . . . abstract rights . . . have never sufficed to assure to woman a definite hold on the world; true equality between the two sexes does not exist even today" (1950, 150; cited in Scott 1996, 170). Joan Scott discusses de Beauvoir's disappointment that

> citizenship had made women men's equals as subjects before the law in a formal, procedural sense, but it had failed to win for them autonomy—social, economic, or subjective. The issue was not that of substantive equality (though de Beauvoir was concerned with securing that too). There was simply no carryover from women's status as abstract individuals to their status as "sovereign subjects," as autonomous beings fully in possession of themselves. In this sense the vote was only a partial victory. (1996, 169–70)

This discovery and disappointment about the necessary-but-insufficient scope of rights has led to two different kinds of feminist developments: either a complete turning away from (further) rights rhetoric and struggles or an attempt to identify the precise limits of rights, rectify shortcomings, and seek to work toward substantial equality. The first is a radical repudiation, the latter a liberal reformist response.[18] Few things, however, are sufficient in themselves, and the expectation that rights would be all-powerful, canceling at one stroke the inequities of history, is also at one level a recognition of the enormous cost of *not* having political rights or citizenship in the world today.

Closely related to the problem of the insufficiency of rights is that of the *mockery* of having them: a matter of their inadequate enforcement, the continuing exclusion of large groups from their ambit, their merely formal observance, the reality of unequal "equalities," and above all the farce of citizenship among a people kept in ignorance, slavery, and destitution by the state. A keenly satirical passage in Mahasweta Devi's story "Douloti the Bountiful" conveys the irrelevance of "India" to tribal people living in bonded labor in the geographical heartland of the country. The holy man who claims that they are all (the untouchables and he himself) children of "Mother India" is quizzed by Rajbi the washerwoman:

—Who is that?
—Our country, India.
—This is our country?
—Of course.
—Oh Sadhuji, my place is Seora village. What do you call a country? I know *tahsil,* I know station, I don't know country. India is not the country.
—Hey, you are all independent India's free people, do you understand?
—No, Sadhuji.
(1995, 41)

Mahasweta's point is this: what is "citizenship" without the consciousness of a "free" nation? What can rights hope to achieve when the people are not aware of having them? Citizenship may be a birthright, but its value and weight are produced only through exercising it. Ensuring the institutions of law and elections, access to education, and the people's participation in local government is the minimal responsibility of the democratic state. T. H. Marshall, in his influential discussion of citizenship in the context of postwar Britain, went further and formulated the demand for socioeconomic rights as a measure of actualizing and making meaningful political equality. The state would have the obligation to institute socioeconomic reforms toward such ends; consequently, the welfare state would direct its efforts toward providing employment, security against unemployment, and other public services to citizens (typically, however, these tended to be male citizens viewed as "heads of households") (Marshall 1950).

There is—my final point—the problem of the *inclusions and exclusions* that are performed by the state in defining citizenship. With national boundaries growing more porous, with the traffic of people as tourists, workers, refugees, and exiles increasing across these borders, the circulation of capital and commodities becoming global, and communications improving with unprecedented ease and speed, national citizenship can begin to appear an obsolete or at least irrelevant identity. (This is a condition that still, ironically, coexists with the intensely parochial or subnationalist identity, its opposite condition, in large parts of the undeveloped world—as Mahasweta Devi's story shows.) At the same time, precisely these same conditions have also led to the passage of stricter immigration laws in the advanced industrial countries as they seek to keep immigrants out, or maintain them as workers with illegal or second-class citizenship status. Thus "citizenship" becomes a rhetoric of exclusion. In India it has been most significantly invoked by the Hindu right to demonize Bangladeshi refugees (Ramachandran 1999). Uma Narayan cautions against feminist deployments of the term that might replicate such exclusion and calls attention to the problems of "non-citizen women," many of whom "also suffer from the effects of poverty and racism" (1997, 64). These arguments must alert us to the dangers of unthinking celebration. But, at the same time, "formal legal definitions of citizenship" do matter "profoundly" to immigrant people, as Stuart Hall insists (1993, 360)[19]—so much so that it is precisely in response to its exclusionary or hierarchizing tendencies that "citizenship" is claimed by the disentitled as a matter of legitimate national identity and equal rights.

These limitations of citizenship—insufficiency, inefficiency, and exclusion—derive from our historical experience of its functioning. They are failures that, in a liberal view, are susceptible to rectification, requiring only political will. But a more profound dissatisfaction that has been articulated with the very concept of citizenship must also be taken into consideration. The conceptual problems are constitutive in a deeper sense than the inadequacy, failure, or regressive uses of citizenship that I have discussed so far, and the critiques that I will identify are articulated from radical feminist positions. This discussion of citizenship is closely tied to the explorations of its political ally, liberalism; the sites of citizenship's operation, state and civil society (often termed the "public sphere"); and the issues of equality, abstract universalism, and justice that underpin it as an ideal.

A major critique of the liberal conception of citizenship is that it enshrines the gendered public-private division of our lives. One of the early projects of feminism was to break down the separateness of public and private spheres by agitating for the penetration of questions of justice into *every* domain of human life, including the familial. (See, for example, Benhabib 1992, 107–09.) Thus the feminist slogan "the personal is the political" argued, and sought to provide, a continuum between the two sharply demarcated worlds. Carole Pateman provides the fullest exposition of the Hegelian equation of citizenship activities with a male public sphere, and of domestic activities with a female private sphere; from this location women could have no access to citizenship.[20] (While citizenship is also classed, the state may arrange equality for working-class *men* by the provision of employment or welfare [Pateman 1989, 182–85].) Citizenship also entails citizens' performance of duties and their recognition of obligations in various realms, the most common being payment of taxes, military service, paid employment, jury service, and, in the civic republican tradition, active political participation. These, too, typically devolve on men; women traditionally do not bear arms, own property, or possess the capacity for self-government.[21] Even in the realm of the normative, in the understanding of what citizenship is intended to achieve and what it entails, differences of gender, as we can see, are elided.

The feminist dilemma in response to this situation, which Pateman locates as first appearing in Wollstonecraft's writings, is whether women's emancipation lies in entering the public world on the same terms as men ("like men"), or whether they should demand that their unpaid work as mothers be deemed central to their citizenship rights and status ("different from men") (Pateman 1989, 195–97). It is a dilemma that continues to exercise feminists: liberal feminists opting for the first, despite the practical and political problems it poses, radical feminists pushing for different versions of the latter, such as maternalist (or "moral") citizenship, which embraces specifically feminine values. In the current Indian situation, while skepticism about citizenship's feminist potential is certainly profound, such radical revisioning of citizenship has not gained much favor. The pros-

pect of women's active political participation in the democratic process, via legislative quotas for example, has instead been largely wel-
comed by women's groups. (Quotas, of course, do not make any less
difficult women's actual negotiations when engaging in public
forums, given their socially prescribed familial roles, their lack of
resources, the burden of domestic functions, and the nature of "politics" as such, so that reflection on gendered citizenship continues to
be an urgent item on the Indian feminist agenda.)

Another major theoretical problem lies with the persona of the
citizen. As represented by the abstraction and universalism of the
liberal subject, it is a conceptualization that is often described as
caricature or outright lie. There are not only no disembodied individuals representing (solely) the abstract qualities of liberal citizenship
such as reason, free choice, individualistic autonomy, freedom; these
qualities are also, and not incidentally, identified as male attributes.
Viewed as a literal *description,* therefore, liberal subjecthood seems to
offer little scope to feminism or other emancipatory projects. Pateman has highlighted the complex sexist history of liberal political
thought: at the very origins of the social contract that brought "the
state" and "citizens" into being, she argues, there is the other, repressed story of sexual relations (1988). The point is to ask how
determining and constitutive is this relation between male power and
political identity, how does it consolidate itself, or what breaches are
opened in it if women's contradictory sexual identity is inserted into
the contract as agent.

For it is precisely in the name of the universal "human being" that
women, working-class men, colonized peoples, or slaves have sought
their rights. As a concept and category that envisages a particular
ideal to apply to "all" "human beings" (both of which terms were not
comprehensively defined to begin with, but may be—as they have
been—stretched to accommodate more and more members of hu-
manity), liberal subjectivity earns its right to the term "universal."
The most sustained theoretical reflection on the question of the universal is to be found in Etienne Balibar's essay "Ambiguous Universality" (1995), to which I referred earlier. Balibar regards feminism's
politics as the "clearest example" of the "ideal universality" in terms
of which it is couched (67). The gender divide characterizes *every*
community, and because the struggle for parity seeks the transforma-

tion of the community, "it is therefore immediately universalistic" (67–68). Universal rights thus has a double politics: it is informed by a (constitutive) betrayal of the promise of universality but also provides the goal and the (historical) grounds of struggle in its name.

The differences on these issues that I have briefly outlined here are not only a matter of *ideological* polarization between feminists of different persuasions. In addition, the different interpretations of women's experience of living with and in the state are informed by the *historical* instances and practices of their interaction—which is fraught with the contradictions and compromises produced by "politics," as such. Since it is these that constitute the subject of this book, there are two imperatives that underlie my exploration. One, the methodological imperative, is to historicize the moment, the decade of the 1990s, as representing a specific stage in the development of the Indian state and of women's position as citizens within it. In other words, we need to move beyond the level of abstract generalization toward an understanding of the concrete contexts of the discussion. And two, in view of the complexity of the debate, the theoretical imperative is to see how or if one might retain, not ignore or refuse, the insights of radical feminist critique even while pushing toward a liberal perspective, by adopting an exploratory rather than tendentious approach in arriving at conclusions.

Women and the State: Terms of Engagement

In this section I will discuss in more specific terms the contexts and forms of the transactions between the state and women in India. Such engagement, I should make clear, is enabled, though it is not wholly determined, by the liberal democratic form of the Indian constitution. While political struggle is an aspect of all regimes— arguably it is more prominent in those where the state is repressive— in the Indian context constitutional equality provides the language for political demands, and a space where the state and women (in this instance) can meet as legitimate adversaries. But also, since democracy in India is an evolving, not developed, institution, democratic norms cannot always be taken for granted.

In considering the relationship between the state and women-as-citizens, there is to be noted, first, the state's pervasive and fundamental construction of gendered identities and roles according to its classificatory and regulatory schemes. Such a regime is an essential technique for producing governmental effects (Foucault 1991). The state, for example, like other patriarchal institutions, implicitly constructs women in terms of their sexuality. State-functions in relation to gendering—what I will describe shortly as the discrimination against, and the control, protection, regulation, and nonrecognition of the work of women—come together within a single logic that is informed by a pervasive understanding of women as sexualized subjects. In such a perception women are at once rendered as a sex and as a group: as, precisely, a "female population."

At the other end from state regulation, but still articulated in response and reaction to it, we will find women's activism in the organized women's movement as well as in other social and political organizations, in variously oppositional, reformist, or collaborative projects in relation to the state and its structures. And, finally, these transactions may be understood in terms of different kinds of formal and deliberate exchange, regulation, address, demand, and negotiation between women and the state, primarily within the context of law and citizenship: these are not entirely determined by the state's control, but neither are they (yet) developed into/as the activism of a women's collectivity.

If I view the relationship between "women" and the "state" as intimate and mutually defining, this is not to imply that the two agents are fully preformed entities entering into a formal relationship of confrontation or dialogue. It is not the case that "the state is the focus for the mobilisation of a social group and a social interest that is already constituted." Rather, "the state, as the focus and antagonist of mobilisation . . . is involved in the constitution of the sociopolitical group 'women' as protagonist" (Franzway et al. 1989, 39). This has particularly been the case in India, where, as historians of the women's movement tell us, "it was in focussing on the state in terms of law, administration and government responsibility, that women's groups came together in a collective effort time and again" (Agnihotri and Palriwala 1993, 3). The usual beginning for the contemporary women's movement, as for many other civil rights and democratic rights movements, is located in the Emergency (1975–76); the first major protest movement was spurred by the judgment in the Mathura rape case.[22] Therefore the state was directly instrumental in calling forth the mobilization of women: at first, and most prominently, around issues of violence and in a climate of repression, and subsequently around other economic and political issues.

Nor do I wish to suggest in speaking of the mutual engagement of state and women that it is in any way a symmetrical interaction. On the contrary, it is clear that more often than not it is the state that sets the terms of the engagement, women's actions being merely reactive; and also clear that the state can and does subvert women's initiatives. But women, their problems and struggles, have also periodically brought the state to crises of signification under specific circumstances. The recognition that "women" exist—whether as a "problem," an instrumentality, or an interest group—shapes the state and its functions in distinctive ways. Unable to easily disavow, as a liberal democratic and secular "modern" state, the ideals of women's equality or its responsibilities for the welfare of its female citizens; or overcome religion, tradition, and the forces of "backwardness"; or resist the forces of developmental imperatives that target women as its victims, the Indian state is forced to reckon with these contradictions, especially when women forcefully bring them to attention.

I identify below the main areas of the state's specifically gendered address to women and, following that, the subjectivities created by women's address to the state, in which these different kinds of relations operate, though in overlapping, not exclusive ways.

The Indian state's discrimination against women, negative and positive, in two areas, in disregard of the constitutional equality provision: Personal laws, which regulate each religious community by its own laws or customs regarding "personal" matters (those relating to inheritance, marriage, divorce, maintenance, custody of children, and the like), are almost all negatively discriminatory toward women. "Positive" discrimination consists of the 33 percent quota for women that has already been established in panchayats (local elected village councils), and which is now being proposed in Parliament. By what logic or illogic are these two kinds of differentiation of women reconciled with each other or kept separate? A clue may lie in the fact of strong resistance to the reform of personal laws from religious communities, as revealed by the fate of the Hindu Code Bill, the passage of the Muslim Women (Protection in Divorce) Act, and the opposition of Syrian Christians in Kerala to the 1986 Supreme Court verdict on the Travancore Christian Succession Act, challenged by Mary Roy; whereas quotas for women in representative bodies have met with surprisingly little opposition, at least in principle. It would seem that the *economic* empowerment of *individual* women that personal law reform or a common civil code might encourage (through changes in inheritance laws or entitlement to maintenance, for example) is perceived as a greater threat to patriarchal privileges than is the *political* empowerment as a *collective* ("women") that quotas might secure for Indian women—or, of course, better yet, fail to. Both these measures, inevitably, have not been viewed solely in light of women's rights but have been substantially displaced onto issues of community identity and caste representation, and we might say that it is in the latter form that they are fought and lost or won. But how women's status is affected thereby cannot be a merely incidental outcome of the enactment of these formal discriminations.

The ideology of "protection": This is reflected in the significant number of laws that are intended to check and punish violence against women (very largely in response to women's groups' demands).[23] But the failure of the state's functioning as a protective agency is indicated by the increase in the incidence of violence despite the laws, the virtual absence of court convictions in most cases of violence, the paucity in the numbers and amenities of custodial institutions for victims, and the instances of custodial rape. Nevertheless its sanctioned institutional role in preserving "law and order" in society—the virtual rationale of the state itself—extends naturally into a paternalistic relation vis-à-vis women.

Population control and other forms of regulation of female sexuality: Population control figures prominently on the agenda of developing countries, primarily as a poverty-alleviation measure. Predictably, it is poor women who are the targets of family-planning programs (especially following the massive resistance to the draconian sterilization campaigns aimed at men during the Emergency) and become victims of cheap, large-scale, and frequently hazardous birth control measures. Despite a new National Population Policy based on the acceptance that growth rates fall voluntarily with economic development, improved healthcare, and the spread of (especially, female) literacy, state governments continue to invoke punitive measures—like withholding food rations under the public distribution system (PDS) to a couple who produce a third child—as a way to check family size. The state's relentless promotion of the small-family norm is also responsible for strengthening the preference for sons within families and leads unambiguously to attempts to eliminate unwanted girl children through various sex-selection methods.

Women's work: By far the majority of working women in India are employed in the unorganized labor sector where there is little legislation and few state-sponsored welfare measures to prevent their outright exploitation. But the problem is more radical than only neglect, for the Indian state has been slow to recognize—even to name—Indian women as workers. Indian feminist historians have expressed puzzlement over the burial and subsequent disappearance from official discourse of the Congress party's radical 1939–40 Women's Role in Planned Economy (WRPE) report, which their researches have recently unearthed (Banerjee 1998; Chaudhuri 1996; Krishnaraj 1995). The WRPE report had proposed a radical mode of citizenship for women as workers. It "concentrated heavily on women's economic rights," proposing that "women's unpaid labour in the family's economic activities be compensated by the right to claim all facilities given by the state to other workers," and that "as compensation for housework they be given absolute control over a part of the family income, and also an inalienable share in the husband's property" (Banerjee 1998, WS 3). However, Banerjee laments, "official policies in independent India showed no interest in women as workers; instead the first [five-year] plan resolved to provide women with adequate services necessary to fulfil what was called a 'woman's legitimate role in the family' . . . Women were back to their iconic roles within the family" (WS 4). Examining the state's welfare policies for women between 1950 and 1975, Nirmala Buch similarly finds a strong "middle-class bias" toward regarding women as "housewives," or as a "weaker/backward/disadvantaged group" needing "special assistance" (1998, WS 19). It was only at the insistence of various women's groups' reports and findings that the National Census, for example, began to record and count women's unpaid work and work in the informal sector in 1993; but regardless even of this, the denial of women's work and of women's identity and productivity as workers predominates in state law and policy as common sense. (See also Mukherjee 1999.)

Women in development: A new kind of identity, indeed of agency, is now being offered to (mainly) rural poor women in India as subjects of development.[24] Both the recognition of women's centrality to the development process[25] and the better returns on credit and aid given to them (rather than to men)[26] are factors that have led to a focus on "gender and development" in various official discourses of international agencies as well as the Indian state, in the contemporary climate of economic liberalization and structural adjustment. Mary John has drawn attention to some of the implications of this new attention, particularly to the "language of efficiency," and to the emphasis on women (rather than the relational concept of gender), which places them, as "good subjects," against marginalized men who are regarded as both "incapable and irresponsible" (1999, 119–20). John reads in this a major shift from the socialism and nationalism of the women's movement's agenda of the 1970s to the market imperatives of the new economy. Her perceptive warning must alert us to the pitfalls and limits of the new visibility of women in development.

Women are interpellated as citizens of the nation-state in a variety of ways, as we can see. Citizenship becomes gendered in the state's acknowledgment of the social discrimination that women suffer (a necessary preliminary to redressing it); via its regulation of sexed (reproductive) subjects; as a consequence of its construction of (gendered) identities toward specific ends; and in its governance of a "female population."

Women, in their turn, respond to—by variously seeking, subverting, refusing, or resisting—this official recognition, interpellation, regulation, and protection, if for no other reason than that the state is so ineluctably present as a force in their lives. Women's response to these relations of gendering may be located, therefore, in both their acquiescence and recalcitrance to the forms they take. They take recourse to the privileges of "universal," that is, unmarked citizenship rights, and, in places, assert a collective gendered identity in voluntary organizations. A schematic and succinct description of women's engagement with the state would represent them in the following ways:

— as electoral subjects, a constituency that can be identified, or projects itself, as having special interests as women;
— as litigants, individually or collectively petitioning the state for their entitlements, in matters of inheritance claims, maintenance, compensation, restitution of rights, employment, fair wages, usually in the court of law;
— as supplicants, usually individually petitioning the state for their

protection, welfare, compensation, or rehabilitation, especially when victims of societal violence (rape, dowry-murder, communal riots) or natural disasters;

— as activists in an organized collectivity, such as autonomous women's groups or other social movements (environmental, communal, caste, left revolutionary, tribal); unions of women workers, particularly in the unorganized sector (Self-Employed Women's Association, sex workers' union) and also trade unions and peasant movements, the women's wings of political parties, and most conspicuously lately in Hindutva organizations.

Though what I call the "transactional" nature of this relationship serves primarily as a heuristic, I also mean thereby to suggest a more positive agential role for women in terms of what might be called a "performative" strategy vis-à-vis the state. Fawzia Afzal-Khan has spoken of "performance" in the literal context of activist theater in contemporary Pakistan, in ways that are suggestive for my invocation of the term:

> [Theater groups] have cast a critical eye through their plays and performances on the way the state's coercive shaping of the constitutional subject of the new nation has had a repressive effect on the identities and rights of women, religious minorities, and the poor. At the same time, as subjects within conflicting ideologies themselves—nationalist, ethnic, secular humanist, feminist, socialist—these drama activists enact or rehearse the very conditions for performances of subjectivity that remain shot through with seemingly unresolvable contradictions . . . (2000, 171–72)

Afzal-Khan's observation on activist theater performance can be used to understand the more deliberate and self-conscious initiatives that women undertake in tackling the state and the subject-constitutive effects that these endeavors generate. But as citizen-subjects we also negotiate (with) the state in quotidian life, and in more mundane ways. Education or welfare, for instance, are spaces in a liberal welfare democracy, Yuval-Davis and Werbner suggest, in which "subjectivity and subjectivism, individual liberty and governmentality, are *performed* as everyday, pragmatic realities" (1999, 8; emphasis in original). Gayatri Spivak offers a suggestive remark on "performativity" as employed by Judith Butler, in its applicability to women in the South: " . . . the gender practice of the rural poor [woman] is quite often in the performative mode, carving out power within a more general scene of pleasure in subjection" (1999a, 43).[27] If *crisis* provides a specific conjuncture for the constitution of female subjectivity in the reactive mode, as we had suggested in an analysis of the Shahbano case (Pathak and Sunder Rajan 1989), then *culture,* in Spivak's/Butler's sense of "conventions in use," is the scene and mode of the performativity of the political as everyday practice. The shuttle between "crisis" and "culture" describes women's mode of "living with/in the nation-state."

It will be clear that I am positing here a somewhat tighter, more dialectical connection, hence a relationship not defined solely as op-positional, between the state and women-as-gendered-citizens than that suggested by the models of a corresponding "nation" and "peo-ple" developed in the work of (nonfeminist) theorists of the nation-state like Homi Bhabha and Partha Chatterjee. Bhabha has spoken of a "nationalist pedagogy," on the one hand, and the people's resistant "strategy of the performative," on the other, which has suggestive implications for an understanding of state-functions and female sub-jectivities as I have been attempting to develop the concepts here (1994, 145). In a somewhat similar vein, though taking the distinction further in the Indian context, Chatterjee develops the opposition between the interventionist, modernizing governmentality of the In-dian state—which he associates with "modernity"—and the political demands and struggles of the "masses" against modernity/elite civil society/state—which he names "democracy" (1998a, 281−82; also 2000). What would complicate this attractive reading of the "people" as autonomous and free agents of political praxis is, I suspect, the gendering of the categories "people," "masses" or "subalterns." How closely can women be identified with these collective designations? In the relationship to the state, the "gendered subaltern," I suggest, requires a separate problematic; and the chapters in this book are an attempt to provide such a perspective.

What are the implications of these interactions between the state and women, and vice versa? In the following concluding section of this chapter, I turn to follow more closely the thinking about law, citizenship, and the state within Indian feminism.[28] Because feminist organizations are made up of women who work with other women and also have experience of direct negotiations with the state, their positions, reflecting consensus in some areas and disagreements in others, are worth exploring in some detail.

Debates Within the Indian Women's Movement

The post-Independence Indian women's movement is usually viewed as having three phases: the period of the 1950s and the 1960s, the decades immediately following freedom, during which there was little organized activity;[29] the period of the 1970s and 1980s, marked by the Emergency, the International Women's Year, and the report of the CSWI on the Status of Women in India, related events which combined to produce the enormous activism of the new autonomous women's groups;[30] and the most recent phase, following the Shahbano case judgment in 1986, a period of withdrawal from the protest agendas of the earlier decade, into introspection, consolidation, and new directions—these latter for the most part turning toward involvement in NGO work in health, literacy, welfare, and development.[31]

Radical feminists argue that the historical phase of liberal faith in the new Indian state's promises is now past, and that continued investment in litigation and law reform is a waste of the movement's energy. Such feminist critiques find support for this broad antistatism in other radical schools of thought that are gaining prominence in India, which I have briefly discussed earlier. These lessons of experience also find support in theoretical critiques—postmodernist, Foucauldian, or deconstructionist (Mukhopadhyay 1998, 12)—that are skeptical of all forms of state-sponsored liberal and homogeneous constructions, such as the individual-as-citizen, law as a fixed and neutral institution, or modernization as teleology.[32] A generational gap, if not actual conflict, among Indian feminists is beginning to be evident.[33]

Women's groups of all persuasions have little disagreement about the perception that their task is to oppose the state's control, exercise vigilance over its moves, alert it to its gender-blindness, and make it accountable. But on the issue of seeking the state's *support* in achieving women's liberation, particularly through the institution of more and better laws, the Indian women's movement is deeply divided, as I have indicated. It is, ironically, the conspicuous *success* of the women's movement in the field of legal reform that led to the doubts about its efficacy as strategy, particularly following Flavia Agnes's appraisal of the laws relating to women in the decade between 1980 and 1990:

If oppression could be tackled by passing laws, then the decade of the 1980s would be adjudged a golden period for Indian women, when protective laws were offered on a platter. Almost every single campaign against violence on women resulted in new legislation. The successive enactments would seem to provide a positive picture of achievement. [But] the crime statistics reveal a different story. . . . The deterrent value of the enactments was apparently nil. Some of the enactments in effect remained only on paper. Why were the laws ineffective in tackling the problem? (1997, 521)

Feminist consciousness of the limitations of progressive laws in the books, when not backed up by implementation or by the judgments of an enlightened judiciary, has grown acute. That progressive and correct laws are a necessary minimal assurance of women's well-being and status is not questioned. But on the matter of pressing for *additional* legislation specifically geared toward women's issues like sexual harassment, sati, rape, pornography and obscenity, prostitution, domestic violence, and dowry, there is an increasing consensus that it is likely to do more harm than good. Feminists are wary of asking for more stringent punishments for offenders or for placing the burden of proof on the accused (as has been proposed in many cases), from fear that conviction rates would then decline further, or that such laws would serve as a pretext for the state's arbitrary use of power.[34] Feminists also fear that a "uniform" law, even if enforced on behalf of women, say in property rights, would seriously undermine customary practices in many parts of the country, for example among tribal communities, some of which may have an already existing and operative structure and practice of gender egalitarianism or, more importantly, which face a threat to their community identities and culture from both the state and the mainstream/majority community.

These criticisms of legal-reform struggles, it can be retorted, view feminist struggles around the law too narrowly since they discount other kinds of effects, those related to the *process* of these struggles rather than their ends—such as raised consciousness and awareness of legal rights among the women involved, the diffusive impact of the publicity (in the media and elsewhere) generated by such demands (even if in the form of hostility), and the value of lessons learned from political experience. Much important feminist legal-theoretical work in India seriously explores the limits and possibilities of law's potential for female emancipation, especially around the question of equality, rehearsing the familiar paradox of demanding that the law both privilege women's difference *and* overlook it in different contexts, according to the ends of real and substantial justice.[35]

Anti-statist feminists demand that feminist struggles be fought on a different terrain than the state in recognition of the local, concrete, and context-sensitive nature of political issues and in response to the heterogeneity of "women's" problems and their imbrication with other struggles. Thus, Nandita Haksar, discussing the efficacy of feminist legal-reform activism, points to the conflict with tribal movements:

> There are alternatives to filing writ petitions . . . there are other ways of dealing with the problem of inequality between men and women in tribal societies . . . there is a need to build a movement based on tribal socio-economic traditions. I strongly feel we should resort to the law only when the movement is strong enough to carry the law reform forward. In almost all such cases a legal battle should only supplement the political battle outside the courts. (1999, 86–87)

But there has as yet not been a clear articulation of what such an alternative politics would look like. The "new social movements" are an indication of a new people's or democratic politics that has much appeal for sections of the intelligentsia. But how far these will be able to successfully operate as autonomous struggles against the "enemies"—feudal landowners, religious authorities, caste leaders, male heads of families, as the case may be—without appealing to the state, or against the state by invoking international support, remains to be seen, as, indeed, do the implications of such a politics.[36] The alliances between these dominant social structures and the state, and vice-versa—which is not, however, a complete identification—also makes the state a major player in all struggles on the terrain of the nation-state. Would the perceived exhaustion of legal-reform and rights struggles also imply that a separate "women's movement" has reached the end of its historical rationale, with the emergence of diverse struggles in each of which gender is an irreducible component? But women's issues have never been extricable after all from struggles around issues of class, ethnicity, community, caste, and other differences. And discrimination and violence against women would still have to be addressed in terms of the specificity of *gendered* difference—autonomous women's movements were, after all, a sign of this recognition—hence a broader coalitional movement rather than a dilution of feminist struggle, as such, seems to be indicated.

If legal-reform activism is one site of dispute within Indian feminism, others becoming equally urgent though not as yet as clearly conceptualized include the consequences of women's groups' participation in state-supported programs, the implications of the "mainstreaming" of the women's movement's demands, and the politics of nongovernment organizational activity in various fields. An innovative experiment in Rajasthan, the Women's Development Program (WDP), was set up in the 1980s (subsequently becoming a model for WDPs in other states), with collaboration between state and central governments, foreign funding agencies, local voluntary organizations, and the women's studies wing of the Institute of Development Studies. The WDP functioned with considerable autonomy in the initial years, mobilizing rural women to perform leadership roles in the community as volunteer *sathins* (helpers) in development projects, which refused state-defined priorities like family planning and engaged instead in various consciousness-raising activities around employment and wages, political participation, reform of child-marriage customs, and education. But, inevitably it would seem, its very success led to the state's seeking to subvert its agenda and ultimately failing to support the volunteers, as the case of Bhanwari Devi made so amply clear.[37]

The entry of feminist concerns into official, mainstream discourse is of course itself the result of protracted struggles on the part of women's groups—a mark of their "success," if anything—but one which has also been a cause for wariness. Apart from the risk of cooptation, feminists also perceive a threat in the state's takeover of programs supported by various civil-society initiatives and fear the consequences of both cooperation and competition between the two. Commenting on the recent National Policy for the Empowerment of Women (NPEW), Kalpana Kannabiran (2001) expresses concern over its faithful echo of the issues that women's groups' interventions first made prominent. The government's proposal in the NPEW to institute "parallel structures under state authority" for implementing women's rights in various spheres might instead end up "replicating," "appropriating," or "undermining" the work of nonstate institutional mechanisms that have already built "legitimacy and credibility" though their work, she fears.

The more radical doubt that engages discussion is about the state's "motive" in "sponsoring [people's] struggles." The women's group Saheli articulated a critique of government's women's development programs:

> In contrast to development plans for other sections of the population, government's emphasis with respect to women is not on policy measures, resource allocation or redefining development, but on awareness building and mobilization or, in other words struggle as opposed to development. With such a definition of development, a bizarre situation has been created where the fight is no longer against the establishment, but is a state-sponsored struggle. (Saheli 1995, 3, cited in Saxena 2000, 31)

Sadhna Saxena is moved to ask whether the state has been so "weakened that it cannot implement its own policies," so that "in exasperation, or for legitimacy" it is forced "to urge the masses to organize themselves against the state" (30–31).[38] Saxena considers also the possibility that (as in the case of literacy programs) the government is only interested in supplying the market's demand for a "cheap workforce with basic skills" (31).

Voluntary agencies as the "human face" of structural adjustment programs in the 1990s are therefore seen to be implicated in supporting the state's economic agendas (Kulkarni 1996). Their role, as the activist Sanjoy Ghose observed, has increasingly been "to explore, or create, spaces for 'official' dissent within the system" (1997, 13). Feminists also express wariness of the "professionalism" of NGO workers, which replaces an earlier "activism"; of the politics of foreign donor agencies from whom they receive funding (Krishnaraj 1998, 394);

and of feminism's "losing its political edge" and being gradually forced to retreat into "social welfare issues and minor sanctioned reforms" (Tharu 1995, 51). Even allowing for some nostalgia among feminists of an earlier generation, the relation of women and the state that they see as dangerously compromised by the mediation of NGOS is a matter for serious consideration. It combats the perception that the broader field of action that women activists come to inhabit through participation in government and nongovernment organizations gives them unambiguous influence in state policy making and clout in international arenas (Sengupta and Friese 1995).

The instances and issues discussed in the following chapters—around nationalism and minority identity, personal law, women's work, custodial institutions, welfare, the female "outlaw"—bring into focus these different dimensions of feminist thinking about women and the state in India. My argument is offered less as a decisive intervention into the current debates than a plea to extend their scope beyond the current polarized terms and enter them into a larger discursive domain.

The six chapters that follow are grouped in three parts that broadly indicate the relations and interactions between women and the state that I have described in the foregoing discussion. In part I, "Women in Custody," are included the essays on "Ameena" and the "Hysterectomies Scandal." Together they indicate the ways in which the state takes women into "custody," in both senses of the word: as protective care and as incarceration. What are the consequences of these for our understanding of the postcolonial state and for the construction of (these) women's subjectivities? In the case of the first, the welfare state in the "developing" world is revealed as an anomaly. And in the matter of women's subjectivities, we see how the state's treatment of the child bride Ameena, as of the mentally retarded women inmates of the welfare home, was crucially dependent on how it constructed them as sexualized (reproductive) subjects, in both these instances primarily on the basis of their age. Both chapters also dwell on the tension between the (nation-)state and the family or community in defining proprietorial rights over and responsibility for the female subject who is invariably viewed as dependent.

In part II, "Women in Law," I am interested in identifying (in the chapter "The Prostitution Question[s]) how feminists might reconceptualize the "work" of sex work in ways that would enable legislation that will empower instead of criminalize sex workers. In the chapter "Women Between Community and State," I rehearse the debates around a Uniform Civil Code in India that places women in the bind of choosing between identification with their communities (by embracing personal law) or with the "secular" state (by asserting individual rights). How may we recognize Indian women as "national subjects" outside these options that are constructed so narrowly, yet so comprehensively? In these two chapters I therefore address women's identity "in law" as a concern but also as a potential feminist resource.

In part III, somewhat grimly titled "Killing Women," I discuss the high incidence of female infanticide in the state of Tamilnadu (chapter 6), and the case of the female outlaw (chapter 7), playing with the grammatical ambiguity of the participle "killing" to describe the two different phenomena. In chapter 6, "Children of the State?" I deliberate on the social phenomenon of *killing women*. What are the state's responses, beginning from the recognition of sex-selective killing and the concern with the demographic problem of sex ratios, to tackling the "problems" of dowry, social "backwardness," and crime? Once again the postcolonial state's failures in reformist intervention and welfare are highlighted. But more centrally, it is the contradictions of the state vis-à-vis women—the "logic" of whose killing lies in their redundancy—that have to be engaged. This leads to my concluding argument, a dystopic vision of unwanted female children in India as "children of the state." Finally, while the question of women's agency is a concern in all the chapters, in more or less muted ways, in chapter 7, "Outlaw Woman," it is foregrounded in the event of Phoolan Devi's voluntary surrender to the police at the end of her career of dacoity, in the form of a face-to-face negotiation with the state. How does the female outlaw define the modern state in this transaction, and what does this eventuality signify about female citizenship?

I Women in Custody

2 The Ameena "Case":
The Female Citizen and Subject

On 11 August 1991 the newspapers announced the dramatic "rescue" of a "child bride" on the previous day. On the flight from Hyderabad to Delhi (en route to Riyadh), Ameena, the child bride, ten or eleven years old, had been spotted crying bitterly by several passengers, who had reported the matter to the airhostess. Ameena then told the airhostess that the old man beside her, Yahya Mohammed al-Sageih, a sixty-year-old Saudi Arabian national, was taking her away after having forcibly married her in Hyderabad (her native town) only a few days before. She wept throughout the flight. As soon as the plane landed in Delhi, al-Sageih was arrested by the city police, and Ameena was produced before the metropolitan magistrate, who temporarily entrusted her to the local Nari Niketan (destitute women's home). The parents, in Hyderabad, were also subsequently arrested. After months of legal dispute over her custody, during which she was moved to a children's home, the Delhi High Court ordered her restoration to her family. No judgment has yet been pronounced in the legal case against her parents for performing the marriage of an underage daughter.

The extent of the national response to Ameena's predicament was unprecedented. In Parliament there were vociferous demands that the government look into "the sale of Indian girls to flesh markets abroad." Newspaper editorials protested that "Indian girls are not for export." When Ameena was produced in court on 13 August there was a "minor stampede" to see her. The case quickly caught the attention of the international media as well. In Canada a "Child Bride Ameena Trust" was formed following the live telecast of an interview with Amrita Ahluwalia, the airhostess who had rescued Ameena and subsequently petitioned for custody of her. Women's groups quickly entered the fray. The national press kept up the pressure with feature articles and background stories.

Primarily and most obviously a discourse of nationalism and nationalist identity, the "Ameena case," as it soon came to be called, also makes visible the functioning of the state in matters relating to gender especially as it concerns female sexuality. It is framed therefore by the problematic of women in / and the Indian state that is the concern of this book. It allows us to see not only how the insertion of women into the discourse of nation has implications for the subjectification of women and the representation of nation, but also how, and with what assumptions and consequences, the postcolonial state addresses "social evils," in this instance child marriage, in its modernizing drive. We might go further and deduce that when the issue is one of "saving" women, the "nation" is the stage on which the state's intervention is most spectacularly performed. In this instance (but not only in this, as my comparison of it with the Shahbano case will show), postcolonial nationalism and the postcolonial state converged on the issue of "reform" of (not coincidentally, *minority*) women's status. The controversy over Ameena's custody and the issue of child marriage also engaged a concerned citizenry (the passengers on the plane, the airhostess), women's groups, "liberal" Muslims, the media, and the High Court, who orchestrated, as we shall see, a liberal, secular, modernizing, and constitutional discourse whose successes and limits it tested. The "Ameena case" serves as a significant site to explore the overlaps and pulls between the concepts and practices of citizenship-as-rights and citizenship-as-national identity (and, even, as compulsory residency) in the case of the subaltern gendered subject. Methodologically, in representing the issue of child marriage in India by / as the "Ameena case," this chapter contends with the problem of having to think *beyond* exemplarity yet well *before* an untheorizable particularity.

Points of Crisis

It is necessary to track closely the development of the case following the rescue of Ameena and the arrest of al-Sageih in order to locate its flash points of conflict, controversy, and contradiction.

Al-Sageih was released on bail but with orders to cooperate with the investigation and not leave the country until the case had been dismissed. He was accommodated in the Saudi Arabian embassy. Ameena underwent a checkup at the government hospital. According to the information on her passport and the *nikhanama* (marriage certificate) produced by al-Sageih, her age was thirty-five; her parents claimed she was eighteen; her own statement and her medical examination suggested she was eleven or twelve.

According to the preliminary reports, al-Sageih had arrived in Bombay on 28 July and met Ameena's family in Hyderabad on 7 August through a marriage broker who arranged such matches. The wedding had taken place the following day. Such marriages are fairly routine arrangements; in the past decade more than 8000 marriages—one report gives the figure as 40,000 since the oil boom—between Arab men and young, poor Muslim Indian girls have taken place in Hyderabad city alone. Al-Sageih reportedly paid the father, Badruddin, Rs 6000 as *mehr* (marriage settlement). Badruddin is an autorickshaw (three-wheeler scooter) driver with eight children; Ameena is the second of five daughters. The Shakkargun locality of Hyderabad city where the family live is a Muslim ghetto, poor and torn by frequent communal strife.

In Delhi, airhostess Ahluwalia passionately pleaded for Ameena's release from the Nari Niketan and outlined her plans for her future if granted custody. She gave several other interviews of a similar kind to the press and on television ("give my Ameena back," etc.). Women's organizations—Saheli and the Janwadi Mahila Samiti—also protested Ameena's stay in a Nari Niketan and applied for custody of her. Their application was refused, but Ameena was produced in court on 13 August and moved to a "short stay" home in response to the outrage over her confinement in a Nari Niketan. The court also refused to admit Ahluwalia's petition, through Saheli, for custody of Ameena. Instead it directed the Juvenile Justice Court to decide on an appropriate residence for Ameena. At this stage, Ameena expressed a wish to return to her parents.

The city police filed criminal charges against both al-Sageih and Ameena's parents under various sections of the Indian Penal Code (IPC): section 366 (abduction), 420 (cheating and forgery), 467, 471, and 486 (using forged documents), 372 (sale of minor for prostitution), 373 (purchase of minor for prostitution), 120-B (entering into a conspiracy to commit all the above offenses), and section 4 of the Child Marriage Restraint Act (CMRA 1929, as amended in 1978). Ameena's parents were released on bail on the basis of bonds provided by two local residents on 3 January 1992.

On 29 August, the arrival of Ameena's parents in Delhi to meet their daughter and file a petition for her restoration to them was occasion for another furor. In interviews Badruddin, Ameena's father, defended the marriage as being in accordance with Muslim custom and expressed resentment at the "interference of outsiders." Shortly after this, the Saudi Arabian ambassador also made a similar statement opposing the intervention of women's groups. The All India Lawyer's Union called for a high-level inquiry into the case.

On 5 September the court rejected all the petitions for custody of Ameena and ordered her kept in a home for children for three months. On 5 December, her three-month state custody over, her case came up for review again, but the Juvenile Justice Board had not arrived at any decision. Responding to these delays and to the Board's indecisiveness, Brinda Karat of the Janwadi Mahila Samiti (JMS) filed a petition for a speedy decision on the issue of custody. Finally, on 21 February, a division bench of the Delhi High Court, expressing dissatisfaction with the Juvenile Justice Board's lethargy in the matter, ordered Ameena to be presented to them the following week in order to formally "ascertain her wishes" on the matter. They then ordered the Juvenile Board to speed up its decision but reserved final judgment over the matter. Meanwhile the case against al-Sageih and Ameena's parents was proceeding independently of the custody case. On 21 February 1992, the court was packed when the three accused appeared before the metropolitan magistrate to face the charges against them. The public prosecutor asked for a trial in the Sessions Court, and the case was adjourned for further hearing.

In the custody issue the Juvenile Board, finding the parents "unfit," ordered (on 4 March) that Ameena be transferred to a service home in Hyderabad for three years. The Janwadi Mahila Samiti protested against this decision, as the welfare institution was meant for women between eighteen and thirty-five and would therefore be unsuitable for a child of Ameena's age; the Samiti urged instead Ameena's speedy restoration to her parents since she had already spent nearly seven months in the state's custody. The decision of the Juvenile Board was subject to review by the High Court.

On 11 March 1992 Ameena appeared before the division bench of the High Court, comprising Mr. B. N. Kirpal and Mrs. Santosh Duggal. She reiterated her wish to go home. The judges examined Badruddin at length to ascertain his fitness and willingness to take charge of Ameena. Badruddin produced three affidavits given on his behalf by respectable Hyderabad citizens. The JMS also supported the parents' petition. The following day the judges ordered Ameena's restoration to her parents but stipulated that she be first presented to a metropolitan magistrate in Hyderabad. They also directed the magistrate's court to verify the state government's arrangements for monitoring Ameena's welfare once she was back at her parents' home. Mr. Kirpal said, "With the passing of this order we hope a nightmarish chapter in the young life of Ameena will hopefully come to a satisfactory end." And, in a sense, the Ameena custody issue comes to a close here.

Later in the year, on 9 September, the prosecution case against al-Sageih and the Badruddins was resumed in court. Al-Sageih's defense advocate, Irshad Ullah Khan, argued that Ameena had never stated in court that she had been coerced into marriage. He also invoked Muslim personal law, which allowed the marriage of a legally minor girl if she had attained puberty—which might happen at an age as early as nine. The court, however, ruled that al-Sageih be tried on all the charges listed against him, including abduction and violation of CMRA. The chief issue here was, clearly, the conflict between the CMRA and Muslim personal law.

This controversy over which system of laws applies—the uniform civil and criminal laws or the differentiated religious personal law—requires some elaboration. India's dual law structure is an inheritance from colonial jurisprudence. The personal law system was acknowledged by British administrators as a way of respecting and guaranteeing the continuation of the traditional laws of the country's diverse religious communities—the majority Hindu as well as the minority

Muslim and Christian—in all "personal" matters (relating to the "person"), such as marriage, divorce, maintenance, succession to property, inheritance, custody, guardianship and adoption of children, etc. The personal laws of *all* communities discriminate against women, though modified reform of some Hindu personal laws has been codified. Though the adoption of a uniform civil code is enshrined as a Directive Principle of the state, to be brought about in time through what was envisaged as a gradual and progressive social evolution, the Constitution of India still continues to observe personal law differences. Muslim personal law is codified under the Muslim Personal Law (Shariat) Application Act of 1937.[1]

In all other matters a uniform law prevails. The CMRA is a civil law, applicable to Indians of all religions. It was first passed in 1929 and was revised in 1978, stipulating an increase in the minimum legal age of marriage, which is at present eighteen for women and twenty-one for men. Any case filed against the marriage of underage children makes the bridegroom (if over twenty-one) and the parents or guardians liable to prosecution under the CMRA. Kirti Jain, an activist feminist lawyer, sees no scope for conflict between CMRA and Muslim personal law (MPL): "The Shariat Act states that the MPL will prevail over custom or usages that are contrary to it, but nowhere does it say that the MPL will outweigh any legislation clashing with it. So legislations like the Contract Act, Criminal Procedure Act, and the CMRA outweigh the MPL." I. U. Khan, however, holds (like several other legal experts) that since marriage, divorce, and inheritance are directly governed by personal law, it is also applicable in the case of child marriage: "The MPL is a special law for a special class of people, whereas the CMRA is a general law. And in the case of a conflict, the former will prevail" (Sahgal and Sarita Rani 1993, 38–39).

Khan argued that Ameena's marriage had after all been performed "openly." Further, "society may have reservations about the respective ages and other aspects of the marriage but where was the legal breach?" (ibid.). Ameena's testimony against the accused, also, was conflicting. The case went on, with several witnesses appearing for the prosecution; but the crucial testimony was Ameena's. On 17 November, when Ameena appeared in court, she formally withdrew her charges. Weeping, she told the sessions judge, Mr. Babulal Garg, that the marriage had taken place with her consent. (At the insistence of the JMS her evidence was taken in the judge's chambers to save her the ordeal of testifying in open court.) The state prosecutor confronted her with her very different statement to the police the previous year, soon after she had been "rescued." Ameena denied the earlier statement and her signature. She gave her age as sixteen or seventeen, not twelve as earlier claimed (but she did not know her date of birth). She said she did not remember what she had said earlier to her interlocutors on the plane and to the police. Ameena's testimony obviously weakened the state's case considerably, though charges were not officially dropped. In July 1993 the newspapers reported that al-Sageih had jumped bail in February and left the country. His sureties paid up the bail amount.[2]

Averting the Crisis

The potential for communal controversy in the Ameena episode was present from the beginning. The scandalous nature of the event, the facts of Ameena's being a Muslim and her husband a Saudi Arabian national, the disparity in their ages, the validity that the marriage was claimed to possess under Muslim law despite being a legal offense: these facts were provocative and sensational. Thus when Ameena's case came to national attention through the media's extensive coverage, its potential for communalization was immediately obvious, especially since its news appeal was highly emotive.

The Shahbano case, which also centered on a Muslim woman's predicament (in her case, unilateral divorce without payment of maintenance), had provoked a national crisis of such dimensions that a decisive turn in the history of post-Independence Indian politics may be said to have taken place around it.[3] The structural similarities between the Shahbano and Ameena cases are striking: the subaltern female subject becomes the object of conflict between community (as Muslim) and state (as citizen) and is therefore perceived as a putative social responsibility; she is invested with agency, all the same, in being called on to exercise her choice between the two sets of regulations and rights, and between her religious affiliation and her entitlements as citizen; she is then restored to the family, which is treated as the appropriate final location for the errant woman—despite the irony of her expulsion from the family having created the crisis of her situation in the first instance; in the process, she becomes a national cause or issue. "Shahbano" has since grown to be the paradigm of the Indian Muslim woman's identity. As a result primarily of "her" case, Hindu fundamentalists began to construct Muslim women as victims of their own community's oppression and implicitly, therefore, as inferior to Hindu women. "This discursive strategy," as Ratna Kapur and Brenda Cossman have pointed out, is one calculated "to strike at the heart of identity—the intersection of community and gender" (1993, 42).

That the Ameena episode, unlike the Shahbano case, did not turn into a pretext for a major nation-divisive communal conflict is attributable to two reasons. The first was a fortuitous conjuncture of events, the historical moment; the second was the success of a certain liberal discourse of secular nationalism in finding the "universal" application of a minority woman's predicament and demonstrating how issues that had primarily to do with class and gender could be successfully articulated in those terms despite the fraught context of communalism and intense nationalist fervor.

The period of the Ameena custody case, August 1991–March 1992, fell between the Shahbano controversy in 1985–86 and the destruction of the Babri Masjid in Ayodhya in December 1992. The last two communal events have been widely connected in political analyses in a chain of cause and effect. The ostensible Muslim victory in the Shahbano case, the consequent disgruntlement of Hindu fundamentalist parties over this, the Rajiv Gandhi government's appeasement of Hindu sentiment by throwing open the disputed Ram temple within the Masjid's precincts, and the growing politicization of the dispute over the birthplace of Ram: this is a well-known sequential reading of events. The destruction of the Masjid was counted as a "victory" for the Hindus that balanced the earlier Muslim "victory" in securing Muslim personal law in the Shahbano case. In the intervening period, the issue of Muslim child marriage exploded around the "case" of Ameena. It was a precarious historical moment, one poised already at the edge of communal tensions.

But, as we have come to recognize, communal conflicts erupt around issues not on the basis of any intrinsic provocation they may offer but as they provide opportunities for specific political use among fundamentalist parties. Between the two charged events,

Shahbano and Babri Masjid, as it happened, Muslim fundamentalism was at a low key, and Hindutva forces were preoccupied with the more pressing issue of mobilizing support for the construction of the Ram temple in Ayodhya. In this lies the (partial) historical explanation for the containment of the Ameena issue, and the reason why it could instead be successfully framed within the problematic of class-gender. It also accounts for the variety of contradictory subject-positions that came to be offered to Ameena within the scenario of rescue.

Thus, though the Ameena case was attended by a sense of déjà vu, in terms of a replay of a recent past event, it was also a conscious *revision* of the event. The conflict between a "progressive" secular and universal law (here the CMRA), on the one hand, and a reactionary personal law, on the other, could have become the central issue, as it did in the Shahbano case, especially since the counsel for the accused did argue, in their defense, that Muslim personal law permitted marriage after a girl reached puberty regardless of her legal minority. But the criminal case was prosecuted at a much lower intensity than the issue of Ameena's custody. And the *communal* identity of the female subject, which had been the primary identity that Shahbano came to be recognized by, was displaced onto the categories of class, gender, and age in a more pronounced way in Ameena's case.

The reasons for this had to do with the alertness of several institutions to the dangers of the first eventuality. Though the overdetermined subaltern status of both women—minority community, female, indigent, dependent (i.e., minor girl/old woman)—was similar in its complexity and contradictions, these facts were appropriated and foregrounded differently by the groups concerned. Thus the reaction of the orthodox Muslim community (the Muslim Personal Law Board, Islamic religious heads) was defensive rather than aggressive about the rightness and rights of Muslim custom and law in the Ameena case; the Muslim husband got no support from the Indian Muslim community; the Muslim intelligentsia intervened promptly to wrest the episode toward a call for reform within the community; the Hindu fundamentalist outcry was preempted by the major role played by the left-wing women's organizations, the All India Democratic Women's Association (AIDWA), and the Janwadi Mahila Samiti on behalf of Ameena; the courts, by separating the issue of Ameena's custody from the prosecution of her husband and parents, shifted the legal emphasis more productively from what had happened to what needed to be done. In the discursive frame of "news," the interest was retained within the focus of the human-interest story and expressed in the idiom of concern for and reform and rehabilitation of Ameena and other minor girls in her situation. It was the nation rather than the community that came to serve as the scene of the drama's staging. Nationalist discourse primarily invoked the strategy of arousing the collective national conscience over the predicament of a young girl who had been dramatically "rescued" in the nick of time and now stood in need of further protection.

We can see how in a case relating to Muslim child marriage certain positions were created for the gendered subject within the contours of the liberal problematic within which sections of the Muslim community, the law, the media, and women's groups operated. In the sections that follow I identify these subject-positions in an attempt to understand their political potential and to ask whether/how they resonated with or were constrained by a nationalist and statist discourse.

The Case of the "Case"

The Ameena story first broke in the newspapers. This fact must be set against the Shahbano case's long gestation in courts of law. What it implies is that Ameena's controversial marriage was not just reported or given publicity by the media but was constructed by them as a narrative, which, as a consequence, *provoked* further developments, both legal and personal/historical. The "Ameena case," as a product of the news, carried from the very beginning the powerful force of the singular human-interest story. The shifts in the subject-status accorded to Ameena, which I will trace in what follows, were accompanied by the typical mode of subjectification of the gendered "case." The "case," in the English-language Indian media, is not merely a shorthand term that refers to the accretion of an entire range of issues around the woman's proper name (with the additional likelihood of these issues being legal in nature, therefore a "case" in the more specific sense as well). It also carries the other notation of the "case"—the example, the symbol, the transcendental signified. The "case," Derrida complains (speaking of Sartre's Genet), is a fixing, an "entrapment" within the logic of example: "So what signs

Genet would be there only to make the example, the case, of a universal structure, which would give us its own key" (1987, 29b).

In the discourse of the news, the operation of the "case" therefore created a double status for Ameena. While, on the one hand, the news story or report kept a steady focus on a singular "Ameena," the editorials freely pluralized her identity: "Save Ameenas" cried the *Hindustan Times* (29 August 1991). "Ameena" is moved at a leap from anonymity to the only kind of public identity she can have—which is not the unique individuality that the proper name signifies but the typicality of the proper name + the "case." In the newspapers' mode of subjectification the singular and individual Ameena figured with identity markers such as age, community, and sex (with the addition of trivial details about her dress, behavior, gestures), an identity reinforced by the extensive publication of photographs.

Narrative is an essential context for embedding identity thus constructed. The typical narrative as framed by press reportage takes the form of the unfolding serial: from mise-en-scène through disclosure, progress, development, reversal to denouement. The "original" happening, the discovery of the weeping child onboard the Indian Airlines flight, was of course a news *event* in its most unequivocal sense and immediately came to be described as a "rescue." The subsequent happenings that constructed the issue as a continuous serial narrative were chiefly the proceedings of the court. The media also played up the appeals of Amrita Ahluwalia, her meetings with Ameena, the parents' statements, etc. Ameena as the "choosing" subject—agent of her own destiny—was likewise a product of this narrative reportage. Ameena was endowed with other characterological attributes: "quiet" and "sullen," observes the writer Anees Jung, who also canvasses other opinions: she is "bossy," according to her mother, and according to the social worker, "Ameena thinks she is a cut above the rest. . . . She wants to be able to read and write and become a big madam, the kind that come to visit her from Delhi" (1992).[4] It was a tendentious narrative that offered Ameena's restoration to her parents, seven months after her rescue at the airport, as closure, the "happy ending" in this case. But postscripts may jeopardize narrative closure by their supplementarity.

I have recorded these odd follow-up details to the Ameena case after the main story died out in the press: the telephone booth that had been talked of as a facility to improve the financial status of Ameena's father does not materialize; Ameena cannot attend the occupational school, one of the many that are set up as a reform measure in the Hyderabad ghetto where her family live, because of her father's insistence on purdah; al-Sageih jumps bail before his trial is over and disappears from the Saudi Arabian embassy where he is lodged; Ahluwalia has reportedly lost interest in Ameena and hardly ever visits her; the "Save Ameena" fund never gets off the ground; the tutor hired for Ameena's home education is invariably absent.[5] The newsmagazine *India Today* added further details in a 1995 report:[6] Ameena's family suffer ostracism on account of the notoriety of her case; her parents are put to the trouble and expense of periodic journeys to Delhi to attend the court hearings against them; the state's Child Women and Child Welfare department has refused assistance to her, on the grounds that the responsibility is really that of the police (Mitta 1995, 157–59). The multiple ironies at play here are only too obvious and need no spelling out.

In contrast, editorials and features, the parallel discursive mode operative in the print media, delivered what Derrida derides as the "the sententious academicism of [an] edifying discourse," which comes about as a result of the "consultation" of "experts": "When one speaks of the case, the doctor, the judge, the professor, the guard, and the lawyer are already in consultation. One sees the robes and the uniforms and the sleeves bustle about" (1987, 29b). Medical, legal, and religious opinions on various aspects of the case were sought and circulated; sociological and economic surveys of the community and the region were carried out. The commentary on the socioeconomic status of poor Muslim (as well as Hindu) girl children came about as a result of the interest in the named poor Muslim girl; her legal story was accompanied by class analysis of the social condition of the poor; the individual is located within the community, but the community itself is placed within the context of the welfare state rather than in relation to its "own" customs and laws. Other "sightings" of victimized Muslim children reinforced the exemplarity of Ameena's case but also functioned as autonomous parallel stories within a climate receptive to such news.[7] The general category and the specific example intersect.

The effacement of the individual subject that is effected in this discursive structure of commentary and analysis need not be deplored as if it were only a strategy of distraction and displacement (as happened in the Shahbano case).[8] The focus on the double dimension of "Ameena" was inescapable, and it carried a double charge. Hannah Arendt has described the doubleness thus: "[The] exemplar is and remains a particular that in its very particularity reveals the generality that otherwise could not be defined" (1982, 72). The Ameena case must be tracked through the intersecting consequences it had for Ameena the "exemplar," as well as for Hyderabad Muslim girls "in general." The discovery of the predicament of the individual protagonist and the widespread publicity it received did annul Ameena's marriage and prevent her exile (the element of chance and contingency in such fortuitous discoveries must be noted), though the subsequent developments in the case led to little more than her return to her former situation, the very condition of poverty and need that had led to her marriage in the first place.[9] Ironically she herself does not benefit from the reform measures her case initiated: the recognition that Ameena was one of many has helped "hundreds of girls," according to a newspaper report about the vocational training program set up by the central government and the Norwegian Development Agency following the media attention to the plight of young Hyderabadi Muslim girls; and the Andhra Pradesh Women's Cooperative Finance Corporation set up twenty-four centers in the old city to provide vocational training to 1600 girls between the ages of fifteen and twenty, according to another (Sheriff 1993b; Jung 1992). Media vigilance about the perils faced by Hyderabad Muslim girls has been active if not sustained. Ameena was both multiplied into and reduced to the "example."

The kind of reformist use made of the singular subject's predicament that characterizes news practice is an aspect of the liberal discourse of the English-language media in India. The pan-Indian medium of the English language, and the nationwide circulation of most English-language newspapers, lead to their privileging putatively "national" over "sectarian" interests. (Most Urdu papers, for instance, gave the Ameena and Kaneez episodes little more than routine attention or tended to champion the Muslim point of view.)[10] English-in-India itself, Vivek Dhareshwar argues, represses caste (and, we might add, community) in the secular consciousness of the metropolitan subject.[11] The alignment of English with secularism and the public sphere that Dhareshwar identifies limits the operation of all three within this narrow conjuncture (1993, 115–26). Further, even as we recognize the national media's decisive shaping of the historical national event within the contours of a "secular," that is, class-gender, issue, its treatment in a trivially sensational and sentimental rather than powerfully reformist mode must be pointed out.[12] In the discourse of the news the "case" is confined to the bearer of the proper name (just as, initially, it was the criterion of "human interest" that determined the entry of the subject into the news). When the story of the individual Ameena ceased to have news value, the attendant discourse of reform also died out. Since women's issues in India have typically tied themselves to the proper name of the woman and been structured as "news," the momentum of change and the pressure for reform have not always been sustained beyond the exhaustion of the news story related to her.[13]

Becoming "Indian"

In India there is a highly visible majoritarian hostility toward the minority communities that arises from the very terms of a nationalism that is "predisposed towards homogeneity" (Zutshi 1993, 136–37). As a result, Muslims in India are forced to occupy "the semantically confusing and psychologically unnerving status of foreigners inside" (Bauman 1989, cited in Zutshi 1993, 136). This identity is reinforced by their perceived connections with and support from Islamic nations. Ameena's husband, the accused Yahya Mohammed al-Sageih, was Muslim, but, more importantly for this situation and in this discourse, it was as a Saudi Arabian national that he became a villain, an adversary, and the public's bête noire.

As representative of the Gulf nations' exploitative attitude toward India's poor, al-Sageih became the Indian nation's hate figure, as much as he was Ameena's repudiated husband. The media has periodically expressed and provoked public resentment and indignation about the flight to West Asian countries of skilled and semiskilled Indian workers for manual employment, of girl children and women for "marriage," domestic service, or prostitution, and of little boys for riding camels in races. But sensitive international relations between India and the Gulf nations—both politically and economically important for India (not least for opening up such employment avenues and generating remittances home)—cannot be jeopardized by overt interstate hostilities. Al-Sageih fitted the villainous stereotype of the tourist sheikh who visits India in search of kicks (though his actual appearance and status reduced him quickly to a figure of fun: "India's most famous bridegroom," one newspaper mocked). Unlike Shahbano's husband, a lawyer himself who was supported by the Indian Muslim Personal Law Board that took his case up to the Supreme Court, al-Sageih, as a foreigner, encountered only hostility or ridicule.

Therefore, one of the major reasons for the differences in the narrative trajectories of the news stories relating to Shahbano and Ameena may be located in the different responses the public displayed toward their dramatis personae, specifically the protagonist's opponent. In the Ameena story, the adversarial role was divided between the Indian Muslim father and the foreign Muslim husband. The father elicited easy sympathy because of the poverty and illiteracy that made him a recognizable dupe of the system of brokered marriages. Women's groups eventually came to support his custody claim for his daughter. At worst Ameena's parents invited derision and contempt as poor, ignorant Muslims.[14] Al-Sageih and foreign "bridegrooms" in general took the brunt of the blame for the marriages that were transacted with Indian (Muslim) girls so that, curiously enough, the issue lost some of its communal flavor by this transference. It was a xenophobic India that embraced Ameena, Muslim identity and all, within the fold of the "Indian" national community.

From a majoritarian point of view that implicitly identifies itself as Hindu/Indian, Ameena, it would seem, called forth a novel form of recognition: she is not "one of us," but she is "ours." As poor, Muslim, child, and female she was severally the "other" of a majoritarian self coded as the bourgeois Hindu adult male; but within the rhetoric of *rescue* and *custody* she could nonetheless be claimed as "belonging to" the nation. It was in this way that Ameena was hailed as "Indian" and as citizen: as one who had (to have) residence within the nation.

The Custodial Subject

If "Shahbano" had operated largely within the discourse of protection—in which the self/other polarity was retained in the benevolent framing of the female subject as the object of protection—"custody" negotiated the relationship more complexly. The rhetoric of custody—"not us, but ours"—was of course generated by the issue of legal custody that came to the fore in the Ameena case, as "protection" had been triggered by the issue of maintenance in the Shahbano case.[15]

The question of who should be granted legal custody of Ameena engaged the courts and the interest of the press for over seven months. Among the many claimants were the airhostess Amrita Ahluwalia, Ameena's husband, her parents, women's organizations, and state-run custodial institutions. The airhostess, despite her claim of having been the agent of Ameena's "rescue" and despite the piquancy of her emotive, much-publicized desire to adopt Ameena, was soon out of the running, presumably because she had no blood relationship with the object of her rescue. The husband, once charged for abduction and illegal marriage, was willing to divorce Ameena and made no further claims on her. Women's groups came around to supporting Ameena's restoration to her parents as the lesser of the two evils confronting her. The contestants who remained in the ring were the parents and the state.

But both these claimants too were palpably disqualified. Ameena's parents had betrayed the family's traditional responsibility toward the safety and well-being of the child by contracting her marriage to an old man for money. And the Indian state has so few adequate provisions for its wards that it could only make a feeble pretense of wanting custody of the child. Its welfare institutions for destitute, indigent women, the insane, the criminal, orphans, beggars, and juvenile offenders are notoriously places of incarceration, abuse, and appalling physical hardship.[16] Ameena's three-day confinement in a Nari Niketan (penitentiary or "home" for women) in Delhi was greeted with public outrage.[17] Indeed "custody" began to carry the weight of its other, here inappropriate, signification, that of confinement, as in "in custody" (reinforced also by the Muslim custom of purdah—Ameena was not permitted to attend school because of the restrictions of purdah).

The concept of custody is thus brought to crisis by institutions—the family and the state—whose conditions both ruled out the possibility of adequate caretaking and placed in doubt the appropriateness of the confinement of an innocent victim within their structures. The broad narrative movement traveled by "Ameena"—the circular trajectory from her ejection/expulsion from home and country, to her rescue and reclamation (by the state), and her eventual return and restoration (to the family)—is blocked at the two points of reentry, nation and home, by the jeopardized concept of custody.

The family and state are of course differently related to the child, and a contest over their respective fitness for custody would not be fairly weighted in terms of either their respective affective bonds or their resources. Skepticism about the family's affective investment in a girl child is too easy a response in a case of child marriage or even the sale of children,[18] for considerations like poverty, social pressures, and poor judgment about the interests of the child overwhelmingly influence these desperate measures. Ameena's parents' reclamation of her and her own wish to return to them offer some evidence of the ties that still bound them.[19] The state, on the other hand, has no *claim* on the child bride it has rescued but rather an *obligation* to fulfill—which is best expressed in terms of *her* entitlements. The question of the child's rights is one I will return to. In this case, state officials were complacent about having rescued Ameena, and indeed the city police and immigration officials in Delhi were extremely assiduous in the months that followed about similar arrests, rescues, and crackdowns on suspected abductions and kidnappings of Muslim minors. In general the Indian state is quick to make a show of criminalizing those who continue to follow the social practices and customs that it has outlawed, while doing precious little to ameliorate the conditions that produce them—especially where abuses against women are concerned. This is by now a well-worn observation. The Ameena case was an embarrassment particularly because none of the institutions the state had established—the Juvenile Justice Board, the Social Welfare Board, foster-care arrangements—was suitable or fit to offer the abandoned child an alternative to the family, even in terms of material resources. They still are not.[20]

The Ameena case was finally "resolved" by renegotiations of the concept of custody: first by the watchdog role played by women's organizations and by the liberal intervention of the media, which pressed for Ameena's rights and for her freedom to choose; and then by the reexamination of the family's custodial role that was forced on the court in the light of economic realities—the conditions of poverty and its concomitant ignorance, illiteracy, desperation, vulnerability to pecuniary temptation and to social pressure that render the family, contrary to received notions, the primary site of the child's/woman's/female child's oppression. Recognizing the need to alter the conditions of her family life through state assistance and intervention, the judges spelled out various directives to the Andhra Pradesh government regarding Ameena's future well-being, such as arrangements for her education and/or vocational training, supervision of her upkeep, and the monitoring of parental care. In this process the traditional separation of the public and private spheres was deconstructed and the interpenetration of the two highlighted, as in the Shahbano case.

The Choosing Subject

How do we read the fact that Ameena's own wishes on the matter of her custody became the central and decisive factor in resolving the issue? In this case custody came to be decided not according to the "natural" (familial) or the legal (state) obligations of the putative custodians but according to the wishes of, and the judgment of their fitness made by, the heretofore passive subject of custody. The judges observed that "in matters relating to custody of children the welfare and wishes of the child are of paramount importance. . . . We have had occasion to talk to Ameena, and she has, in no uncertain terms, expressed her desire to go back to her family. Ameena appears to us to be quite mature for her age and does not seem to be under any influence and has been quite unhappy in not being restored to the members of her family."[21] The High Court thereby helped to create a subject-position for Ameena that moved her, in the narrative we are tracing, from being the object of property (contracted by a sale by her father to another man in marriage for the sum of Rs 6000) to a passive subject of custody and then promoted her to the active, agential role of the subject who is called on to make crucial decisions based on her own wishes and choices.[22] Her first decision, intended to resolve the case of her own custody, is made when the High Court seeks to ascertain her wishes about her future. It strikes down the Juvenile Board's decision to make her an inmate of a women's welfare home as unsound. When Ameena pronounces in favor of her return to her own family, it respects her wishes and restores her to them. Subsequently, Ameena is called on to offer further crucial testimony. As witness in the state's prosecution of al-Sageih and her parents, she states that she had "consented" to her marriage, and that therefore her parents were not guilty of forcibly marrying her off. She retracts her earlier statements to the police about her forced marriage. In the context of her wish to return to her parents this retraction is, of course, only logical. Members of the AIDWA, which had been supporting her return to her parents, observed that "the exoneration of her parents by Ameena should come as no surprise." Clearly "her statement is determined by her concern for her family and their protection and not necessarily by what happened" (*Hindustan Times*, 18 November 1992). She is entirely consistent in this second move to reinforce her restoration to the family, however inconsistent her different versions about her marriage may appear.[23]

In Islamic marriage, since the woman's consent must be given in the marriage document, the child bride may annul the marriage on reaching puberty if she so chooses. (This option is also permitted by the CMRA, in a clause that has been taken over from Muslim marriage law.) When "consent" is called on to define the legal subject so that she is endowed with the right to grant or withhold it, parental, social, legal, religious, and sexual norms and demands intersect and conflict on the terrain of the female child's sexuality. It is not, of course, merely fortuitous that women's consent, otherwise so rarely called on, comes to bear the weight of legal and social significance when the issues at stake are sexual offenses committed by *men,* as in child marriage, rape, abduction, or prostitution, since then the offenders may be exonerated if the women in question (invariably the victims of the offenses) can be proven to be complicitous with the crime, as they only too often can be shown to be.[24] The issue of consent becomes complicated only when the female subject is still a child by certain definitions of "maturity," here legal ones. I will return to the issue of age in relation to legal identity.

Ameena's "voice" therefore put in doubt the presumption that she was coerced into marriage. And if her testimony was instrumental in restoring her to her parents, it also meant that her supposed "consent" to the marriage weakened the case against her husband.[25] The framing of laws like the CMRA enshrines, as we will see, a deliberate contradiction at its very heart, so that the immediate benefit of "consent" expressed by the individual (to protect her family) undermines the long-term reformist consequences for the class (abolishing the institution of child marriage). And even this option has been known to be denied by courts where the guardian is believed to have been "well-intentioned" in contracting the marriage. We must be careful, then, not to exalt agency as defined by the exercise of choice or the expression of consent from within a conceptual vacuum. However radical this assertion of the child's rights may have been, in reality the "choice" exercised by Ameena could only be a heavily compromised pact with the circumstances in which she was enmeshed. "For a concept like 'choice' to make sense," as Mary Poovey cautions, "it will have to be conceptualized as a social issue and in a social arena: that is, a variety of options will have to be made available and supported with equal social resources" (1992, 253). In the absence of such options choice can turn out to be at best an ironic freedom.

It is important as well not to overstress the radical boldness of the judgment that granted custody of Ameena to her parents. Legal judgments are contextualized within, if not actually influenced by, the social and political circumstances of the case. The high-profile publicity that attended the Ameena custody case, and the pressure of influential Delhi women's groups, were factors that counted toward not only a relatively speedy disposal of the case but also the most popular judgment in the circumstances. The law is in any case ideologically inclined to support the reinsertion of women and children into the family whenever this option is legally available. The fact that both Ameena and the women's groups involved sought such a move accorded well with its own conservative family-oriented views. The fact of consensus rather than conflict on the issue among the parties involved helped in resolving the matter to reflect Ameena's "choice."

If the centralization of the issue of choice in Ameena's case, in particular the judges' emphasis on the significance they attached to it, is a subjectificatory move that I have wished to draw attention to all the same, that is because it entails a significantly marked departure from previous resolutions of the child marriage question. Janaki Nair has described the (non)place of the child bride in the controversies over child marriage in pre-Independence India:

... the child wife was irreducibly the victim, placed at the centre of a legal-juridical discourse that often made criminals of her parents, husband and other members of her natal and marital families and yet permitted her no more than a name and an age. On some occasions, she was subjected to medical examinations to establish her age, but her own voice remained muted and muffled throughout the period when the government of her sexuality passed uneasily between the system of alliances of which she was a part and the state. (1996a, 174)

Nair offers two reasons why the discourse of reform, which had been able to offer only this diminished subjectivity to the child wife, the object of its reform, subsequently died out: one, the project of modernization, here the achievement of "a reformed patriarchy," was deemed to be complete; and two, an increasingly visible women's movement "had transformed the agenda of social reform by speaking more directly of women's rights," thereby "enabling sections of Indian women to sculpt entirely new subjectivities" (184).[26] The Ameena case is shaped within this new discursive and political terrain. To dismiss the impact and the effects of the campaign that women's groups waged on the ground of the rights of the girl child would be to slight a significant site of struggle. I will return to the issue of child marriage within the movement for rights (children's and women's), to explore how "reform" is being reconstituted within these new agendas.[27]

Gender, Age, and Sexuality

The doubt about Ameena's correct age, and consequently about her status as child or adult (girl or woman), was central to the controversy surrounding her forced marriage. That there should have been a controversy at all was, as I have pointed out, merely a function of the notoriety of the circumstances of its "discovery" as news, for child marriage in India is the norm, despite its illegality. Some of the complexities of this situation, and their implications for the construction of Ameena as "Muslim child bride," require further elaboration.

The age relating to consent and marriage was legislated five times between 1860 and 1929 in British India, and its reformist purpose was addressed primarily to Hindu practices.[28] The first legislation, the Age of Consent Act of 1860, related to the legal "age of consent" for sexual intercourse, that is, the age of the girl below which intercourse with her would be regarded as rape. It was one of a number of legislations undertaken by the colonial government as a measure of reform of Hindu society, in this case the perceived evil of widespread child marriage, which was closely related to the "problem" (as it was then regarded) of regulating the sexuality of widows.[29] The movement for the abolition of child marriage was spearheaded by the social reformer Ishwar Chandra Vidyasagar. The first Age of Consent Act, fixing the minimum permissible age for sexual intercourse with a woman (married or unmarried) at ten, was passed with relative ease and incorporated into the Indian Penal Code. The second Age of Consent Bill, passed in 1891, following the sensational Phulmani case, the child wife who had died of sexual injuries, sought to raise the age of consent to twelve. This, in contrast to the earlier bill, became a center of extreme controversy. The Indian nationalist Bal Gangadhar Tilak led a fierce opposition to it on the grounds that the act interfered unwarrantably in Indian religion and custom, hence all Indian nationalists should oppose it. In Bengal, orthodox Hindu patriarchs offered ingenious explanations as to why, while ten had been an acceptable legislation for the age of consent, twelve would seriously impinge on the sanctity of Hindu marriage since by that age girls would have attained sexual maturity (T. Sarkar 1996, 230–38). The Child Marriage Restraint Act of 1929, more specifically intended to regulate marriage customs, raised the marriage age to fourteen for girls and eighteen for men. Only in the 1920s did discussions surrounding the issue of age of consent and child marriage come to focus on the medical dangers of intercourse and early pregnancy of the young brides, but even in this later discourse the concerns expressed about Hindu motherhood were only "metaphors" for nationalism, as Judy Whitehead has argued (1996, 187–209). The earlier discourse, whether of defenders or reformers, centered largely on the issues of Hindu tradition and on the eugenic and class and racial aspects of early marriage for the Hindu male and female. As was the case in much social-reform legislation in the colonial period relating to women's issues, the consent acts sharpened the conflict between traditionalists and modernizers, nationalists and reformers, indigenous patriarchy and colonial rulers. The outcome of these reform measures, as Meera Kosambi sums it up, while it "ensured legal protection for child-brides, and . . . introduced a more humane perspective on their condition," also meant that, because of the intense controversy, "the cause of women's emancipation was relegated to the background over the next decades" (1991, 1868).[30]

At least one consequence of this relentless focus on the question of Ameena's age in relation to the validity of her marriage was that, like the gendered subject of representation in general, she was inescapably sexualized. While the law subjected Ameena to medical examinations in order to ascertain her age, the news media frequently featured her in photographs that offered her appearance (large eyes, full cheeks, diminutive stature) as self-evident indication of her youth. The law and the media admittedly played an active and reformist role in ensuring Ameena's "rescue" and restoration, as I have pointed out, thus providing what Parker et al. have termed "counter-narratives" serving the purpose of "civic education." At the same time, "newspaper, films, novels and theatre all create sexed bodies as public spectacles, thereby hoping to instill through representational practices an erotic investment in the national romance" (1992, 12). These child women, Ameena, Fatima, Kaneez—nubile, pretty, vulnerable—were clearly easy to eroticize within narratives that, further, related them in marriage to men who (apart from being foreign) were also old and unattractive. The sustained and (as the Kaneez case that followed "Ameena" proved) persistent interest in the fate of Muslim child brides cannot be separated from the prurience and sensationalism associated with much media representation, as I have earlier held. The large-circulation English daily the *Indian Express,* for instance, reported the Kaneez story as follows: "Another minor girl was saved from being sacrificed at the altar of lust on Wednesday as alert Delhi Police rescued sixteen-year-old Kaneez Begum from the clutches of three Arab Nationals" (10 December 1993).[31]

The state too, by its laws, as Jacqui Alexander has pointed out in her analysis of the Sexual Offences Bill (1986) of Trinidad and Tabago, "eroticizes girls from the outside by sexualizing them and constructing them as untouchable" (1991, 142). The legal issue at stake in the Ameena case, as we saw, was the different positions of CMRA and Muslim personal law on the permissible age of marriage for girls. Muslim law equates maturity with puberty but also permits child marriage (i.e., marriage before puberty) at the discretion of the guardians.[32] Female subjectivity, both CMRA and MPL seem to agree, inheres in a certain "maturity," which in turn is defined by the female subject's readiness for sexual intercourse and reproduction. The disagreement is over whether this is reached at the time of physical eligibility, that is, puberty (according to MPL), or at or over the specified legal age of eighteen (according to CMRA).

Medical and pseudomedical definitions of puberty formed part of the nineteenth-century debates about age of consent, as Tanika Sarkar has shown, revivalists insisting that it could properly be said to begin with the onset of puberty, and reformers arguing that "puberty was a prolonged process." But either way, consent was "pegged to a purely physical capability, [and] . . . made into a biological category, a stage when the female body was ready to accept sexual penetration without serious harm," without regard to questions about "free choice of partner or sexual, emotional or mental compatibility" (T. Sarkar 1996, 230–31). A purely legal criterion of maturity is equally difficult to establish, given the absence of birth registration in most parts of the country. But it is increasingly clear that the criterion of age itself is a problematic one, as a basis for both sexual activity and the exercise of choice/consent, and that it has to be radically reexamined and restated.[33]

Reforming Child Marriage

If we locate the Ameena case within the problematic of child marriage in contemporary India, we are led to ask how its "solutions" are envisaged. Unlike the colonial state, the Indian state's concern about early marriages is not primarily (or at least explicitly) addressed to families' and communities' anxiety about the chastity and sexual "protection" of young women (and men—the defense that early marriage is "better than premarital sex" [in the West] is a familiar one). Delayed marriage is instead viewed within a problematic of development (family planning: as a measure that will reduce births; and health: as a medical argument that women beyond their teens bear not only fewer but also healthier children).

But the state's straightforward address to child marriage as a developmental issue is hampered because as a social practice it occupies yet another ground of contention beyond those we have been examining so far (personal law versus universal civil law, and consent versus coercion): that of custom and tradition versus modernity. Since successive Indian governments have notoriously used progressive laws in cautious and noninterventionary ways because of their professed respect for social custom and tradition, the law against child marriage remains completely unenforced, in disregard of the developmental concerns of the state.[34] It is not surprising that virtually nobody has so far been successfully prosecuted under CMRA, despite nearly 50 percent of all girls in the country being underage at the time of their marriage. According to the 1991 census, the all-India mean age at marriage among females is 17.7 (Rustagi 2000, 4281).[35] The marriage of minor children is a widespread practice in many parts of the country, especially rural areas, among Hindu as well as minority communities. It has been defended on grounds of practical necessity and "common sense" as well as tradition. The sale of girls into prostitution is also virtually a ritual annual practice in some parts of the country. Neither practice is checked by law enforcers. Ameena's parents were to demand with genuine bewilderment, as also Kaneez's mother, where their transgression lay, given the commonplaceness of the situation, especially in poor families (Sheriff 1993b; Sarita Rani 1993, 42).

The emphasis among feminist activists opposing child marriage is more exclusively focused on the health of young married girls and is expressed as concern over their loss of "childhood" as such, their removal from school, their compulsory entry into household labor at an early age, and their sexual exploitation and violation in marriage unions like Ameena's. This concern has recently prompted some feminists, led by the National Commission for Women, to demand an amended law and stricter law enforcement, while others are both skeptical and wary of the impact of state-sponsored legislation in social-reform issues. Those demanding legal reform point to the contradictions of the present CMRA, which does not attract the penalty of the law unless a case is filed against the parents and husbands, and according to which the marriage is not declared illegal even if performed illegally. As Vasudha Dhagamwar, an activist lawyer involved in drafting an amended CMRA, mocks: "The Child Marriage Restraint Act is perhaps the only Act in the world which says that something—in this case child marriage—is legal and yet an offence" (2000). The amendment proposed by the NCW includes "appointment of Child Marriage Prevention Officers by the state governments, stringent punishment under Section 23 for violation of the Act, declaring as void marriages performed in contravention of the law, and making it legally obligatory for every person attending a child marriage to prevent it or report it to the concerned authorities" (UNI report, September 2000). Dhagamwar argues:

> The only way to tackle this situation is by a mix of law and practical steps. First step is to abolish child marriage. The second is for every State Government to publicise the law widely. The State must stress the fact that
> Your girl (or boy) is still not married.
> The state will confiscate the dowry.
> The girl will still be your responsibility.
> You will not get a daughter-in-law to do free manual work.
> Instead, all four parents and guardians, the priest and the adult guests will be punished.
> In short, we need a law that is as draconian as the Sati law. (ibid.)

Since in many communities mass weddings of children are performed on specific festival days in the year, it is possible, Dhagamwar argues, to publicize the law widely among such target groups: "Prevention is always better than cure" (ibid.; see also Dhagamwar 1997, 156–60).

Alongside a stricter law, stricter law enforcement, and prevention measures, Dhagamwar, like others of her persuasion who would vest these responsibilities (and powers) in the state, also supports free universal compulsory education (FUCE) up to the age of fourteen, "as the Constitution enjoins us to do" (ibid.); another supplementary measure that has been proposed is registration of all marriages and births.[36] The United Nations Children's Fund (UNICEF) regards birth registration as the "first" right, the "right to official identity" (as expressed in Article 7 of the UN Convention on the Rights of the Child). According to Unity Dow, writing in the organization's *Progress of Nations* report in 1998,

> Registration of birth is the State's first acknowledgement of a child's existence. It represents recognition of a child's significance to the country and his or her status under the law. This

ticket to citizenship opens the door to the fulfilment of rights and to the privileges and services that a nation offers its people. . . . An effective system of birth registration is fundamental not only to the fulfilment of child rights but to the rational operation of a humane government in the modern world. (Dow 1998, 5)

Though Dow does not include the prevention of child marriage among the benefits of birth registration, she does list others like protection against military service, child labor, and sex trafficking; and the importance of being "counted" when the state has to provide services like health, immunization, and schooling. Many countries in the developing world, however, have no systematic birth registration procedures, especially in sub-Saharan Africa and South Asia. (In India, less than 50 percent of births are registered.) Clearly, those who insist on the "rights" of the child are calling on the *state* to make them enforceable by, in turn, enforcing measures like registration of births and marriages, compulsory primary education, and the criminalization and annulment of child marriage. The implications and politics of such an approach are not free of problems, as we will see.

In the first place, many women's groups point to the strong resistance among communities to the imposition of a law that would criminalize their entrenched customs; these women's groups would rather tread warily in this issue, pointing to the adverse impact of annulling marriages on the young brides who would then be effectively "abandoned" (Dhagamwar retorts: "their lives are already ruined by early marriage"). In 1992 the case of Bhanwari Devi, a "saathin" in the Rajasthan Women's Development Project, brought home the dangers of even cautious propaganda against child marriage as Bhanwari was assaulted and raped by upper-caste landlords in the area as warning against her "interference." This is *not* to advocate withdrawal from activism but to indicate its difficulties. In rural areas where the safety of unmarried girls is an acknowledged problem, and in general where dowries are a burden, child marriages, especially performed at mass weddings, make practical sense. The received wisdom, which approaches a truism, is that any change must first prepare suitable conditions for the new situation, in this case by providing the girl child with alternatives to early marriage. The issue of child marriage remains suspended, therefore, in a dilemma that is now familiar to feminists in India, between an indefensible custom that supports it and an impotent "modernity" that opposes it.

Secondly, when practices are deemed "backward" or criminal, it is minorities and lower caste groups who often tend to be scapegoated; and, as a consequence, the issue becomes communalized. While it is true that Ameena's marriage could not sustain an exclusive communal focus because the superiority of women's status in the Hindu community could not be as easily vaunted or even implied in an issue of child marriage as it could be in the Shahbano case (relating to provision for divorced women), the attack on Muslim child marriage could and did insidiously take on a communal coloring. This was mainly because the Muslim bridegroom is not only an Arab/outsider but is also invariably already married (a "polygamous" Muslim) and, contrary to the upper-caste Hindu practice of dowry, he pays bride-price, which leads to these transactions being described as the "sale" of girls. Travesties of such marriages are common and include "temporary" marriages, desertion, reduction of the wife into servitude, and sale of "brides" into prostitution.[37] There is yet another aspect of early marriages and polygamy among Muslims that comes in for attack from the Hindu community: the complaint, based on serious misperception or fundamentalist propaganda, that the Muslim birth-rate is so high that their numbers threaten to overrun Hindus in the country.[38] Ameena's mother pointed out bitterly in an interview that even her poverty was blamed on the size of her family.[39] Similarly, Shankar Singh and Nikhil Dey have argued that the "akha teej" festival in Rajasthan is wrongly viewed as a dalit or OBC custom and is used to oppress these groups "in the name of being modern," while shifting the focus from oppressive upper-caste Hindu customs (1994, 1377–79). Therefore what was and continues to be a widely prevalent upper-caste Hindu practice is rhetorically displaced onto Muslims and lower-castes in the current climate of the politicization of social-reform issues.

Finally, there is the more abstract dimension of the issue, which focuses on the concept and politics of "rights." Like the question of liberal individual rights in general, that of the rights of children is open to a number of objections derived from historical and cultural relativist critique. We are reminded by its critics that any universal conception of children's rights assumes a Eurocentric conception of childhood, which is itself a product of modernity, as a norm. It over-looks the culturally variable structures of family and of the place, nurturance, sex-differentiation, and socialization of the child within the family. In particular, when the rights of the child are pitted against the rights of the family, it leads to "denuding the child of whatever support structures are available, i.e. family, clan, community etc." Notions of "correct" childhood only narrow the alternatives available for productively addressing the problems of children in non-Western societies (Raman 2000, 4059, 4064).[40]

The problem of the *nation-state* becoming the inescapable agent of enforcing rights (here, the rights of the child), and of (or by) modernization (here, removing child marriage), is a crucial one. Talal Asad argues that when the "universal character of the rights-bearing person is made the responsibility of sovereign states, each of which has jurisdiction over a limited group," then it is *populations* that are in question. "This limited population—as Foucault argued—is at once the object of the state's care and the means of securing its own power" (2000). The individual's rights therefore become the double-edged property of the state. And the requirements of counting and recording instituted by modern governmentality can also compromise these rights.[41]

Conclusion

A person, the proper name, is both constituent and component of a population but also has another interest and significance for us that derives from the fiction, if we like to call it that, of the uniqueness of the particular self, one located historically, at a particular conjuncture of events. The difficult task that this imposes on one is to think the individual (citizen-) subject and the population together. A law of the Indian state, making the forcible marriage of a minor girl punishable, prevented one such girl's entry into a life of servitude and indignity. We cannot make many or further claims for the law's efficacy or the state's role, given the vast majority of girls who are not similarly "saved"; and we must acknowledge even here the far greater role played by other agents in her rescue. In such a situation a liberal problematic would view the case (and the solution) as one requiring greater efficiency of the state's reform machinery (policy, law, policing, welfare measures), while the Foucauldian problematic of governmentality would ask us to be wary of the implications of the all-too-efficient intervention (reform/management) of the state. If in the postcolonial ("developing") nation we are called on to be aware of and responsive to both perspectives, the figure of the individual historical subject-as-citizen in question is the necessary point of reference that rescues us from theoretical aporia.

The particularity of the historical subject is mediated by the categories that define her identity—as also classify her for legal/administrative purposes—in terms of gender, class, community, age, sexuality. But this list becomes something more than a ritual incantation when we note that the predicament of Ameena, and others like her in the South Asia region, has also made necessary the construction of *new* categories for addressing it and describing the subject: in this case, as the "girl child." The problematic of age has emerged from the need to distinguish between the different forms of oppression to which women are subjected at various stages in their life, from the foetus to old age; and the problematic of gender from the need to define how sex and gender construct children differently in society, as in law and policy. It is primarily women's groups that have insisted on the need for a "disaggregated" analysis of the female and the child populations in order to identify the "girl child" as a specific category and identity.[43]

The Ameena case traverses some of the fraught areas in the transactions between the gendered citizen and the postcolonial nation-state. I have attempted to show how Ameena, from certain subject-positions, that is, as a citizen before the law, as a "case" (a representative victim of gendered oppression, here child marriage), and as a protagonist of the women's movement, was able to exercise significant agency. This agency was, however, compromised in various ways: by the limitations of individual choice or consent, the reduction of the individual to example, the regulation of female sexuality by the community and the state, and the contradictory operations of law. I have also identified the problem of—and with it the difficult and problematic solution (i.e., state intervention) envisaged for—child marriage in modern India.

Such an even-handed analysis of the possibilities and limits of citizenship, rights, and the law is a predictable if necessary exercise to perform in this exemplary fashion. My attempt has been to conduct this inquiry within the limits of the "case." I have provided the details of the Ameena case—as matters involving communal crisis, media interest, policy issues, feminist activism, the behavior of the law courts, the agency of the chief actors in the drama—as a way of arguing that some such density of context and narrative must help us locate both the historical subject and the issue she exemplifies, and to show the process toward her identification and identity as "girl child." One of the discoveries (rather than purposes) of the exercise of writing about the Ameena case, for me, has been that such a narrative of the singular—single and particular—sexed individual is a relevant context for understanding the state's ideology, practices, and functioning in relation to gender—and that her destiny is not by any means an excessive measure of judging the latter.[43]

3 Beyond the Hysterectomies Scandal: Women, the Institution, Family, and State

My reflections on institutionalized women in relation to the family and state in India, in this chapter, derive from and focus on a widely reported case of mass hysterectomies performed on women inmates of a state-run home for the mentally retarded in Pune, Maharashtra, in February 1994.

It is important to clarify at the outset that I offer the following discussion of the hysterectomies scandal as a case study not serving solely expository purposes but also exemplifying a conjuncture of issues that I regard as useful and significant for an understanding of the postcolonial situation. Let me clarify further: I do not intend simply to rehearse the terms of the debate over the hysterectomies, much less resolve it by referring to some transcendent third term above the opposed ones that structure it. Nor is there much to be gained by shading in greater "complexity" to the issue; no one suggests it is a simple one. Least of all is this intended as an exposé of Third World "underdevelopment"—though, as a plea for reform, my argument will attempt to probe the meaning and making of the postcolonial "scandal." I am more interested in *extending* the implications of the issue. By placing it at the juncture of a number of lines of inquiry (which are suggested by the chapter's title), I hope to reveal their overlooked interconnections. Implicitly, I hope also to rebut the currently influential intellectual position that, in the name of cultural relativism, indigenous values, historical contingency, social heterogeneity, or communitarian liberalism, seeks to rationalize, with reference to a certain "India," various aspects of the status quo—and these include, needless to say, the position of women.

The news story of the hysterectomies was itself a brief one, but the debate in the press over its pros and cons, along with feature articles on various aspects of the issue, continued to appear for several weeks.[1] On 4 February 1994, eleven women inmates of a home for the mentally retarded in Shirur had their wombs surgically removed at the Sasoon Hospital in nearby Pune city. The women were between the ages of fifteen and thirty-five; their average mental age was below four. Activists from several women's groups in Maharashtra protested outside the hospital but were unsuccessful in canceling the operations. A former member of Parliament of the Communist Party of India (Marxist), Ahalya Rangnekar, sought the intervention of the Maharashtra chief minister to prevent the operations, who then stayed the next batch of operations scheduled for the following day and ordered an inquiry. Shortly thereafter, however, he lifted the ban and these and similar procedures have been permitted to continue. The chief minister declared that it would be the responsibility of the bureaucracy and the doctors to decide what to do and that his government would not interfere. He only recommended that the operations not be performed in mass surgical "camps."

The Shirur home had about fifty inmates of whom thirty were in the specified age-group for the operation. Of these, eighteen were declared medically fit to undergo the procedure. The operations were performed free as a social service by a leading Bombay gynecologist, Dr. Shirish Seth, and his team. According to him and the director of the Department of Women, Child, and Handicapped Development (wchd) of the Maharashtra state government, Ms. Vandana Khullar, hysterectomies have been a standard procedure in the care and maintenance of mentally retarded women of reproductive age.[2] The protests of women activists of such groups as the Sarva Mazdoor Sangh, Bombay, Forum Against Oppression of Women, and Forum for Women's Help, Pune, were directed at the "fascist encroachment on the personal rights of the individual." Charnika Shah of the Forum for Women's Help held that "Nobody has the right to decide on such a major intervention on the body when there is no reproductive health problem." The activists therefore viewed the hysterectomies primarily as a human rights violation. The protestors found the reasons for sterilization offered by the government unconvincing, namely, the problem (for the caretakers in the home) of managing the inmates' menstrual periods and the official anxiety about their susceptibility to sexual assault. The first could not be regarded as a problem warranting such a serious step, and as for the second, protestors pointed out that the removal of the uterus would in any case not protect the women against sexual attacks or from sexually transmitted diseases but would only prevent pregnancy. "In fact, by doing away with evidence of assault, it will make them more vulnerable" (*The Telegraph*, 6 February 1994).

An organization of the parents and guardians of the mentally retarded in Pune, the Umed Parivar, came out in support of the sterilization. A writ petition questioning the legality of the operations was filed in the Bombay High Court in June 1994.

So much for what may be termed the facts of the event. Here, I first set out the implications of "welfare" in an underdeveloped economy, as an issue of import for women in the postcolonial state. In the discussion that follows, these aspects of the case are significant for my argument: the conflicting discourses of "expert" knowledge generated by the hysterectomies scandal, those of the institution, the law, and medicine; the implications of the controversy for questions of the family; and the politics of feminist interventions in this issue.

The State and "Victim" Citizens

In the Constitution of India the role of the state in the promotion of the people's welfare is recognized in unequivocal, if large and general, terms, first foreshadowed in the preamble, then included in the Fundamental Rights within the broad category of equalization of gender, caste, and class differences, and then explicitly identified in the Directive Principles.[3] Article 41 of the Directive Principles particularly directs the state "within the limits of [its] economic resources and capacity" to "ensure the right to work, to education and to public assistance in cases of unemployment, old age, sickness and disablement and in other cases of undeserved want." Justice Krishna Iyer has praised these provisions as reflecting the Indian Constitution's faith in "administrative engineering" and its "comprehensive backing for humanitarian jurisprudence in the area of retardates and handicapped classes" (1980, 193).

Directive principles, however, are only goals; they do not (yet) have the force of law. Further, despite the constitutional commitment to creating a welfare state, successive governments have placed critical limitations on achieving it. Barbara Harriss-White points out that "the institution to preside over this [the welfare state], the Planning Commission, does not have a constitutional status, and many of the interventions required were under the jurisdiction not of the central government but of the states" (1999, 146).[4] And a limiting factor to the scope of welfare is already indicated in Article 41: "within the limits of its . . . resources."

Here we come to the crucial question of government policy and the implementation of constitutional rights and directives. Developing nations of the Third World are beset not only by constraints of resources but by a concomitant predominance of the numbers of those in need of relief, the frequency and scale of disasters, and the limited and tardy means of legal recourse available to those denied their rights. Thus the larger question framed by the hysterectomies scandal relates to the welfare commitments of the developing nation in the Third World: in the first place, what are the responsibilities acknowledged by the state toward those citizens who have second-class status as a result of disability or other forms of deprivation? More crucially, how far is it able, or willing, to fulfill them? But beyond this, what are the consequences to citizenship-identity and other forms of subjectification for those viewed in terms of such negativity?

As Harriss-White points out, the alleviation of disability in all countries, but particularly in the developing nations, is bound to be an issue of low priority in "public choice theoretic terms." For the state, the "political and economic costs" of such welfare measures are high and its benefits low (135). Translated into the language of state policy, this consideration (supported by widespread social apathy about the condition of disabled people) means that welfare programs require "*ab initio* convincing justifications that the social health of disabled people is a necessary precondition not only for economic growth but also for social welfare" (143–44). Cost-benefit considerations, she ruefully concedes, have become a universal "institutional *lingua franca*" (146).

Though scarcity of resources is no longer the powerful pretext it once was for the Indian state's inability to meet the basic needs of the population and provide the necessary infrastructure for their attainment, the issue of resource allocation remains an important one in defining the obligations and functions of the state. As a matter of the common sense of the state, the welfare of the disabled figures among its lowest priorities. Even by the standards of a poor nation, the Indian government's budget allocations appear to be no more than a token gesture of its recognition of the needs of the disabled. The sum of Rs 980 lakhs allotted by the Union Ministry of Welfare for disability-related programs in 1988–89 was "less than the budget for a medium-sized municipality" and "less than what neighbouring Sri Lanka spends on a population under 2 per cent that of India's" (Harriss-White 1999, 150). Out of an estimated four million mentally retarded people requiring services, only eighteen thousand received any through institutions funded by the National Institutes of Mental Health (151).

These priorities of the central government are reflected in state governments' budgets as well. In Maharashtra, for instance, the Shirur home is the only government-run home for mentally retarded women in the state (the government gives aid to 65 other institutions run by nongovernment organizations). There are only 22 state-run institutions for the disabled, and 252 state-aided institutions. The expenditure on the state-run homes is a "meagre" Rs 1.75 crore (Iyer 1994). The allocation for social welfare as a whole in 1993–94 was Rs 35 crores, of which 17.59 was earmarked for the welfare of the handicapped. The 65 state-funded schools are intended to serve the needs of an approximate 59.2 lakh mentally handicapped children in the state. The expenditure on social services fell in nominal as well as in real terms between 1989–90 and 1992–93, in both the Union and Maharashtra state budgets ("Butchers in the Guise of Saviours" n.d., 8–11).

Meager resource allocation is of course only part of the sorry story. Rampant and virtually routine corruption at the administrative levels ensures that funds intended for developmental and welfare programs are siphoned off at various levels before reaching the intended recipients. Even at less extreme levels, governmental functioning ensures inefficiency and bureaucratic slowness of process. And like those of any developing country, the concerns of the Indian government are predominantly statist, macro-economic, and demographic in the administration of welfare and development-oriented programs. As a consequence, it disregards and, in case of conflict, overrides individual rights and community interests. Examples are not hard to find: the displacement of tribal people in big dam projects, forcible sterilization "camps" (especially notorious during Indira Gandhi's Emergency), the disregard of hazards to local people living close to nuclear test sites, batches of institutionalized mentally retarded women undergoing sterilization simultaneously—these are all instances of the policies and practices of the Indian state that have been justified by such rationalization.

Institutional studies in developing nations are therefore obliged to take into account the state's neglect of and simple lack of interest in those of its population who need special services, rather than fear the systematic and intrusive forms of regulation that are read as the mark of the modern welfare state. Harriss-White concludes: "For the mass of disabled people, the state does not exist" (19). Needless to say, such a situation is not informed by any libertarian-anarchic freedom from rule—quite the opposite. Deprivation is also a systematic form of discrimination, and its consequences can be, as they have been, antidemocratic and authoritarian, as my examples above should indicate.

This broad picture of the so-called welfare state in India is valid for most of the post-Independence period; but it must now be qualified by some recent developments. One visible recent trend in welfare administration by the Indian state is the increasing relegation of care functions to voluntary, that is, nongovernment, organizations. This is offered as a matter of administrative convenience: since bureaucratic functioning is top-down, cumbersome, and slow, the state seeks to rid itself of low-priority functions, ostensibly those better served by smaller, decentralized mechanisms.[5] The NGOs receive varying degrees of funding support from the state government but are otherwise autonomous bodies.[6] While it may be true that many such organizations are motivated by greater commitment and run with better professional skills than state-run institutions, the dispersal of responsibilities between the state and NGOs cannot be considered a viable solution to the need for more and better welfare planning, including institutional resources. Harriss-White lists some of the limitations

NGOs suffer from: they have "small and insecure funding"; "their provision is unsystematic and discretionary"; and they are "minimally regulated," so that "redress by disabled people for incompetence is practically impossible to obtain" (137). Nor can the other recent trend, toward privatization, serve as an answer for the majority of the needy disabled poor for whom high-cost care in private institutions is impossibly beyond reach. Harriss-White is equally pessimistic about the role of markets in responding to disability, given their logic of acknowledging "purchasing power" over "need" (137). We must agree with her that the state in India will therefore continue to have a central role in matters of large-scale welfare, if only "by default" (37).

Ironically, however, given that World Bank–directed structural adjustment policies call for further cuts in welfare expenditure and more private-sector participation in health,[7] the currents of liberalization are likely, however incidentally and diffusively, to effect some social transformation. A liberalized economy has been, in certain areas—for instance, literacy, environmental protection, public health, free primary education, urban planning, sanitation, public transport—a stimulus to reform initiatives. The expansion of markets has been accompanied by factors that have contributed to interventions in the social sector: among them, the increase of funding from foreign agencies both to governments and to NGOs working in these areas; pressure from governments of developed nations to boycott goods produced by child labor; the recent establishment by the United Nations of human rights agendas covering the disabled and mentally retarded; the presence and scrutiny of their observance by international as well as national human rights organizations; and the diffusive but real influence of the gaze and the example of the West. The last, for example, was a persistent aspect of the discourse surrounding the hysterectomies issue. It is another matter that the actual human rights record in the United States, for instance, will not stand up to scrutiny, that welfare is an area of considerable political-ideological conflict and compromise in advanced countries, and that the humanitarianism of Western governments' strictures on Third World market production dissimulates real commercial and political considerations.

Nor is there any real contradiction between this observation about piecemeal reform and improvements in specific social sectors, on the one hand, and the increase in gross levels of poverty under the new liberalization, on the other. However, I would wish to avoid the suggestion that the former is achieved only at the expense of the latter, or that one must wholly deplore wished-for outcomes that are (by)products of overall harmful economic processes.[8] An aspect both directed by and reflecting the changed climate of economic liberalization is an increasing middle-class sensitization to some of the, let us say, more unpleasant conditions of existence in India.[9] The issues that engage this new middle class may admittedly be selective and self-interested—urban conditions, environmental pollution, public transport, sanitation, and conservation are now causes that have something of a radical chic about them. But there is also, beyond this, visible popular support for issues that earlier had engaged only activists in movements, a significant contrast to the usual pervasive public indifference to larger social injustices said to characterize Indian society.[10]

The mechanism by which such matters are brought to the public notice has typically been the scandal. The name of "scandal"—in this context the exposure of the wrongs of the state and its functionaries—describes a form of crisis in postcolonial civil society that in recent times has most often and most successfully initiated measures for reform.[11] The government's response, though reflexively consisting of disavowal or cover-up, will sometimes result in a commission of inquiry, and in rare cases in acceptance of responsibility and promises of change.

I wish to conclude this section by some reflections on the self-representation of recipients of the state's so-called welfare in India. These citizen-subjects are generally viewed, and described succinctly, as "victims." "Victims" belongs to a terminology that prompts specificity: victims of what (whom)? While the term does refer also to those who are, always already by social status—class, caste, gender, minority identity—"traditionally" underprivileged, as well as those who, as a result of age, disease, or handicap, are "naturally" disadvantaged, victimization is more specifically and especially identified with the plight of individuals in exceptional crises: manmade and natural disasters like the Bhopal gas tragedy, or communal riots, caste wars, periodic drought, flood, and famine; and large-scale or routine violence, often gendered, like rape, abduction, prostitution, bonded labor, domestic brutality. Though contingencies of the latter sort may uniformly and democratically occur among any people—disasters, for example, are often moralistically viewed as "levellers"—their victims invariably, and not coincidentally, belong to the categories of those I have identified as "traditionally" underprivileged and "naturally" disadvantaged. Built into the definition of victim, further, is the notion of *blamelessness:* the Indian Constitution, for instance, guarantees the right to assistance of those suffering from "undeserved want" (Article 41), and the United Nations Declaration of Human Rights of 1948 specifies the right to security of a person in the event of lack of likelihood due to "circumstances beyond his control." Let us note, though, that blame can be a criterion that is ambivalently judged—victims often get blamed for their misfortune either by the curious logic of divine justice or the harsh one of existential responsibility or, more mundanely, simply for not being smart enough to avert it. Where blamelessness is a criterion for compassion and/or compensation, the suggestion of blame can insidiously deprive victims of both.

Persons or populations viewed thus, in terms of victimhood, emerge in any case as a category of political beings who do not have a relationship of full equivalence to citizenship. They are at once less and more than the normative (tax-paying) citizen: less, because often denied the rights available to other citizens, subjected to further exploitation on account of their vulnerable status, and blamed for their misfortunes; more, because by the terms of a liberal democratic constitution they are (arguably) entitled to the special provisions that actualize "equality of opportunity." (In India, these exist, at best, in the form of a "weak reservation policy" in education and employment for certain categories of the disabled, for example [Harriss-White 1999, 147–48].) Between the actual discriminatory treatment they receive and the abstract entitlements of their status, victim-citizens fall into the category of the exception in our understanding of political identity.

This exceptionalism is pronounced in the case of the disabled.[12] Even where the state is moved to acknowledge their difference, bureaucratic administration requires the "labelling, categorising and prioritising" of the disabled population, especially in conditions of scarce resources, leading to their further marginalization and segmentation (Harriss-White 1999, 144). And even a discourse of civil rights that provides access to compensation and other privileges to the disabled, as in the liberal democratic welfare state in the West, bears, according to Judith Monks, connotations of "exclusive rights and identity." Such exclusionary status stands in the way of the "inclusion, mutuality and belonging" and even the civic involvement that many disabled seek (1999, 66). Thus a stigmatized (or, more correctly, re-ified) identity, even one that provides access to exclusionary *rights* and the mechanisms of compensation, is a consequence that the disabled or their advocates would be quick to contest in the West. When the difference of disability is used to *deprive* the handicapped of liberty and choice, as involuntary sterilization appears to do, the consequences are vastly graver.

My attempt in the foregoing discussion has been to show how constitutional commitments and state policies in the matter of welfare have been translated into—for the most part, betrayed by—the practices of the Indian state; and to describe the contemporary pressures and processes by which it has been, intermittently, brought to accountability. I have touched on the exceptional citizenship identity borne by the disabled as a consequence of bearing the mark of "victim" status. This serves as a prelude to my discussion of the state's rationale for and response to the sterilization of the mentally retarded destitute women in institutional care in the Shirur home, offered in the language of "expertise."

Outside in the Institution: "Expert" Discourses

The hysterectomies controversy, which at first sight appeared to be a straightforward issue of institutional expediency versus human rights, eventually became a battleground of conflicting "expert" views. The absence of unanimity among those in these fields was due partly to the real complexity of the issue, partly to their incomplete access to the facts of the case, but largely to differences of opinion among the participants in the debate. The claims or citations of expert knowledge tended to override the prejudices and principles that informed this ethically and politically fraught issue. The women victims' mental condition rendered them ciphers in the issue of their well-being, leaving the field clear for other "concerned" parties to battle it out.

The emergence of the acknowledged (or self-proclaimed) expert is never, in any context, entirely the natural procedure that it may appear to be. The appeal to the expert as adjudicator and voice of truth, a function of our society's desire for certitudes, is made primarily by and through the media. It is also the media that sustain the layperson's faith in a singular truth even in the face of varied, changing, and conflicting "expert" pronouncements. The arguments in the hysterectomies debate, as will become apparent, would appeal to professional opinion, precedent, the practices and positions in the field in advanced Western societies, tradition, common sense, the vox populi, endowing each of these with legitimacy, expertise, authenticity, and ethical validity, while at the same time invalidating whoever and whatever lay outside these valorized sources of the "truth."

I must draw attention here also to the intermittent instances of a "humanistic" perspective, which, in opposition to the prevalent appeal to "experts," drew on popular sentimental ideas and beliefs in an attempt to arrive at an empathetic understanding of the victims' "own" subjectivity. The regulation of the sexuality of the inmates of the Shirur home by means of sterilization brought to the fore the fact of physical maturity coexisting with mental underdevelopment in mentally retarded women. Any understanding of their situation would accordingly be obliged to reconcile these two aspects of their plight. So while, on the one hand, sympathetic activists argued that mentally retarded women's "emotions" could not be assumed to be "gender-neutral," and that a hysterectomy could conceivably lead to feelings of "loss of womanhood" in them,[13] on the other hand, the Government Director could evoke the dismay of a "three-year-old" having to contend with the onset of the monthly menses or, worse, with motherhood: "If we look beyond their bodies into their minds, we will realise it is stupid to talk of their 'right' on par with normal women. They have no concept of motherhood" (Khullar 1994). If "expert" discourses pronounced on mentally retarded women's sexuality in terms of its problems and dangers, an attempted "subjective" understanding of female sexuality in a state of presumed childhood was both inadequate and confused. In the overwhelming context of expert pronouncements and, simultaneously, the nullity of the subjects of the issue—indeed the comprehensive and frustrating impossibility, as it was deemed, of ascertaining their wishes, choices, and reasons, of reaching into their consciousness, as it were—these statements have a poignant theoretical and political interest.

The sources of the expert discourses generated by the hysterectomies issue reveal them as essentially a *textual* production, where the "text" has to be read in the material contexts of reproduction, distribution, production of surplus value, and circulation. The textualization of the discourse points as well to the social text of *literacy*. In a situation where those who represent the women—that is, speak of and for them—do so as a literate class, the women themselves must necessarily, not just actually, be "illiterate." While the scandal of their situation circulates *outside* the institution, the conditions of seclusion define those *inside* it as ignorant, even of the scandal. These oppositions—of expertise versus ignorance, literacy versus illiteracy, (objective) text versus (subjective) consciousness, the outside and the institution—come to constitutively define knowledge about institutionalized subjects. The politics of this issue was played out on the different sites of professional expertise that were invoked, these being, chiefly, the institution and the state's welfare bureaucracy, law, and medicine. I enter into a more detailed consideration of each of these areas of expert discourse below, so that both the complex politics of the issue and the subjectification processes they engendered may be more fully understood.

The Function(ing) of "Welfare":
The Institution and Its Norms

The institutional defense of the hysterectomies became an expert discourse by virtue of the "experience" it claimed to rely on and which, more importantly, it denied to those who denounced them. The opponents of the government—in this issue, mainly activists in the women's movement—were held to be irresponsible, naive, or merely "antigovernment."[14] (Subsequent researches, however, revealed that a number of institutions run by other agencies, even in Maharashtra, do not sterilize the women in their care under similar circumstances.[15]) The authorities invoked precedence, pragmatism, and procedural correctness for their action—and support on these grounds was forthcoming from both the medical community and the families of retarded women.[16] The language of expediency was particularly handy to justify the mass operations (each operation took no more than an hour, the dean of Sasoon Hospital explained). Typically "state" and "institution" define problems and seek solutions in the gross and by bureaucratic procedure. Accordingly, the conflict with the concept of individual human dignity remained unresolved even when the protestors could be persuaded that the hysterectomies were correct in other respects.[17] Undoubtedly it was also the scale of this operation that brought it to the attention of the press in the first place. Nothing reveals the gap between the opposed discourses of human dignity and institutional practice more starkly than the government's promise, in response to the furor, to be more "discreet" in the future!

More significant, however, than the putative correctness of sterilization as a "solution" to the "problem" of mentally retarded adult women in institutional care is the fact that the Shirur case opened up a scandal. Too often reports about the state's sins meet with public indifference, if not apathy, since inadequate resources and bureaucratic negligence are the well-known and even widely accepted explanations for all official (mal)functioning. But the value of such reports must not be downplayed: facts about the "inside" of an institution are not easily made public; when they are, they have the force of an exposé. Custodial institutions are secured by a stringent secrecy enforced by the "closed" system in which they operate.[18] Instances of resistance, escape, and rebellion by inmates of institutions suggest that their administration is barely effective in many cases. Reports of remand-home breaks periodically appear in the press.[19] Sex workers similarly resist "rescue-and-rehabilitation" operations by crusading government officials since their relatives are forced to meet the demands of the police for money for their release from the institutions they are lodged in following their so-called rescue (Dey 1996). Thus its intolerable material conditions and the opportunistic corruption and abuse practiced by its employees would seem to inhibit the institution's successful functioning—even if the criterion of "success" we invoke in this instance be only the *effective* incarceration, not the well-being or security, of the inmates.

It is from the escapees that information about the abysmal conditions in the institution is periodically gleaned; the institutions are unwilling to give outsiders, and in particular journalists, permission to visit the homes, and the constituted Boards of Visitors perform their functions at best lackadaisically.[20] The intermittent exposure in the press of aspects of state-run institutions by such revelations, especially when they are protested by activist groups and further publicized by the media, occasionally provokes wider public outrage. (In official circles, as we might expect, the breakouts are read not as crises of institutional malfunctioning but as failures of "security.") In the Shirur case, the rumors escaped from the institution's closed bounds, since the surgeries were scheduled to be performed in a public government hospital, and then grew into a scandal.

Thus the significance of the Shirur scandal lies in the knowledge of the conditions of this institution, and of state institutions in general, that the public came to possess, and the concern that knowledge set in motion about the problematic legal implications of institutional custody for women and the mentally ill, several times compounded when they were both mentally ill *and* women. The report of the voluntary organization Action for the Rights of the Child (ARC), as well as several newspaper accounts of the Shirur government home, unanimously decried the conditions that their investigators found there. The institution is described as a large building with few amenities, and the living conditions were found to be appalling. There was no hot bath water, the inmates were found to have inadequate change of clothing, the surroundings were filthy. The staff was limited to a superintendent and a probationary officer ("who are there by virtue of a transfer they cannot wish away"), a sweeper, a cook, and six caretakers. Three posts of teachers had not been filled since 1990–91 (Kshirsagar 1994). Though the Social Welfare Department claimed that the District and Sessions judge, Pune, made regular supervisory monthly visits to the home, no records of these visits or reports based on them were available. Other state-run institutions—whether jails, homes for women, mental asylums, juvenile homes, or orphanages—were found to have similar stories of neglect and misery.[21]

This account of the institution has relied largely on a description of its (mal)functioning, which, analytically, leads to reformist solutions. The call for reforms—for both more and better institutions—is understandable, given the numbers and the needs of those requiring their services. But equal attention needs to be paid to the *normative* structure of the institution.[22] An examination in such terms uncovers the ideologies that underpin institutionalization and the powers of control that the state wields by means of its confinement of sections of the population. Hence, before insisting on the *obligations* of the state, such a view prompts us, more radically, to question its *rights* in matters of institutional administration. This reflexive view derives from recently developed positions on reform that revise earlier progressive histories. These new theoretical premises are now well established in studies of disciplinary knowledges and institutional practices in the West. Revisionary explanatory and theoretical accounts—whether they be Foucauldian/poststructuralist/European/anti-Enlightenment epistemic studies, or Marxist/materialist/Anglo-American/anti-Whig historical analyses—are agreed that the segregation and incarceration of large sections of populations considered deviant and/or unproductive, consisting of the insane, the criminal, the poor, or the sick, have in view not (only) their care, cure, reform, and rehabilitation but (also) their disciplining and punishment; and that this is a historical innovation of "modernity."[23]

The history of the development of the institution in the colony was linked to but not identical with its history in modern Europe.[24] The first modern penal institutions, hospitals, and mental asylums in India were established by the British colonial government, though with peculiarities and differences that are only now beginning to be investigated by historians.[25] Many utilitarian Benthamite experiments for administrative efficiency were in fact introduced in the "laboratory" of the colony before they were replicated, modified, or abandoned in Britain. Most existing institutional facilities in India are colonial legacies that have undergone little change or expansion in the years since Independence—so that whatever "modernity" they represented has now passed into obsolescence.

The reformist position expects that the state will provide care and security to those in need of them and attacks its failure to do so adequately. But the institution is also a place of confinement and hence of control. So, while the government may divest itself of more and more of the actual responsibility of providing institutional *services* (especially as a response to "scandals"), it is unlikely to surrender or dilute the *authority* of its custodial powers—and its targets are specifically women and juveniles—even when the very excess of this function may prove, as we have seen, to be self-defeating. A gap opens up between the executive functioning and the legislative logic of the state, and even while we attend to (the failures of) the first as a matter of immediate and urgent necessity, we must not lose sight of the laws that define the institution as such, whose assumptions operate the state's machinery. Usha Ramanathan accuses the law of acting as a "protective shield" for the problematic aspects of institutionalization, or even as an "instrument of state power" itself (1996, 200). It is in support of this contention that I turn to the understanding of custody in law.[26] Since custodial confinement, or "protective custody" as it is called, has specific implications for women, this involves attention to the specifically gendered aspect of the institutionalization of women, a crucial aspect of the hysterectomies issue. As will become apparent, it is through the law/logic of institutionalization that, first, specific forms of subjectification of the institutionalized are produced, and, second, a mutually defining relationship is established between them and "society."

Sweeping powers of arrest and confinement are available to the police in India under draconian political laws.[27] "Criminal" is an elastic and potent category that the state invokes to identify and punish "antisocial elements," male and female. The jails are filled with political detenues, undertrials, prostitutes, the vagrant and homeless, and those arrested on suspicion as "habitual offenders" (often on nothing more than the basis of discriminatory socioeconomic criteria like caste, [un]employment, etc.). In addition, women (and women alone: Ramanathan 1996, 200) may be taken in on grounds of (noncriminal) "immorality." The vulnerable and the dangerous are indistinguishable from each other in relation to a normative society. Thus individuals in the state's care—the deviant, destitute, handicapped, ill, all often female—are routinely lodged in jails. This is partly because of the inadequate numbers and facilities of care institutions, partly because the distinction between crime and misfortune is legally as well as socially blurred, and to a great extent because the differences in the conditions of penal and nonpenal institutions are in any case not very significant. Penal sentences may be considered, in fact, preferable to nonpenal institutionalization since they at least have fixed terms whereas custodial confinement is in effect indefinite (Ramanathan 1996, 203–11). Nonpenal institutions—healthcare centers (mental asylums, leprosy asylums, infectious diseases hospitals), remand homes, short-stay homes and shelters, and hostels for juveniles and working women run by the state—notoriously operate under jail-like conditions. Though legal remedies are repeatedly sought and legal strictures equally regularly passed to enforce these distinctions, the practice of jailing noncriminal men and women continues.

Formally, a distinction exists between "protective homes" and "corrective institutions," but actually they are put to use interchangeably (Ramanathan 1996, 203–06). Destitute or sick women for whom the first is intended are placed along with women accused of "victimless crimes" like vagrancy or solicitation identified for the occupation of the latter, and all of them are indistinguishable from criminals. (My argument here does not venture into the questionable appropriateness of incarceration, the conditions of prison, and other regimes of correction, discipline, and punishment for convicted "criminals" themselves—or the question of who they might be, and the powers of naming them as such—but I would like it to be understood that the appropriateness remains a question.) Admission to institutions is usually not at the initiative of women themselves. The irony is indeed that, as Ramanathan notes, "the law does not recognize a *right* to shelter or protection from the state where the woman seeks entry into an institution *as a matter of choice;* a choice that is often dictated by desperation" (200; emphasis in original). Women therefore find their way into institutions only because they have been forcibly admitted there by their families or by the police. Families wishing to be rid of the social stigma or the burden of caring for mentally ill, retarded, or leprosy-afflicted members commit them to asylums. Or the police, aided sometimes by social workers, pick up prostitutes, vagrants, and beggar women on grounds of soliciting and lodge them in custody— the argument being that a "single and especially poor woman, without any male support, must either already be working in prostitution or will soon be 'corrupted' into joining it" (Joint Women's Program Report 1995, 69).

But if suspected deviance is one cause for a woman's getting locked up, then her powerlessness is another (Ramanathan 1996, 200–01). A(ny) woman's perceived "incapacity to make decisions for herself or to care for herself" is the ostensible reason for not releasing her except to the custody of a member of her family (ibid, 202). Despite the fact that women with mental illness and similar "problems" end up in institutions of the state primarily because their families delivered them there, the institution, as if in a reciprocal gesture, will only release them back to the care of the family. It is the "ideology of the family"—the conviction that women's sexuality must be both protected and controlled—that underpins the ideology of institutional confinement, making a vicious circle of the passage of women from family or community to the institution and back. The processes of discharge/exit are highly bureaucratic. Women are released only if they have a family ready to receive them, but families, as we saw, are either reluctant or unfit to receive them (Joint Women's Program Report 1995, 73).

Institutions for women are marked by cruel regulations, ostensibly in conformity with bureaucratic norms of "discipline" and motivated by "reformist" intentions. Institutional rules therefore would require women inmates to give up all marks of personal identity, enforce uniforms, mandate shaving of heads, etc. There are other genderized forms of "brutality and bullying" that are specific to women's institutions (ibid., 71–72). The effect and logic of punishment in such forms of supervision, confinement, and deprivation are not hard to see. Such brutality, in conjunction with the dismal material conditions, the corruption of functionaries, and the sexual abuse suffered by inmates, unequivocally renders custodial institutions as hell-holes, places to which human excrescence may be removed, there to remain forever, forgotten and out of sight, and suffer damnation.

Why and how women enter institutional spaces; how and why they leave them (or fail to); what kinds of discipline and other forms of violence they are subjected to while "in custody": the ideologies and modalities of these processes reveal the contradictions of as well as the profound complicities between the patriarchies of family and state. What is at stake, of course, is not, or at any rate not only, the protection of victimized women but the putative protection of society *from them* (Murlidhar 1999, 318). The anxieties produced by women's sexuality—real and imagined fears about promiscuity, commercial sex, sexually transmitted diseases, unregulated fertility, infertility, deviant sexuality—are widely recognized as coexisting with the exploitation and regulation of aspects of woman's sexuality by social, religious, legal, communal, and state sanctions. The institutional confinement of certain women—usually "single women without obvious family," therefore in need of support but therefore also potentially threatening—thereby serves the purpose of "securing" them: in the double sense of confinement and protection. As Rokeya Shekhawat Hossain ironically pointed out in her fable "Sultana's Dream," "Men, who do or at least are capable of doing no end of mischief, are let loose, and the innocent women shut up in the zenana!" (1905/1988, 9). The logic of women's confinement has always been built on this paradox.

As a direct and pragmatic measure of care and discipline, the sterilization of the mentally retarded women inmates of the Shirur asylum was clearly, then, a response to the prevalent beliefs about female sexuality. The institution had little difficulty in accepting the widespread cultural prejudice about menstruation as "polluting," and menstruating women as "unclean," and therefore it respected the refusal of caretakers to attend to the women's hygiene.[28] In institutional thinking, the feeble-minded are promiscuous and/or vulnerable to sexual abuse, though the authorities tacitly admitted that institutional lodging was by itself no safeguard against rapists' attacks and indeed in many cases actually invited such danger. The prevention-of-pregnancy motive, however covert, is based on the conventional understanding that these women's pregnancy would be undesirable, not merely in consideration of their own interests (when, for example, a consequence of forced intercourse or a threat to their health) but as a eugenic measure. It followed from this that a uterus not useful for reproductive purposes is dispensable. The hysterectomies are an instance of advanced medical technology serving the ends of traditional patriarchal control, similar to the widespread use of amniocentesis for fetal sex detection. The different logics of institutionalization that I have identified, though opposed, are not contradictory. They feed into corresponding modes of subjectification offered to women, which coalesce and are resolved in terms of the widespread social beliefs about female sexuality. Thus institutions offer protection *to* women (from the world "outside," as the familial "home" does) because women are vulnerable; and they offer protection (to society) *from* women because of the threat, nuisance, or danger they represent.

Feminist legal activists, whose positions I have reproduced extensively here, rightly see institutionalization as a device of normalization and a manifestation of state power—and, for these reasons, a threat. But I have noted their repeated calls, at the same time for reforms of the laws relating to commitment and discharge, for the protection of the human and civil rights of inmates, for greater transparency of institutional functioning, for government's accountability. These positions could rightly be considered contradictory had they subscribed to the Foucauldian view that institutions are *constitutively* regulatory. Such a position, however, would not answer a situation in which Indian women, caught in the travails of a rapidly changing society, are desperately *in need of* the services of institutions like shelters, short-stay homes, hostels, old age homes, and vocational training centers that only the state can provide in the numbers and at the cost that can answer to such a massive (and as yet unrecognized and unmet) demand. An analytics that pursues more intellectually consistent and rigorous conclusions, or functions only as a disciplinary theoretical exercise, must do so at the cost of ignoring this situation. The idea(l) of the institution as an alternative (temporary) space for a community in transit or in search of rehabilitation, sponsored by a *welfare* state, animates the reformist discourse.

The Mentally Retarded in Law: Questions of Guardianship, Rights, and Identity

In the Shirur case, the institution, we must take note, perceived the problem and devised the solution in relation to not only the sexuality of the women inmates of the home but also their mental condition. This had very specific implications for their subjectification and the consequent handling of their predicament.

The legal provisions defining the status and rights of the mentally retarded in India occupy at present a curious limbo. Originally they were covered by the Indian Lunacy Act of 1912, whose definition of "lunatic" as "a person who is an idiot or of unsound mind" has clearly little scientific or medical meaning today. As Geetha Ramaseshan (1994) points out, this law "simply reflects the bias that existed in society towards the mentally ill and the mentally retarded in the early twentieth century." The act, rightly considered outmoded and irrelevant given changes in the definition and treatment of mental illness, was replaced by the Mental Health Act of 1987, which came into effect in 1993. The new act, however, excludes retardation from the scope of mental illness, but there are yet no legal statutes pertaining specifically to the mentally retarded.[29] What remains on the books are the different personal laws of different religious communities, and certain other uniform provisions, that pronounce on issues relating to them in various contexts such as marriage, divorce, reproduction, guardianship, and inheritance. Ramaseshan provides a partial listing of these:

> Under "Hindu law" and "Special Marriages Act" (which governs interreligious marriages), a party at the time of marriage should not be suffering from any mental disorder so as to be unfit for marriage and the procreation of children. . . . [M]ental retardation and mental illness are treated on par. The Indian Divorce Act, governing Christians, considers marriage with a "lunatic" or an "idiot" (sic) as a nullity. It is only under customary Islamic Law that a mentally retarded person is treated as a minor. The guardian can validly conduct a marriage on behalf of the mentally retarded under Islamic Law. The Indian Succession Act however treats the mentally retarded (though it uses the term lunatic) on par with a minor. Thus, a guardian of a mental retardate (either appointed under a Will or a court) will administer the property on behalf of the mentally retarded. . . . The Medical Termination of Pregnancy Act, 1971, permits the termination of pregnancy of a "lunatic" (as defined under the Lunacy Act and hence will include the mentally retarded) with the written consent of her guardian, provided the doctor is of the opinion that the pregnancy will cause injury to the woman's physical or mental health. The doctor can also take into account the woman's actual or reasonably foreseeable environment. (1994)

The last, however, does not specify that sterilization may be legally performed on retarded women. While the need for legal recognition of rights of persons with mental disability is conceded, in general legal activists suggest that rather than focusing on making special laws, it would be "more appropriate to adapt existing laws to the needs of disabled people" (Autism Network 1998, 11).[30]

If certain laws define the mentally retarded, by analogy, as "minors," thus entrusting decisions regarding their welfare to their guardians, Justice Krishna Iyer demands their recognition as "minorities," as those with a claim to the state's "ameliorative" measures, by analogy with economically disadvantaged and racially discriminated groups (1980, 196). The logic operative in these differing arguments by analogy highlights the conflict in the state provisions for the mentally retarded between welfare measures (as minors) and legislation for rights (as minorities). When the state regards destitute disabled in its care, especially the mentally retarded, metaphorically as "minors," it constitutes itself as a custodian. The state's custodianship is, however, legally defined by limits and safeguards. A custodian is in any case not identical with a guardian, as the activist lawyer Indira Jaising argued, and the state "cannot appropriate the rights of a guardian."[31] Using the Mental Health Act of 1993 as a guide, she points to the "elaborate" procedures, requiring judicial as well as medical clearance, for such appropriation (cited by Iyer 1994). The state becomes a guardian only if the individual has been legally made its ward. In the Shirur home, no responsibilities for the well-being of the inmates other than or beyond the sterilization—such as training them to some degree of independence, the maintenance of their general health, providing recreation and skills education—seemed to have concerned the state as custodian.

Recent judicial activism in the field of mental health has itself tended to privilege the suffering of the mentally ill over their right to autonomy, by focusing too exclusively on their "unjust deprivation of liberty" (i.e., wrongful or overlong confinement in mental asylums) and on "the dismal living conditions and treatment in mental hospitals" (Dhanda 1995, 25). As a consequence, there has been insufficient emphasis on the "constitutional basis" of the various declarations that would instead have highlighted the rights of mentally ill persons. This emphasis is necessary because persons with mental illness, necessarily dependent on "surrogates," also need protection "*from* them." This point is made with special reference to the need for "accountability" on the part of medical functionaries and psychiatric institutions (ibid.).

The position that would guarantee a person with mental illness "an uninterrupted right to her psychosis" (unless her mental condition infringed on the rights of others) is identified by Dhanda as the human rights position. (In describing her rights thus, the nature and degree of mental illness are obviously relevant, as would be discriminations about levels of retardation and competence in retarded individuals; neither group can be homogenized.) The "problem-centric" "interest-based" perspective, by contrast, sanctions or even insists on interference by the state or the family to promote the alleviation of her condition (22–23).[32] Justice Krishna Iyer would formulate the rights claim differently: as the right *not to be retarded* where it is "the adversities of poverty, medical neglect or environmental pollution" suffered by pregnant mothers that may be responsible for the retardation of the child.[33] If the retardation and other disabilities are caused by accident, the victims must be adequately compensated (1980, 195, 202).

It will be clear that in the debate over the hysterectomies the government's most elevated defense of the practice was based on the "alleviation of suffering" argument, while the activists' opposition to it drew from the human rights defense of the women's autonomy, liberty, integrity, and privacy. By extending and applying these constitutional rights to mentally retarded women, activists were making a radical claim for a subjectivity grounded in their *identity* with others (others as *citizens*), rather than their differences from them. This move toward equivalence clearly calls for a complex negotiation of disability in law—between welfare and rights claims, exclusionary and inclusionary status, alleviation of suffering and preservation of autonomy. In contrast, the state's adoption of a "guardianship" role is reductive of those in its care. In a single stroke, the sterilization procedure wholly and comprehensively defined the identity of the inmates of the welfare home as "mentally retarded women": as *women,* in terms of the "problems" of female sexuality; and as *mentally retarded,* in terms of their incapacity to make rational choices. The individual's spaces of selfhood, subjectivity, and citizenship are thus entirely usurped by the state and the exigencies of institutional "care."

Medical Perspectives

The opinions of medical experts were, on the face of it, amazingly diverse on the different medical aspects of the issue as they related to mental retardation, to surgical and other procedures regulating menstruation and reproduction, and, more broadly, to the biomedical ethics of sterilization.

Psychiatrists, psychotherapists, and other mental health experts point out that there are varying degrees of mental retardation. The IQs of most patients can show considerable improvement over time with proper stimulation, and all but the most incompetent can be trained to some degree of self-sufficiency in their everyday lives, including the observance of menstrual care and even the management of parenthood. None of this was seriously disputed by others in the medical profession who, nonetheless, implicitly supported the institutional measures followed at Shirur. Under the circumstances—namely, that the mental age of the inmates was below four, that the hygiene of the menstruating women was so poor that they were highly susceptible to infection, that no facilities were available to train them in this matter or in any other—they held that sterilization was the best solution.[34] In other words, whatever may be the drawbacks of the sterilization of mentally retarded women in general, the lack of alternatives (read: Third World exigencies) was grounds for exemption from these concerns for those placed in state-run homes in India.

A common medical response was the argument that hysterectomy was the only method that could at one stroke medically solve the problems of both menstruation and unwarranted pregnancies. (One doctor went so far as to suggest, in addition, sewing up the vaginas of the women.)[35] Other alternatives that were suggested, such as endometrial ablation of the bleeding surface of the uterus to prevent menstruation, or tubectomies to prevent pregnancy, do not offer this dual benefit. Some doctors did express reservations on medical grounds: that hysterectomies involved a major surgical operation not free of the risks that any invasive procedure poses; that they required extensive postoperative care (of which there was no guarantee at the home, given the poor attendant facilities); that they could produce hormonal imbalances with long-term consequences if not properly followed up. But many others robustly denied any such risks, especially since the medical fitness of the inmates had been ascertained by the regulatory tests, and no doubts were raised about the competence of the Bombay gynecologist who led the surgical team in the

Sasoon Hospital. The risk element, then, was not the paramount consideration.

The chief issue, therefore, was not so much the narrow or technical medical viability of the hysterectomies as the *ethics* of sterilization. On these grounds, the protest against it was led by a doctor, Sunil Pandya, founder of the Forum of Medical Ethics in Bombay. He reasoned: "Hysterectomy is an irreversible process. If a family does it, it is okay but it is not so for the State. Because it helps the State to set a precedent. Uncensured, it will lead the State to extend it to other areas to circumvent its own responsibilities" (quoted in Iyer 1994). The agency of the state produces anxiety. This was echoed by other doctors, including those in charge of institutions of mental health, like Dr. Sarada Menon, who had served as superintendent of the Madras Mental Hospital: "I think the operation is necessary.... But if you make it legal, then there is the possibility of people misusing it." She therefore advocates using it extremely selectively (quoted in Bhagat 1994). State surrogacy in matters of agency and care, it is suggested, must be defined in cautious and minimal terms.

Inevitably, reference was made to and clarification sought from the more advanced discourse on biomedical ethics in the West.[36] In these countries the sterilization of mentally retarded women requires the permission of the court and certification by medical practitioners, regardless of whether it is sought by the family or by the state.[37] The Ethical Committee of the Medical Council of India has pronounced hysterectomies without consent unethical. Since sterilization can be regarded either as a violation or as a beneficial measure, depending on the specific situation of the person concerned, those who are in no position to take a decision about it themselves can legally be said to be deprived of a right if the state does not act responsibly either way.[38] The state, either voluntarily or by unambiguous judicial direction, is called on to discharge the responsibility by entering into widespread consultations with medical experts, social workers, and the family. There is no indication that the hysterectomies performed on the inmates of the Shirur home were accompanied by any such procedure. (The justification for this procedural short-circuiting was that precedent for the hysterectomies existed; nevertheless, the force of precedent as a legal and legitimizing argument must not be underestimated.) In short, while sterilization is not ruled out as such, either as a measure of protection or of eugenics in the case of the mentally retarded, it is always treated as a last resort rather than a routine practice.

In a medicalized discourse the subjecthood of the women inmates all but disappears in the technical discourse of risk and the discourse of the female body—or more accurately, of its functions—until redeemed by the ethical argument. But a formal (and quasilegal) biomedical ethicism is also bound by difficulties and limits: difficulties because of the inevitable number and complexity of the factors to be considered (which is what makes it an issue in the first place); limits because of the aporetic shuttle of most issues, including this one, between the necessity for simultaneously holding an absolute/abstract moral position *and* adopting a contingent/particularized relative perspective, when each risks undermining the validity of the other. Nevertheless, by stating the ethical humanness of the subjects as an unqualified premise, the medical opponents of the hysterectomies made an important gain in the protagonists' stakes and status in the argument. What makes their assertion especially significant is that there is clearly a pervasive skepticism in Indian society about the fully human status of the disabled, especially mental retardates. Justice Krishna Iyer was driven to argue the case for the recognition of the disabled individual as a "human being" and a "full member of [any] society that does not subscribe to a project of the survival of only the fittest." Given the necessary accessories, training facilities, and milieu, he pleads, the "high human potential" of the handicapped can be realized, and they can be made contributing members of society (1980, 189, 195).[39]

Inside the Family: Feminist Critiques

The rhetoric of reform in India is most likely to be couched in the language of "modernization," as we have seen—in relation to not only institutional structures and practices but also legal and medical provisions for those in institutions, invoked invariably with reference to the West. But if this reflects an aspiration to a "modern" universality via equivalence to the West in matters of human rights and social development, there is also another and opposed tendency to stress the *differences,* treated as the superiority, of "traditional" societies like India's to the West, especially in the matter of care of the needy. This argument is located within a broader antimodernist critique that harks back nostalgically to earlier social formations. In this view, the "premodern community" accommodated the deviant and the handicapped more easily than contemporary societies do, and the extended family uncomplainingly provided care and shelter to unproductive members.

Whatever measure of truth there may be in such imaginings of the past, the suggested recreation of such solutions in the present, given the beleagured condition of family and community in a rapidly changing society, is problematic. Suggestions that welfare programs for the care of the handicapped, sick, and aged be returned to the family must take into account the high likelihood that this task will once again fall to the women in the family. Moreover, social-service activists are also quick to point out that the destitute and disabled in India who are outside institutional care are not automatically absorbed into adoptive families or communities, as is sentimentally claimed, but are, on the contrary, exposed to the most horrific threats of public abuse: stoning, jeering, stripping, and rape (Bhagat 1994).[40] The institution, obviously, is not the only space that lies "outside" the family. There are large populations that sleep, roam, work, beg, in short live their lives in anonymous public spaces—the streets, parks, alleys, abandoned buildings, fields—vulnerable to the state's and the populace's hostility. The "homeless" are those who have slipped through the net of the containing structures of any institution.

The family, or specifically the *crisis* of the family, is nevertheless diagnosed as the origin and source of the condition of "homelessness" in modern society, alongside and as an aspect of a critique of the regimes of modernity as such. Read in relation to the *failures* of the family in modern society, the institution presents itself as a response to the neglect, abandonment, or cruelty of the family toward its so-called unproductive members, the disabled, the aged, orphans, widows, disobedient wives and daughters. It aspires to the ideal surrogacy of the "home" in terms of the quality of the care it offers, the security of its shelter, and other affective satisfactions. Alternatively, read as a response to the *needs* of the family in modern society— nuclear, often dislocated from community, transient—it offers itself as a solution. Typically the institution is larger, more efficient, more resourceful, and more impersonal: both in scale and service it is different from, and therefore better than, the family-home where care functions are concerned. The institution, as I noted earlier, is undeniably a phenomenon—product and manifestation—of modernity. But to read it solely in terms of the crisis of the family is, as I have suggested, to both subscribe to an unexamined critique of modernity and problematically assume that family and community are spaces standing completely outside the modern state. I have drawn attention instead to the continuities and complicities of ideology and actual praxis between these structures, especially as they pertain to the institutionalization of mentally ill women in India.

The critique of the family is one of the most intellectually powerful and politically radical interventions of feminism, and it has been enabled and reinforced by the mutual insights of feminist disciplinary-theoretical work and feminist activism. Scholarship as well as legal and other forms of activism have contributed to the critique of the family in different but interconnected areas. Thus major findings and their questioning—the recognition of women's unpaid labor in the home and the fields; the hierarchies in the access to food, attention, and services within the household; the legal inequalities of inheritance and other forms of property between men and women; the implications of the compulsory heterosexuality (and reproduction) enforced by the family through norms of marriage, kinship, and inheritance; the prevalence of sexual abuse and physical violence within the family—have all been the product as also the basis of feminist endeavors.

Yet the family has also been the ideology and structure most resistant to critique and change. The reasons are not far to seek. The power of the family draws from many sources: ideologically, the religious sanctity with which its values are invested; the sociocultural legitimization of its control over dependent members, predominantly of course women and children; and its legal control of sexuality for the ends of reproduction and the production of heirs. Equally, the family represents powerful material interests through its monopolistic patriarchal ownership of property and patrimony. Above all, the family in the modern nation-state lays claims to autonomous status and to the right to privacy, and hence to immunity from state "interference." These reasons have combined to make feminist attempts to open the family to scrutiny and reform largely ineffectual.

Feminist constraints derive also, of course, from a significant aspect of the family as social institution: the fact that it is an affective realm of great potency and meaning in contemporary society, the "haven from a heartless world" that it is not merely sentimentally claimed to be, and a structure that feminists, no less than other women, are implicated in through their several roles as daughters, mothers, wives, lovers, or sisters. Its susceptibility to attack is protected by its self-representation as a nonpolitical arena, operating by consensual values, animated by love, altruism, and care, which lies outside the rational calculus that informs the functioning of the public world. A simple denunciation of this representation as ideological mystification, or of those who live by it as victims of false consciousness, does not take critique very far.

Ironically, Indian feminists have had to take on the championship of families in instances where a diagnosis of the family's sole agency in women's victimization would be grievously misplaced. Such attribution, further, and as a consequence, succeeds in eliding the responsibility of the state or the market. When families sell their children into prostitution or send them out to work, kill infant daughters, marry them off too young, pay dowry, or sterilize mentally handicapped daughters—in all such instances, the state has found it convenient to blame the failures of parental responsibility. (See chapter 2, on the Ameena case, and chapter 6, on female infanticide in Tamilnadu, for specific examples of this kind.) Feminists have been quick to rectify such analysis by emphasizing instead the conditions of poverty that provoke such desperate measures and by insisting on the direct implication of the state and market in creating these conditions.

Above all, feminist analysis of issues cannot afford to rely on the family/household as a *unitary* institution. As Bina Agarwal, among others, has insisted, this leads to a skewed set of assumptions about resource allocation within the household, for example (2000, 3). By recognizing that women within the household occupy positions of subordination and often victimization, one can readily see the need to disaggregate the "family" into its constituent members by age and gender. Thus in the instances of ostensible failure of the family, such as those listed above, the positions, responsibility, and roles of (often younger) female members cannot be assumed to be identical with those of the male head of the household.

Feminists are called on, therefore, to hold that *the family* is a patriarchal institution while refraining from condemning *families*, on the basis of the actual circumstances of each issue and the socioeconomic condition of the families concerned (for example, minority, poor, regionally backward, and so on). Thus in the Shirur case, the protesting women's groups were inhibited from condemning the families of the patients for a number of reasons—delicacy about intrusion, the imputation of self-righteousness, and the recognition of the burdens borne by women in the family in such situations, among others. The significant differences between the family and the institution, in terms of structures, resources, and attitudes in the matter of care of the handicapped, cannot be gainsaid. Mothers of mentally retarded girl children interviewed in the wake of the hysterectomies scandal poignantly described the difficulties of caring for their daughters (Bhagat 1994).

At the same time, the ill-repute of the institution in India discourages (perhaps is meant to discourage) simple recourse to commitment as an alternative to home care. Emerging among feminists is a cautious endorsement of other alternatives that will combine residence at home with support from the state, a trend visible in countries like Britain that have a well-developed public health system. Thus outpatient services, the state provision of (only) training and equipment, day care centers, community health visiting schemes, visits by social workers, or (as in Singapore) state incentives of housing etc. for those families willing to keep aged members at home—such systems mediate the stark alternatives of home or institution for the disabled and aged. These are as yet fledgling initiatives of the Indian state. The theoretical and political problem of the family remains, therefore, central to an understanding of the institutional question and feminist critiques of the state.

One of the ways in which the problematic has evolved is by way of representations of women inside the institution and those outside (in the family), or of feminists and "other"/victimized women, that seek to enforce the distinction, in ideology and practice, between women who are differently positioned thus in relation to the family. As the foregoing discussion has intermittently indicated, the distinction may be interrogated by both the organized women's movement and institutionalized/"other" women in organized or spontaneous resistance. I consider the problems and possibilities of this politics at greater length in the concluding section of this chapter. Here I wish to pursue the exploration of the complex ideology of family in relation to the institution, and for this I turn to examples from Indian cinema that engage these issues. Film is a major ideological site for the shaping and reflection of public opinion and is particularly significant in defining gender relations. In the films I choose for discussion, Jabbar Patel's *Umbartha* (1982) and Rajkumar Santoshi's *Damini* (1993), the representation of the (predominantly) middle-class female protagonist exemplifies as much as it explores the contradictions that underlie the "concerned" or activist woman's relationship to (her) family and to "other" women.[41]

Some preliminary clarifications are in order. First, it would be misleading to collapse the two films into mere thematic sameness. They belong to different and distinctive genres of Indian cinema, as I will explain; further, the decade that separates them is responsible for the operation of a "feminist consciousness" that has now penetrated commercial cinema, though in the compromised forms of ideology that I have discussed elsewhere at length.[42] Nevertheless, their representation of women in institutions, and their interest in relating the predicament of middle-class women's domesticity to that reality, are rare enough preoccupations in Indian cinema. My choice of these films for discussion is therefore not arbitrary; and the common assumptions about family, women's politics, sexuality, and the institution that they share despite their different genres and contexts make the point about ideology I began with. Finally, though I do not connect them in any specific way to the hysterectomies issue, I do mean to suggest that the films partake of the latter's discursive, cultural, and political moment.

The earlier film, *Umbartha*, belongs to the Indian new wave or alternative cinema that (most significantly in the 1970s and 1980s) made a conscious departure from the themes and conventions of mainstream commercial cinema by engaging social issues, using a stark neorealist idiom. Thus *Umbartha* was offered as a bold and novel feminist statement about the middle-class woman's aspirations to career, her sympathetic understanding of fellow or destitute women, her recognition of widespread patriarchal double standards, and her growth to individualistic selfhood. Sulabha, the film's protagonist (played by Smita Patil, virtually an icon of the new wave cinema), leaves her home, containing husband, child, and extended in-law family, to work as superintendent of a *mahilashram* (remand home for women) in a small town in Maharashtra. The film has an extended middle section that is offered as a grim exposé of the depraved conditions prevailing at the mahilashram. Sulabha is placed in the position of a bewildered mediator between the women inmates and the governing body of the institution. She fails in this situation and returns home, only to find that she is no longer needed there. She leaves home again for an unknown destination, with determination and hope for a new life.

The film places Sulabha's career in specific opposition to her mother-in-law's lifelong involvement in social work in various charitable organizations. Unlike her mother-in-law, Sulabha has been professionally trained for her work: she has special credentials for working with women and she has progressive ideas about the administration of institutions for them. The mahilashram is a dumping ground for mentally ill, sexually deviant, abandoned, prostitute, and vagrant women. The women are powerfully depicted, not only as pathetic but as unruly and disobedient. Equally revelatory is the corruption rampant in the running of the institution, the sexual exploitation of the inmates, and the ignorance and apathy, as well as authoritarianism, of the governing body's members. There are inmates of the mahilashram seeking freedom from their confinement, but also those seeking shelter in it from the world outside. But the governing body is oblivious to these different purposes and proceeds to decide their fates in exact opposition to their wishes, "in their own best interests." This leads two of the women to commit suicide, and a third to commit infanticide.

These are the film's strengths as a feminist statement. Its weakness lies in what we actually see of Sulabha's "work" at the institution—and we are not sure whether her failures point to her limitations as custodian or to the limits of the filmmaker's imagination about the relationship between women of different social classes. When Sulabha is not recoiling in horror and distaste from the women under her supervision, she is punishing them (shutting them up or scolding them) or enforcing discipline (organizing prayer meetings, putting the attendants in uniform, and so on). Her self-righteousness is in no way different from that of her social-worker mother-in-law, an observation that can only be ironic in the context of the film's message. A series of disasters take place, some due to her own bungling, since she evinces major failures of sympathy and understanding. But, more importantly, the film fails to undertake any radical rethinking of the functions of institutional space for noncriminal women. Even as the mahilashram experience ostensibly moves Sulabha to the realization that she is "one of them"—as she progressively loses the privileges of marriage and familial security—it insists on her superior self-sufficiency and her superior resources in terms of education and professional prospects. At the same time, the unremittingly bleak visual representation of the mahilashram (despite the presumably ironic accompaniment of the voice-over lyric that celebrates love and springtime) marks her voluntary departure from the institution as an escape—one, let us note, that is not available to the inmates.

The most ambivalent aspect of the film—perhaps a necessary ambivalence given the power and appeal of the ideologies underpinning it, and an inescapable one given its formal resolution—is the attitude it expresses toward marriage and family, the alternative not only to the institution but also to women's independent careers. By making Sulabha's husband a sympathetic and attractive figure (a representation overdetermined by the choice of Girish Karnad for the role), Jabbar Patel makes out a "fair" case for the man's culminating infidelity, in terms of tolerance stretched to its limit by his wife's neglect and of "natural" male sexual need.[43] The extended household—which includes the mother-in-law, who is just despite her harshness, and a brother-in-law and sister-in-law who are affectionate and supportive—is therefore not oppressive except in being *too* comfortable and well-run. For most audiences, as for the characters in the film, Sulabha's decision to seek a career elsewhere can seem irrational, even perverse. The situation therefore becomes one of choices that she must make, as a matter of not being allowed to have one's cake and eat it too. Smita Patil gives the role of Sulabha a fine edge of hysteria cutting into brooding unhappiness: a rendering that enhances the imputation of blame, or at least of culpable ignorance, that attaches to her actions. Because of its commitment to a realistic representation, the film's criticism of patriarchal bourgeois values is not able to penetrate the strength of their ideological pervasiveness but remains instead fixated on them.

Paradoxically, it is the commercial cinema's melodramatic mode that achieves this unequivocal identification. Commercial or mainstream Indian cinema, in Hindi or one of the score of regional languages, commands a vast viewership as a *popular* cinema. It subscribes to the star system, relies on song-and-dance interludes, and is usually made on large budgets—all this in contrast to the "parallel" cinema. In *Damini,* which became a major success of Bombay cinema, the eponymous heroine is played by the glamorous star actress Meenakshi Seshadri. Like Sulabha, she is located within a love-marriage and a comfortable extended family; and although she too is responsible for her eventual ejection from the family, that is only because her principled integrity is in conflict with their wickedness. Damini is eyewitness to the rape of the family's servant-girl by several drunken revelers at a Holi festival, including her brother-in-law. She decides to speak out against them and files a police report, while supporting the raped woman, who is admitted to hospital. The family hopes to cover up the incident and succeeds in doing so by throwing Damini out of the house, bribing the police, hiring a corrupt lawyer, and discrediting Damini as a madwoman and confining her in a mental asylum. Damini escapes from the asylum and is rescued by a lawyer who shelters her and takes up her case, ultimately vindicating her in court. She is then reconciled with her estranged husband.

The asylum interlude, phantasmagorically depicted, opens the film, which then moves into a flashback of the events that have led to Damini's incarceration. There is a certain horrific credibility about the swiftness with which the "respectable" bourgeois domestic woman is pitched into the outer darkness of destitution and confinement in an asylum. The asylum scenes are impressionistically rendered with all the stereotyped features of popular cinema's conception of the "mad." Nevertheless, Damini's reduction to one among many women in terms of a shared predicament does point to her vulnerability and qualifies her moral superiority to some extent. After this point the film works in the genre of the psychothriller, deploying fear, excitement, and suspense toward the triumph of good over evil in the denouement.

Both Damini's mode of departure from her home—relucant, bewildered, and clutching an idol of the goddess Lakshmi—and her reconciliation with her husband at the end (despite what might well have, but is never allowed to, become a romantic involvement with the young lawyer) keep her actions safe from feminism. Her stand is attributed instead, in the film's credits, to a Gandhian adherence to "the truth of conscience." By thus keeping a presumably *personal* feminist politics separate and different from a *disinterested* ethical praxis, the film manages the contradictions in Damini's behavior. Within this explanatory frame there is thus no surprise in her un-shaken allegiance to her husband and in her return to the institu-tion of marriage and family though it has been revealed as hollow and corrupt.

Both films show that, for women, the divide between safety and danger, freedom and confinement, sanity and insanity, respectability and criminality is a tenuous one and is secured only by the condition of their conformity to the values of family and marriage. But since these values are finally upheld, or at least held to be unshakable, the solidarities among women across class and circumstances are never consolidated into a politics of gender. For the female protagonist of *Umbartha*, "fallen" women are an episode on the way to feminist self-realization; for the heroine of *Damini*, the raped woman is a moral and sentimental cause. The limitations of these films, even with their broadly feminist pretensions, clue us in to the difficulties of women's struggle for gender equity and justice, whether regarded in terms of their solidarities with other women or in terms of a politics of rights, when the appeal (in both senses of the word) of the family divides their loyalties.

The Politics of Intervention: Who Speaks for the Shirur Inmates?

The state's strategy in addressing women's issues is to target their "welfare," "development," or "upliftment" (as the titles of govern-ment departments and ministries indicate). Social workers (usually but not always women) support measures in the spirit of such "con-structive" reform, and these find favor also among broad sections of the intelligentsia for the same reason. It is hard to draw an absolute distinction between social-work activism among NGOS and similar groups and feminist activism: clearly the first has subversive and destabilizing potential even where it functions within the broad parameters of patriarchal reformism, while the latter may seize on the concessions and the opportunities made available by the state and society in order to wrest greater rights for women. Feminist arguments and interventions have more than localized relevance, of course, and their resonance with larger questions of gender equality marks the major distinction from community and social work. Feminist initiatives therefore call forth popular as well as official disapproval, helped by their identification with the activists' class and urban location and with the Westernized tag of "feminism" itself.

Activist groups in Pune and neighboring Bombay involved in the Shirur case found themselves in a familiar situation: their interest in the women whose case they were supporting (the inmates of the Shirur asylum whose sterilization they had tried to prevent) was met with skepticism. "Familiar," since in recent years the intervention of women's groups in other similar instances of perceived injustice and violence toward women, such as the Shahbano case, the Deorala sati, and Banwari's rape, has met with resistance from the so-called concerned parties—these being, generally, the religious or caste community to which the women belonged, their families and guardians, and the institutions of the state. The politics of feminism has not been considered sufficient justification or authentic motivation for intervention. The charge of alienation directed at women's groups remains a provocative one at the level of polemic and political expediency, since women in the organized women's movement in the metropolitan cities are self-evidently nonidentical with victimized women, in this case, of course, not themselves mentally deficient or every one a guardian of the mentally deficient. (In a letter to the editor of *The Hindu,* a prominent neurosurgeon of Madras asked, with a rhetorical flourish, "Will the so-called activists make arrangements all over the country for the care of these retarded unfortunates?") (14 February 1994).[44] Women activists are also accused of being selective in the causes they espouse and the abuses they protest—hence hypocritical, interested, or reflexively antiestablishment. Above all, the activists' recourse to rights arguments—constitutional, human, gender equity—is anathema, because it is pitted against what are invariably described as complex situations, traditional values, the force of custom, or competing rights demands.

In analyzing the fallout of the hysterectomies issue, I have been able to identify different (but necessarily overlapping) kinds of feminist activist responses to both the scandal itself and to the politics of their intervention. One of these is a strategy of finding shared ground among *all* women by stressing the commonalities of the "female condition" as such. Thus a piquant, and to my mind by no means insignificant, aspect of the Shirur case that illustrates the ideological divide I have described as the tradition-modernity dichotomy was the prominence the subject of menstruation came to have in the discourse. Menstruation is still a largely forbidden or at least ignored topic in polite public discourse in India. In this instance, however, it allowed feminists to speak *as women* in alliance with the women in the Shirur home—even as their no-nonsense demystification of the female body's functions marked them, once again, as alienated from prevalent social norms and conventions. Such openness and oppositionality are treated negatively, as a mark of modernity, by feminism's opponents; but their usefulness in asserting a politics of the female body was considerable. (The "modern" is, however, visible in other guises. Female-hygiene products—marketed predominantly by multinational companies—have recently entered public advertising space: here the idiom of freedom and confidence produces even a dissimulation of feminist rhetoric.)[45] In line with the feminist politics generated by the breaking of a social taboo, a recent short story by Manjula Padmanabhan, "The Stain," ends in a sturdy, unapologetic assertion of feminist individualism when the (African American) female protagonist refuses to be cowed by her (Indian) fiancé and his mother into observing traditional Indian menstrual rituals. When asked by him, rhetorically, if she would compare "five thousand years of civilization to . . . feminine hygiene products," she answers, quite simply, "yes" (1996, 229). This unequivocal stand on priorities is as unexpected as it is stimulating. The story must be viewed as part of the discursive regime of the female body that Indian feminism has begun to construct.

I do not wish to suggest that this gain, tangential if also noteworthy, marks the unqualified triumph of a "modern" feminist ideology. Feminist arguments, we must note, were also appropriated by the government's spokesperson, Vandana Khullar, to argue precisely the reasonableness of the solutions sought by the hysterectomies: "Is it not a gross invasion of a woman's privacy and independence to have someone else take care of her menstrual hygiene, to even change napkins for her?"; and, further, "Suddenly the 'wombs' of a few unfortunate women have become news, as if its [*sic*] removal will eliminate her femininity. In fact this operation does not even affect their capacity for sexual enjoyment. Why then are we equating womb with womanhood?" Khullar blames feminists for their projection of their own "preconceptions of what a woman must feel about her rights" (1994). Such appropriation of feminism's arguments by its opponents is by no means rare in the contests over women's rights, and it must alert us to the limits of the purely debating aspect of such issues.

A second major initiative that addresses questions of locus standii is that of public-interest litigation, or social-action litigation, as it is more accurately called (Baxi 1988, 388). In recent times it has become a method of political intervention frequently deployed by concerned individuals and activist groups to alleviate the sufferings of others. As we saw, the women's and healthcare groups that took the lead in the protest against the hysterectomies followed up by litigation against the state. Dr. Anant Phadke, founder of Paryaya (an organization for the welfare and rights of mentally handicapped women), and Jayshree Velankar of Forum for Women's Health (a society that engages with issues of women's health, in particular reproductive technologies), filed a writ petition in the Bombay High Court against the state of Maharashtra, questioning its authority in ordering the hysterectomies.[46] The problem of locus standii is thus *legally* met by resorting to this form of activism, through which "outside" parties are permitted to agitate matters in the courts on behalf of the "oppressed and weaker sections of society." What is equally important is what this mode of recourse tells us about the state of the state: the fact, first, that the expansion of the role of the courts—their direct intervention in "social and political problems"—is a consequence of the "obduracy and non-response" of state institutions to prevalent injustices; and, second, that the actions are often directed (especially in the early years, following the Emergency) against cases of "*state lawlessness*" (emphasis added) as these resulted in "violations of individual rights and liberties" (Suresh and Nagasila 1995, 37–41). While the general effectiveness or otherwise of judgments on public-interest litigation (PIL) is open to debate,[47] there is no doubt that they have allowed

Beyond the Hysterectomies Scandal   109

people or groups of people with poor resources access to legal remedies from the Supreme Court—and these have included those in custodial institutions, specifically mental asylums. (See, especially, Ramanathan 1996, 221, note 8, and 217–18; and Murlidhar 1999, 294, note 16).

A recent and, in India, not yet widespread institutionalized means of "speaking for" takes the form of advocacy groups. The first of such groups was recently set up to lobby for legal reforms relating to the mentally retarded. Since many families of the mentally disabled and many concerned NGOS were by and large ignorant of the laws relating to their legal status and rights, and, conversely, legal experts knew little about "the capacities and incapacities of persons with mental disability," the need for their interaction and mutual learning was keenly felt. From February to September 1997, therefore, a core group of ten NGOS, some of them Parent Organizations (such as Action For Autism), met and interacted in a Legal Advocacy Workshop facilitated by Dr. Amita Dhanda of the Indian Law Institute and initiated by Jan Madhyam, an NGO concerned with mental retardation. The group felt that as a preliminary to law reform "there has first to be a change in attitudes and mindsets of the community. There is a strong need to first aim at changing societal attitudes in order to reform law."[48] Clearly, such an initiative is urgent and necessary—its priorities, those of generating public awareness as a preliminary and adjunct step to lobbying for legal reform, are undeniably correct. But its uniqueness is also an indication of the high degree of organizational resources[49] and commitment that it calls for, both commodities in short supply in the general Indian context. Though they may well be a forerunner to similar self-education, publicity, and pressure-group lobbying tactics for similar constituencies among the disabled, NGO initiatives in India are unlikely to put the state out of business, as Harriss-White, among others, has pointed out. Their significance here is mainly to indicate one of the ways in which the intervention of "other" groups may be legitimized in the eyes of the state and the larger public.

Finally, in the terrain of oppositional politics the voices of the victims themselves are beginning to be raised in protest and demand and are beginning to be heard in the spaces available in a democratic civil society, predominantly, of course, the press. The role of activists is to assist such endeavors.[50] Thus we witness a spate of organized movements for social justice, based on civil liberties demands, on broad class, caste, and gender interests (trade unions, self-employed women's associations, peasant movements, student unions, urban women's groups) and on the solidarities forged from the shared experience of specific disasters (e.g., the Bhopal Gas Victims' Association, the Sikh Riots Victims' Association); or arising from spontaneous opposition to the state on specific issues like price rise, liquor sales, power and water shortages, custodial death of a member of the community, etc. This raises the issue of the politics of organized resistance by those within the institution, a possibility to which not much significance has as yet been attached. For instance, the draft report for the Beijing Conference, while rightly calling for institutional reforms and also for more institutional spaces for women in need, does not envisage the possibilities of a libertarian organizational politics initiated by the inmates of the institutions themselves. Instances of spontaneous revolts and breakouts, though numerous, lead, as I earlier pointed out, to repressive measures—though they have also contributed to the makings of a scandal whose repercussions may come to have some significance and impact. Lately, historical studies of the institution from a subaltern perspective have begun to address such a politics: Sanjiv Kakar's study of patient unrest in the colonial leprosy asylum between 1860 and 1940, to which reference has been made earlier, analyzes the combination of factors that led to inmates' revolts against poor living conditions in asylums in this period and attributes them to the patients' knowledge of the medical advances in leprosy treatment as well as their responsiveness to the wider political climate (Kakar 1996, 78). Such organized resistance cannot, of course, be seriously envisaged as a possibility among the mentally retarded in custodial institutions, making them the most vulnerable even among the most marginalized of groups, the destitute disabled—a fact that made the question of custodianship a crucial one in the hysterectomies issue. In general, as Harriss-White mourns, "disability has a weak constituency" (154), and there are severe constraints on disabled people as activists.

The combination of protest, media exposure, and judicial intervention that I am projecting here as an oppositional politics—the trajectory followed in the hysterectomies case—does not, of course, by any means guarantee success, in the sense of restitution of rights or correction of wrongs.[51] But a scenario in which such an oppositional politics is absent or even weak would undoubtedly be one of unbridled social injustice. Within an ethical rationale of social struggle, we must consider the check on the absolute powers and the calling to account of state and elites as the sufficient sign of success. We are nonetheless led to ask, plaintively, whether social justice is to be won only by the unceasing struggle of disadvantaged victim-citizens and their advocates against their opponents. The intellectual is tempted to invoke, in answer, the establishment of ethical absolutes. There is a basic, though not for that reason self-evident, argument to be made for the protection and well-being of the retarded and other disadvantaged on the basis of humanitarianism, as a matter of basic civilizational decency, even while we may admit that definitions of disability are culturally relative. "The test of any civilized society lies in the way it looks after those who cannot look after themselves," insisted S. D. Sharma, director of the Institute of Human Behavior and Allied Sciences, Delhi, in a polemical response to the hysterectomies scandal (quoted in K. Jain 1994).

This shift from the mechanisms of the welfare state to questions of ethicality is one I wish to mark in conclusion. The ethical state must be reflected not only in the original mandates of a constitution but in a government's repeated and alert responsiveness to the varied needs of different but equal people according to a calculus that transcends cost benefit, a (self-) control that checks the abuse of power, and an impersonality that yet accepts responsibility greater than that of any guardian. The protests raised in cases like the Pune hysterectomies are directed, beyond the immediate issue at state, toward the establishment of such norms.

The foregoing discussion must be viewed as an attempt—difficult, but necessary in my view—to extend the implications of a women's issue to the fullest, while at the same time grounding it in the specificity of gendered analysis. I have been concerned to raise questions about institutionalization in/and the postcolonial state—about the extent of the state's responsibilities and the limits of its control in relation to dependent citizens—and to explore strategies of social protest and struggle—specifically, how feminists in the women's movement may strategically define their relationship to victimized women.

In theoretical terms the issue may be read, for the first, in light of Rawlsian welfarist moral theory, that is, as a means to judge the goodness of a state of affairs, in this case the contemporary Indian, in terms of "the greatest benefit of the least advantaged," in this case, of course, that of the hysterectomized women (Rawls 1971, 83). Second, since the issue concerns destitute mentally retarded women—women who inhabit the undecidable ground between adult/child, women/not-quite women, victim/citizen, social responsibility/social threat—it may be invoked as a *deconstructive* tool. It is the deconstructive method that has taught us to reconceptualize the center in relation to the margin, to interrogate the positivity with reference to the differenced, and to invoke the contingent and singular to bring the normative to crisis: a methodology for reflexive feminism. Above all, the ambiguities within and the overlaps between schemes for social *control* and social *welfare* that a feminist politics brought to light as the scandal of institutional care illustrate the intimate, indeed constitutive connections between (actual) violence and (ostensible) protection in the relationship of women and the state.

II Women in Law

4 The Prostitution Question(s): Female Agency, Sexuality, and Work

This chapter is set out as a series of reflections on the prostitution question as conceived in terms of feminist politics, legal reform, and prostitute rights. Its context is provided by the widespread demand to amend the present set of laws relating to prostitution in India, chiefly the Prohibition of Immoral Traffic Act (PITA) of 1986.[1] Changes in the existing prostitution laws have been deemed necessary and urgent by sex workers and women's groups, NGOs, legal activists, health workers, state functionaries (health administrators, police, etc.), and others in the field, though the reasons and the directions for change proposed by different participants have been widely divergent.

The "prostitution question," as we may term in short the contemporary debates around women in prostitution, is fraught today because of the acute divide it has created among feminists and between feminists and sex workers, not to mention among others in the field, in India and elsewhere. It challenges us, as well, to ask whether prostitute interests are being truly represented in these debates.

The urgency and force of the disagreements arise not only from the issues relating to prostitution but also from the fact that the prostitution question has gathered around itself many of the issues that remain unresolved in feminism, such as the relationship between feminists and female "victims of oppression"; the construction of the female subject in terms of "agency" (choice, autonomy, desire, "voice"); the conceptualization of women's work and female sexuality, and the public and private domains of these; the assumptions about First World/Third World difference and sameness in women's status; and the narrativization-as-progress of women's (here, especially, prostitutes') history.

Inevitably the prostitution question(s) feed into the feminist interrogation of heterosexual relationships (especially marriage), family, work, and economic exchange, based on the recognition, more or less overt, of women's equivalence to each other at the level of function and structure, and of women as the universal objects of exchange in every kind of transaction, social, economic, familial, sexual, psychic, aesthetic, religious, and linguistic.[2] As Evelina Giobbe, a prostitute-activist, observed: "Prostitution isn't like anything else. Rather, everything else is like prostitution because it is the model for women's condition" (cited in Baldwin 1992, 47). This is a perception that radically overturns the sharp disjunction traditionally maintained, in both ideology and social arrangements, between the categories of respectable bourgeois womanhood and prostitution. But the slippages between the two categories are frequent and significant in both discourse and practice. They are visible in such matters, for instance, as the contractual terms of bourgeois marriage, the "normal" forms of heterosexual dating, many women's confessions to "occasional prostitution" or sex for favors, and the name-calling of women accused of promiscuity as "whores."[3] The recognition of *continuities* among women is crucial to any understanding of prostitution, even while we must necessarily attend to the *specificities* of the phenomenon in our endeavors to understand and contend with it as a feminist issue.

Feminist interventions in prostitution have been significantly located within the legal arena because law is one of the discursive structures that constructs "women" and "prostitute women" as separate groups. As Margaret Baldwin has astutely observed, "a woman's claim on justice . . . crucially depends on her success in proving that she is not, and never has been, a prostitute" (1992, 81). It is the law's hegemonic role in the production of gendered identity that, as much as any social practice, enforces this separation.[4] And prostitute women both define and are reciprocally defined by implicit concepts of "normative" femininity, which is a major site of investigation and questioning for feminist theory.

As a central issue for law and feminism, prostitution becomes a significant site also for attending to the relations between women and the state. The state approaches prostitution in two contradictory but well-established ways. First, for the patriarchal state, prostitution serves as an instance of deviant or criminal female sexuality, to be therefore placed under surveillance and control by its instruments, the police, the courts, and social-welfare bodies. At the same time, prostitution also services what is generally viewed as an incessant and urgent male sexual need, especially in the absence of or in excess of marital or "legitimate" sex (this is especially so for populations like men in the armed forces)—and it is therefore to be safeguarded in more or less overt ways for this purpose. And second, prostitution as female sex *work* is an aspect of the economy—either as a sex trade that furthers national tourism and other leisure industries and as such is promoted by the state (even if it may disavow any such association), or as part of the vast informal labor sector, predominantly occupied by women workers, that remains unprotected by wage or labor legislation despite its substantial contribution to the economy. State intervention in prostitution has recently received a further major impetus as sex workers are believed to represent a public health threat as carriers of HIV/AIDS infection (a mostly erroneous impression). But as a result of all these perceived reasons, distorted as well as accurate, prostitutes—as practitioners of illegitimate/deviant/criminal sex, as workers in the informal sector in large numbers, and as potential public health hazard—have also been able to emerge as a collective with significant bargaining powers with the state, especially in their demand for recognition, rights, and removal of stigma.[5]

In what follows, I outline first the current different legal positions on prostitution and their highly contested forms. I then describe how these are advocated or opposed by feminists according to their understanding of the politics of prostitution. In the third section I identify what appear to me to be the chief conceptual and theoretical areas of contestation in the debates, highlighting the aspect of the prostitution question that seems to me to have received the least theoretical elaboration in these discussions, namely, the representation of prostitution as work. In the concluding section, I speculate on some of the reasons for such divisions on the prostitution question and attempt a recasting of the question in terms of a dialectic of theories and historical forces.

The State, Law, and Prostitution

The legal-reform debates turn on whether prostitution requires special laws and how such laws will address the problems relating to prostitution today—but also whether laws (of any kind) are not themselves the problem, and hence whether it is legal measures that will best serve the purpose of effecting change. One argument is that existing criminal laws have sufficient means and strength to deal with the unlawful aspects of prostitution (such as abduction, coercion, and exploitation of women, especially minors). For instance, Margo St. James, founder of the prostitute rights group COYOTE (Call Off Your Old Tired Ethics) observes: "I want to use the laws that are on the books and go after the people—mostly men—who are using force, fraud, violence, and deceit. The laws needed to do that are on the books already; we don't need special laws to prosecute men who do this to prostitutes" (in L. Bell 1987, 86). But the question goes beyond that of a narrow legal-reform agenda, into the question of the state as the source and repository of such authority. Calling on the law to regulate, shape, or control social practices can only lead to the empowerment of an already draconian state, while also providing loopholes for wrongdoers to exploit. Or the state's intervention would lead to its getting "saddled" with the "supervision of a vast and organised system of prostitution" (as Annie Besant feared as long ago as 1876 in the context of the controversy over the passage of the Contagious Diseases Acts in the British parliament) (Jeffreys 1987, 91–99). Participants in a conference on the politics of pornography and prostitution in Toronto cited in Laurie Bell's *Good Girls, Bad Girls* were divided about the role of the state. One of them remarked on the "different attitude on the part of different feminists towards the state and how much of an ally it can be of ours in the present context and how much it can't be" (1987, 185). While in general there was fear of state control and interference, another participant admitted, "I'm not convinced that the state is the worst and most awful repository of power at this time" (186).

True, prostitution is not solely a legal issue, nor are laws the sole determinants of cultural and social practices. But because the laws bring sex workers into much more immediate, constant, and pressing proximity to the state regime than any other population group, law reform has become a central and tendentious issue in the prostitution debates. As an influential mechanism of regulation and control, the law becomes a site of contestation for various groups seeking change. The democratic state is urged to be responsive to pressures from rights movements and interest groups to reform or remove existing laws or introduce new legislation, even as it may itself initiate change in social attitudes and traditional practices through legal measures. These pressures are inevitably in conflict with the status quo, the often powerful moral majority, the elite or majoritarian groups supporting both these, and the compulsions of the state itself (where prostitution is concerned, for instance, these are reflected in the unspoken or actively denied economic interests served by sex tourism in certain countries, especially in Southeast Asia), whose mandates invariably dictate the shape of the laws and the ways in which they are interpreted by the courts. In India as elsewhere, it is now sex workers themselves and the groups supporting them who are framing these demands for change. This identification, however, by no means provides clear indication of the desired changes or the means of their achievement since, as I have pointed out, they themselves are divided on the issues occasioned by prostitution.

Broadly, states have addressed prostitution by regulating (or deregulating) it in one of several ways. The two poles of these alternatives are its abolition on the one hand and, on the other, decriminalization (with or without laws actively supporting prostitution). Abolition seeks to remove prostitution by criminalizing every aspect of the prostitution system and all the people involved in it, prostitutes themselves, their clients, pimps, traffickers, brothelkeepers. According to the "radical" or abolitionist view that supports prohibition, the commercial sex system is and can never be anything but an exploitation of women, whose entry into prostitution is always involuntary and who are degraded by the sale of their bodies. Prostitution in this view is, further, profoundly and *constitutively* implicated in a system that is criminal, that is, its existence depends on the support of criminal elements, pimps, brothelkeepers, crime mafias, sex-tourism operators, and other organizational middlemen who exploit both the prostitute and the market. Radical reformers therefore seek the legal abolition, prohibition, or stricter regulation of prostitution. They solicit the aid of world organizations like the United Nations, voluntary groups, the Church, and other influential organs of social regulation and change in order to achieve these ends. In a deeply revealing analogy, Jean Fernand-Laurent, a special rapporteur for the United Nations Economic and Social Council, compared prostitution with slavery when he concluded his report with a plea for abolition: "Despite persistent prejudices and considerable economic interests, the nineteenth century, which did not then have a League of Nations, abolished the traffic in blacks. The process took less than a century. . . . Is not the twentieth century, which is better equipped in all respects, able to act as well and as quickly with respect to the traffic in women and children?" (1985, 36).[6]

Arguments based on the rights of individuals to engage with mutual consent in any kind of sexual transactions in private or, less loftily, a pragmatic acceptance of prostitution as a necessary evil, have led to a more "tolerationist" version of the antiprostitution position. This, and the recognition of the double standards involved in penalizing the (female) prostitute but not her (male) client, have led to the exemption of the prostitute from prosecution by the law—at least in principle—while penalizing her associates (pimp, brothelkeeper, dependents) for their activities. The United Nations Convention for the Suppression of the Traffic in Persons and the Exploitation of the Prostitution of Others, held in 1949, was based on such tolerationist principles. India is a signatory to the UN declaration and passed the Immoral Traffic (Suppression) Act of 1956 broadly in accordance with it (subsequently amended in 1986 to the Prohibition of Immoral Traffic Act PITA).

But in spite of progressive laws that "decriminalize" the prostitute, in *practice* it is she who continues to bear the brunt of punitive law-enforcement measures and legal strictures.[7] This is particularly true in India, where the revision of the law in the direction of exempting the prostitute from prosecution has had little impact. Persecution of the prostitute seems likely to continue in spite of the laws—or even because of them.[8] Further, the laws that circumscribe the practice of prostitution—making solicitation and living off the earnings from prostitution illegal and criminalizing pimps and brothelkeepers—drive sex workers deeper and deeper into covert practices and thereby make them more vulnerable to police harassment.[9] Some of these provisions, such as the magistrate's powers to convict a woman of solicitation in a "public" place or turn her out of a house deemed to be a "brothel," are also in violation of a citizen's civil rights of residence and mobility.

State regulation of prostitution in certain countries, notably Germany and the state of Nevada in the United States, may *legalize* the activity, a third option for the state. This move is usually less concerned with sex workers' well-being than with regulating their work in the interests of their clients and with other considerations about the "public good." Thus, legalized prostitution would impose registration, licensing, zoning laws, mandatory health checks, and taxes, which would enable the state to perform surveillance and strict supervision of prostitute activities. But some sex workers' organizations believe that the legalization of prostitution, by bringing it unambiguously within the sphere of legitimate work and granting them full legal rights, will improve their condition despite these risks.

The demand for the complete decriminalization of prostitution comes from "liberals,"[10] who view all forms of state intervention as violation of the rights of prostitutes to practice their profession. They do not believe that it is state intervention, in the form of legislation, police controls, health checks on prostitutes, or closure of brothels, that will provide the solution to the perceived problems of prostitution (crime, exploitation and coercion, health hazards). Rather, the solution will be found in the individual and collective right of prostitutes to act in their own best interests. Indeed pro-prostitution feminists maintain that it is criminalization (by the law) that is solely and wholly responsible for the problems encountered by those in the sex trade. "Where it [prostitution] is decriminalized . . . sex work can immeasurably expand and enlarge the choices available to women," maintains Anne McClintock (1993, 4). And beyond these there is the hope and expectation that the state can and will empower prostitute women as citizens and workers, by enacting labor and other legislation on their behalf and by supporting prostitute movements that will mobilize and organize them to achieve control over their professional activities.

It is not only state and international laws relating to prostitution that these different positions support: they are also reflected in the reform agendas and activist strategies relating to prostitute welfare and rights. Antiprostitution activists have tended to concentrate their energies on promoting rehabilitation, legal assistance, job training and placement, and other welfare measures for women removed from prostitution. The emphasis of prostitute activists, in contrast, has fallen on opposing police excesses, social pressures, discriminatory legal decisions, and on agitating for improved work conditions, benefits, and protection for those within the sex trade. While antiprostitution radical reformers use the *human* rights approach (the United Nations declaration in 1950 is framed as a human rights document on behalf of women in prostitution), pro-prostitution liberals prefer to focus on the *civil* rights of women in prostitution, either as individuals or as a professional collective. The human rights perspective is a global one, formulated in light of the realities of the international sex trade, white slave traffic, sex tourism, the adverse impact of wars, migrations, or natural calamities on regional economies.[11] The liberal perspective was developed in the context of the prostitutes' rights movement in the United States and Canada, especially in the 1970s and 1980s, as a response to increased police repression, illiberal laws, and other forms of state control, as well as the dominance of the moral right. Prostitute rights movements have since spread globally and are particularly visible in Southeast Asia (Philippines, Thailand) and in India as a consequence of other developments, prominently sex tourism, the migration of sex workers or trafficking across international borders, and above all mobilization around the HIV/ AIDS threat.[12]

In India the present PITA is widely regarded as inadequate, and therefore a number of proposals for reform have emerged in response to its antiprostitute provisions and to the demands of sex workers, some at the initiative of the Indian government itself. Some of the problems with the tolerationist law in general, and particularly as it applies in India, have been identified earlier. An alarming aspect of the PITA concerns the Indian state's welfare provisions for the so-called rescue and rehabilitation of prostitutes and the nature of the "protective" or "corrective" institutions to which prostitutes are sent. As I have shown at length in chapter 3 on the institutionalization of destitute mentally retarded women, these provisions are few and miserable; and the period to which women are sentenced in these institutions (between which, and among which and regular prison, there are few if any differences) is often an indefinite one, in contrast to fixed period criminal sentences.[13] Thus, as a memorandum prepared by the Centre for Feminist Legal Research (CFLR) has argued, prostitute women are effectively criminalized or treated solely as victims in need of rehabilitation (any person found in a brothel or believed to be a prostitute is compulsorily "rescued") (CFLR memorandum 1997, 4–6). The act also empowers the state to remove the children of prostitutes from their custody and even guardianship.

Not all groups demand a change in the existing laws. Sleightholme and Sinha argue, for instance, that until major reforms are achieved the existing laws can be successfully interpreted in favor of sex workers if they are made to work in the spirit in which they were intended, to punish not them but the organizers of the trade (1996, 70–71). There are other organizations, like the Ashaya Tirskrut Nati Sangh, formed by three hundred brothel owners in Bombay with the Indian Health Organization, that favor the licensing of prostitution. A bill drafted by the Maharashtra state government (the Maharashtra Protection of Commercial Sex Workers Act of 1994) is also similarly a proposal for legalization, requiring compulsory registration and medical testing of all sex workers (Gangoli 1998, 504–05).

Other proposals for reform have been drafted by the National Law School (NLS) in Bangalore, and, along with proposals by other groups, were discussed at a conference on women and the law organized by the NLS in 1994. These have been reported at length in the CFLR memorandum (1997) and in Kotiswaran (2001, 182–95). Some of these proposals recommended variations on the existing law, emphasizing, for instance, greater stringency against trafficking and coercion, and improved rehabilitation methods. Others were more radically in favor of decriminalization. According to one such proposed bill, legal intervention would consist only of labor laws to protect sex workers (on the lines of the Consumers Redressal Bill). Another, named the Sex Worker (Legalization for Empowerment) Bill of 1993, recommended legalization but in a very different way from the usual state-regulated, legalized prostitution. The bill instead completely decriminalizes all sexual services; provides a series of nondiscriminatory measures against sex workers; and frames clauses to prevent violence against them, provide adequate wages, and ensure other welfare measures (Kotiswaran 2001, 190–92).

The CFLR memorandum presented a working draft of a new bill at a workshop in Delhi in 1997; it incorporated several of the radical

NLS proposals.[14] The draft pushed for complete decriminalization through repeal of PITA and suggested in its place "a three-pronged law reform strategy." The provisions of the Indian Penal Code (IPC) are considered sufficient to prevent and punish offenses like trafficking (though even here the draft suggests caution in invoking these against women suspected of being trafficked). The draft further sets out a list of the rights often denied to women in prostitution, which the state is called on to enforce: the right to work, to safe conditions and benefits at work, to freedom of association, to education, to free movement and residence, to privacy. It also considers at length the redressal mechanisms and alternatives that the state must offer to women in prostitution in place of the existing corrective/protective custody for rescued prostitutes. Labor legislation is discussed, but the prevailing view at the workshop was that labor laws in India have been extremely ineffectual even in the factory sector and were unlikely to be successfully implemented in the unorganized sector; and even if used to regulate sex work legislation would apply only to a small portion of the sex trade that actually has provision for a "workplace," such as brothel prostitution.

The National Human Rights Commission, the National Commission of Women, and the Joint Women's Program discussed the CFLR proposals at a later conference, also in 1997. The main resolutions that emerged were to crack down on South Asian regional trafficking, protect prostitute rights more rigorously, and amend the laws in light of the proposals made by Jean D'Cunha. (Jean D'Cunha, a longtime legal activist in this issue, does not support complete decriminalization or legalization, recommending rather the removal of the excesses and loopholes in the existing laws to prevent the prosecution of sex workers.) At present PITA awaits change/replacement in the wake and in light of these proposals and those in the CFLR draft.

The CFLR draft is entirely prostitute-centered, and it is unlikely that the state will actually push for enacting such radical legislation to empower sex workers. It does ask whether prostitute rights need to be enforced by legislation, or whether decriminalization is sufficient in itself to allow prostitutes to exercise their legal rights in the same way as other citizens; and also whether prostitute rights groups cannot lobby for welfare measures more successfully than statutory endorsement can (CFLR memorandum 1997, 19–22).

Despite the varied nature of the proposals for legal reform in India, we notice that two assumptions are constant: one, that the prostitute is not engaged in criminal activity and indeed it is she whom the laws must protect (though there is disagreement in that case about whether she is primarily a coerced "victim" or, instead, a legitimate (voluntary) worker in a bad trade); and two, that the state is a central agent in bringing about this transformation, both because its laws and personnel, the police and the judiciary, bear responsibility for the criminalization and degradation of prostitution in the first place, and because it possesses the necessary influence to rectify this situation. The discussion that follows attempts to connect these perceptions of the law with feminist positions about prostitution and its politics.

Feminism and the Politics of Prostitution

The differences among contemporary feminists, particularly in the West, were sharply drawn in the significant years 1983 to 1987, when two major conferences on prostitution met and an international movement and network of prostitute-feminists began to be visible. The first was a workshop held in Rotterdam in 1983 called "International Feminist Networking against the Traffic in Women: Organizing against Female Sexual Slavery," whose agenda, as the title indicates, was to draw attention to the international dimensions of the problem, insist on the forced nature of all prostitution, and organize a campaign for its removal. The participants were feminist activists and researchers from all over the world. Prostitutes were not participants, but Margo St. James, the founder of COYOTE, the first prostitute organization in the United States, shared her experiences with the workshop participants as a "resource person" (Barry et al. 1984). The second major conference was the Second World Whores' Congress in Brussels in 1986. Gail Pheterson, one of the organizers of the event, drew attention to the significance of the participation of prostitutes themselves in the debates on prostitution: "It is almost unprecedented for prostitutes to speak on their own behalf and on behalf of other oppressed people in a large well-publicized forum. It is also almost unprecedented for non-prostitute women to work as equals with prostitute women in shared struggle" (1989, 3). The conference stressed the rights of prostitutes to organize to achieve "economic and sexual self-determination" and drafted a Charter of Demands as well as founded the International Committee for Prostitutes' Rights.

Pheterson deplored the traditional separation of feminist and prostitute movements, criticizing especially the politics of the Rotterdam conference, which had not included prostitutes among its participants. Kathleen Barry, the chief organizer, had refused to appear on a television discussion program with Margo St. James, on the grounds that "the conference was feminist and did not support the institution of prostitution" and that it would be "inappropriate to discuss sexual slavery with prostitute women" (Pheterson 1989, 17–21). The accusation that feminists have chosen ignorance about the realities of sex-trade workers' lives and experiences was freely expressed by the participants (strippers, hookers, and porn artists), who said that they "feel isolated not only from society but also from a women's movement that has, they believe, ignored or dissociated itself from [them]. . . . We don't know each other. We never talk to one another. We perceive each other's struggle to be separate" (Bell 1987, 14).

It is true that feminist campaigns, even when they were on behalf of prostitutes, beginning with Josephine Butler's opposition to the Contagious Diseases Bill during the years 1870 to 1886 in Britain, had not sought out prostitutes as participants: on the contrary, they implicitly maintained the separation of "good girls/bad girls" (feminists/whores) that the prostitute conferences mocked and mourned.[15] If then it was a matter of feminists' claiming the moral high ground, contemporary women's movements, while less likely to endorse traditional sexual morality, are nevertheless still prone to view prostitution solely in terms of an exploitative practice and, consequently, to regard women in prostitution in the light of victims to be saved.

The pro- and antiprostitution feminist positions today have also been identified with "postmodern" and "modern" versions of prostitution, respectively, an identification whose usefulness I want to explore here, especially in terms of the opposed categories First World/Third World, which it also inhabits. The liberal position on prostitute rights is usually identified with a postmodern feminist politics in the West. In a recent book Shannon Bell historicizes the phenomenon of postmodernist prostitute discourse by marking its discontinuities from the "modern" form prostitution took in nineteenth-century Europe under the aegis of the new industrial capital. Bell diagnoses the proletarianization of the prostitute during this process, which also produced increased state regulation (1994, especially chapter 3, "The Making of the Modern Prostitute Body"). She establishes its continuities instead with the valorized "premodern" institution of the Greek hetaerae. By this means she seeks to recuperate the prostitute as "sexual, sacred, healing female body." Further, and more insistently, she asserts that, within the contemporary postmodern historical moment, prostitutes have been enabled to "assume their own subject-position and produce their own political identity" (2).

Many Indian feminist activists would argue that this liberationist postmodern position may be valid under the conditions of prostitute activism in the West but would be completely inappropriate in India and most other Third World contexts. (See, for example, D'Cunha 1992, 42.)[16] But prostitute activism, including unionization, as I noted earlier, is now a spreading phenomenon in many parts of the non-West. It has dovetailed into a "sex radical" politics, as it has been called, which includes gay-lesbian movements and a broadly liberationist sexual politics among women's groups, to produce the contours of a pro-prostitution feminist politics. This conjuncture describes the situation in North America and Europe,[17] and also, generally, in Taiwan and in India.[18] But a postmodern feminist theory like Shannon Bell's has a particular North American fix, Lillian Robinson suggests. Here prostitution is identified with power, as reflected primarily in the *discourse* of the "prostitute body and prostitute identity." This is because Bell draws from and relates it almost exclusively to prostitute performance artists rather than those in other kinds of sex trade. Robinson regards this as a severe limitation of the radical potential of the theory, since by privileging the mere "assertion" of power, it overlooks the interactions between the "world of the performance" and "the one in which prostitutes ply their trade" (Bishop and Robinson 1998, 235–42).[19]

Those feminist texts that offer what we might regard as a postmodern take on prostitution in India also similarly represent the work of performance artists within a closed and autonomous world. Mira Nair's film *India Cabaret* (1985)[20] and Veena Oldenberg's essay on the courtesans of Lucknow (1992) are both interesting and problematic works. Nair's film presents cabaret dancers as "survivors" who express a subversive, independent view of their profession. Nair's foregrounding of the dancer's "voices," her stress on their "ease with their bodies," and on cabaret as a way of making a living, that is, as a professional activity, replicates postmodern Western feminist views on sex performance artists. In an interview Nair attributed the negative responses the film generated among Indian feminists and other sections of the audience to its being at odds with their expectation of seeing female passivity, shame, and oppression. She casts the opposition in too-simple terms, as one of "complexity, irony and contradictions" (her representation of the dancers) versus "stereotypes" (the moral right's expectations) (Nair 1986–87). Similarly, Oldenberg sets out to consciously reverse the stereotypes about prostitution, specifically about courtesans in Lucknow. While marking the decline in their condition and status since their heyday in the Mughal period, she nevertheless insists on the continuation of the traditions of autonomy, sexual skills, and alternative sexuality in the courtesans' "lifestyle" that has been remarked on as an aspect of "premodern" prostitution in different cultures by other historians (for instance, Bell 1994; Srinivasan 1985). She concludes her essay by explicitly linking the courtesans' attitudes to work with those of New York hookers, thereby diluting her description of the historical practice and profession of their work into a broad perspective on prostitution as such.

Both Nair and Oldenberg give us full, richly documented accounts of their subjects' lives, grant their voices authority, and forcefully argue the feminist implications of the construction of such alternative female subjectivities. However—without either disagreement or disbelief—we might still experience reservations on finding that in these texts prostitutes are exhorted to serve primarily as adversaries or critics of a "society" whose representatives are (all) men and "respectable" women. What such a representation fails to acknowledge is that prostitutes are necessarily and complexly *connected* both to patriarchy and to women as a class, in ways that cannot be only antagonistic and would in fact include dependence and emulation— an acknowledgment that complicates our view of them as consistently subversive agents as much as it does the view of them as invariant "victims" that it sought to displace.

Clearly, postmodern positions are available for feminists within the context of prostitution in India, even if problematically. While prostitute-activists in India are vocal and articulate about their demands and about the legitimacy of their work, there are not many instances of the celebration of commercial sex as representing sexual freedom *tout court*,[21] of the kind to be found in the work of North American prostitute-activists like Annie Sprinkle or Scarlot Harlot.[22] But for certain nonprostitute feminists, commercial sex has precisely this kind of *symbolic* meaning of power and resistance and is therefore read wholly in terms of a subversive, dominant, and autonomous sexual praxis. The work of Annie Sprinkle, for example, introduced as resource material in a workshop on prostitution organized by the Centre for Feminist Legal Research in New Delhi, found many takers chiefly because it had this kind of extended relevance for sexuality questions in feminism;[23] and a recent article on Indian sex workers and the law begins with a lengthy quotation from Scarlot Harlot as a way of signifying itself as an act of "civil disobedience" similar to Scarlot's description of prostitution (Kotiswaran 2001, 161–2).[24]

The chief issues on which feminists disagree, as the debates on prostitution I have sketched above indicate, relate to prostitute *agency*, *sexuality*, and *work*. Though these terms are analytically distinct, they are connected and overlapping aspects of sex work, such that a position on one logically entails the others. I follow these differences further in the next section.

Prostitute Agency, Sexuality, Work

The issue of *agency* relates to the subject-position accorded to the prostitute, broadly in terms of coerced woman (victim) or freely choosing and willing sex worker. The current definition of prostitution in Indian law reveals the ingenuity required to decriminalize the prostitute in keeping with the coercion/volition framework: while, according to the earlier act of 1956, the volitional act of "a female offering her body for promiscuous sexual intercourse for hire whether in money or in kind" was criminal and rendered her liable to prosecution, under the revised 1986 Act, "prostitution" means "the sexual exploitation or abuse of persons for commercial purpose, and the expression 'prostitute' shall be constructed accordingly"—so there is not only no criminality if there is "offering by way of free contract," there is not even prostitution! And when the prostitute subject is legally represented only in terms of coercion or of volition, as Margaret Baldwin has pointed out, the need and the violence that sustain prostitution tend to be overlooked (the need in the first case, and the violence in the second) (1992, 60).

Gail Pheterson has deplored the way prostitute agency gets framed by the antiprostitution lobby: "Whores are dishonored as lost women (the victims) or as bad women (the collaborators)" (1993, 58). As a result of liberal-feminist intervention, prostitute agency (the voluntary decision to enter into and stay within sex work) has moved from equation with deviance or legal criminality to an issue of prostitute autonomy and rights; just as nonagency (coerced entry into and terrorized existence within prostitution) has shifted from being viewed as nonculpability and victimization to a denial of rights. If prostitution's central figure is regarded as an individual to whose action/behavior a certain measure of choice must be accorded—however restricted such a choice may be—then she is a social agent and the privileged "voice" of prostitution.[25]

But what of the fact that, at least in many parts of the Third World, women (often young girls) are forced or tricked into entering the sex trade? Pro-prostitute feminists demand that instances of explicit coercion, such as abduction, violence, and trafficking, be exempted from the argument, as well as child prostitution. The problem is how to determine positions in the vast gray area that lies between the extremes of coercion and volition, for instance on the matter of choices made from necessity: are these circumstances of coercion, or do we argue that necessity is a factor in all existential choice? Sleightholme and Sinha's account of the sex trade in Calcutta, for example, makes use of a survey conducted by the NGO Sanlaap in 1994 to find out why women entered prostitution; they identified poverty as the single most overwhelming reason, followed by violence, family problems, fraud, destitution, and abandonment—all of which are reasons suggesting force or necessity rather than choice. Only ten out of the 257 respondents said they came from "choice" (1996, 16–33). This is likely to be generally true in the Third World context, and perhaps in a majority of First World situations as well. Pro-prostitution feminists argue, however, that since this is not the situation of *all* women in the sex trade, it is not generalizable. Additionally, such compulsions are equally at work among others in professions of a like nature that are unskilled and poorly paid and hence do not indicate "coercion" in any significant way.

As a matter of ethical concern, too, if we oppose coercion on the grounds of the individual's rights, must we not by the same token support voluntary choice in the matter of prostitution? As Margaret Baldwin puts it, "if no means no, yes should mean yes under whatever conditions a woman chooses" (1992, 31). On the other hand, Kathleen Barry refuses the possibility that prostitution could under *any* circumstances be treated as woman's choice: to do so is "a way to reduce all women to the lowest and most contemptible status of women in any male dominated society" (1979, 28). Such a declaration invalidates and dismisses the protestations of many practicing prostitutes.

Increasingly, feminist theorists are beginning to realize that "agency"—in short, arguments to determine coercion/consent—is not a useful terrain on which to debate issues relating to women's behavior or social roles and status.[26] In understanding the conditions of contemporary prostitution, it is perhaps less useful to frame the agency question by asking why women are in prostitution than to attend to the forms and politics of *prostitute activism.* The latter arguably provides a better exemplification of the independence and control that sex workers seek, as collective rather than individual practitioners of the trade, and is a more reliable indication of their wishes, intentions, and attitudes toward their trade. Sex workers' collectives in Calcutta, for instance, have successfully formed cooperative ventures[27] and won legal cases against eviction and other forms of harassment; in Delhi they have prevailed on the courts to have their children admitted to schools without having to give the names of their fathers on the application forms; everywhere they are now demanding that clients use condoms and that the state provide safeguards against violence and create better conditions of work, through widespread mobilization as a National Network of Sex Workers.

Despite such successes—and the evidence of a worldwide prostitute movement itself—the problems, limits, and contradictions of prostitute groups' politics, of prostitute-feminist/NGO alliances, and of prostitute freedom in general have to be borne in mind. Thus

Prabha Kotiswaran concedes that many prostitute women's groups in North America are not truly representative of prostitute interests, and many of the members are not active sex workers or even former sex workers at all (2001, 227). In India several prostitute organizations are led by brothelkeepers who have links with politicians. Most of all, of course, there is, as Sleightholme and Sinha warn, the problem that all of them encounter, that of organization itself, especially as a stigmatized group. Since "so much is at stake, and so many vested interests would be threatened" [due to their organizing], they encounter a great deal of hostility and opposition (1996, 143).[28]

For feminists supporting sex workers' groups, the valorization of prostitute agency raises questions of politics and ethics that are no less urgent than the complaint that their opponents are refusing to respect that agency. How acceptable is it that nonprostitute women's groups and NGOs assume a vanguard role in these movements?[29] Do feminist academics risk looking like impresarios by showcasing prostitute activists in their publications? Do feminist legal scholars have to validate prostitute experience before it can count, as Kotiswaran fears (2001, 227)? Or, in celebrating such agency ("sex workers have *on their own* devised ways to utilize/improvise discourses and practices to fight off domination and exploitation"), are feminists instead left with no role except that of "affirming, and even whole-heartedly supporting such demonstrations of power and agency," as Josephine Ho (2000, 295; emphasis added) seems to be suggesting?

I will return to these questions, while now moving on to the second key area of contestation as it follows from this, relating to prostitute sex. The functional argument that implicitly—and often explicitly—supports prostitution as a phenomenon is that of male sexual need. This is viewed as a "natural" phenomenon that requires fulfillment outside of monogamous marriage, and the institution of prostitution is widely understood to exist to service this need. Its theoretical defense is given in what is termed the "contractarian" argument, according to which "the need for sexual gratification is a need similar to the need for food and fresh air (and hence should be as readily available)," and, further, that under conditions of "sound" prostitution sexual services may be freely sold in the marketplace.[30] Abolitionists in the prostitution debates not only repudiate the urgency of such an invariant and natural male sexual need, they also find contemporary feminist support of the legalization of prostitution too uncomfortably complicit with this premise. Susan Brownmiller expresses the typical feminist outrage at this argument and links it with forms of male violence: "My horror at the idea of legalized prostitution is not that it institutionalizes a female service that should not be denied the civilized male. Perpetuation of the concept that the 'powerful male impulse' must be satisfied with immediacy by a cooperative class of women, set aside for the purpose, is part and parcel of the mass psychology of rape" (1976, 392).

Liberal feminists supporting prostitution have, however, shifted the sexual issues in prostitution from male to female sexuality, with the argument that a woman in sex work is in greater control of her sexuality than women in general in other (noncommercial) heterosexual relationships. Margo St. James marks the significant difference between the prostitute's disempowerment in *public* life ("she has absolutely no rights—no civil rights, no human rights") and the power she wields in *private,* that is, in the sexual transaction ("she is in charge, setting the terms for the sexual exchange and the financial exchange") (in Bell 1994, 82). Liberal feminists and activist-prostitutes are able to claim that sex work is a form of indifferent sexual service offered to a variety of clients to whom the sex worker is bound only by the terms of payment—which, therefore, gives her greater and less ambiguous control over her body. Gail Pheterson opposes the *Oxford English Dictionary*'s definition of prostitution as "indiscriminate sexual intercourse," by contesting both of these terms: while sex workers do have multiple partners, they choose (or would like to be able to choose) their clients and, further, they negotiate the terms of their services, which do *not* always involve sexual intercourse (1993, 39–42).

Prostitute accounts themselves can be contradictory and varied about the sexual act: its performance may lead prostitutes to see themselves either as free, fully expressive, in charge; or as degraded, used, and manipulated.[31] These differing positions on female sexuality in prostitution remain confused, an aspect of what Cora Kaplan identifies as the "central contradiction" of female sexuality itself in general within contemporary feminism (1986, 32). Prostitutes who feel empowered and in control in the performance of the sexual act in the absence of desire or affective bonds may also as a consequence feel shame when they do inadvertently experience desire or gratification.[32] Josephine Chuen-Juei Ho reports conversations with sex workers in Taiwan who experience not just control and power but also uncomplicated pleasure in the interaction with the client: " 'It's like I am the client and he serves me.' " She concludes that "in this process of negotiation and exchange, the dominant person is obviously the sex worker: the one who is served is the sex worker, who enjoys the pleasure is the sex worker—and the one who gets paid for it is still the sex worker" (2000, 288). Others have deplored the regular "mechanical" performance of "tricks" and the frequent distancing from the act that leads to the development of a "split identity" (Baldwin 1992, 117). The connection between affect ("love," desire, sexual gratification) and the sexual act is obviously complexly negotiated by many sex workers, and therefore describing it as either empowering or degrading, in the service of different feminist ideologies, cannot hope to be definitive. Such claims are not particularly useful or accurate when invoked as arguments in the prostitution debate.

Morever, whatever the sexual *practices* of prostitute women may be, the undeniable fact remains that *institutionally* prostitution exists and exists particularly in its present form as a global sex trade, primarily to serve the need/pleasure of large male populations; the pleasure, empowerment, or other gains that prostitute women may wrest from their encounters is secondary, if not incidental, to this reality. It is in the context of international sex tourism that Lillian Robinson has returned male sexuality insistently and forcefully to the center of these debates. Drawing on the sex chat to be found on the Internet's World Sex Guide, she accesses the "heterosexual male perspective" that she finds missing from most "vanguard sexual theory" (Bishop and Robinson 1998, 222–23). The sexual discourse she uncovers is that of an "alienated sexuality," one constructed, Robinson suggests, by the "current economic and social forces" of global capitalism (220). When the customer is so much a "law-abiding citizen" of a "world system designed to privilege him," he can hardly be viewed as the "swashbuckling transgressor" that feminist theory would like to turn him into, she mocks (228).

The strongest argument against condemning prostitute sex must remain, therefore, the familiar relativist one: the questionable superiority, moral, affective, or gender egalitarian, of other (nonprostitute) sexual relations. The prostitute defense of payment for sex comes from showing how women "prostitute" themselves in the marriage relationship.[33] Pheterson quotes a sex worker as baldly stating, "Women who have sex out of duty or submission are the real 'whores'" (1993, 47). The moral condemnation of prostitute sex has to do with more than the threat of nonreproductive sex: it is caused by the disapproval of nonaffective sex. Commercial sex is viewed as an inferior version of "real" (or free, romantic) sex, which reflects adversely on both the prostitute and the client.[34] But, argues Margo St. James, "why should the women be considered deviant because they're separating sex and love? I think separating sex and love is a good thing personally. I think romance may be oppressive" (in Bell 1987, 63). Prostitute sex's most subversive charge is, therefore, the way it functions as a challenge to the moral majority; I have also alluded to the symbolic meaning it offers to feminists as a way of opening up issues of sexual freedom.

Questions of sexuality in prostitution overlap, in this way, with a third major concern in the prostitution debate, the nature of prostitute work. The claim that prostitution is *work* was itself one of the first gains made by sex workers in the contemporary debates.[35] It remains, however, a disputed claim. Kathleen Barry is the most prominent among those who continue to refuse it that recognition, since doing so would "normalize" it (1995, 70). Similarly, Indrani Sinha, who heads the NGO Sanlap in Calcutta, argues against viewing prostitution as work since "it is rooted in oppression and violence" (cited in M. Menon 1998). Logically, denying prostitution the state of work is the grounds for calling for its abolition, while granting it that recognition would lead to reformist measures. Clearly, what is at stake is to determine what kind of "work" sex work might be. The contradictions and unresolved ambiguities of "sex work" in prostitution, which I wish to pursue at somewhat greater length here, may be found in three broad areas.

The first is that of the *legitimacy* of the work. As long as sex work is associated with crime, health hazards, and other antisocial aspects, it would be hard to normalize it legally or professionally within the protocols of normative (i.e., socially useful and productive) "work." At the same time, as we saw, state and society construct a functionalist human (male) "need" for female prostitute services and also recognize prostitution's contribution to the economy. Hence attempts to regulate prostitution legislatively (in the interests of the client and the "public") have always paradoxically accompanied the attempts to criminalize it. The foundational unease with the unresolved status of commercial sex is reflected in the ambivalence of most legislation on prostitution, including proposed labor legislation. Prostitute groups have seized on this ambivalence to suggest that removing the legal classification of prostitute activities as criminal and improving the conditions of sex work would at once remove its stigma and its risks.[36] Reforms are demanded (a) to eliminate the use of force in inducting and keeping women (and often, children) in the profession, and (b) to make provision for the adequate livelihood of prostitutes and the safety and health of both prostitutes and their clients. But, as argument, this is only as much as to say that all work that is bad (i.e., performed under poor working conditions) is bad. There cannot be any disagreement over the need and urgency of reforming these conditions. But viewing sex work as work like any other, while being an important legitimizing move, is not necessarily also a demystifying one. It does not help us to understand it in its specificities, which (and not only social hypocrisy) have led to the difficulties that inform the concept of it as work.

The reductive view of sex work as (any) work, especially in the arguments of socialist feminists, Margaret Baldwin complains, is the result of separating the work from the sex (the "libidinal adventure" that liberal feminists celebrate), though prostitution is the significant site of their convergence; and it is achieved at some cost. It is the sex in "sex work" that produces the particular dilemmas of defining and judging it for feminist theory. This may be identified as the second broad area of disagreement in feminist prostitution debates. The discourse on prostitution is prey to what may be termed catachresis ("application of a term to a thing it does not properly denote; abuse of a trope or metaphor," according to *The Shorter Oxford English Dictionary* [1973]). As productive work prostitution has been viewed, in catachrestic terms, indifferently and at various times and contexts as wage-labor, as a sale or trade of a commodity (the female body, or "sex"), and as service. Lydia Nead reads this conceptual uncertainty as in fact constitutive of and specific to prostitution in nineteenth-century Britain in the historical context of industrial capital and urbanization. Nead argues that prostitution deconstructed the differences among the terms of capitalist production:

... the prostitute does not behave like any other commodity; she occupies a unique place, at the centre of an extraordinary and nefarious economic system. She is able to represent all the terms within capitalist production; she is the human labour, the object of exchange and the seller at once. She stands as worker, commodity and capitalist and blurs the categories of bourgeois economics in the same way as she tests the boundaries of bourgeois morality. . . . . As a commodity, therefore, the prostitute both encapsulates and distorts all the classic features of bourgeois economics. This is the full nature of her threat and it is also the key to her power. (1988, 99)

We may value Nead's insight into prostitution's deconstructive potential without necessarily agreeing that it is also a potential for the empowerment of the prostitute's social or economic condition. Luce Irigaray makes a similar observation about the prostitute's "value": neither pure use value nor entirely exchange value (the mother and the virgin, respectively, represent in her taxonomy the female "types" of these values), "prostitution amounts to usage that is exchanged." But Irigaray finally sees the prostitute as "at least as exploited as the mother and virgin," for she is only an object of exchange between men, the pimp and the client (1985, chapter 8, 186 ff). Shannon Bell recuperates Irigaray's observations about prostitution to suggest, with Nead, that this "ambiguous unity in the prostitute body of use and exchange value . . . positions her as a speaking subject" and that she is therefore "an active participant who *exchanges her own use value*" (1994, 91; emphasis added). The opposite position, as expounded by Carol Pateman, is that prostitution is primarily an aspect of the "sexual contract," which is different from other forms of contract because it is constituted by the subordination of women to men. Though labor of all forms inheres in the body, sex labor is different from other labor. Pateman argues that while the capitalist employer uses the labor of his workers only to produce commodities (he may therefore replace the worker by machinery), the men who engage a prostitute "have only one interest; the prostitute and her body. . . . In prostitution, the body of the women, and sexual access to that body, is the subject of the contract" (1988, 203).[37] Even if the prostitute is regarded only as a seller of sexual *services* and not of her body itself, as the contractarians argue, "property in the person, unlike material property, cannot be separated from its owner" (202–03). "Selves are inseparable from bodies," and sexuality and self are integrally connected (206–07).

Pateman's position has been repeatedly challenged, chiefly by those who view it as "too absolutist" (Fraser 1993, 179). Her opponents seek to render her structure of (male) domination/(female) subordination "more complex" (ibid.), by highlighting prostitute practices of resistance. But reformed prostitution legislation would require more than the defense that sex workers do successfully devise forms of survival or subversion within the constraints of their situation. It demands a description of the precise agential work role of the prostitute. In this case there is an obligation to recognize or identify female "sexual labor" as a unique kind of labor having specific kinds of social usefulness and/or demanding skills possessing economic value. Prabha Kotiswaran argues, for instance, citing Kamala Kempadoo, that commercial sex, in line with wet-nursing, temple prostitution, surrogate child-bearing, and donor sex, "could serve as illustrations of the historical and contemporary ways in which sexual labour has been organized for the re-creation and replenishment of human and social life" (2001, 235). Many such arguments, like this one, remain tentative; or they tend to fixate on a valorization of prostitution's function either in an earlier golden age or in an emancipated future state. Nevertheless, such imaginings must form a component of thinking on the subject of prostitute work.[38] In the absence of such an attempt, prostitution's legitimacy will remain complicit with contractarian arguments.

There still remains a third and closely related aspect of prostitution that requires consideration in terms of work. This is its *gendered* aspect, the reality that prostitutes are invariably women (though not always or necessarily so: but the fact that the users of sexual services are always men places the prostitute *structurally* in the position of the female even if he be biologically male). The sexual component of sex work genderizes it, but so do the material conditions of the profession, which connect it with other forms of women's work. Commercial sex is denigrated even in a sexually liberated society because it is posed against "free" sex. Prostitution falls within the ambit of the "commercialization of traditional female roles" that is the cause of so much ambivalence in our contemporary economy (Schwarzenbach

1990–91, 108). When women place a monetary value on and claim payment for the work that they traditionally perform within the family out of love or "instinct" for "free" (or for intangible nonmonetary rewards), then their demand is viewed as a "betrayal." Teachers, nurses, secretaries, and women in similar service professions are idealized but they are also, in the same way as sex workers, trivialized by being paid low wages in keeping with the ideology of "service." This is one of the reasons why any profession that becomes "feminized" in the wage market also gets devalued (the others have to do with low skills or with general gender discrimination).

As women's work, in any case, the economic circumstances of many prostitutes are commonly "marginal to impoverished" (Baldwin 1992, 105). Sex workers are not the primary beneficiaries of the global sex trade despite its magnitude and profits. As women in the international division of labor, they are susceptible to the worst forms of exploitation. But it is also precisely as women's livelihood that pro-prostitution feminists see the value of sex work. There is no doubt that sex work represents an important labor market for women. The fact that it is often the only livelihood option available to poor and unskilled women is a strong argument against its legal abolition, especially when alternative schemes for their "rehabilitation" are either entirely absent or practically useless. And women in the sex trade, at any level, make better money than those in other comparable trades that may be available to them. Sex workers and their advocates are convinced that unionization and other reforms in the trade will alter the situation of wages, profits, or returns. But the point about viewing it within the parameters of female work in the unorganized sector is to indicate that it is formed by the larger structures of an international capitalism that depends on the surplus of women's labor as much in the sex/entertainment/leisure industry as in other areas where women predominate. Labor-reform proposals remain necessary but insufficient (and, many activists urge, also ineffectual, given the nature of the sex trade).

To sum up: we stand in need of an "explanation" for prostitution that is both more complex and more compelling than that provided by a functionalist explanation or a mechanistic demand—(male) sexual need—and supply—(female) sexual availability—paradigm; and this includes contending with the strongly residual stigma of criminality, illicitness, and deviance that attaches to prostitution. We must also identify the form of work involved in prostitution and find its value in the specific function (such as sexual therapy) that it may serve. And, finally, we must view it as a gendered activity, requiring resolution in terms of the conditions of and payment for "women's work" in our culture and economy.

I have tried to show that none of the three chief areas in the prostitution debates—the agency of the prostitute, female sexuality in prostitution, and prostitution as work—that provide opposed positions for feminists of different persuasions to occupy is susceptible to such clear-cut resolution as each may wish to suggest. The issue of volition is a compromised one; the affect of the sexual act for the prostitute is not generalizable, nor is it possible to define commercial sex in terms only of the female sex worker's professional sexuality and leave the male client out of the picture; and, finally, the nature of prostitution as work is as yet undertheorized. In the next and concluding section I pursue an attempt at an explanation of these conflicts in the prostitution issue: in terms of differences of feminist politics, disciplinary frames of understanding, and the object of study, prostitution itself.

Prostitution as System and as Practice

What, we might ask, accounts for these vastly different and conflictual positions in feminism on the matter of prostitution? I do not wish to reduce the theoretical postulates labeled, for purposes of quick identification, liberal, radical, or "postmodern" to reified identities by suggesting that the positions are solely the products of (pre-given) ideological preferences. If we believe that politics is instead necessarily generated from the social realities that surround us, then we must acknowledge that the different feminist positions on prostitution are contingent on the circumstances of the sex trade that operate in different contexts. Thus it is as *description* that the discourse of prostitution often functions.

In view of this, we would therefore have to contend with the variety and heterogeneity of "sex work" as practice, in place of a singular phenomenon "prostitution." Unlike other professions that create, despite the inevitable hierarchies within them, a certain homogeneity of identity and socioeconomic status among their practitioners, prostitution varies widely in terms of both, depending on a number of factors, as we have seen. Historical changes in prostitution (primarily in the direction of increasing proletarianization); differences in the "levels" of prostitutes in terms of clientele, income, work and lifestyles (from call girls to streetwalkers); differences in the function and social prestige of prostitution according to the cultural context in which it operates and according to the practitioners' skills and accomplishments; and, above all, international differences in prostitution systems, broadly, between those in First World and Third World countries, are facts that have been repeatedly invoked to account for the widely different ways in which "prostitution," as such, is understood. But, of course, "description" is not simply a neutral activity, a transparent record of what lies "out there." Over and beyond the actual differences in the conditions of sex work in different contexts, differences in prostitute accounts are also marked by their narrators' or researchers' tendency to "find the stories we expect," "the ones most suitable for our political purposes" (O'Neill 2001, 26, paraphrasing Chapkis 1997). Desire or political intent can inflect the interpretation of even similar stories in strikingly different ways. If, for Lillian Robinson, the interviews with Thai sex workers "rely a great deal on euphemism," so that she reads "pain and fear" even in their matter-of-fact accounts of their sexual experiences at work (Bishop and Robinson 1998, 229), then Josephine Chuen-Juei Ho (2000) determinedly finds in very similar words only effective and subversive strategies of sex workers' "management" of their profession.

The different disciplinary frames and methodological imperatives that structure prostitution research also influence how feminist meanings are generated. Robinson points out that accounts of prostitution drawn from interviews by journalists or social scientists, are "all negative";[39] while statements by prostitute activists, especially performance artists, "have a more positive story to tell" (Bishop and Robinson 1998, 236). The representations of prostitution in Indian texts, if we might generalize, are similarly structured by the sharp polarities of literary "realism" and "romanticism." "Realistic" accounts of prostitution, whether in documented research and journalism or in imaginative literature and film, contextualize it within the broad frame of the Indian socioeconomic structure, describing rural poverty and bonded labor, the gross exploitation of tribal, lower-caste, and refugee women, urban red-light areas, disease, and police brutality and corruption.[40] The genre of the popular Hindi "courtesan" film, on the other hand, romanticizes the female protagonist either by rendering the pathos of her condition as the very type of female abjection (as in Kamal Amrohi's *Pakeezah* or Guru Dutt's *Pyaasa*) or by celebrating her beauty, her artistic skills, and her sexual expertise in the form of (the male filmmaker's) appreciation and homage (as in Girish Karnad's *Utsav* or Muzaffar Ali's *Umrao Jaan*).[41] Typically the realistic mode stresses the *work* of prostitution, the romantic mode the *sexuality* of the prostitute.[42]

The prostitution debate is fueled, therefore, by the differences in the objective conditions of prostitution in different contexts feeding into divergent political positions in feminism (chiefly as they relate to sexuality). But above all, the differences in the understanding of prostitution, as my analysis of the debates about prostitute agency, sexuality, and work has suggested, arise from a fundamental divergence of emphasis: abolitionists read prostitution as structure or *system*, decriminalization advocates as *practice* (sex work).

The latter position has emerged from, and turns toward, some relatively recent developments within feminism that I have noted: among others, attention to the voices of prostitutes; research into their experiences; dialogue between feminists and sex workers; the feminist politicization of sex for payment and of sexual pleasure/danger; and feminist support of and identification with prostitute movements. By recasting prostitution as sex work feminists have added a necessary and significant dimension to, and indeed altered, earlier positions on prostitution. The knowledge of sex work as praxis, lifestyle, and labor therefore can and must be used to supplement a structural and historical analysis of the prostitution system. But in many pro-prostitution arguments, the former tends instead to supplant, or even actively counter the latter, often in unproductive ways. An idealized representation of prostitute life as fun and games, and of sex workers as feisty, fun-loving, philosophical, feminist women (i.e., not weepy "victims"); the contention that prostitution exists primarily to provide women with a livelihood (rather than serve male sexual needs); the denial of any essential difference between the feminist and the moral right opposition to prostitution; the appropriation of prostitute sex as sexual liberation as such; the uncritical celebration of prostitute movements: these counterarguments, while necessary correctives to existing stereotypes, nevertheless fall into overstatement and seriously undermine the structural understanding of prostitution. Almost any system we deplore and hope to reform or eliminate—slavery, child labor, the class system, marriage, for example—is, after all, susceptible to similar rewriting in terms of practices of subversion, survival, wresting spaces of resistance and even enjoyment on the part of the oppressed subject. But such rewriting must not be achieved at the cost of turning into a defense or a demand for the perpetuation of the systems. While we must acknowledge and accord due respect to the subjectivities and capacities of those otherwise regarded solely as victims, and also perhaps grant the functionalism of these systems, these must not hide the perspective of structural domination and oppression that sustains them.

The demands of contingent description, undoubtedly urgent in the context of prostitute rights and legislation, tend to obscure the issues that emerge in understanding prostitution *as such*. As Margaret Baldwin retorts to those worried about the possibility of generalizing prostitution, "that *prostitution* may forge a connecting link in the experience of 'prostitutes' is a notion [often] suppressed . . . by the suppression of prostitution itself as a topic of analysis" (1992, 84). While no one denies that prostitution is deeply inscribed within contemporary systems of patriarchy, global capitalism, and racism, those who support what Margaret Baldwin calls the postmodern ideal of a "decentralized, individualized practice of prostitution" tend to overlook its systemic aspects. In this view, "as the *economic* conditions urged by these advocates approach the ideal, the entailed *sexual* conditions approach the normatively non-economic. The better a 'job' prostitution is, that is, the less it looks like a job, or the less it looks like prostitution" (107). Prostitution itself thus tends to get written out of the picture.

Recent scholarship on the global sex trade by feminist/activists like Swasti Mitter (1986), Ryan Bishop and Lillian Robinson (1998), Cynthia Enloe (1992), Kamala Kempadoo and Jo Doezma (1999), among others, while not replicating the straightforward abolitionist position advocated earlier by Kathleen Barry, nevertheless offers a powerful indictment of the forces that support the prostitution system today. Based on extensive research and, in many cases, the writers' participation in sex workers' struggles and grounded in the acknowledgment of the realities of global capitalism—the dimensions of the sex tourism and leisure industry, the role of women in the unorganized labor sector, national economies that depend on the sex trade, and exploitative center-periphery relations—these works are opposed to prostitution in this larger sense.

Feminists who are seeking to reconcile these positions—and their numbers are increasing—hope to embrace the contradiction of abolishing the system while empowering the practice, indeed, to achieve the first by means of the latter. Lynn Sharon Chancer, for example, advocates a "two-pronged" "synthetic" stance, "at once immediately pragmatic and with some vision of the longer run," which would support *prostitutes* while opposing *prostitution,* and pursue the decriminalization of prostitution while envisaging its transformation into something other than it is today (1993, 166). The theoretical resolution is envisaged by Martha Minow as a combination of "the constructive impulse of reformers" with "the celebrat[ion] of the gaps and conflicts among possible meanings of sexual identities and differences" by postmodern feminists (1992, 1100–01). Pursuing this strategy of doubleness and conscious contradiction into questions of the state (law) and women (sex workers), we are led to the suggestion that a reformed *national* law must allow sex workers full access to civil and human rights of every kind through decriminalization or empowering legalization of sex work, while at the same time at the *international* level propaganda, policy, and prostitute movements must oppose the prostitution system in all its manifestations. In this way the local and the global, the contingent and the systemic, practice and institution, sex workers and the market, enter into the dialectic of struggle.

5 Women Between Community and State: Some Implications of the Uniform Civil Code Debates

This chapter is an attempt to think through the question of women's position in relation to the state and to religious communities, a position that is invariably played out as a conflict between the exercise of their citizenship rights and the claims and protections of the religious communities they belong to. It is an issue that figures in the conflict around a uniform civil code (UCC) for India. The UCC debates are among the most vigorous and divisive in the present Indian intellectual and political scene, centering as they do on whether such a set of laws should replace the present personal laws, and, if so, the manner of doing it and the content of such laws. The chapter has two parts. In the first I set out the main positions on the UCC, identify the relationships among individual, community, and state that they are premised on, and highlight the feminist interventions made on grounds of gender, citizenship, and rights. The second part seeks to locate women as "national subjects" in relation to, but also beyond, the state and the religion-based community that the UCC debates implicitly regard as providing the only two alternative resources and identities for the female Indian citizen.

Personal Law

The operation of separate personal laws for different religious communities in India is a legacy of colonial administration. Four religious communities—the majority Hindu, and the minority Muslim, Christian, and Parsi communities—have their own personal laws (other religious groups such as Sikh, Buddhist, Jain, and tribal and scheduled castes are subsumed under Hindu law). No one is exempt from or may opt out of a religious identity (Indians may choose, however, to be married under a nondenominational Special Marriage Act). Personal laws operate in matters relating to inheritance, marriage, divorce, maintenance, and adoption, which are regarded as "personal" issues, understood to be matters that relate to the family or "personal" sphere. Despite differences among them, the personal laws of all communities are discriminatory toward women. Personal law, since it is envisaged as a means of securing community identity and respecting religious difference, operates therefore within rather than despite a constitutional commitment to the secularism of the Indian state. Any proposed reform or removal of personal laws becomes a fraught issue and is perceived as a threat to community identity and/or traditional patriarchal arrangements. Following the Shah-bano case in 1986 (which resulted in the passing of the regressive Muslim Women's Protection of Rights in Divorce Act of 1986), a uniform civil code became an issue of moment on the Indian political scene.[1] Since the Bharatiya Janata Party (BJP), subscribing to a Hindutva ideology and politics, came to power at the center in 1998 with the promise of instituting such a code, it continues to be a prominent issue on the agenda of the Indian state.

The Uniform Civil Code: Positions

In the contemporary debates on the UCC, the following broad positions may be identified:

— *Constitutional secularism:* The Indian Constitution approves a UCC in principle but not in practice. The main consideration, in principle, is that legal uniformity will serve as a means of overcoming religious differences and achieving national unity. The subtext, at least at the time of Independence, was also that secular laws would be in keeping with the modernizing agenda of the postcolonial nation-state. However, the difficult communal situation at the time of Independence and the opposition to removal of personal laws at such a time led to the accommodation of a UCC only as a directive principle in the Constitution (directive principles are constitutional injunctions, viewed as policies to be kept in abeyance and implemented in the fullness of time).

— *Religious patriarchy:* The opposition to reform in personal laws was most vociferous when a reformed Hindu Code bill was proposed in Parliament in the early years of independence. Its proposals included measures like women's equal rights of inheritance and rights in divorce, which were viewed by the majority of Hindu parliamentary members as threats to the hierarchy and traditional gender relations within the family. The personal laws of other communities have remained untouched by any reformist impulses since Independence (except for the regressive Muslim Women's Protection in Divorce Act passed in 1986). This position continues to prevail, though the explicitly gender-discriminatory arguments are in recent times more muted in lip-service to women's rights. These broadly and transparently patriarchal concerns among all religious communities are additionally inflected by different political anxieties in different groups, as the next two items indicate.

— *Minority communities:* Their opposition to UCC is articulated on the grounds that it threatens the sanctity of their communities' religious laws and therefore threatens their religious identity— more recently, it arises from resistance to what is perceived as the likelihood that a UCC will really be a version of Hindu law, which will then be made uniformly applicable to all.

— *Hindu political parties:* Following the passage of the Muslim Women's Act of 1986, Hindu political parties have stepped up their advocacy of a UCC, primarily as a means of removing the "privileges" of minority men. The UCC that is envisaged will be a version of Hindu law and will thereby secure Hindu hegemony. Much is made of the so-called progressive reform of Hindu law in the 1950s as a model for a UCC. (But note that Hindu ideologues seeking a UCC would still be bound to resist reform of personal laws in certain directions, those that might empower women.[2] The positions of both minority communities' representatives and Hindu ideologues are undoubtedly covertly patriarchal as well as overtly communitarian, grounded as they are in the will to preserve gender hierarchies as well as retain their own religious authority and autonomy.)

— *Communitarians:* would oppose the imposition of a UCC because of their opposition to coercive state secularism, their advocacy of a pluralist and decentralized polity, and their support of autonomy for religious communities.

— *Liberal secularists:* would support a UCC on grounds of egalitarianism, uniformity of law, and democratic politics but would hesitate to unequivocally support its imposition in view of the actual situation of conflict with embattled minorities in which it is enmeshed, as well as the dubious credentials of the government, in this instance for securing a secular and egalitarian substitute for the present personal law structure.

— *Women's groups:* The agenda of *women's* rights in discussion of personal laws has been systematically foregrounded only by the women's movement, and that only in its most recent phase.

The UCC debates among these last three categories—communitarians, liberal secularists, and women's groups—occupy two distinct discursive realms whose overlaps and disjunctures are important to note. Though the Shahbano case led to the revival of the UCC question, it was perceived in sharply different ways, and the political and intellectual discussions it prompted moved in two different directions, one toward the nature of "Indian" secularism and the other toward women's rights in the context of personal laws. The latter is by no means at the center of the secularism debate between the communitarians and the left/liberals, and the former has impinged on feminist thinking specifically only in terms of defining democratic political space, as I will elaborate later. As will be clear from this exposition, there are problematic convergences to be found in this situation: between the liberal/left and the Hindu right favoring a UCC, for instance, and between secular communitarians and fundamentalist representatives of minority communities that oppose it; as well as contradictions between a secular constitution and a state that administers religious laws and is indulgent toward religious communities' demands. The content of these positions cannot, therefore, be looked at in isolation from their context. We must be alert to ask who speaks, why, and what is his or her politics.

A further point by way of clarification: both the liberal multiculturalism debates in the West and women's struggles against religious fundamentalism in other parts of the world are relevant to the issue of the UCC in India, and they are useful parallels to draw on to facilitate understanding. But the Indian debates are considerably more complicated because of two factors specific to India: one, *religious* laws in a secular democracy, and two, a multireligious nation-state. Thus the "secularism" debate, as I call it here, like the multiculturalism debates in the West from which it draws, is similarly polarized between communitarians and liberals; but since the communities under discussion in the context of Indian personal laws are *religious* communities, the place and function of religion in the modern democratic state becomes a central issue, rather than (only) the question of group (cultural) rights versus individual (legal) rights as in the latter case. Further, feminist politics around the issue in India are more complicated (I mean theoretically and ideologically, not necessarily in actual political struggle) than similar movements in other countries because of the multireligious situation in India in which majoritarian community organizations have sway over and pose a threat to minority communities.[3] Feminist activists may oppose the state and/or community straightforwardly when there is a clear polarization of positions between women's interests (gender justice) and religious/state patriarchies—but in India women's groups have also to respond to and negotiate minority claims for recognition. This means that Indian feminists, because of their liberal, secular credentials (which does not exempt them from "having" a religious identity), cannot confine their struggles to women's interests "alone" (if such a thing were clearly identifiable in the first instance) but are expected to be sensitive to the identity crises and threats experienced by members of minority communities, including women. This double commitment can lead to acute dilemmas for feminist understanding and to the paralysis of feminist praxis. I will examine in greater detail, below, some of the positions in the secularism debate between communitarian and left-liberal intellectuals, who share a common discursive space despite the divergence of their views on the UCC, and in the following section I will highlight the issues in the debate around women's rights within feminist groups.

State and Religious Community in the Secularism Debates

The modern Indian state, by definition secular, nevertheless—indeed precisely in the name of that secularism—grants considerable recognition to religion, not only by retaining personal law, as I have explained, but by actively regulating religious institutions in the name of a vastly expanded definition of secularism: for example, by having the courts administer personal law, managing religious trusts, opening entry to temples for lower-caste Hindus, administering religious holidays, constitutionally securing freedom of religious belief, and other similar interventions. This is clearly in contrast to the modern secular state in the West, which operates with a definition of secularism that places religion, treated as a matter of *faith* (worship, ritual, custom), in the realm of the private, to which it makes the promise of noninterference and offers a minimal guarantee of protection of freedom of practice, and little else, and that relegates the *institutions* of religion—church, religious law, religious authority—to minor functions in the public sphere related to the community's practice of its religion. Beyond the constitutional investment in "secular" control of religious matters, the Indian state, as Sandra Freitag has pointed out, has also showed a marked shift from the "initial constitutional emphasis on the relationship between the individual and state" to an increasing reliance on direct relationship with communities, both in terms of "state policies (e.g., reservation policies for scheduled castes and tribes)" and in terms of "political strategizing (in the wooing of vote blocs)" (1996, 228). It has also responded to demands for decentralization and greater autonomy to local bodies, regional blocs, and religion-based organizations in politics.

Despite, or some would say because of, the state's concessions to religious groups' demands, the Indian polity has been riven by communal conflict. Conflict is the product of two aspects of communalism (as it is called): the existence of many religious communities within the single space of the nation, and the consequent struggles among them for supremacy or survival, as the case may be; and the conflict between communities and the state. The latter takes different forms. The mobilization of the majoritarian religious community, organized around Hindutva or Hinduness as a claim of cultural nationalism, is of course a direct challenge to constitutional secularism and the state's secular authority. The problem posed by minority communities is different: it takes the form primarily of intransigence to state-led change in an attempt to preserve their religious identities. Both the conflicts as well as the complicities between state and different communities show unmistakable signs of ascendancy. In such a context, the Indian state cannot adopt the West's secular program of domesticating religious practice, relegating religious institutions to an enclave, and treating religious faith as a "private" concern. Religion in modern India is not simply a survival of premodern belief systems and religious authority—a familiar stereotype of civilizational backwardness in the Third World—but a crucial signifier of community identity and hence a player in state politics.

It is in the face of this enlargement of religious communities' political influence that communitarian arguments are becoming prominent in India. Religious community (along with other forms of linguistic, regional, caste, and ethnic communities) is rescued from the illegitimacy it has acquired in the modern state. All these groups are described as various "fragments" in opposition to an inauthentic and totalizing nation-state. Located within powerfully orchestrated critiques of modernity, the community is cast in the role of the only alternative to modern life and its institutions (including, indeed above all, capitalism). The argument goes that, along with the family, the community is the primary site of the individual's socialization and hence of identity, affiliation, and the formation of affective ties of loyalty and solidarity with others; it offers the idiom of love and bonding in place of the sterile terms of the modern contract in law and marketplace; religion, of course, provides spiritual solace, in contrast to secular rationalism. However, none of this, we might think, is in real conflict with the place assigned to it in the contemporary secular state.

But the fostering of communal sentiments has also led to community identity politics, communal mobilization, and ultimately communal conflict, in the view of others. Left-liberal secularists attribute the eruption of hostilities between communities in the form of riots, arson, and other acts of violence and destruction (whose apogee was reached in the destruction in 1992 of the Babri Masjid in Ayodhya) to the problem of communalism. Refusing this explanation, or rather perceiving communalism as only a symptom, communitarians would instead blame modernity. They argue that it is the failures of the totalizing modern nation-state and its belief-systems—liberal individualism, the rhetoric of rights, bourgeois capitalism, secular rationalism, science, "development"—at whose doors the responsibility for the pathology of communal violence must be laid. The resurgence of indigenous community values is a consequence of people's disenchantment with alien (European) Enlightenment values, even a rebellion against their imposition by the colonial and then the postcolonial state. It is in this context that the communitarian defense of "minority cultural rights" and "toleration" of different religious laws for different communities is put forward. As we can see, here it is the defense of community rights and cultural pluralism, articulated as a politics of recognition, that provides the larger argument within which a UCC is opposed.

In the left-liberal secular position the concern with a UCC tends to be only an aspect of a larger discussion of secular modernism, the role of the state, and the "real" issues for postcolonial nation-statehood. Sumit Sarkar, for instance, complains about the neglect of urgent problems like poverty, underdevelopment, caste and gender inequalities, or land reform in Indian political praxis and discourse as a consequence of the claims of cultural nationalism and identitarianism to political centrality (1996, 270–94). A recent collection of essays by prominent Indian left-liberal social scientists offers a specific focus on "state and politics" in response to these claims, in which the *state's* centrality to the Indian nation's development is reaffirmed. Even as they stress the need for state-led development, the writers acknowledge that the *actual* record of the Indian state as the central secular, liberal, developmental agent and authority of the postcolonial nation is a dismally poor one. They argue that, nevertheless, what this poor record would entail is a "censure of governance" rather than the wholesale "denunciations" of modernity, science, and reason (which is loosely combined with anti-statist critiques) of the kind engaged in by the anti-Enlightenment intellectuals (Bose and Jayal 1997, 7).

Both Amartya Sen and Pranab Bardhan, in essays in this volume, address the state-versus-community debate. They insist that the state is called on to play a "protective role vis-à-vis inequities within the community" since the community is not necessarily the egalitarian, democratic, and intimately affective space that it is claimed to be in communitarian discourse (Sen 1997, 10–35). Communities often insist on compulsory loyalty from their members; religion-based parties like the Rashtriya Swayamsevak Sangh (RSS) are closely modeled on fascist organizations in their modes of discipline and regulation. The individual's exit from communities is not easy, and there is violent opposition to conversion, mixed marriages, or disobedience of norms; and the question whether religious leaders—sometimes self-styled—or a vocal fundamentalist minority among a community can be regarded as truly representative of its position is often raised by its moderate members. There is also a well-founded belief that community institutions are in any case caught up in a process of "decay," which is accompanied by changes in other spheres of social and political life. The displacement of communities' authority by the state's may well be the result simply of an "institutional vacuum" caused by these changes, rather than active or aggressive state intervention (Bardhan 1997, 190–95).

Some clarifications to introduce greater nuance and complexity into this too-quick summary of the secularism debates are in order before I move into the next stage of my discussion.

First, I must repeat that communitarians, though opposed to the state's imposition of a UCC, speak as "secularists": they are critical (only) of official or Nehruvian secularism. In its place they advocate religious *tolerance* as being both more authentically "Indian" and more effectively "secular." The problems of identifying some essentialized cultural "Indianness" in this formulation are obvious. Second, there is a spectrum of communitarian positions, which I have so far described in a somewhat undifferentiated way, ranging from the strong antimodernity stance of Ashis Nandy, who nostalgically conjures up a premodern vision of community derived from the Gandhian idealization of village societies; to Partha Chatterji's Foucauldian antigovernmentality from which derives his advocacy of autonomy to communities as a (indeed, the only) way of resisting the state's totalizing and sovereign power; to Akeel Bilgrami's critique of Nehruvian "Archimedean" secularism whose corrective is a state-initiated "negotiation" with communities for reform.[4] Much creative energy is evident in the ways that communitarians seek to make the rights of communities not only *not* in conflict with, but central to, democratic politics.

In general we may say that, despite the initial strongly polarized opposition between the parties, these debates have brought them to agreement about some positions. One concerns the limits of the model of secularism as the separation of state and religion that Jawaharlal Nehru, the chief architect of post-Independence Indian secularism, hoped would prevail in India as in the West: its failure (even impossibility) has been conceded by left-liberals. The failure, as I have explained, has been variously attributed to India's multireligious polity, the persistence and strength of religious faith and affiliations among the "people," and the Indian Constitution's version of secularism as the official protection of all religions. Significant attempts to evolve more historically and socially sensitive theoretical paradigms for secularism, as well as to search for and interpret models of intergroup amity, have been made from broadly liberal premises.[5] Even more clearly, the initiatives of the state in the matter of a UCC, as a matter of actual politics, and especially under the present government, are suspect: they are therefore resisted by both communitarians and left-liberals.

A final observation, which will lead me into the discussion of gender and feminist politics in the next section. In the secularism debates, as I have indicated, the question of gender is nowhere directly addressed, though the conflict that is noted between the Constitution's equality provision (Articles 14 and 15) and the freedom of religion and rights of minorities provisions (Articles 25 to 30) marks the space of such an address. The reasons for the repression of gender in these different positions are different and complex. I will not belabor an explanation here, only quickly sketch one: for communitarians grounded in an anti-Enlightenment agenda, women's rights are problematic (though they are not explicitly rejected as such) because they fall within the arena of modernity, egalitarianism, and secular law. For the left, there is the familiar conflict between the categories of gender and class for primacy in understanding social structures and in conducting political struggle.[6] In liberal thinking, the individual is necessarily conceptualized in unmarked terms as the bearer of universal rights.[7] In all these ways of thinking, the claim of women's rights in the UCC question tends to be fudged, or at least marginalized, in contrast to the way the issue is addressed by women's groups, as we shall see.

Gender, Identity, and Citizenship: Feminist Positions on the UCC

The UCC debates both in the Indian Parliament and in other forums remained for a long time restricted to arguments about uniformity versus minority rights, secularism versus religious laws, and modernization versus tradition, in the context of the new nation-state. Though the threats to patriarchal norms and the control of female sexuality, especially in relation to inheritance and marriage, were explicitly brought up in the discussions around the Hindu Code Bill, women's rights even in these contexts appeared only fleetingly as a consideration. Even women's organizations like the All-India Women's Conference stressed the need for a UCC mainly for the reason that uniformity of laws would unify a nation split along religious communitarian lines.[8] It was only as of the 1960s that the AIWC and other women's groups began to press for a UCC as a means of ensuring gender-just laws for women of all communities, a demand that became considerably more complicated following the communalization of the Shahbano issue in the mid-eighties. In the subsequent years the differently evolving positions on the UCC among different women's organizations have resulted in sharp divisions on a range of fundamental issues related to and emerging from it. This discourse is both different from and yet closely related to the positions articulated in the secularism debates (Chhachi 1994, 90). The major difference of emphasis is the primacy in feminist discourse of securing gender-just laws, a matter of little concern and sometimes active repression in the secularism debates. The parallels are to be found in a similar split between left-liberal and anti-statist/communitarian positions, though it is important to recognize how feminist imperatives inflect these positions in significantly different ways.

The only unanimous feminist perception in the matter of the UCC is that all religions' personal laws are at present gender-discriminatory. To some extent all women's groups also agree that therefore these laws must change and that women must be involved in bringing about these changes. Beyond this, major disagreements divide feminist thinking on the subject. Nivedita Menon has usefully outlined the different positions on the UCC issue discoverable within the women's movement, which variously advocate:

1. compulsory egalitarian civil code for all citizens;
2. reforms from within communities, with no state intervention;
3. reform from within as well as legislation on areas outside the personal laws;
4. optional egalitarian civil code;

5. reverse optionality, i.e., all citizens to be mandatorily covered by a gender-just code across "private" and "public" domains, but with the option to choose to be governed by the personal law of their religious community. (1998b, PE-10, note 2)

The first of these, a compulsory egalitarian civil code for all citizens, has been more or less given up as a feasible or even desirable demand and ceded to the Hindu right. The compromise version of this is envisaged in the last two positions, as an optional or reverse-optional civil code. The idea of a uniform civil code that will replace and exactly take the place of the present personal laws (as envisaged by Hindu right groups) has also been discredited: instead, the third option envisages a common civil code of much wider ambit, which will include domestic violence, homosexuality, and women's rights in work in its place, in this way refusing both the division of "private" and "public" as well as the restriction of gender relations to the sphere of the "private"/"personal" alone that underpin the structure of "personal" laws.[9] The broad options are those of the issue of reforms from within communities as in the second position, versus versions of a state-sponsored common civil code.

These opposed positions derive from and correspond to the division between communitarians and left-liberals that was reflected in the secularism debates. Women's groups who concede religious communities' rights to personal laws do so, however, less from a recognition of the legitimacy, even less of the value of communitarianism, than a pragmatic reconciliation to the realities of the Indian situation. Thus even the All India Democratic Women's Association (AIDWA), the central left women's organization in the country, conceded at their convention on equal rights and equal laws (December 1995) that a two-pronged strategy would be necessary to achieve this reconciliation—both common gender laws as well as reforms from within—and, specifically, that Muslim personal laws must be reformed "within the scope of Islam."[10] This is a concession to the current crisis of minority identity in the context of majoritarian fundamentalism and an attempt to distance feminist positions from the Hindu right's demand for a UCC. The most influential proponent of this view, Flavia Agnes, has argued that that it is outcomes that are important, in this case, gender justice, not uniformity for its own sake. This is best achieved by reform from within communities, by piecemeal legislation, and/or an optional civil code, and this is all that may be reasonably expected in the present context. There is also the recognition that in India women are closely tied to their communities and to their religious identities, for reasons of both an inegalitarian multireligious social arrangement and an inherently traditional social structure, and that therefore women's groups cannot assume an "isolationist" stance by pressing for a "secular" civil code (Agnes 1996, 68–94).

It would be incorrect, however, to identify the support for internal reform of personal laws as only a strategic position. Increasingly, more substantial and foundational grounds for feminist opposition to proposals for reform from outside are being advanced. One source of dissatisfaction with outside initiatives is a problem internal to the women's movement, while the other reasons for resisting it occupy the theoretical ground proposed by communitarians. Flavia Agnes has criticized the mainstream women's movement for an implicit "secularism" that disavows and refuses recognition to differences among women deriving from their community identities, especially religious ones (1996; see also 1994). Agnes, and most recently the Anveshi group, maintain that this has led not only to the homogenizing of "Indian women" but also to the hegemony of implicit upper-caste majoritarian norms in defining "women" (Anveshi Law Committee 1997). Feminists on the left have issued denials of such designs and assumptions on their part (Chhachi et al. 1998, 487–88). But the real question surely is not one of the intentions and good faith of the left-liberal wing of the women's movement but rather whether differences among women are best recognized and respected by having separate religious laws. This would continue to be a problematic issue even if the accusations were valid.

If the question of "women" is one of the theoretical issues that the UCC debate has made urgent in feminist political struggle, other radical questions have been raised with equal political urgency from an anti-statist position that resonates with communitarian arguments (especially those of Partha Chatterjee, who has figured prominently in these feminist debates). The hostility of many in the women's movement to the state, to legal reform, and to the promises and premises of liberalism—individual rights of citizenship, legal equality, and state-sponsored secularism—draws support from their experience of activist struggle. The limits of nationalist ideology, the fiction of citizenship, and the dubious progressiveness of the law are all exposed by women's issues like the Shahbano case, to mention only the most prominent among innumerable instances.[11] The most radical formulation of this anti-statism, the Anveshi group's statement referred to earlier, is critical of the women's movement's preoccupation with self-evident gender issues such as personal law reform—Anveshi identifies instead with the struggles of minority communities and oppressed castes (Anveshi Law Committee 1997, 453–58).

The most explicit cultural/communitarian position among feminists engaging in this debate is that of Madhu Kishwar, editor of the feminist journal *Manushi*. Kishwar has been a major advocate of India's "living tradition," like Chatterjee deriving impetus for this position from opposition to the totalizing and leveling moves of the modern state. From this position she opposes both personal law and a UCC, because codification of the law only fixes and homogenizes the diversity and flexibility of customary laws. Even today "each caste and sub-caste and occupational grouping continues to assert its right to regulate the inner affairs of its respective community and does not pay much attention to either ancient textual authorities or modern parliament-enacted laws" (1994, 2148). But in general there is strong feminist resistance to a position such as Chatterjee's—even where his communitarianism may be otherwise supported—on account of its gender-blindness. Nivedita Menon, for instance, complains that he ignores a particular trajectory of community formation in India: "the very selfhood of religious communities as they have come to be constituted is contingent upon marking their difference as male in the 'inner' realm, so that to challenge this is to threaten their very existence as communities" (1998b, PE-8). We might link this to Fatima Mernissi's observation about the "feminization" of the male in the postcolonial state as a consequence of the "access of women as citizens to education and paid work" in the modernizing state (1991, 23). This might explain why the impulse for men to retain control over women within the bounds of religion grows reactively stronger, in India as in Morocco. Another objection, the failure to distinguish between different kinds of communities, especially those based on caste as opposed to religion, and between majority and minority religious groups while valorizing "community" in the abstract, has been noted by the Working Group on Women's Rights in their response to the Anveshi group: "Anveshi equates community with minority community, and caste with dalit. Would they grant the same rights to custom and practice where the majority community and brahminical customs are concerned?" (Chhachi et al. 1998, 488). Anti-state women's groups recognize the bind: that most religious communities cannot be valorized as protectors of women's rights in rivalry with the state, that democratic space for reform within them is hard to win, and that support for "community" in a loose sense may well implicate them in an undesirable support for hegemonic and majoritarian caste and religious groups as well.

At the same time, feminists on the left are by no means unequivocal in their support of the state. The Indian state's record in the matter of protecting and promoting the rights of minorities, scheduled castes, and women would in any case be hard to defend. The liberal defense of reform movements, legal activism, rights struggles, and citizenship is instead based on more modest claims for their efficacy than the attacks of its opponents would indicate—and surely it need consist of nothing more resounding than the simple belief that having rights is more empowering than not having them, that progressive laws are better than regressive ones (though not, perhaps, than none), and that universal citizenship is preferable to a political system that reflects social differences and hierarchy.[12] The main point to note here is that the conflict between the two feminist positions I have been outlining does not arise from an absolute defense of either state or community but rather a muted and qualified support of legal reform from "outside," that is, by the state, on one side, versus a muted and qualified support of reform from "within," that is, by religious communities themselves, on the other. This is accompanied, however, by strong opposition to autonomy for communities in regulating their internal affairs by the first group, and strong opposition to state intervention by the second.

While secular and feminist discourses valorize or criticize state and community differently according to the liberal or communitarian positions they support—feminists particularly as they relate to women's identity and the benefits or costs of allegiance to one or the other institution—both would appear to share the view that there is no third ground that is available to women, and that the only recourse from the one is the other. The national crises provoked by events like the Shahbano and Ameena cases have resulted in this dilemma's coming to be viewed as a paradigm of women's destiny in contemporary India. It is this impasse that I seek to negotiate in the second part of this argument.

The space that lies outside the state and its institutions, commonly referred to as "civil society," is traditionally regarded as the forum for debates on issues such as the ucc in a democratic nation-state. What kind of participation in civil society is possible for women? What social place is available for them that is not coopted by family or religious community, from which they might negotiate with the state? What identities, social roles, or social formations might secure for them the influence of a critical mass *as women?* In what follows I briefly rehearse some of the ways in which women are presumed to relate to the community, the state, and other women before I examine their relationship to civil society. I am specifically interested in the collective subjecthood available to them in terms of each of these affiliations/identities/locations.

Women in Religion-Based Communities

It is useful to think of religious community in two distinct ways, one as a political identity, and the other as an actual anthropological and historical entity. Religion has undeniably come to provide a strong sense of identity to people widely scattered geographically who may share little else by way of class, language, custom, history, or even nationality; and it is this identity that is upheld by even as it upholds personal law. It is also this politicized religion that is increasingly seen to take over the public sphere (often literally invading the streets), occupy various forums of public discussion, and set the agendas for regional and national issues. Necessarily such groups appear reactionary and resistant to change, mobilizing only to assert identity in increasingly fundamentalist ways.[13]

The second kind of understanding of people within living communities in a bounded geographical territory is provided by ethnographic studies that explore the interaction among and between men, women, family, religious leaders, the state's personnel, and other communities. Kalpana Ram's work on the Christian Mukkuvar fishing community in southern Tamilnadu is a valuable example of such an undertaking. Ram shows how both Catholic clergy and state intellectuals make interventions into the reform of the Mukkuvar community in the name of "modernization" and "development," impinging in particular ways on the reform of "bodily regimes," which includes women's sexuality (1996, 298–99).[14] This study and similar ones[15] point up the importance of marking the heterogeneity of "communities": the differences between minority and majority communities; the differences between different minority communities such as the Muslim, Christian, Parsi, Sikh (relating to their size, status, beliefs, origins, politics, transnational affiliations, and political clout as a consequence of all these factors); the fact that religious denomination is inflected by other aspects of identity and location such as region (north versus south, the northeast versus the rest of India, urban versus rural, for example), occupation, class, caste. As historical studies reveal, religious communities are constructed, not "natural," entities. Personal laws were codified by colonial administrators for the sake of administrative convenience, in many cases by overriding or fixing customary laws, and do not in every case have scriptural sanction. Communities are far more heterogeneous, their boundaries far more permeable, and their norms far more flexible than the political rhetoric or the state's classificatory schemes would lead us to expect (Kaviraj 1992; Sangari 1995).

Our understanding of women-in-communities would differ according to how we read the community in the postcolonial nation. If we understand communities primarily in the political sense, we emphasize their separateness, their isolation from the "mainstream," their stasis and their resistance or refusal to change: all in the sole and supreme interest of maintaining their identity. Religion-based communities in this sense—like families, with which they are closely tied, and the nation to which they are culturally allied—are self-evidently centered on and led by men. But women are not excluded from or marginal to them; on the contrary, they form a crucial component of them. Their inclusion is indeed central to the identity communities, as well as women themselves, come to bear. But women—in specific contrast to men—are not viewed as *constituting* these spheres; they are described instead as *belonging to* them. (Though religious identity is legally inescapable in India, it is not for that reason nonvoluntary or merely passive—more or less active agency is permitted depending on the class, caste, or gender of their members.) The primordial nature of religious identity, which is an aspect of being born into a religious community, is not automatically available to women but is conferred on them as an aspect of their relationship as daughters and wives to the men of the community. The complexity and contradiction of such "belonging" is indicated by the double meaning of the word as both "affiliated with" and "owned by," the one indicating voluntary and participatory membership, the other the status of appendage and symbol. For women, even where the first, more agential meaning is operative, "belonging" is a reactive mode. They arrive on a scene that is always already set, and their membership is conditional on their conforming to the preexisting rules, roles, practices, conventions, histories, and meanings that have been instituted. In every case obedience and loyalty are rewarded by (the promise of) accommodation, protection, or praise; while disobedience and disloyalty are punished by (the threat of) boycott, expulsion, violence. (This is the reason for the paradoxical conformity of women even in situations of power within religion-based political parties in India, and it explains why they have only ingratiated themselves with these structures, not transformed them.) It is in this sense that women become symbolic figures for communities, especially at moments of real or perceived crisis.

Within such an understanding of religious community, as an autonomous enclave within the space of a larger public life from which it is isolated, it is difficult not to see women as merely pawns, prisoners, or deluded subjects. Ram's conclusions about the Mukkuvars' relations to both religion and modernizing reform are developed, coincidentally, in opposition to an essay on the Shahbano case that I coauthored some years ago (Pathak and Sunder Rajan 1989). She objects to the concept developed in it of family and religion-based community (especially a minority community) forming a "state-within-a-state," which ignores, she holds, the "dynamics of historical change within the 'inner state.'" Such a model is, in her view, "inadequate at the intellectual level," not only because it is inaccurate—since it does not record the changes occurring within communities—but also because it stigmatizes (minority) communities and, as a result, "isolates and damages the prospects of minority women by further reinforcing the taint of 'backwardness' associated with minority status by a dominant modernity" (1996, 298–99).

In her own study of the Mukkuvars, Ram convincingly shows the changes that modernizing reforms in the areas of marriage and sexuality bring about in Mukkuvar women's behavior, their status, and their well-being, in opposition to the assumption of minority communities' stasis and backwardness that many feminist studies, like our own, worked with. But in the end she marks the limitations of the modernizing project, the "relations of power in each model of emancipation and reform," and the renewed attempts, ultimately, to recontain the sexuality of women (316). Such a concession must not be taken to negate the lessons of her work. While it reinforces the reading of women's relation to the community as one of subordination and subjection to control, it also in important ways opens the door, as she maintains, to the larger context of "postcolonial nationalism, and its allied legitimizing discourse of development" (ibid.), a context I explore more fully in the last part of this chapter.

Women's Rights

The recourse to legal remedies and the assertion of rights and autonomy by individual women are often viewed as isolating and individualizing moves, especially when posed against the affective solidarities offered by family and community. The trade-off between (gaining) legal rights or legal victories and (losing) family and community support is invariably one that must give women pause. That such choices have to be made is a problem, it is argued, arising from the liberal conception of rights as inhering in the individual. The perceived limits of individualism and liberal rights for women have been responsible for calls issued by some feminists to abandon them as failed promises and return to family and community solidarities and values.

The politics of legal rights is a complex and charged issue, and not one that I wish to explore here in any depth in terms of an abstract debate.[16] What is relevant for the present discussion is that, for Indian women, the state is not in any case a readily available recourse from the problems of violence, injustice, discrimination, exploitation, or oppression experienced in family, society, or community. Legal pro-

cesses are tardy, the police corrupt, welfare and employment opportunities negligible, and the individual's knowledge of her rights and
entitlements vague. To speak of women as rights-bearing individuals
in this context is to invoke a situation that does not exist in any
meaningful way.

It is not hard to see that in addition to the conceptual and practical
limitations of the law and state-sponsored welfare or protection,
there would also be the problem of significant patriarchal resistance
to women's access to or deployment of these resources. The social
status quo is defined by women's place within the structures of family
and community being maintained; it is challenged when attempts are
made to change it in the direction of greater egalitarianism, autonomy, or freedom. The powerful moments of rupture occur when
women are disaccommodated within these structures and a process
of moving outside a given orbit ensues. These, in recent Indian history, have been the moments when women challenged their religious
laws or customs and became public and nationally visible figures,
as in the widely publicized cases of the divorced Muslim woman,
Shahbano, and the child bride, Ameena. That these cases developed
into national crises of significant dimensions was unprecedented
and indicates as nothing else does the political reverberations of
women's issues.

Women as Communities

Though the concept of *group* rights, gaining increasing prominence in
communitarian thinking, has sought to extend rights beyond the individual by insisting on identitarian claims based on race, religion, sexuality, region, and minority status of different kinds, it does not engage, as we have seen, with the problem of women's rights within or
in conflict with the community. Nor have women been envisaged *as a
collectivity themselves* in any significant rights-bearing sense. Archana
Parasher holds that this inability lies at the heart of the explanation
for the Indian state's continued discrimination against women in the
conflict between their fundamental right to equality and the community's right to religious freedom that supports personal law. By way of
illustration, she asks us to substitute women with any other group:
"For instance, in the case of the Hindu community it would be almost

unthinkable for the State to enact or enforce laws to discriminate against the scheduled castes on the ground that the right to religious freedom of (higher caste) Hindus prevents the State from modifying the untouchability rules of Hindu law" (1992, 19).

The question of "women" remains one of the unresolved issues for feminism itself. Real difficulties remain in conceptualizing women even as a viable category of analysis once forms of biological and other essentialisms have been refused. As "difference" theorists have been insisting, women are divided by caste, religion, class, race, and nationality, and so their interests cannot be identical; they are so deeply embedded in structures of family, neighborhood, religion, and community, which offer them their primary identity, that these would claim their loyalties in a situation of competing rights; they do not naturally cohere in groups in any significant numbers or situations.[17]

Elizabeth Fox-Genovese dismisses, rightly in my view, the political valence of "female communities" that some feminist theorists and historians have sought to resurrect and valorize in response to the failure of individual rights in addressing women's oppression. Such female communities, whether found within existing social arrangement or in more "formal" associations, would continue to be "hostage to the legal and political relations of our society as a whole," she argues. Moreover, separatism does not offer a "practical model for a society that still requires cooperation and fellowship across genders in order to survive and reproduce" (1991, 53). Even in the organized women's movement, women are brought together in a problematically identitarian unity, as we have seen. Therefore, beyond the terms of gendered difference (from men) and (shared, but not identical, or even equally shared) discrimination (with other women), what do women bear by way of a *positive* collective identity in the modern democracy?

Women in/and "Civil Society"

If it is true that women are only secondary and subordinate members of religion-based communities, and, worse, subjected to severe controls in any fundamentalist resurgence; if both their individual and collective/communitarian gendered identity as rights-bearing citizens is of limited potential for securing their well-being; and if the search for recourse from subordination or oppression in communities that might drive them to seek recourse in rights will only push them back into the arms of community again because of the limitations or failures of rights, (how) can this situation be broken out of? Are women doomed to enact this aporetic shuttle between community and state in any struggle, or can and do they occupy another space as citizens of a democracy, the space of a certain "civil society"? And if so, (how) does it provide a leverage to their position within communities and the state?

The political and social space that lies outside both the state and the family is loosely defined as "civil society."[18] Civil society is by no means a utopian social formation but is itself marked by hegemony and exclusions, gendered, classed, and ethnic—but for that reason it has also been a site of internal struggles for participation and influence. Civil society is identified with the "public sphere," distinct not only from the state but also from the "private sphere" of the family. The exclusion of women has been *constitutive* to the notion of the public sphere (in ways unlike the exclusion of working-class men or minorities), since it is the private sphere to which women are traditionally relegated and confined. In other words, the public-private divide is constitutively gendered.[19] The admission of women to political citizenship, while it broke this barrier—and has indeed provoked discussion about the emancipatory potential of voting for women, the extent of their participation in the democratic process, their (lack of) representation in electoral bodies, and similar issues—has not as yet generated any significant discussion of women as members of civil society. To a great extent their absence from the discourse of civil society reflects their actual absence from the institutions, associations, and other spaces of the public sphere.

Civil society is of course a fraught term in political debates. We are warned about the limits of both its emancipatory potential and its applicability outside the liberal discourse and actual political context of Western democracies. There is a well-founded and pervasive belief that civil society is an underdeveloped or at least distinctively different phenomenon in postcolonial countries.[20] But most analysts are agreed that voluntary associations do constitute a significant aspect of Indian democracy: political parties, trade unions, new social movements, peasant movements, and NGOs are examples of voluntary groups formed outside the state's initiatives and often in opposition to them that bring people with shared interests together in solidarity and/or in pursuit of self-interest, even if they do not conform to the normative description of bourgeois civil society as it has developed in the Western democracies.[21]

While women are not overwhelmingly present in terms of numbers or significance in these organizations, they are not negligible either. The terms and interests of their participation deserve some scrutiny. Before I amplify, however, I want to mark a parallel development. As we attend to contemporary public discourses in and on India, we cannot fail to notice that women now figure prominently in them as "national subjects," as we might term this figuration, to whom considerable influence is being attributed.[22] This stands in contrast to the conspicuous earlier blindness to the production-related activities of women in the public domain.[23] Developmental agencies of the state and international organizations target women as beneficiaries of reforms and welfare schemes (literacy, health, employment, credit) from the recognition that they are deserving recipients and that the improvement of their status produces immediate and significant developmental benefits.[24] Political parties view them as a significant vote-bank by identifying issues like prices, water, sanitation, and prohibition as "women's issues" and wooing them accordingly with promises of delivering these benefits.[25] Above all, the market, newly liberalized, has been quick to identify them as consumers having money and decision-making powers and has brought them into the ambit of advertising and customer profiles.

It would be naïve to report these phenomena as all equally empowering, or as solely empowering. There is no denying that these forces and institutions can and do view women in merely instrumental terms, add to their burdens and responsibilities, delude and exploit them, and subject them to new forms of coercion and regulation in the interests of development. Women are also here viewed in terms of specific class, urban-rural, and age factors, so that no singular collective identity is activated by this new visibility. Nevertheless, neither this collective influence nor the signifier "women" that is in circulation in these discourses is easy to dismiss as irrelevant when we are seeking to identify spaces for women in the public sphere that derive from functions and identities other than the reproductive, the symbolic, or the legal that family, community, and state respectively have traditionally granted them. Nor should "market-related liberties" be regarded as solely responsible for this development, Amartya Sen argues, for they are complementary to "freedoms that come with the operation of other (nonmarket) institutions" (1999, 116).[26]

The interpellation of women in these ways marks the acknowledgment of their entry into an economic sphere of *consumption* and *production*. Mary John points to the contrast between the emphasis on middle-class consumerism in a liberalized economy on the one hand, and the World Bank reports on poor women's economic productivity on the other, as precisely being the way poor women are classed and gendered in development discourse (1999, 112–14). But though manufacturers may represent the middle-class woman in their market research and advertising primarily as the leisured wife who spends her husband's money, there is at the same time an implicit acknowledgment of her as working woman, in the form of a canny recognition of her (independent) earning capacities as well as her association primarily with household *labor* products, such as food, detergents, gadgets. Though different subjectivities are produced in the discourse of women based on class differences, the important point to note here is that a certain agency of citizenship is emerging within the economic scene of labor, production, and consumption from which women are, conspicuously, no longer excluded. Women's work, both waged and nonwaged, is clearly no longer denied or deniable in the public discourse of gender generated by state and market, in contrast to earlier positions.

If we return to the question of women's participation in social movements, we note that their concerns too in each case relate primarily to *livelihood*—whether in the matter of the environment and the conservation of natural resources, microcredit societies and cooperatives, protests against liquor sales, or, predominantly, nonformal labor women's organizations like Self-Employed Women's Association (SEWA).[27] If we bring together these two observations—the acknowledgment of women's productivity in a variety of sites of discourse and policy, and women's active involvement in struggles around livelihood—we are led to ask if *work* might serve as a possible locus of women's collectivization and identity, hence an opening for them within civil society, an alternative to the all-subsuming private sphere of the family and the (sole) public sphere of the religion-based community to which they are otherwise limited.

I view "work" here, over and above its economic definition in terms of production and wages, as also a subject-constituting category ("worker"). The identity of women as economically autonomous (nondependent) individuals promotes their self-respect and feelings of equality, strengthens their entitlements, and increases their bargaining power. Paid work's empowerment of individuals in these ways is of course well known. But, in addition, "work" brings women into visibility in at least two other ways: by designating a work*place* and by mobilizing them in struggles around livelihood.

Without idealizing workplaces, where admittedly several and multiple kinds of oppression exist—sexual harassment, hierarchy, discrimination in wages, to name only the most obvious— or overlooking the double burden that wage-earning women carry, we can visualize the possibility that the shared conditions of (similar) work may produce solidarities among women workers and provide the grounds for their mobilization. The most striking examples of women's collectivities in India today are organizations like SEWA (whose members are women workers in the informal, unorganized sector) and peasant women's organizations.[28] The urban women's movement as well is largely made up of professional women—lawyers, journalists, teachers, social workers—whose initial politicization often occurred within professional associations.[29] The workplace enables first the identification and then the furtherance of shared interests; it is a place of close physical proximity among its members; and it offers freedom of membership and exit: for these reasons we may view it as a voluntary community. It is not my point that the places and conditions of work are more egalitarian or democratic than nonwork spaces—undoubtedly, as part of larger social structures and practices, they are gender-, class-, and caste-segregated to a greater or lesser extent. But they do provide the conditions of work-related activism (such as unions), which call for a transcendence of internal differences. This, ultimately, is a route to women's participation in the political process.

This argument admittedly takes too little account of the problems and contradictions of women's work. Some of these are obvious. Work is the site of class exploitation and, for women, also of domestic oppression, and so skepticism about its liberatory potential is well-grounded. Women's autonomy as workers is likely to be as threatening to patriarchal structures as are their abstract political entitlements and legal rights. It could be argued that differential relationships to means and mode of production, variations in kinds of labor, and consequently hierarchies in earning capacities create inevitable class divisions among women workers. The difficulties of organizing women workers, the vast majority of whom are in the unorganized sector, are enormous—and this does not take into account women performing nonwaged work within the household. Most crucially, women's entry into world production markets, especially in the Third World, is significantly related to multinational capital and its industries, a well-documented form of exploitation especially as it results in the increase of informal labor. Even where women's work is recognized as central to national productivity, as in the East Asian economies, this has only meant increased controls and exploitation of their labor. Above all, the protection of wages and work conditions are inescapably dependent once again on the state's intervention and its laws, which are at best fitful, and even this would obtain only in the organized sector.[30] All of these are valid and major arguments in countering a belief in any absolutely emancipatory potential of work for women that I do not seek to refute.

My point in any case is not an exhortation to women to join the paid workforce, as if it were membership in a club. And needless to say, my brief is not for working women as a category separate from women who are considered not to work, but an argument that all women are always already contributors to production, even if often in ways different from male waged work, a recognition that has entered official discourses belatedly. Even less is my argument about women's work an endorsement of the common, if implicit, expectation that productivity should be a criterion for citizenship. Mine is not an abstract argument about work as "worth" but a more tangible description of it as a praxis.[31] I deploy women's agency as workers and its acknowledgment in national life as a form of visibility in the public sphere as grounds for a collective identity ("women workers") even if not actual collectivization, and as a space for participation in civic affairs.[32] The official recognition as well as the actual material aspects of economic improvement, political mobilization, and social solidarities that work facilitates have seemed to me significant for women in the current context of the state's discriminatory personal laws and religious communities' controls. It is a meager and compromised space, but precisely for that reason one whose resources we should seek to expand, not write off.

The exploration of the anomaly of personal law in a modern secular democracy has brought this chapter to an unexpected destination. The official, public recognition of the agency of women as workers in national life, not a guarantor of rights but nevertheless a form of attention and an opening for participation in its affairs, along with meaningful signs of women's involvement in organizations mobilized around issues of livelihood, are, I have suggested, facts that may be brought to bear usefully on the debates around the UCC. By pushing the terms of the debate on personal law beyond the dispute between the state and the rights of religious communities, Indian feminism has already identified *women* as not merely the subjects but the rightful agents of change. My location of this agency in the fact of their productive capacities is a next step, as is also the demarcation of work as a public domain in a certain "civil society" where alone such issues may be rightly determined.

III Killing Women

6 Children of the State?
Unwanted Girls in Rural Tamilnadu

This chapter is concerned with female infanticide in contemporary India, specifically in the state of Tamilnadu. Even the question of how to pose the problem of female infanticide in relation to the state and to questions of gender is less simple and straightforward than might at first appear. I pursue two lines of inquiry in this discussion with a view to exploring these relations. The first is to explore the implications of the state's different approaches to the problem: as crime or "social evil" (the latter typically relating to caste and gender), as a development affecting demographics, and as violence against women. My second line of inquiry is to ask: is infanticide more productively examined in terms of its sex-discriminatory aspect or in terms of the extinction of human life? I do not mean by the latter only infanticide's aspect as crime or as human rights violation; nor do I intend by this question to set up the false though familiar opposition between (the particular) "female" and (the universal) "human" as categories of analysis. I offer this as a quick preliminary clarification.

Son-preference is a widespread attitude in India, but its degree, and the consequential degree of discrimination against girl children, varies in different regions. Neither the preference nor the discrimination is much camouflaged. The abhorrence of female children is intense enough to affect their chances and rates of survival. In her 1981 book, Barbara Miller, reading the signal of falling sex ratios soberly, not sensationally, described females as the "endangered sex."[1] Active

Table 1. Sex Ratio for India and the States

State	FMR[a]	State	FMR[a]
India	927	Maharashtra	934
Andhra Pradesh	972	Manipur	958
Arunachal Pradesh	859	Meghalaya	955
Assam	923	Mizoram	921
Bihar	911	Nagaland	888
Goa	967	Orissa	971
Gujarat	934	Punjab	882
Haryana	965	Rajasthan	910
Himachal Pradesh	976	Sikkim	878
Jammu & Kashmir	—	Tamil Nadu	974
Karnataka	960	Tripura	945
Kerala	1,036	Uttar Pradesh	879
Madhya Pradesh	931	West Bengal	917

Sources: Census of India; Negi 1997: Annex I.

a. FMR = Number of females per thousand males

killing of female babies, termed neonaticide, has been reported in various parts of the country, including, most recently, Tamilnadu. Tamilnadu, ironically, had one of the highest sex ratios among the Indian states and displayed other positive indices of the high status of women for a long time. (See table 1 for sex ratios in India and the states.) In the past decade, however, female feticide following sex-detection technologies such as amniocentesis and ultrasound tests has become a large-scale phenomenon. Various other forms of discrimination against girls, beginning at birth, such as lower levels of nutrition, neglect in sickness, imposition of household work, and denial of schooling, especially in the northwestern states of India, have been identified by those working in a variety of fields—anthropologists as well as demographers, economists, nutrition experts, journalists, public officials, activists, and NGO workers. Whether the killing of girl children at these different stages and by these various means, active and passive, is actually reflected in or primarily accounts for the adverse regional and national sex ratios that the 1991 census revealed is still a matter of debate among experts.[2] The actual number of female infants killed before or at birth is difficult to establish, given the covertness of the act; hence the magnitude of the

Table 2. Causes of Infant Deaths (in Konganapuram Block, 1990–91)

Causes (1–7 days)	Konganapuram		Vellalapuram		Chittor	
	M	F	M	F	M	F
Respiratory	3	4	3	14	1	4
Prematurity	—	—	2	4	—	2
Diarrhea	2	3	1	3	1	3
Fever	1	2	—	2	—	6
Social Causes[a]	5	28	11	72	3	51
Umbilical cord around neck	—	2	1	1	—	—
Total	11	39	18	96	5	66

Source: Arulraj et al: PHC records; Negi 1997: 8
a. "Social causes" is the term used in the Primary Health Centre (PHC) records to refer to infanticide.

problem, as a matter of numbers, is also in dispute. (Some estimates are available: according to one, about 35,000 to 40,000 female infants are killed in India every year. In Tamilnadu female infanticide accounted for 8 percent of all female deaths and 16 percent of all female infant deaths in 1995 [Kher 2000]. This would amount to approximately 3000 deaths. These figures are showing a decrease, from 1081 cases in Dharmapuri district in 1996 to 659 in 1999, according to a recent study, which I will be citing later [Philipose 2000].) In Tamilnadu the strikingly low sex ratios in specific districts, together with reports based on journalistic investigation, some empirical evidence, and reliable regional estimates derived from birth records in Primary Health Centres (see table 2), lead to the reasonably certain conclusion that the killing of female children at birth is a widespread practice in these regions (George et al. 1992; Chunkath and Athreya 1997). Disaggregated figures for specific districts and blocks and for different age groups tell a different story, as Chunkath and Athreya's tables show (see tables 3 and 4).

Situating the Problem for the State

The perception of female infanticide by the postcolonial Indian state may be said to be structured by three predominant modes of understanding it: as crime; as a demographic problem; and as violence

Table 3. Juvenile Sex Ratio Trends: India, Tamilnadu, and districts

Territory	1941 (0–4 Years)	1951 (0–4 Years)	1961 (0–4 Years)	1971 (0–4 Years)	1981 (0–4 Years)	1991 (0–4 Years)
India	—	—	976	964	962	945
Tamil Nadu	1010	999	995	984	974	948
Dharmapuri	—	—	—	993	955	905
Madurai	1011	978	988	981	970	918
Salem	1010	1016	990	966	900	849
Tiruvannamalai Sambuvarayar	—	—	—	—	—	964
Dindigul	—	—	—	—	—	934
North Arcot Ambedkar	1013	995	998	988	999	962
South Arcot	1007	1015	1017	981	973	970
Pudukkottai	—	—	—	—	999	976
Periyar	—	—	—	—	964	929
Coimbatore	1006	979	987	978	969	966
Chidambaranar	—	—	—	—	—	964
Kanyakumari	—	—	966	978	997	970
Nilgris	921	—	998	985	987	968
Thanjavur	1017	1008	997	984	987	965
Tiruchapalli	1035	1017	1005	994	969	955
Kamarajar	—	—	—	—	—	946
Chengai	999	999	1015	986	996	970
Nagai Quaid-e-Milleth	—	—	—	—	—	971
Tirunelveli Kattabomman	990	1042	986	995	973	955
Pasumpon Mutharamalinga Thevar	—	—	—	—	—	958
Ramanathapuram	1042	1015	995	998	969	960
Chennai	942	928	976	969	987	962

Sources: Census of India, various volumes; Chunkath and Athreya 1997: WS 21.

Table 4. Total Infant Deaths, Female Infanticide Deaths, and
"Female Infanticide Rates" (Sample Survey for 1995)

District	Total Infant Deaths		Female Infanticide Deaths	Female Infanticide Rate = Female Infanticide Deaths as Percent of Female Infant Deaths
	Male	Female		
Dharmapuri	182	308	183	59.4
Madurai	149	208	112	53.8
Salem	146	174	58	33.3
Tiruvannamalai Sambuvarayar	89	99	9	9.1
Dindigul	128	135	28	20.7
Villuppuram Ramasamy	118	134	1	0.7
North Acrot Ambedkar	99	111	—	—
Perambalur Thiruvalluvar	108	110	1	0.9
South Arcot Vallalar	129	135	1	0.7
Pudukkottai	114	109	—	—
Periyar	101	88	—	—
Coimbatore	74	65	—	—
Chidambernaar	84	80	—	—
Kanyakumari	33	27	—	—
Karur Dherran Chinnamalai	96	91	9	9.9
Nilgris	45	38	—	—
Thanjavur	94	76	—	—
Tiruchirapalli	136	120	1	0.8
Kamarjar	111	91	—	—
Chengai MGR	96	81	—	—
Nagai Quaid-e-Melleth	102	77	—	—
Tirunelveli Kattabomman	130	95	—	—
Pasumpon Muthramalinga Thevar	86	63	—	—
Ramathapuram	135	98	—	—
Tamil Nadu	2585	2613	403	15.4

Sources: DPH survey; Chunkath and Athreya 1997: WS 24.

against women. I discuss below the implications of each of these modes of viewing the problem.

Female Infanticide as Crime

Infanticide figures as murder in the Indian Penal Code.[3] Infanticide has always been a covert act, and it has never claimed religious sanction, unlike sati, for example.[4] Consequently, the prosecution of female infanticide is, or ought to be, easier than that of other comparable "customs" that are no longer acceptable by modern legal and social norms. But since infanticide is committed by large numbers of people, and like sati has the sanction of custom, it is difficult to apprehend simply as criminal behavior. If in one view it may be unequivocally regarded as crime, in another there is also the reality and realization of the extremely minimal usefulness of treating it as such. "Illegality" becomes the imposition of an alien norm, as the anti-sati law in Rajasthan recently proved to be. But more crucially there are the problems of detection and identification of the criminal. Who is to be punished when so many participants are involved, given that midwives, parents, other family, and the community collude in the act and in its cover-up? Criminalizing the act has also had the result of pushing it further underground and has encouraged the turn to forms of killing that are less detectable, and more painful, than the ones used earlier. The state's wholehearted pursuit of a project of abolition is thus blocked by the futility of treating it as crime. There is also the questionable justice of doing so: in a recent well-publicized case of actual arrest and trial of those accused of infanticide, it was the mother who was found guilty and sentenced (to fourteen years' rigorous imprisonment), while the father was let off, a judgment that we must find deeply problematic as an instance of punishing one who is already a victim. There are ambivalent issues as well: for instance, are the more passive forms of killing, such as neglect, exposure, and starvation, to be regarded as murder?

Moving from legally defined crime to a broader framework of *deviance* within which child maltreatment may be placed, we must acknowledge the paradox that Nancy Scheper-Hughes formulates: "infanticide-tolerant" behavior in the Third World does not necessarily involve "direct violence" or "hostility" toward the child, in contrast to the "abortion- and abuse-tolerant" behavior in societies of the advanced industrial West, which does (1987, 14; 187–208). There is therefore, arguably, a larger normative sense in which passive neglect even leading to early death does not fit within the cognitive framework of crime/deviance/violence. In an expansively relativist view the argument may be stretched to include active infanticide (true, this is not explicitly suggested in Scheper-Hughes's volume). A few studies undertaken on the "psycho-social" causes and consequences of infanticide in rural Tamilnadu suggest that while there is "predictable grief" among the mothers, there is also "a marked absence of guilt" (Negi 1997, 19–20). However this may be, in contemporary India the awareness of infanticide as a prohibition by law and a punishable crime is by no means absent, and it exists in clear tension with the custom and/or social compulsion that permit (or even demand) it. The state, both colonial and postcolonial, has found it a useful alibi to present practices it labels "social evils" as both preexistent and deeply embedded, not amenable to reform through its intervention via modern law and education.

Female Infanticide as Demographic Problem

The fact that feticide and infanticide in India are modes of sex-selective family planning that seek to eliminate unwanted female children leads to two distinctly different kinds of concerns for the state and for feminism. For the Indian state it is a fact that translates into a problem of demography, both (and contradictorily) that of overall population figures and of male-female sex ratios. For feminist analysts, on the other hand, female infanticide is another example of a pervasive misogyny in Indian society, expressive of discrimination and aggression against women, to be addressed therefore as primarily a gender issue.

For the state the progressive decline in sex ratios is a matter of concern both as an indisputable reflection of the poor status of women in the country and as an anarchic meddling with "nature" with consequences for "society." Fewer women available to larger numbers of men would provoke, it is feared, an increase in prostitution, abduction, rape, polyandry and other abuses of women.[5] (Nor are there lacking careless explanations that yoke demographic find-

Table 5. Comparison of Sex Ratios: India and the World

Region	Sex Ratio (1980)
World	0.990
Western Europe	1.064
Eastern Europe	1.056
United States	1.054
Latin America	0.999
Asia	0.953
India	0.931
Pakistan	0.929
Bangladesh	0.939
Western Asia	0.940
Eastern and Southeastern Asia	1.008
China	0.941
Africa	1.015
Northern Africa	0.986
Non-Northern Africa	1.024

Sources: A. D. Sen 1987; Agnihotri 1995: 2074.

ings to crudely economistic supply-and-demand models to argue that the status of women might be *improved* if their numbers were limited, by whatever means.)[6]

There is, more seriously, a fraught if not openly articulated conflict of state interests in this matter, as a consequence of its vigorous programs and propaganda for population control meshing with the family's logic of killing unwanted children. I must make clear that it is not a line of thinking that is consciously entertained by any official bodies, and certainly not one that has been adduced to explain their indifference to the prevalence of the killing of females. There is, nonetheless, an established connection between population control and female children's declining life chances. As fertility rates decrease—as they have in Tamilnadu and other southern states—for a number of reasons such as developmental gains, increase in female literacy and employment, lower infant-mortality rates, and higher life expectancy, female disadvantage is seen to increase.[7] When the desired norm (as stipulated by the state) is the small family, then the birth of girl children in the place of the desired sons is an even greater catastrophe within families. "The small family will always be at the expense of girls," as Sabu George explains (2001). Female children are suspected to have been killed in China under the pressures of draconian population-control programs that restricted children to one or two to a family (Kumar 1983b, 1076, citing from a report in *The Economist*, 16 April 1983). A nation that achieves an absolute reduction in population at the expense of vastly unequal sex ratios—India's is among the lowest in the world (see table 5)—is in the grip of a major crisis for the state. While individuals, families, and communities typically look to their immediate gains and interests rather than consider the long-term consequences of their choices, the state must recognize an obligation to balance the different interests of the nation's different constituencies and evaluate its goals in noncatastrophic as well as just ways.

Female Infanticide as Violence Against Women

Feminist analysts in India include female infanticide on their list of expressions of patriarchal violence (and not just discrimination) against women. (See, for example, Karlekar 1998, 1743–44.) Female infanticide is regarded, however, not as gratuitous violence but as instrumental killing, like feticide a method of sex selection. This feminist perspective on female infanticide as violence-against-women occupies a central space in our understanding of the issue. The question of women as a constituency/class/sex becomes the issue for feminists engaging the state in a situation of sex-selection and elimination of females. In developing this argument, feminists resort to two strategies: insistence on the *rights* of women and arguments about women's *value*. I will focus on the question of rights here because it conditions the state's response in terms of deterrence, returning to the discussion of women's social value later in the chapter.

Rights discourse and demands have always had a tenuous and vulnerable status—and in recent times a controversial one as well[8]— in Indian political struggles. How does the rhetoric of rights resonate in this instance? One way of articulating a feminist rights position in the case of female infanticide is to argue the right of the newborn (female) child to live, based on her autonomy as an individual. But this is a controversial claim that requires more extended scrutiny, especially as female infanticide is inked to its extremely recent counterpart, female *feticide* based on sex-detection technologies. Though I have not come across any actual conflation of female feticide and infanticide in the contemporary Indian discourse,[9] it is logical to assume that it is only because some women have no access to medical means of detecting the sex of their fetus that they wait to kill their female infants soon after they are born. Vina Mazumdar reports that women practicing infanticide argue that "if the sarkar thinks abortion is ok what is wrong with what we have done? We do not want to risk our health through abortions, so we wait till the babies are born" (1994, cited in 1999, 360; see also Bumiller 1990, 108–09, 124ff.). There would appear also to be empirical evidence that a decline in female killings in infanticidal regions is offset by an increase in sex-selection and abortion facilities in these parts. There has been a major feminist campaign in the country against sex-determination testing, which has resulted in legislation prohibiting such technologies (the first of these to be passed was the Maharashtra Regulation of the Use of Prenatal Diagnostic Techniques Act). This has not been an easy campaign since antifemale feticide arguments fall within the same framework of rights discourse as abortion: in both cases the right-to-life claim of the (female) fetus conflicts, it has been argued, with the mother's right to autonomy and control over her body.[10] Female infanticide uneasily inhabits the discursive space of this debate over female feticide.

There is a feminist position that supports nonintervention in the female feticide position for other reasons than that of the difficulty of articulating it as rights discourse, which I will only briefly state here. It flows from a kind of radical pessimism and hopelessness about the magnitude of the problem. Some feminists succumb to a market model of demand-and-supply of females because its operation is perceived as inexorably determining; others argue that the girl child's early death is preferable to a life of extended hardship;[11] and yet others foreground a mother's right to choose.[12] The argument about women's "choices" in this matter of sex selection is murky. But whether they are compelled by husbands, families, and communities to eliminate female children, or are moved by independent altruistic reasons to "spare" their female children a life of deprivation and suffering,[13] or are pragmatically motivated to choose the number and sex of their offspring, it is true that women *do* make these choices, however undeniably the choices are an outgrowth of social prejudice against their sex.

Does this bring female infanticide within the same terms of feminist debate as female feticide? How may the rights of the newborn female infant be articulated differently from those of the fetus? The infant child, one may argue, of course, is a more fully formed individual than a fetus and thus has stronger claims to a right to life. But this too is a double-edged response. When questions about the developmental *stage* at which the fetus is a viable separate entity have predominated in the context of anti-abortion/pro-fetus rights arguments—to the severe consternation of feminists who have sought to retain the focus on the issue of women's autonomy and control over their bodies—the insistence on the newborn's fully developed individual status in contrast to the fetus's dubious one is likely to fall into the trap of endorsing pro-life arguments. I want to suggest that we may avoid the conflation with the abortion debate by recognizing instead that there are different assertions made by the mother in relation to the fetus and the infant, respectively, in these different contexts: in the case of abortion she says, "It is my body"; in infanticide, "She is mine." "She is mine" is a claim that does not have the same compelling moral and legal force that "It is my body" does.[14]

A related argument would be that, where the mother is (or ought to be) the sole agent where abortion decisions are made (as a matter relating to her autonomous body), she is virtually negligible or overridden in decisions about the killing of newborn female infants, where the concern is a different one, that of the child's upbringing. These differences—in the articulation of the mother's competing claims and in the kinds of maternal agency at stake—also mean that the state or any other institution would be able to intervene in the context of female infanticide (that is, once the child is born), in a way that it cannot into the privacy of pregnancy. The Tamilnadu government's "cradle-scheme" provides women an alternative to the killing of the newborn female infant by offering to take in unwanted girl children. I therefore wish to accord this scheme a *conceptual* significance (which it undeniably lacks in actual practice), in that it differentiates the issue of killing the female child from that of aborting the female fetus. I will return to this point.

In view of the postcolonial Indian state's modernizing drive, the issue of infanticide might be located within a consideration of state policy about parental rights and duties toward children. "The shift from rights to duties is a profound one in the history of the relationship between children and the state," Myron Weiner observes, in the context of the debates over compulsory schooling (1991, 181). "The notion of duty denies parents the right to choose [whether to send their children to school]" (ibid.). When institutions like the family and religious communities are no longer trusted to ensure their members' well-being, the state either directly protects these vulnerable members as "citizens" or directs the institutions to treat them (or refrain from treating them) in certain ways. At the same time, if the parents have a (state-mandated) *duty* toward the well-being of the child, the (mandating) state assumes a similar duty: hence, as we see, its initiatives in providing resources to parents for maintaining children (alive), or its intervention to provide them care. Both state and society in India are caught in the transition between shifting conceptions of the rights of children.

Further, a major limitation of rights arguments, as political theorists have been insisting, is that they are always embedded in a situation of *competing* rights. What if the situation of female infanticide is cast as a conflict between the competing claims of the child (to live) and the family's (to do as it chooses toward "its" children)? Though it may appear from the position of liberal individual rights that the former, that is, the child's right to life, is self-evidently more powerful than the family's right to privacy or property (which might be extended to cover how "its" children are treated), the conflict can be a fraught one. The patriarchal male-headed family may not be legally recognized as a rights-bearing unit, but implicitly it is accorded the greatest privileges in regulating its internal affairs without interference from outside forces. These privileges, as the women's movement has been insisting, include the infliction of violence on women within the family by men (husbands, fathers), with the immunity provided by a widely accepted ideology of privacy. The close surveillance of the family that was required as part of the colonial strategy to prevent female infanticide—the detection of pregnancies and the supervision of their progress, the registration of births, the monitoring of the welfare of female infants, the information about marriages, and so forth—was considered its most repugnant aspect, and the one even the hardliners in the debate found most difficult to advocate. The modern postcolonial state is equally bound by these considerations, more so when the family partakes of the larger community's norms. Its attempts to secure children's rights in the matter of forbidding their labor or making schooling compulsory have been conspicuous failures for this reason. Turning a blind eye to what transpires within families and closed communities then becomes a politic move.

The feminist response to this staging of rights conflict would be to presuppose, on the contrary, the wish of the parents, and in particular the mother, to *preserve* their child(ren)—even in the face of their agency in performing the act of killing—by arguing their situation to be one of necessity or social compulsion prevailing over desire or intent. Though there is some danger of reproducing a popular and sentimental ideology of "maternal love," a feminist position would seek to separate the mother from the family, as such, in judging cases of infanticide.[15] The fact that "the social cult of maternity is matched by the real socio-economic powerlessness of the mother" (Mitchell 1966, 33) operates with a particular and ironic force in the context of female feticide and infanticide. The killing of female infants, even though it may be impelled by the logic of sex-selective family planning, therefore produces a situation of conflict *within* families, one which activists seek to encourage by providing support to the unwanted infant's mother.

At the same time, the proprietorial argument can be a poignant one. In the slave narratives of the American South, the killing of the infant by slave parents was an act of assertion in a situation of abject absence of freedom—as, for example, in the claim made by Sethe (in Toni Morrison's *Beloved*) about the infant daughter she killed: "Beloved, she my daughter. She mine" (1988, 200). Homi Bhabha views infanticide as a form of "slave resistance": "Infanticide was seen to be an act against the master's property—against his surplus profits" (1994, 16–17). Such resistance, in Elizabeth Fox-Genovese's view, "led some of the most desperate to feel that, by killing the infant they loved, they would be in some way reclaiming it as their own" (1988, 329). In present-day Tamilnadu, a similar possessiveness is evident, especially in the resistance of the poor to the state's intervention. S. H. Venkataramani quotes Kanthammal, a village woman, as saying,

"The village panchayat and the village administrative officer have no right to investigate or interfere in our personal affairs. If I and my husband have the right to have a child, we also have the right to kill it if it happens to be a daughter and we decide to kill it. Outsiders have no right to poke their noses in this" (1986, 30–31). As Mitchell has pointed out, in the context of capitalist production relations, "parenthood becomes a kind of substitute for work," of which the child is the "product"—and hence a "possession" to which parental claim is made. And since "possessions are felt as extensions of the self"—and "the child as a possession is supremely this"—we are able to see how a certain logic of infanticide may be produced within a problematic of "property" (1966, 33).

The discourse of rights in the issue of infanticide is, therefore, not by any means a simple one, though rights claims undeniably have compelling force. Within the context of the postcolonial Indian nation, we may translate the demands of female infant-citizens at risk to the following obligations of the state: to maintain demographic equality of sex ratios; to recognize the rights of women as a class; and to provide destitute parents with the means of raising children and/or providing institutional care to unwanted children. I have highlighted, alongside these, the difficulties, limits, and contradictions of these rights claims and of the fulfillment of state obligations.

If these three frames—those of crime and deviance, demographic control, and the rights of women—are the predominant ones that we can identify in the state's address to the problem of female infanticide, there are others, emerging from locations I will term collectively as activist-academic, that need to be taken into account both to contextualize the state's address in order to place the former, as well as to provide a broader critical perspective for our understanding. The following section offers a brief discussion of some of the more significant of these.

Other Frames: Activist-Academic

As a cultural practice specific to certain regions, periods, groups, and cultures, infanticide has been the subject of cultural-anthropological studies, and the anthropological perspective continues to be a valuable one in contemporary studies and interventions. Selective infanticide in human societies is a phenomenon that has eluded systematic anthropological study, however, as much because of the stigma attached to it as to the difficulty of finding firsthand information. Though a number of studies based on fieldwork in specific districts have been conducted, the need for more extensive and more reliable data is constantly reiterated among social workers and policy makers (Negi 1997, 37–38). In media reports based on interviews, the people of the community are understandably reluctant to admitting to actual killings themselves (though many claim to know of others who have done so, and most can produce arguments to defend the practice).[16]

One of the attributes of contemporary infanticidal communities that such studies have identified as being relevant to the phenomenon is that they are most likely to be found in rural and isolated regions. George et al. found, in a study covering the years from 1986 to 1990, that these villages are located in hilly areas, and they have no bus service (1992, 1155). This may no longer be the case; more recent studies suggest that the practice is spreading out from the "core" districts where it was initially predominant to more populous and "developed" parts of the state (Chunkath and Athreya 1997). Many of the larger villages and towns are now, in addition, equipped with clinics specializing in sex-detection technologies and abortion facilities. The "development" of a region, in terms of transport, jobs, health facilities, cinemas, and so forth is no guarantee, as we saw, that more enlightened norms will prevail, and indeed George et al. do not suggest that it is. All the same, the kind of monitoring that a good public health system provides, especially the home visitation scheme, has proved an effective deterrent to infanticide elsewhere in India, they point out (ibid.). For activists, such intrusion raises the problematic issues of investigation, propaganda, and surveillance to consider and pause over, especially in view of the suspicion and hostility felt by the communities to outsiders' presence. They feel the need to create awareness of different values and norms in these regions, but not at the expense of singling out communities in terms of specific class, caste, and regional "backwardness." A double focus on female infanticide is necessary as a consequence: as a practice specific to particular castes, communities, and classes of people, but one, at the same time, based on widespread patriarchal values.

The identification of groups practicing female infanticide as "criminal" castes/tribes or "martial" races is only rarely invoked in responsible reports today, though it was a staple of explanation in colonial analyses. Nevertheless, caste and religion remain significant aspects of cultural practices and customs, by no means irrelevant to accounts of female infanticide. The important difference is that they no longer result in culturalist explanations of an essentialized character of a group and its unchanging and invariant traditions but are instead inflected by an understanding of other social and economic factors that influence social behavior. Unlike classic functionalism in anthroplogy, which tends to view culture (or certain cultures, termed "primitive") as fixed and unchanging, contemporary understanding locates infanticide within a narrative of social and economic *change* within communities, especially that of development—as reflected in the increase in prosperity and standard of living of certain groups, overall decreases in female fertility and infant mortality rates, social changes such as consumerism, rapid transport, availability of advanced medical technologies of sex-detection, etc. The earliest of the reports on the Salem infanticides, the 1986 *India Today* cover story, for instance, connected the revival of the custom among the Maramalai Kallars in Usilampatti district with specific developmental changes in the region: the construction of the dam on the Vaigai River brought water to agricultural lands in the area, and the new prosperity gave rise to dowry customs (Venkataramani 1986, 32). Similarly, the Gounder caste in the districts of Salem and Periyar, also upwardly caste mobile and given to large-scale expenditure on daughters, is an infanticidal group (Venkatachalam and Srinivasan 1993, 37, 68). Infanticide is practiced only by Hindu communities and is not known among Muslims and Christians even in the same regions. Scheduled castes do not know the practice, and in general sex ratios among scheduled castes and tribes have been healthy, but this is yielding to a new trend toward dowry giving and, consequently it seems, discrimination toward daughters, though no significant infanticidal tendencies are apparent.[17]

Activists and NGO groups working in the field consider ethnographies based on fieldwork essential for their projects. One Chennai theater group reports, for instance, that it undertook extensive research into local song traditions and into the customs and rituals marking stages in a woman's "life-cycles" (the continuing compulsory observance of which places huge economic burdens on her natal family) (Mangai 1998, WS 71). But beyond the necessity of such knowledge of local customs is the larger issue of the ethics and politics of understanding "other" (and putatively inferior: "backward," "primitive," "criminal") cultures, a process both sophisticated and complicated, in which contemporary anthropology self-reflexively engages. Cultural activists, in particular, who regard such understanding as the first step for bringing about change and who are sensitive to their own identities and locations as urban, educated intelligentsia to whom infanticide is alien, scrupulously avoid the difference and division of "us and them," which condemnation or other aggressive methods of propaganda in their interventions would create. They avoid naming and stigmatizing infanticidal groups or individuals, adopting instead a systemic analysis by broadening the situation to include all forms of patriarchal discrimination and violence, and they emphasize the structural basis of this oppression (Mangai 1998; Natarajan 1997).[18] While these strategies reflect what is undoubtedly a (post)modern anthropological sensibility, cultural relativism as it operates in the context of bringing about social change in certain districts of Tamilnadu is nonetheless seeking to make productive intervention possible by promoting sympathetic identification and dialogue between the two groups.

In contrast, cultural relativism in recent historical and social scientific studies of infanticide produced in more exclusively academic contexts, especially by scholars in the West, has a more "objective" cast. Such studies, as in the case of Scheper-Hughes 1987, discriminate between two *kinds* of infanticide. Accordingly, infanticide may be either "traditional," therefore "normative," informed by an "instrumental" rationale and a "cultural logic" for the killing of disvalued offspring; or it may be pathological, caused by the "social trauma" of factors like "extreme poverty and deprivation, rapid culture change and cultural disintegration, and the catastrophe of famine" (Scheper-Hughes 1987, 17). And scholars of both kinds of phenomena share skepticism and wariness about "altruistic" projects for saving disvalued children (ibid., 20).

Some of this work comes close to adopting a sociobiological approach, as Scheper-Hughes concedes (21). Sociobiological approaches, based primarily on primate research, are concerned with understanding infanticide among animal groups in similar ways, as either an "adaptive" strategy or as a "pathological" response to stress.[19] Indeed, we might ask whether the construction of typologies of infanticide does not reflect a struggle with questions of interpretation: the construction of limits—what counts as deviance or pathology and what as rational or adaptive response—is an important point at which moral distinctions are made, the most crucial ones being those of intervention and its methods.[20] Understandably, therefore, infanticide is also a crux of biomedical ethical discourses, especially those generated by the abortion debates in the contemporary West, in which the question of "moral status" predominates (Warren 1997). Positions on infanticide vary from opposition on the grounds of its intrinsic wrongness (for example, Tooley 1983) to historical and cultural relativist tolerance (for example, Warren 1997, 165).

Selective infanticide in contemporary human societies raises questions of life, corporality, and populations that bring it inevitably into the frame of reference of the biopolitics propounded in the work of Michel Foucault and, following from and extending his arguments, that of Giorgio Agamben. The Foucauldian argument about a modern biopolitical regime allows us to go beyond the usual anthropological "culture-norm" and the typical social-scientific explanation in terms of the economy of "value," by asking us, instead, to view sex-selective infanticide in contemporary societies in light of *technologies of rule*. Foucault argues that modern governing techniques target the "disciplining of individual bodies and the regulations of the life process of aggregate human populations" (1980, 139–46). Agamben's critique addresses the point at which Foucault's biopolitical models of power intersect with the juridicoinstitutional models of power: "Placing biological life at the center of its calculations, the modern State therefore does nothing other than bring to light the secret tie uniting power and bare life" (1998, 6). Bare life is the life of *homo sacer* (sacred man) who, according to an archaic Roman law, "*may be killed and yet not sacrificed,*" who is defined by this (inclusive, constitutive) exclusion. Agamben offers this law as the "key" to the "very codes of political power," the "hidden foundation on which the entire political system rested" (8, 9; emphasis in original). In a modern democracy man is both object and subject of political power. In positing a constitutive link between power and the body, the radical proposition that human biological life is integral to modern political life would contest any understanding of phenomena such as female infanticide as exceptional.[21] It would propose larger, foundational answers to questions posed in a larger frame: what explains the pervasive misogyny of such acts? What is there that in every society sanctions certain killings within a universal prescription against the taking of life?

But ultimately a diagnosis that views politics itself as bare life does not provide the necessary purchase for those asking why this group or that is targeted for discrimination: a purchase necessary so that they might fight back, or make the state accountable (the concern of interventionists). The interventionist projects in present-day Tamilnadu involve locating female infanticide as a historically and geographically defined and limited phenomenon (looking at disaggregated figures at the district and block level, tracking dicennial sex ratios, etc.). It by no means assumes the universality of the practice, and can therefore only sit uncomfortably with an Agambenian diagnosis of a founding and ineradicable violence at the very heart of our political existence. In order to identify the female neonate in rural Tamilnadu as a case of *homo sacer* (alongside Agamben's examples— the camp inmate, the human guinea pig, the neomort), a different approach must be embraced. It would seem that interventionary, liberal-reformist feminist projects cannot afford such globalized theory. The aporetic point of my argument is to retrieve the liberal democratic state for a project of welfare and development in the postcolony where its limits have not yet been reached. For Agamben the entire population of the Third World is transformed into bare life by the "[global] democratico-capitalist project" (180), but for those of us contending with the conditions that operate *within* the Third World a more differentiated, or at least a less radically comprehensive, interpretation of this world that we inhabit is needed.[22]

Strategies for Intervention: Government Schemes and NGO "Cultural Activism"

The different perceptions of female infanticide have translated into strategies for intervention, social change, and reform initiated by the state and by concerned activists in the regions where it prevails. These regions and the communities who practice it are broadly identified by, respectively, their socioeconomic conditions—understood in terms of "backwardness," poverty, and isolation—and their cultural practices, specifically linked to caste and marriage customs (dowry).

I turn to the specific measures adopted by the Tamilnadu government in the nineties with a view to gauging the sense of the postcolonial state's approach to social reform and women's issues. The Tamilnadu government's immediate initial response to the publicity generated by media accounts of female infanticide in parts of the state, which began to appear from the mid-eighties on, was to announce a series of highly publicized measures to tackle the issue primarily as a socioeconomic problem, grounded in a diagnosis of extreme poverty in these areas.[23] In October 1992, accordingly, the Tamilnadu government announced the Puratchi Thalaivi Jayalalitha Scheme for the Girl Child (named after the then chief minister of the state, and subsequently renamed the Girl Child Protection Scheme), and the following month the Cradle Baby Scheme, both as responses to the female infanticide problem. The first was a long-term incentive plan to help families maintain their girl children: a sum of Rs 500 would be deposited in a public fund for each girl child enrolled in the scheme; smaller sums would be given to her when various milestones were reached—on her first birthday, on enrollment in school, on the completion of class VI and class X; and finally a lump sum of Rs 20,000 would be awarded to her at the age of twenty-one provided she passed class X and remained unmarried until then. There were other eligibility conditions attached to this scheme: one of the parents should undergo sterilization, the parents should have no sons, the beneficiary child should be below three years of age, and the family's annual income should not be above Rs 12,000 a year.[24] The Cradle Baby Scheme was envisaged as an immediate rescue mission: in the districts of Salem, Dindigul, and Madurai, where female infanticide is known to be rife, cradles were to be prominently placed outside Primary Health Centres, hospitals, and orphanages to receive the newborn infants that parents may have otherwise intended to kill.

Evaluations of the schemes began to appear shortly thereafter. The larger program, the Girl Child Protection Scheme, was flawed, its critics argued, even conceptually. Practically, it was financially too modest, the outlay being only Rs 400 lakh, covering 20,000 girls, and the eligibility criteria were made needlessly restrictive. To make a real impact it would have to be more substantial and cover more families. The monetary incentives offered by the state to families to preserve and raise their children, as also the income-level limit imposed for a family's eligibility, are proposals based on the assumption that poverty is the chief underlying cause of the problem. But though poverty is never an absent cause, almost all those who are acquainted with the issue relate the sex-specific elimination of infant children to caste considerations in marriage practices—specifically, to the recent upward class/caste mobility of certain groups, especially newly rich agricultural communities.[25] Colonial analysis of female infanticide tied it without hesitation to the "pride and purse" of designated Rajput castes, poverty rarely figuring as a factor in the regions of the northwest in question. The poorer classes, on the contrary, especially among the scheduled castes, recognize the occupational value of women, especially in agricultural work; consequently, it seems, there is no dowry, there is greater egalitarianism of the sexes, and there are no reported cases of female infanticide (this situation, as I mentioned above, is changing with changes in the socioeconomic status of scheduled caste and tribal groups).

The premise of the official understanding of the female condition is based on an acceptance of the social perception that girls are an economic burden since they are not wage-earners for their families and since their marriage involves major expenditure on dowry for them, a perception shared by activists. The economist Jean Dreze has questioned the wisdom of bribing parents to keep their daughters, thereby "*reinforcing* the notion that [they] are a liability" (1997; emphasis in original). I will return to this argument in the last part of this chapter. According to Sabu George's findings, the incentive money itself is sometimes used for dowry (2001).[26]

The Cradle Baby Scheme had been met with skepticism from the start. Even the earliest of the newspaper reports, which carried photographs of the Chief Minister fondling babies at the inaugural function, cynically viewed the cradle "solution" as only a government public relations scheme. The number of babies "saved" as of 1998 was 134—of these 28 died shortly after they were received, and 12 were returned to their parents. The remaining were placed in various orphanages run by voluntary agencies, from which 20 have been given away in adoption. The explanation given for the large numbers of children who have died in institutional care is that most of them suffered from ailments of one kind or another as a result of earlier attempts to abort or kill them (Mana 1998, 18). Another report blames the high mortality rates on the actual modalities of leaving the babies in the cradles: most of the children are left at night to avoid detection, and they are not taken in until hours later when exposure has done its work; worse, because it is the department of health that handles the cradle scheme but the department of social welfare that must take the infants into institutional care, bureaucratic conflict results in further delays (Negi 1997, 30). There is also predictable moral resistance to the scheme among some officials because of the "irresponsibility" they feel it is bound to encourage (Vaasanthi 1995, 83). One social worker explained that the Jayalalitha government had itself lost interest in the program by the end of its term, while the Dravida Munnetra Kazhagam (DMK) government that took over in 1997 recognized little commitment to the earlier regime's prom-ises (Mana 1998, 20). According to a recent media account of the scheme's (non)functioning, few cradles are any longer evident in the designated spots (most of them were found locked up in storage in a building donated by a Japanese voluntary agency); officials are vague or shifty about the operation; most people in the area seem not to have any knowledge about it, a largely self-defeating fact if the cradles were meant to be used (ibid., 17–20). All reports agree that there is little knowledge and less enthusiasm about the scheme among the people of the region toward whom it is directed: government schemes do not inspire trust and confidence, but also there is a wide-spread aversion, it seems, to giving away daughters and consigning them to an unknown fate—their death is the preferred option.[27]

How do we read this narrative of ineffectual state intervention? One friend asked, after reading an earlier draft of my account of the Tamilnadu government's schemes, if they weren't some kind of "bad joke." I myself have not been able to decide on the right register in writing this chapter. Indignation is too easy, and I have wished to engage seriously with the question of the state's failures in this as in almost every issue that touches on women. The Tamilnadu state's minister for welfare argued that the cradle scheme could be counted as successful if even one child's life was saved (Krishnakumar 1992, 105). Numbers are admittedly not the whole story. But even granting this, there can be no reason, except lack of political will and official indifference, that more children could not be saved, or that even existing incentives for girls are not availed of. Incentive schemes and rescue are well-intentioned but necessarily limited interventions, and I don't wish to exaggerate their significance in policy and state ideology. Nevertheless, the failures even at the level of implementation—which my analysis has shown to be rife with inefficiency, delays, and apathy in bureaucratic functioning—bear further probing. Undoubtedly there are limits to state-led initiatives, but it would be naive to believe that the Indian state operates at those limits.

A comparative study of colonial British attitudes to female infanticide can be instructive.[28] Female infanticide was one of the earliest major social-reform issues tackled by the British colonial administration. There were significant disagreements among colonial administrators on whether and how to abolish it, which bear comparison to the way the issue of sati was deliberated. Broadly, the debates related, as in the case of sati, to the likely adverse political consequences of colonial intervention in native customs (especially when these were practiced by influential landowning upper castes), as against the righteous conviction about the need to stop the "barbaric" practice. Strategically the dilemma was whether to treat infanticide as a crime or as a social evil. Eventually the doubts were overridden, and in 1870 the Female Infanticide Act, making the practice a crime equivalent to murder, was passed by the Viceroy's Council. Officials of the British government were very clearly moved by reformist zeal in the matter, however divided they may have been about the measures to be adopted, and however ambivalent about the enforcement of the measures decided on.[29]

A present-day Indian government is in a different situation from a colonial government deploying a discourse of civilizational otherness and simultaneously concerned with the pragmatics of rule in the colony. For one thing, while the colonial state was anxious about the nature of native "consent," the postcolonial state claims for itself a more absolute mandate for intervening in social/women's issues by claiming a consensus that need not be reiterated. The modern Indian state at the time of Independence was, after all, programatically entrusted with and committed to a modernizing agenda that involves the removal of resistant earlier or so-called traditional practices not in keeping with "civilized" norms. This, together with the demands for government action by a visible and influential urban professional middle class—including journalists, lawyers, teachers, NGO activists, and public officials—and the negative publicity on the national and international scene when instances of "backward" practices in the state come to light, demands a show of concern and a declared policy of intervention on the part of a ruling government.[30] The issues of women's rights and human rights are also sufficiently prominent to require its prompt responsiveness.

The most significant difference, of course, is that in an electoral democracy, as opposed to colonial and other authoritarian forms of rule, political parties come to power as a result of populist agendas. Aside from the question of how far the state can be held distinct or even distant from a traditional patriarchal illiberal society in the values that it supports, there is also the consideration of how radical or sustained a political party in power will be in its opposition to social norms in a virtually universal case such as daughter-aversion. The strength of popular feeling about an issue and the confidence enjoyed by the party in power would be important considerations in whether a government at the center and in the states would pursue a policy of radical reform. The All India Anna Dravida Munnetra Kazhagam (AIADMK) government headed by Jayalalitha in Tamilnadu in the 1990s was well entrenched in terms of its majority, and therefore well placed to implement wide-ranging social policy changes, had it chosen to. Furthermore, the chief minister developed the image of a saviour of the people and sought special support among women's constituencies. The responsiveness of the Tamilnadu government to the female infanticide issue was therefore prompt and highly publicized, though short-lived—as is the nature of such popular initiatives. It set out to directly counter the popular, social, and cultural rejection and devaluation of girls—the rejection by offering to raise them in "its own" care, the devaluation of investing them with monetary value. By projecting female infanticide as an issue of poverty, the Jayalalitha government was able to offer sympathetic economic assistance to affected families, without interference in their traditional attitudes. The schemes implicitly endorsed the communities' perception of girl children as a burden that the state would help them to bear.

But it is true that the Tamilnadu government has not reduced the problem entirely to one of poverty. It has not overlooked the larger and more diffuse ideological situation of gender discrimination, since it has a progressive record to live up to.[31] It therefore produced a few educational television spots, slogans, and billboards and supported other methods of propaganda on behalf of the girl child. For the most part the Tamilnadu government left it to NGOs and other activist groups, at least initially, to work independently or in tandem with district-level government organizations to operate in these areas of change.

Community-based groups, of which there are nearly thirty in Madurai district and over twenty-five in Salem district, have adopted a wide variety of strategies to counter the devaluation of female infants in these regions. Elizabeth Negi, in a monograph on female infanticide in Tamilnadu, lists some of the approaches used by these different organizations: advocacy and lobbying; socioeconomic development of the region, especially improvement of women's status within the community; gender sensitization programs (such "cultural activism" is promoted via "jathas," consciousness-raising theater movements, films, etc.); working through panchayats or local councils; monitoring pregnant mothers, providing support and advice to them; legal intervention; providing temporary care to unwanted female infants in shelters with the option extended to parents of reclaiming them; active intervention, such as protests; and networking among groups. The success rate and popularity of these different strategies vary, and as might be expected, legal remedies are the least favored. For the most part activists in these groups envisage a gradual change in social consciousness, along with significant material changes in the condition of women. Toward the latter end they recommend jobs, special self-employment schemes, educational scholarships, and reserved seats in local and state government bodies for women, which will empower them in various ways and help them both to oppose infanticide and also not be liable to such vulnerability in the first place (Negi 1997, 33–36).

It came to be recognized that NGO interventions, while strategically more appropriate (and politically more "correct"), could not have the large-scale impact that government-sponsored initiatives typically can achieve. As Athreya and Chunkath observe, "there is the critically important question of scale. . . . It is evident that upscaling operations to cover an entire block or district definitely requires involvement of government machinery." Government-led schemes also have greater "political and social legitimacy" (2000, 4345). Therefore, and largely at the initiative of this team (one a development economist and the other a government official), the Tamilnadu government began a scheme of large-scale social mobilization against female infanticide in Dharmapuri district in 1997, as part of the Tamil Nadu Area Health Care Project (TNAHCP), assisted by the Danish International Development Assistance (DANIDA). This program appears to have largely superseded the earlier government initiatives. The method used was one that had worked well in literacy projects and already in use by NGO groups, "kalaipayanam," or itinerant street theater. The message and method closely resemble those of earlier activist groups: the use of songs, sensitivity to local situations, no overt propaganda, the involvement of audiences, and so on. Because local bodies (panchayats) were involved, the performances' outreach was substantial. Athreya and Chunkath are able to show that there has been significant decline in female infanticide rates in the district, from 1,244 in 1997 to 997 in 1999; in Dharmapuri health unit district itself even more "unambiguous" results are evident: the figures show a decline from 1,048 in 1997 to 657 in 1999 (2000, 4347). The significant decline of female infanticide cases, as a result of the state's initiative in community mobilization with the involvement of activists and panchayats, is a cautious sign of success. However, the authors warn in conclusion that the decrease in infanticide may be offset by an increase in feticide and that "the road ahead is far from easy" (4348).

Clearly, the state may embark on less and more successful schemes for removing practices like female infanticide. The government's apathy and failure in the *ameliorative* Girl Child Protection and Cradle Baby schemes it undertook indicate that such instantaneous and literal problem-solving methods are both heavy-handed and suspect. Its relatively more successful *pedagogic* intervention would suggest that consciousness raising and social mobilization programs make its presence felt in the community and function as surveillance in effective but nonintrusive ways. In speaking of the "state," or even of specific governments, we cannot also discount the initiatives of its personnel or the effective forms of newly forged collaboration among government, nongovernment, and foreign funding agencies.

In the foregoing discussion I have tried to refuse the suggestion that the state has all the law and reformist zeal on its side, and the people all the criminality and backwardness on theirs, by offering some complicating factors: namely, that the Indian government's strategic interest in reducing overall population may lead to a covert, even unconscious, willingness to overlook discriminatory practices against girl children leading to their death; that the continuities and complicities between the state (at the level of policy and personnel) and the ruled are often a matter of shared ideologies and perceptions about a problem; and that the populism inherent to electoral democracy may constrain the government's aggressive or effective pursuit of social reform—but also that the contrary pulls of modernization, the pressures for reform (from women within the affected communities as well as from the women's movement), the parental desire to preserve offspring, and the involvement of voluntary bodies are factors that operate in tension with these. In what follows I return to this analysis in order to identify the deep-seated assumptions about women's social value and the instrumentality of killing, in an attempt to arrive at a more comprehensive understanding of the continuance of forms of femicide.

Resituating the Problem

As we have seen, explanations based in socioeconomic, demographic, and cultural factors feed into the contemporary understanding of female infanticide in India, with significant differences between the official and the feminist interpretations of and intervention into the problem. Nevertheless, analytically both the state and feminists converge on the same proposition: that female infanticide is primarily a manifestation of larger forces of prejudice against the female sex, and that the basis of the prejudice is the problem of dowry.[32] Dowry is an overdetermined phenomenon, a site where explanations drawn from different disciplines converge. I don't question its explanatory force— for female infanticide as well as other forms of oppression that women in India experience—but I want to ask here what is the *necessary* connection between dowry and death, as an argument leading into my concluding reflections on the subject.

Dowry and Death

The liability of girl children is attributed to the burden of finding dowries for them at marriage. This burden is eliminated by eliminating girl children, infanticide being one of the methods. At this point, it seems to me, the "explanations" stop short of explanation. As Miller, among others, has pointed out, there are regions in India where large dowries are the norm and in which female infanticide is unknown (1997, 21). The issue of dowry is of course embedded in a complex and complicated matrix of causes and effects, which include the sexual control of women, religious laws of property inheritance, hypergamous marriage practices, caste-norms and upper-caste emulation by other groups, custom, ritual, and social status, female labor participation and other forms of female empowerment, and the nature of development. The intricacies of this analysis have been unraveled in numerous studies, and I will not revisit them here.[33] I am far from suggesting that these explanations are irrelevant or invalid; on the contrary the understanding of dowry practices takes us a long way in understanding the situation of women in India. In terms of effective intervention, by the state as well as other organizations, attacking the problem of dowry is urgent and necessary, as is the parallel endeavor of empowering women in every way possible. But to counter the pessimism of the Indian state (as well as of other analysts of Indian women's condition), which has long found itself in an impasse in its mission to reform "social evils," so called—which are considered both too pervasive and too long sanctioned to be amenable to the power of its laws to change—it is important to identify the situations and spheres in which dowry is *not* practiced, or where it has been eradicated: not only among the scheduled castes and tribes among whom women's occupational status is high, but also the effective social-reform movements in recent history that initiated changes in marriage practices (Brahmo Samaj, Dravida Kazhagam), "modern" marriages of choice as against arranged marriages, mass weddings/marriage bazaars, etc. that economize on wedding expenses, and others.

Further, an answer to femicide that is formulated in terms of the problem of dowry only begs the question. I want to offer as puzzles those places where the phenomenon of dowry veers into the irrational, taking on a compulsive repetition that is not explained by social norms, much less religious prescription. How to explain the convoluted logic of love/hate directed at daughters, in which the family announces in paradoxical terms: "we love our daughters" (so much that we will kill them by feticide, infanticide, neglect?); "we hate our daughters" (so much that we will sacrifice our life's savings to marry them off and keep them happily married?)? A structural understanding of dowry as an institution and social practice must always be intertwined with the contradictions of its operation at the level of the subject. I do not wish to subsume this understanding of the subject's "unconscious" participation in the "objective" effectivity of an ideological field within an explanation of the workings of "power," as such, but rather to locate its contradictions as marking a *tension* in these relations, one that might even develop into a source of resistance.[34]

There are other questions that arise in understanding dowry as a "tradition." How does it resist the impact of modernization—as reflected in the diminishing importance of community norms, the increase of the numbers of women in the workforce, rapid urbanization, larger numbers of marriages of choice over arranged marriages—which might be expected to erode its hold? Why, when dowry is so widely decried, does its practice spread instead of diminish?[35]

A fact that has been relatively overlooked in the dowry debate—Madhu Kishwar has been one of the few to draw attention to it—is that dowry givers and dowry takers are not neatly divided into two separate and opposed groups, the first of whom might be expected to offer resistance to the second (1989, 5). It is entirely likely that families accept the burden of giving dowries for their daughters so that they may reap the benefit of receiving dowries for their sons. When we view the matter within this broad social framework, there are no victim families pitted against oppressor families. To be sure, not all actual families naturally achieve the right balance of sons and daughters. So complaints about dowry are made and heard by families with more daughters than sons. But, significantly, few oppose it as *system*. The logic of the lottery works to make the system acceptable in terms of risk, with the further correspondence that the players can hope to "fix" the numbers to their advantage (by sex selection at or before birth).[36] Given this calculation, the emphasis in this discussion must shift from the "problem of the daughter" to the "benefit(s) of the son." We are led to ask how the latter has become such a major prize.

The answer lies in the fact that modern dowry inhabits another world than the private one of families: it is an important aspect of the public world of the Indian economy. The drive toward new sources of wealth, earned by way of, for example, "black" money (money on which tax is not paid), bribery and corruption especially in government offices and projects, nonresident Indian (NRI) wealth via remittances and investments, increases in entrepreneurship and in levels of competition in the professions and higher education, corporate culture, "yuppiedom," and nouveaux riches of many other kinds; the kind of instant status-elevation that dowry provides to the bridegroom and his family; the forms of consumerism that are promoted by a new liberalized economy: these developments would give us clues to important aspects of dowry. These are also areas in which the state is implicated and in which it can intervene to some effect. It is in recognition of this that Barbara Miller has suggested, more than half-seriously, that the government resort to a "son-tax" to check unbridled son-preference (1997, 212–13).

I am arguing here against too close an identification of dowry with the "problem of women," and vice versa, the first because I believe a wider frame of reference is possible (one that admittedly I have only sketched here because to elaborate would take me too far afield), the second because I believe we must not subscribe to a valuation of human beings that is linked to their social and economic usefulness. This leads me into the discussion in the next and concluding section of this chapter.

Women's Worth

The major argument of Barbara Miller's *The Endangered Sex* is the "etic" ("objective") observation that it is women's participation in paid labor, mainly agricultural labor, that determines their status differently in different regions of the country, in opposition to the "emic" perception (that is, a "subjective" perception intrinsic to the group in question) that daughter-aversion is prompted by dowry compulsions. Thus women in the south who perform several of the most labor-intensive tasks in rice-growing agriculture have a higher status, with smaller dowries, than the women in the wheat-growing regions of the north, where it is the men who carry out all the tasks of agriculture (1997, chapters 6 and 7).[37] Women's survival and status are linked to (the perception of) their social and economic usefulness, their death and devaluation to its denial.

This is a powerful insight. If indeed dowry explanations act as a screen to hide the instrumental rationality of the valuation of women in society, then this has serious implications for our understanding of cultural misogyny. The feminist counter to this has been, predictably and understandably, to establish and emphasize women's substantial nonwaged labor: their centrality to social reproduction and their contribution to household work, marginalized tasks, agricultural and other work in the unorganized sector. The women's movement's demand for recognition and equal wages for such work done by women has had a significant impact in this area.[38] Simultaneously, the struggle to provide women with better legal access to inheritance and property, to employment, and to political influence is also a strategy of "empowerment." Activists working in infanticidal areas, as we saw, are engaged precisely in bringing about such changes.[39]

But necessary and important as such countermeasures are in feminist thinking and praxis, they should avoid falling into the trap of accepting social value as a measure of the right to live. The tautologous and deterministic argument about women's (lack of) "worth" is, of course, an ideological move requiring demystification and resolute opposition in every way. Women's worth is a fact that must percolate into official discourse and inform the economic and legal issues of compensation.[40] But even if we grant women's "inferiority" in conventional gendered terms it still cannot constitute acceptable grounds for killing them when they are judged to be unwanted! There are other categories of human beings who would be (and are) equally endangered if their social and economic usefulness were to serve as the criterion for their survival—the old, the handicapped, the terminally ill, and, all too often, denigrated racial, caste, and ethnic "others." The stronger proposition to put forward therefore is that human life has value regardless of its social function or the meaning attached to that social function. In the absence of such a belief, female infanticide's terrible logic takes hold.

It is in this connection that I offer the suggestion that the "killing" requires a differently inflected idiom in the contemporary discourse of female infanticide. I have been tracing in the course of this chapter the differences between female infanticide as a problem for the state (crime, the problem of population, "social evil") and as an issue for feminists (violence and sex discrimination), so far only implicitly suggesting that the suffusion of empathy and pity for the human "matter" of death seems to fall outside, or be positioned athwart, the agendas of both—that the issue of life and corporality has to be talked about in a completely different language. I want to push the question of language and representation a little further here.

Some discussions of female infanticide in India exhibit, as a consequence of its stigma in civilizational terms, an acute form of deferral: they sidestep the use of the phrase itself. In official language this involves the euphemistic choice of a more innocuous sounding (but revealing) substitute: the phrase "death by social causes" that is entered in the official records of infant deaths at Primary Health Centers in Tamilnadu (Chunkath and Athreya 1997, WS-25). Admittedly, "infanticide" is an ugly term; it is avoided also because of the legalistic difficulty of establishing beyond doubt the cause of death as active killing. It therefore falls under the heading of a "sensitive" topic, particularly as it might touch on the denigration of a community.[41] But in much activist language, too, the phrase is rejected for reasons of rectitude, its sensationalism reserved for journalism. Activist-reformist arguments strategically avoid condemnation of the actors and sidestep sensationalized descriptions of the act. Equally, both moral outrage and pity are such predictable responses that they are presumed to exist without expression or the need for it. For all these reasons there is a perceptible ambivalence about exploiting the affective dimensions of the issue. The discussion of the street-play *Paccha Mannu* by its director, Mangai, describes the group's attempt to create a Brechtian alienation at the end that will provoke thought and discussion on the issues raised by the play (Mangai 1998, WS-71).[42]

It is as a response and reaction to this reticence in speaking the horror and pity of female infanticide that I suggest that the creation of a climate of an ethical sensibility about human life, its value, worth, and meaning, by such means as literary affect, would offer an important counter to the logic of "explanations" such as the social devaluation of women and its causes. The structural explanation of the instrumental rationality of female infanticide is already complicated, as we saw, by the subjectivity of the "irrational" motivation underlying the dowry-death connection. It is this destabilization of rationalist logic that I wish to push further, rather than invoke an argument about human rights, as such. The appeal would not be to a universal moral prohibition against killing,[43] therefore, but to a pity that will override social compulsions and even sanction. Human solidarity, Richard Rorty has argued, does not require the premise of a universal "human nature" but typically is achieved through identification and sympathy with (even) those "different" from ourselves (1989, 14).[44] Sympathy, of course, can serve as a mere ruse of power and is deeply implicated with liberal bourgeois invocations of the "human."[45] Nevertheless, there is a need to define it in a way that doesn't get subsumed within that ideological nexus.

Such representations are not entirely absent in the discourse surrounding female infanticide in India today. I find it significant that *Pacha Mannu* begins with a powerful invocation of grief—the *oppari* (customary mourning song), here sung about the fate of the woman. It describes the "painful moment" of a mother's decision about the fate of her infant daughter, though given the play's formal and programmatic structure it does not build to a cathartic conclusion but throws open the decision to the audience (Mangai 1998, WS 71).[46] Similarly, the Telegu revolutionary poet Gaddar has written a poignant song about a mother's dilemma about killing her child; it ends with her expressions of pity and her assertion of maternal bonding and female solidarity that finally will not permit her to go through with the killing.[47] The uses of literature and art in extending our sympathies by offering representations of human suffering, and in bringing about social transformation by this means, have been widely remarked and are indeed something of a pious truism;[48] and infanticide has figured notably in the literary works of Western humanism.[49] (Needless to say, a "change of heart," even if successfully effected, must be attended by material transformations in the socioeconomic and political spheres). Repugnance toward killing, parental love, feelings of protection toward the vulnerability of the newborn, alongside the moral dilemmas and emotional conflicts experienced by those called on to kill infant children, are "experiences" and states of mind that do not only stand in need of communication in a situation such as this: they are, radically, in need of a language or semiotics in order to be articulated and recognized in the first place.[50]

The concerns of the state are, necessarily, macrological. In the Third World, the pressures of poverty and overpopulation are routinely invoked to explain the trivialization of human life, reflected in the state's indifference to natural disasters (floods, earthquakes, cyclones, drought, and, questionably, famine), its neglect of safety measures in public life, the frequency of epidemics and other public health problems. Within such a macrological perspective femicide is regarded as significant only if its incidence is high enough to warrant attention. The feminist address to female infanticide as a problem of discrimination is still based on the identification of "women" as a (gendered) population. Even the description of it as a manifestation of misogyny overlooks the fact that it is not women but *daughters* who are the victims. The understanding of the complicated parental love that both sustains and undermines rational calculations of daughterly value would fall outside the affective realm into which the "literary" alone, it would seem, can attempt insights. This argument is not prior to but it *is* different from that of gender justice. While human rights as a *globally* validated counter of legal justice may have (more or less effectively) breached the nation-state's sovereignty in matters viewed as violations of its mandates, it is only a pervasive *local* cultural-social belief in the value and preservation of human life that can make the state seriously responsive to the well-being of—and hence the avoidable deaths among—the nation's people.

Postscript

I end with two scenarios, one imagined, the other real. For the first, envisage a future when women have been eliminated or so drastically reduced as to provoke a state of crisis—when patriarchy's solution to the problem of female children has resulted in a situation of, precisely, *overkill.* The crisis is a result of the realization that, as Dharma Kumar has pointed out, "*Fathers may not want daughters, but men want women*" (1983a, 63; emphasis added). It would not be fanciful, then, to conclude that in order to avert this crisis, while patriarchal *men* will continue to do their best to expel women, the patriarchal *state* may seek to preserve women for them. And as a consequence, girls in India in the future will be children of the state, while boys alone will be the children raised by their families. The Cradle Baby Scheme is an indication of such thinking, its significance operative at the unconscious rather than operational level at this point (which is just as well). Families will keep some female children, of course, if they are first-born or only girls. But in its broad lineaments we may retain this intriguing scenario of a division of labor and sexes between state and fathers in the upbringing of children. What would be its implications? There is no cause to feel sanguine about the state's institutional welfare provisions. But a more dangerous probability looms: if the preservation of female children were to be regarded purely in terms of population requirements and specified social functions for women, hierarchies not only between men and women but also among different *kinds* of women according to these functions are likely to be established anew. Feminist dystopias like Margaret Atwood's *Handmaid's Tale* (1986) allow us to imagine a society arranged along these lines. Such projections are admittedly far-fetched, but skepticism about the ends and wariness about the means of large-scale sociobiological engineering are never misplaced.

My second scenario is as yet an emerging one, and it is the market that has stepped in to manage the problem of unwanted female infants, beyond state intervention. On 1 April 1999 the *Deccan Herald* from Hyderabad announced that 228 girl babies were discovered in the custody of two nongovernment organizations—and these organizations had already sold 156 female infants bought from the nearby Banjara tribal districts to adoptive parents in various countries abroad. The scheme was reportedly "busted" and the organizers arrested (Akhileshwari 1999). What is uncovered is an emergent (global) market and its (local) middlemen. If familiar cynicism about the state's promises and provision of relief is likely to prevail, then a newfound faith in the market may well take over to separate the custody of female children in India in the future, with consequences that have now to be newly imagined in the context of the global.

7 Outlaw Woman:
The Politics of Phoolan Devi's
Surrender, 1983

There is a strikingly iconic scene embedded in the imaginary of modern India: the figure of a woman, her arms upraised, rifle held aloft, facing a vast crowd. This is a scene from the drama of Phoolan Devi's surrender to the Indian government. It was disseminated by the media, as such images are in our time, and made memorable in cinematic recreation. How may we read the meaning and significance of the surrender—in terms not only of this spectacle but also as historical event? As explanation the image tends to be self-sufficient in its own terms, the representation, in the form of the freeze-scene, overwhelming the narrative that precedes or follows it.[1] I want to examine the intriguing force of the image, while also working it into the narrative of Phoolan Devi, centering my discussion on the period immediately leading up to and following her surrender to the police in February 1983.

As I was developing the larger concern of this book, the relationship between women and the postcolonial Indian state, the figure of the female outlaw began to obtrude—first as a theoretical puzzle and then, increasingly, as a "supplement."[2] Her figure is not quite contained within this relationship, but it has nevertheless come to be central to my understanding of it. The female outlaw, directly confronting and confronted by the executive and judicial authority of the state, stands outside the usual transactions between women and the state that I briefly outlined in chapter 1. Such exemption, which constitutes her also as exception, indeed contributes to the definition of the outlaw. While the rest of this book has exemplified these other relations in the chapters dealing with the Ameena case, the Indian prostitution laws, the sterilization of mentally retarded women in state-run institutions, and the phenomenon of female infanticide, Phoolan Devi's dealings with the Indian government raise questions for both post-Independence Indian nation-statehood and gendered agency that alter the terms of this relationship. This negotiated relationship will be the matter of this chapter. I suggest that at the very least this is an intriguing crisis of citizenship, but I am inclined to think that it is also a significant one—that it uncovers certain usually repressed aspects of both that are revelatory.

The *surrender* resonates in this argument for two reasons. One, it was a direct, face-to-face, and (precariously) symmetrical encounter between the singular citizen-subject and the officials and representatives of the state, uncommon in the dealings of citizenship (here both "encounter" and "singular" are deliberately double-coded words), which forces us to ask: what are the conditions productive of such a crisis? And two, it is a point that marked, as it were, a baptism, Phoolan's entry into a novel territory of citizen-identity, the conditions of which also made visible the contracts that are otherwise naturalized in citizenship. If Phoolan promised to be law-abiding (in/law) as a condition of the state's pardon, the state's pardon too signaled the suspension of its dubious use of force as an instrument of law. This engineered event thus brought to crisis both citizenship and law as aspects of the state, as I hope to show.

I draw my account of Phoolan Devi's surrender from an authorized biography by Mala Sen, *India's Bandit Queen: The True Story of Phoolan Devi* (1991 / 1993). Phoolan Devi's life story has been made familiar to an international audience through Shekhar Kapur's film *Bandit Queen* (1994), which is largely based on Sen's book. I have also drawn on reports and feature articles about Phoolan Devi in the Indian media.

This is a brief recapitulation of the events of her life as we know it from these sources. Phoolan was born the second of five children into a poor family in rural Uttar Pradesh (UP) and was married off as a child to a much older man. She then escaped to or was abducted by a dacoit gang (the Chambal valley has long been notorious as the home of dacoity). Her evolution into an outlaw is usually explained as rebellion against her exploitation as a poor lower-caste woman. She quickly attained legendary status as leader of her own dacoit gang. But after the death of Vikram Mallah, her lover and co-leader of the gang, and following the notorious massacre at Behmai village, which she was accused of leading, she was on the run. Eventually, early in 1983, she voluntarily surrendered to the police when assured of fair terms of trial and rehabilitation by the government; and after eleven years in jail awaiting trial, she was conditionally released. Since her release her life has been an escalating sequence of media fame, bourgeois respectability, and political influence. She was elected to Parliament as a Samajwadi Party candidate from UP in 1996, lost the seat in the general elections of 1998, and was reelected in 1999. A significant aspect of this time was the making and release of the film *Bandit Queen* and the controversy surrounding it.

The reliability of these accounts of her life as "facts" is admittedly controversial, especially since what have been regarded as the relevant, even crucial, events of her outlaw career—her stripping in the village square, followed by her revenge on her enemies in Behmai— are contested by the issues that Phoolan raised about the film version of her life, namely, her right to privacy and her right to control her version of events, especially about her alleged crimes, which are still pending court trial. This chapter is bounded by these constraints and by the ethical and political considerations involved in any discussion relating to the life of a contemporary figure. The surrender, however, was a public event in an incontrovertible sense, though its political meanings are admittedly open to differences of interpretation. As an event in her life (as much as in the nation's), it appears to me to be legitimately available to the kinds of inquiry to which I open it. It is important, also, not to mystify the reversals in Phoolan's biographical trajectory. There is an inevitability, even inexorability, in the sequence that turns the dispossessed toward dacoity in a particular conjuncture of postcolonial underdevelopment and caste-and-politics nexus and subsequently propels the reformed outlaw (like, for example, the film star) toward electoral politics in a populist democracy. Our understanding of the politics of the surrender must be informed, then, by both the exceptionalism and the paradoxical representativeness of Phoolan Devi's career.

By way of clarifying the position from which I speak, I pause briefly here to explain where Indian feminism stands, first in relation to the state, and then to Phoolan Devi.

First, let me quickly recapitulate the exposition of the introductory chapter of this book. The state has been an important issue for Indian feminism and its "most constitutive site of contestation," as Mary John has described it (1999, 108). The postcolonial Indian state has been a strong, centralized, and initially socialist state that assumed powers and responsibilities that the autonomous women's movement sought to call to account. In the early post-Independence years, women's organizations displayed conspicuous liberal faith in the constitutional guarantees for gender equality and in legal measures for instituting reform, as well as in the executive machinery of the state—law enforcement, development programs, implementation of quotas, etc. But inevitably and in time Indian feminism has developed a critical relation to the state, without, however, relinquishing that relation. The failures of the Indian state in these fifty years of independence are not only those of the gaps between promises and delivery, progressive laws and their failed implementation, but a betrayal at a deeper level: the "neutral" state has been exposed as a myth as successive governments' support of patriarchal and upper-caste and majoritarian religious interests has become impossible to ignore. Following the Emergency, increasing numbers of anti-state movements have sought to question the powers of the state, its human rights violations, its control of resources, and its monopoly of the television medium. Lately feminists have insisted that the women's movement's focus on legal reform activism has limited potential in the absence of the state's commitment to implementation of laws, and that the state's intervention through increased and more stringent legislation only further strengthens its powers; that the struggle for social transformation by democratic processes requires equal attention to other sites, family, religious communities, caste relations, and, increasingly, the market, and to their connections to the state. At the same time, the Indian women's movement, never monolithic in any case, has begun to develop differences even among its broadly left-secular-democratic sections, which I will not address here since they were discussed at some length in chapter 5. The phenomenon of women's mobilization in Hindu right-wing organizations, along with the growing communalization of politics, has also led to a great deal of introspection.

How may we locate the figure of Phoolan Devi within the scenario of feminist politics? The contrast between, on the one hand, a certain low-keyed and ambivalent attitude toward Phoolan on the part of Indian feminism, and on the other the widespread popular recuperation of her as the type of female heroism cannot have escaped anyone's notice. The recuperation has utilized the idiom of the female goddess, a myth widely spread locally, as well as the image of a commodified underclass/Third World/female heroism established internationally by a certain kind of populist feminism.[3] If, by contrast, Indian feminists have been noticeably reticent about Phoolan Devi, the reasons are not hard to seek: Phoolan is not a feminist figure or a figure for feminism. This, needless to say, is not a criticism of the historical Phoolan, for there is of course no reason why she should be either; nor does it indicate a dismissal of her life's vicissitudes as irrelevant to feminism's concerns. Indian feminism has in general been unenthusiastic about embracing militant feminist models, and skepticism about the value routinely attributed to female "agency" and "empowerment," as such, has tended to increase in the context of militant Hindutva women leaders. Also, as I have argued elsewhere, feminist theory has found the singular figure, the biographical subject, problematic as the subject of feminism, especially when, as in the case of Indira Gandhi, she exemplifies a unique or exceptional achievement or power (Sunder Rajan 1993).

This, on the one hand. On the other, there is a more complex feminist unease about engaging with the historical "actual" Phoolan Devi. Mala Sen was quick to point to the failure of the urban, middle-class Indian women's movement to connect to Phoolan's oppression: "the women at the heart of the events on which they campaigned [in the 1970s] remained faceless, if not nameless. . . . Nothing they did or said made any difference to the course Phoolan Devi's life was to take" (1993, 54). The unfair and illogical expectation that the women's movement must serve and save all women, everywhere, is one commonly held and is quite often advanced to score points against it. At the other extreme is the criticism that the women's movement espouses only a victim feminism, and hence women who display initiative and individualism are of no interest to it. Thus, if the "victim" Phoolan (lower-caste poor rural woman, raped and humiliated by upper-caste landlords) escaped its attention as a cause, then the Phoolan who became a dacoit and subsequently a political figure on her own initiative was irrelevant to its concerns as a personality.

Unlike Shahbano or Ameena, proper names around which causes were mobilized, Phoolan Devi became a personality whose cause was quickly appropriated by other interests.[4]

I share the caution about recuperating the exceptional woman for feminist meaning. But Phoolan's destiny and the destinations she sought at various points of her life (the surrender marking one crucial turning point) tell us much that is of interest about social and political processes, and it is in pursuit of such an understanding that I undertake this exploration of Phoolan Devi's surrender as an episode in the life of the nation.

The dacoits, locally known as *baghis* (rebels), of central India (mainly the states of Uttar Pradesh and Madhya Pradesh) are men (and, rarely, women) who leave their villages to join gangs of varying sizes (numbering from seven or eight to as many as fifty or sixty). They camp in the jungles and ravines of the Chambal valley, moving frequently from place to place, periodically entering and raiding a village and quickly departing from it. They are known to slip back into their villages to visit their families and to come and go freely, sometimes even to return to their former lives; but for the most part they live as outlaws. Because many of them deliberately cultivate a code of honorable and even altruistic behavior—robbing only the rich, giving to the poor, settling local disputes, following devout religious practices, instituting summary justice by punishing landlords and priests, protecting and honoring women, taking care of their own—they gain considerable support from poor villagers and can rely on harborers and informers among them, as well as on caste- and kin-networks, to protect them from capture. In the popular imagination they are also dreaded and admired figures of heroism. For these reasons dacoits have powerful enemies among upper-caste landlords and rival caste groups and are susceptible to betrayal for money or revenge; hence their lives are precarious. Men join dacoit gangs either because they have already committed a crime in their village—arising from a quarrel, a property dispute, an assault on a woman's "honor"—and wish to escape or because the gang life supports them in the absence of other means of livelihood. This is a region known for its harsh living conditions, rife with caste conflict and corruption.[5]

This is not the place to explore in any depth the divergent interpretations of dacoity in a criminal framework, but a quick rehearsal of the most influential explanations will be helpful for an understanding of the context of Phoolan's surrender. Historians of the British eighteenth century have been the first to emphatically shift the study of crime from its "conservative orientation" in viewing it as a problem of policing, to the "broader framework" of social history (Linebaugh 1992, xviii–xix). The category of "social crime" was made distinct, though not in any very clear-cut terms, from ordinary crime (Hay 1975, 14). More radically, crime's "challenge to law" shifted the historian's focus from state power to the "views and actions" of working-class criminals (Linebaugh 1992, xxii–xxiii). This shift was greatly influenced by Eric Hobsbawm's *Primitive Rebels* (1965 / 1959). "All kinds of rioters, smugglers, poachers, primitive rebels in industry" were regarded as "good" criminals, in fact "premature revolutionaries or reformers, forerunners of popular movements," who often gained the support of "the community and its culture" (Hay 1975, 14).

This is clearly a useful way to understand dacoity, and by now a widely accepted one. While the mythical stature and heroism of dacoits may have suffered considerable diminution in post-Independence India, there is little doubt that they wield considerable regional clout (though whether as benefactors or as terrorists would be a contested point), and police and politicians act in acknowledgment of this reality. Their influence is also borne out by the fact that many "criminal elements" enter electoral politics successfully.[6]

Hobsbawm holds that instances of banditry in later times are only "odd survivals" from a precapitalist period, and that they are provoked by the uneven development of capitalism or by other sudden disruptions of the social order. "En masse, they [social bandits] are little more than symptoms of crisis and tension in their society—of famine, pestilence, war or anything else that disrupts it" (1981, 24). Despite its persistence in South Asia and Latin America, "on the whole," he writes, "social banditry is a phenomenon of the past, though often of the very recent past. The modern world has killed it . . ." (24). If we accept this, we must regard, as many do, its occurrence in modern India solely as a survival.

For the modern Indian state dacoity is a severe embarrassment, not least because it is viewed as an anachronism in this sense. In most explanations dacoity figures as a custom with a long tradition, changed but with a persistence of "memory and habit of mind" that keeps the tradition alive (Jayprakash Narayan, cited in Sen 1993, 196), a remnant of a feudal past, in a part of India that has been overlooked in the development process. Geographical heart of darkness (inaccessible, hostile territory, harsh climate, drought); economic failure (industrial backwardness, lack of employment); social marginalization (feudalism, rigid caste-structures, local community justice): these are the plausible reasons offered for the continuation of dacoity into the modern present. All analysts of dacoity in contemporary India—including politicians—are willing to lay the blame for the phenomenon on the conditions of underdevelopment, hence a problem of administration rather than merely policing.

It is an article of faith of the postcolonial Indian state (as of its predecessor colonial government) that the premodern aspects of the nation must be brought into the fold of modernity by administration—through development, education, rule of law. But these aspects (whether dowry, sati, or dacoity), while appearing to be survivals, are instead considerably altered phenomena produced by and feeding into the circumstances of modern social and political realities. In the states of the Hindi belt the nexus of party, caste politics, and criminals is well known, as is also the fact that dacoits illegally acquire high-powered weaponry from police, military, and government arms factories. The notorious sandalwood smuggler Veerappan, operating in the southern states of Karnataka and Tamilnadu, skillfully uses the media to publicize his exploits and demands. This adaptability, and the pressures of contemporary Indian realpolitik, complicate the paradigms of both primitive rebellion and feudal survival, calling for a more radical revision of our understanding of dacoity in modern India.

One link in pursuit of such an understanding is with the colonial discourses and practices around the abolition and reform of *thuggee,* dacoity, and criminal tribes. The continuities between police practices in post-Independence India and their colonial nineteenth-century past was attested by Ayodhya Nath Pathak, the Deputy Inspector General (DIG) of police in Gwalior, when he suggested that Mala Sen read Francis Tuker's book on Henry Sleeman, the colonial police officer responsible for wiping out thugs in central India, because "We still use it as part of our syllabus in the Police academy, you know" (Sen 1993, 25).[7] Here, as elsewhere, colonial bureaucracy provides the systematized knowledge and understanding that the modern postcolonial state draws on for its own rules and strategies of government.[8] Sleeman's exploits constituted a subculture of police lore that, as much as the official protocols of law, informed the operations of the force in their work. At the same time, while the Indian police forces may demand "special legislation" to increase their powers, of the kind Henry Sleeman sought—such as the Prevention of Dacoity Act (which was in fact promulgated at the height of Phoolan's activities)— the postcolonial state can no longer draw on the reformist legitimation that empowered Sleeman's campaign against thuggee.[9] The tension between the police approach in apprehending dacoits and the political compulsions that recommend either coexistence (willfully turning a blind eye to their activities) or negotiation with them is a visible manifestation of the problem of the adoption of a simple law-and-order approach to their "abolition" by the modern state.

Developing the analogies with insurgency—or, broadly, political crime—is another productive or at least suggestive move.[10] In post-Independence India there have been and continue to be many kinds of insurgencies, secessionist movements, or movements for regional autonomy; Marxist-Leninist people's "war" groups; and other militant and revolutionary peasant groups, which use violence, mainly in guerrilla warfare and terrorism, to fight the state. Dacoity is not identical with these since its action is not directed at the state, for one thing, but at upper-caste men of property, and it is pursued as a way of life and a livelihood rather than followed as a political program. All the same it constitutes a challenge to the modern state as it invariably shades into, or is taken over by, political demands. The composition of dacoit gangs in recent times—predominantly men belonging to the lower castes, especially significant in Phoolan's and Vikram Mallah's gang—has given dacoit activity a distinct political aspect as underclass and caste resistance.[11]

It is often the case that it is *how* the state actually contends with the problem of civil strife that confers the status of "criminal" or "insurgent" on its adversaries rather than accordance with some pregiven definition of these types. In the case of terrorism, for instance, Paul Gilbert points out that "despite their constant insistence that terrorists are simply common criminals, states seldom consistently treat them as such": thus, for example, there are Prevention of Terrorism provisions, special extradition policies, refusal to prosecute for treason, and so forth that implicitly place (even as they resist placing) terrorists in a special political category (Gilbert 1994, 47). The legal understanding of dacoity as a criminal phenomenon is contradicted by the state's invocation of such special procedures in dealing with it—among them both the Anti-Dacoity Act and the engineering or acceptance of surrenders—based on the acknowledgment of the local realities of its status and practices in a different category, or at least a different register from that of "ordinary" crime.

In a complex argument, Upendra Baxi has avowed that in the postcolonial state the discourses of "development" and "criminality" are interlinked, the latter regarded as a concomitant of the former. While "progressive criminality" (as instanced by the Bhopal gas leak) is condoned as an aspect of development, "regressive criminality" (which refers to both economic crimes and certain "traditional" practices in need of reform or abolition: dacoity falls into both categories) is seen "to foil or frustrate the objectives of planned development." "Criminality" therefore is a "notion contingent on the very nature of class and formative practices through legislation and legal administration (enforcement, adjudication)" (1994, 55−57).

The state's power of naming "dacoity," or "terrorism," serves important functions for its institutional image. Naming the "terrorist" is a scapegoating technique, as William Connolly has argued, for covering the deficiencies of the advanced industrial state in the West (Connolly 1991, 207). In postcolonial India, the dacoit is a less unambiguous scapegoat for a state that, given the uneven development of constitutional rule—its use of force in counterinsurgency or anti-crime crackdowns has always to contend with the problem of legitimacy—seeks to disavow both the phenomenon itself and the use of force, as I will shortly elaborate.

Dacoity is thus suspended between crime and social crime, as well as social crime of the prepolitical kind and a more up-to-date model of terrorism/political insurgency/civil strife, and between developmental issues and electoral politics, placing it in a unique position for police and administrative agencies. The different contradictions it thereby poses for the state, both as a matter of naming and constructing it as a "problem" and in framing strategies for countering it, shed light on the specific politics of Phoolan Devi's surrender.

This brings us to the state's resolution of the conflict by negotiating a surrender. Was Phoolan's surrender a defeat or a victory, and whose?

Mala Sen's book gives a closely detailed account of the political background of the event. The government of Uttar Pradesh had escalated its attempts to put down dacoity in the state during the years of Phoolan Devi's activities, by promulgating an Anti-Dacoity Ordinance in 1981 that gave the police unlimited powers to arrest individuals on suspicion, while simultaneously intensifying operations to hunt dacoits down (there were schemes to flood the ravines, to train leopards to track them, to use aircraft to strafe them in hiding, and so forth, according to reports cited in Sen, 176). These measures led instead to police corruption and to the killing of innocent people in staged "encounters," against which protests were mounted.[12] The chief minister of the state, then V. P. Singh, having staked his reputation on eliminating the most notorious gangs—he was considered to have a personal stake since he was a Thakur himself and had lost his brother and his family to a dacoit attack—had no choice but to resign following the Behmai massacre and the killings in Dastampur. There was considerable friction between the police forces of Uttar Pradesh and neighboring Madhya Pradesh, and their morale was low. Malkhan Singh's surrender had been successfully arranged by the Madhya Pradesh police, and many dacoits began to consider giving themselves up. The Phoolan–Man Singh gang was running low on men and supplies and finding it hard to commit dacoities under such intense police surveillance. At the same time, the police felt that it would be impossible to catch Phoolan, given the vastness of the territory in which she could hide. Phoolan was tracked down by the superintendent of police of Madhya Pradesh, Rajendra Chaturvedi, a man trusted by the gangs operating in the region for having successfully arranged Malkhan Singh's surrender the previous year. After meeting with her several times over a long period—nearly a year—he persuaded her to accept the state's offer of amnesty ("The choice is between dying like a dog in the ravines or being hanged by a court"). Phoolan's surrender therefore came out of both parties' sense of impending defeat, but both could turn it to strategic account.

In the 1960s and the 1970s, Sen reminds us, the Gandhian leaders Vinoba Bhave and Jayprakash Narayan had persuaded large numbers of dacoits to surrender voluntarily in response to their call. These had been greatly admired moral conversions, coded in the language of reform and redemption and masterminded by respected national figures who were not themselves politicians. The climate of the 1980s was a vastly different one. Jayprakash espoused a Gandhian view of human nature and social transformation. But Gandhian interventions had become awkward for an independent Indian state that had set course on a different—modern statist—trajectory. (Jayprakash himself was anxious to defend the surrenders' philosophical basis for "change of heart" as an axiom of "modern penology"; Bhaduri 1972, 190.) In addition, there is a requirement of uniformity and predictability in the conduct of public affairs, especially in the rituals of the state, which makes cultural difference in itself a matter of embarrassment, even without the added imputation in this case of the government's inefficiency and failed toughness in matters of law and order. There was consequently no attempt—as how could there be?—to represent the surrenders of the 1980s as similar to the emotionally charged mass conversions of the earlier years, or as motivated by benevolence on the part of the government; they were an entirely pragmatic negotiation. The moral aura that had given the government its authoritative high ground as well as legitimized the surrenders by representing the dacoits as "converts" to the right way of life had by now entirely dissipated, rendering much more dubious the profit-loss calculus of this transaction.

However, a closer look at the events surrounding the surrenders to the Sarvodaya leader, Jayprakash Narayan, in the early 1970s, reveals them to have been a controversial development even then.[13] There was at the time considerable resistance from the police force to promising amnesty to the dacoits as a condition of their surrender.[14] But the main opposition came from the Congress party's chief minister of Madhya Pradesh, P. C. Sethi, to what he regarded as Jayprakash's upstaging of the state government's initiatives. Jayprakash was an opposition figure in politics and was soon to become a critic of Indira Gandhi's regime. Sethi complained frequently about the politics of the surrenders: the dacoits were being glamorized, Jayprakash had "smuggled in" BBC and news agency personnel to film the events,[15] the dividends paid by the show of force of his government's police was not given due credit, and so on.[16] Jayprakash went to the press to defend his intervention while also offering to withdraw from further participation.[17] Though such third-party intervention was absent in the negotiations in 1981 (it was the Madhya Pradesh police who took the initiative in contacting the dacoits and arranging their surrender, with the active backing of the state's Congress chief minister, who in turn was authorized by Prime Minister Indira Gandhi herself), there was still a different kind of murky politics around the event—notably caste politics in Uttar Pradesh, and the personality politics of the chief ministers of the two states and their relationship to the Center. The government of Madhya Pradesh scored political points for securing Phoolan Devi and put on a show of the surrender to highlight its success. Chief Minister Arjun Singh's prestige was never higher, and he continues to retain the loyalty of the dacoit constituency.[18] Given such a high degree of politicking around the issue, Phoolan appeared to be a puppet who was manipulated by various parties to their own ends. Kamini Jaiswal, Phoolan's lawyer during her jail term, was emphatic in her view that the surrender was no more than a "political gimmick" (personal communication).

Framed within such a perspective, one that would grant little initiative to Phoolan's leadership or at best would make her secondary in significance to her gang as an adversary of the state, how far would we be justified in viewing the female outlaw's career and its culminating surrender as a unique transaction between the individual historical woman and the impersonal state having implications for the question of postcolonial citizenship for women? Was she an agential subject in any meaningful way? Is the politics of her identity best understood in terms of her gender or her caste?

Let me address the last question first by way of a preliminary clarification. To separate Phoolan Devi's identity as lower-caste woman into its component parts, even for analytical purposes, is an unproductive exercise, since they are so constitutively interlinked. There is no doubt, however, that one or the other element could be played up by the different parties involved in projecting her persona and the problem she represented, not least by Phoolan herself. Thus caste certainly predominated in the internal politics of the hostility of the state government and the regional elite against her, and it consequently also provided the strength of her own mobilization of a following against her opponents (both as a gang leader and later as a political party candidate).

Her gendered identity was one that demanded negotiation in several contexts. That traditionally male bastion, the dacoit gang, accepted Phoolan's presence and her leadership in large part because she was their leader's mistress and also because an available cultural rationalization of women's vigilante violence is sexual vendetta. In a brief appendix on "Women and Banditry," Hobsbawm observed that "the most usual role of women in banditry is as lovers" (1981, 135), though women who are bandits themselves are celebrated in the myths and legends of many regions. The woman bandit, like the *serrena* (mountain woman) of Andalusia, "turns to outlawry in general and revenge on men in particular, because she has been 'dishonoured,' i.e. deflowered" (ibid.). Phoolan's career follows this general pattern, her dishonor being both (her) motive and (their, the community's) acceptable reason for her turn to lawlessness. In practice, her presence and role within Vikram Mallah's gang, and within the larger dacoit community and the villages of their operation, seems to have been naturalized by the quick and relatively easy acceptance of her resemblance to the legendary Putlibai or the goddess Durga (just as, at the other extreme, denigration of her was expressed by equally facile sexist abuse, for example, "Mallah whore"). Both Phoolan and Vikram played up her identification with the militant, fearful, avenging righteous female figures that were available within the repertoire of the culture, and there is no reason to think that it was not also deeply internalized. In the discourse of the impersonal modern state, however, this face-saving idiom was not permitted.

What was significantly absent in the official discourse, as well as in the media discourse at the time of her surrender and later of her release from jail, is any recognition of the events in Phoolan's life as *gender* issues of any significance, other than the routine acceptance that her actions were to be understood as "revenge" for the sexual violence she had been subjected to by upper-caste men in her village.[19] It was Mala Sen's book and, however problematically, the film *Bandit Queen* that first projected a "feminist" interpretation of Phoolan's story, foregrounding the humiliations she suffered—child marriage, police harassment, threats, rape, public stripping—as typical of lower-caste rural women's oppression. The media typically sought a feminized image of the female dacoit and was not slow in expressing disappointment in sexist terms: for example, "Phoolan means flower but the bandit queen who surrendered is neither delicate nor meek.

She is a short and tough woman" (*Times of India,* 13 February 1983). The politics of the image is, however, a separate issue.[20] What is relevant at this point is to note the active process of demythicization that her surrender initiated in the media, which seemed to involve mainly the offer of a "realistic" representation of her (lower-caste female) speech and appearance.[21] Following her surrender she was represented by activist women lawyers, first Kamini Jaiswal, who successfully petitioned the Supreme Court for her release in 1994, and then Indira Jaising, who represented her in the *Bandit Queen* controversy.

More crucially, for the state there was the *symbolic* significance of Phoolan's gender to contend with. The genderedness of the state as masculine and its role in gendering and sexualizing its citizens has been extensively argued, among others by Franzway, Court, and Connell. At the most general descriptive level, the state, they hold, is a patriarchal state, implicated in the "overall social advantaging of men and subordination of women," in part because "men have greater access to power in and through the state" (1989, 10). Further, the state is constituted within a "specialised 'public' realm marked out by sexual ideology and the sexual division of labour" (6–7). It is constituted in a realm "culturally marked as masculine": for example, the personnel of the state are predominantly male, especially at the higher levels, a fact that will have significance when I turn to the details of Phoolan's surrender negotiations.

But the state is not only "gender-structured," as Franzway et al. call it; a great deal of what it *does* is also gendered, especially in the legal system, police, courts, and prisons since the "process of criminalizing people is markedly gendered." The majority of criminals are men (just as the majority of welfare clientele are women) (9). (Women in prostitution are an interesting exception—they "meet" the state as criminals, but of an anomalous kind.) The genderedness of crime as male, and the actual fact that the great majority of criminals are men, is a necessary counterpart to the phallocentrism of the state, given that they are viewed in a structure of antagonism.[22] For the masculinity of the state must always be in evidence (however discreetly) for its authority to stick. It figures not only in the state's militaristic displays and in the rituals and paraphernalia of national symbols and ceremonies but also in the paternalism of its justice and welfare functions, in the professed objectivity and neutrality of its functioning, in the institutional supremacy and authority it represents: signs and claims everywhere simultaneously displayed and disavowed.

Therefore the embarrassment created by the successful *female* outlaw for the state (and for society) can be readily imagined. Phoolan's exploits threatened the state not only as a problem of law and as regional caste conflict but also as one of image. The failure of the Indian state—its government, political leaders, police—to capture her did not make it *look* good. Pressure for her capture was mounted most insistently, of course, by the Thakur community, powerful in Uttar Pradesh politics in the early 1980s. But the interest of the national media (with the international media never far away) was clearly in the sex war. That this encounter was widely perceived as one between a female outlaw and the male personnel of the state is evident in a detail from a newspaper report that Mala Sen quotes to highlight the popular disaffection about the government's amnesty to Phoolan: " . . . boys from the local students' union threw broken bangles towards the dais" (1993, 216). (Bangles are a symbol of womanhood, and they are offered to men as an insult to their manhood.) In her encounters with the police, Phoolan herself appears not to have been reticent about taunting them about their masculinity—this was an available script for defying the state's armed force, especially given Phoolan's own acceptance of traditional ways of conceptualizing male and female sexualities and gender roles.[23]

If we are to follow citizen-state transactions in the realm of politics and the everyday, the state must be viewed in terms of the actual contradictions of its institutions—interstate rivalries, political parties' conflicts, center-state relations, the relations between police, government, Parliament, judiciary—and in terms of its functionaries' status, provenance, attitudes, and attributes (which include to a significant extent their class, caste, and gender identities), as of its abstractions and symbolic centers. In this instance the figure of Rajendra Chaturvedi, superintendent of police of Madhya Pradesh, was a crucial agent in the procedures. Chaturvedi inspired trust because he was a middle-aged Brahmin man from Kashmir—his age, sex, official seniority, and distance from regional affiliations gave him prestige in Phoolan's eyes and provided the assurance of his neutrality. Chaturvedi's approach to Phoolan in persuading her to surrender was one of paternalistic condescension, familiarity, and even affection. The terms in which he most often referred to her while speaking to Mala Sen are those of hysterical woman, infant, or untamed animal. We move here from a politics of identity to a discourse of behavior, specifically gendered female, as Phoolan is reduced from outlaw woman at large to the more familiar figure of unruly female.

Phoolan was also responsive to calls of sisterhood. When Chaturvedi brought his wife to meet her, carrying food, he struck a chord; Kiran Bedi, at the time inspector-general of Tihar jail, was her supporter; most interesting of all were her feelings for Indira Gandhi, a combination of respect, identification, and the conviction that the prime minister as a woman herself had great sympathy for oppressed women. It was true that Gandhi had played a major role in Phoolan's surrender (both Arjun Singh and Chaturvedi himself had consulted her), and while this had primarily to do with wooing votes in the rural Uttar Pradesh–Madhya Pradesh belt, the prime minister's intervention did give Phoolan considerable clout while she was in jail.

There is little question therefore that Phoolan's sex had *relevance* in a variety of contexts and registers: for the myth of the Bandit Queen, for "politics" as such, for the representations of her in the media, for the image bestowed on the government that sought her capture, for providing a strategic psychological understanding of her for the surrender negotiations, for feminist politics. But the *significance* of Phoolan's identity as lower-caste woman who negotiated with the state following, and as a consequence of, a successful outlaw career requires some further exploration of the politics of her surrender. I do not mean by this to aggrandize her career and her role, or to offer the surrender as a romanticized confrontation between a female David and a Goliath state. On the contrary, granting all the ambiguity of "surrender" itself (how) does it nevertheless provide a space for viewing the transactions of the not-quite-not-citizen (woman/outlaw) with the state?

He [Chaturvedi] said . . . "Phoolan, we will make a human being out of you!" I asked, "Will you convert the UP police and make human beings out of them too?" Mala Sen, *India's Bandit Queen*

Phoolan set out the terms of her surrender, and once these were accepted the public event took place in Bhind, Madhya Pradesh, in the presence of the state's chief minister and other officials. Phoolan was then taken away to be lodged in Gwalior jail where she remained for most of the next eleven years until released by the orders of the Supreme Court. I want to explore here some aspects of the agreement.

The terms for the surrender were based on what Phoolan knew of earlier surrender agreements. They included: no death penalty; no trial in the Uttar Pradesh courts; settlement of her family with land and house in Madhya Pradesh; employment in the police force for her brother and brother-in-law; a prison term of no longer than eight years; rehabilitation in Madhya Pradesh after the jail term (Sen 1993, 212–13).[24] She also stipulated that the police would not be armed at the time of the surrender (to guard against the possibility of being shot "while trying to escape").

A negotiated surrender usually offers the edge to the dacoit over the state. The option to surrender at the culmination of a career in dacoity is one that is always in the cards for the dacoit as an attractive option to capture, while for the state it is a last resort.[25] For the duration of the negotiations Phoolan became not only the equal but the equivalent of the state, an external adversary rather than a local criminal. This was a moment of power, but also, let us note, only a moment. Once Phoolan gave herself up she had no further bargaining point, leaving all the power in the hands of the authorities. She had therefore to do her utmost to get the best possible terms for herself before surrendering. Where the surrender was a unique and final act for Phoolan, for the state it was only one in a series of possible moves. Thus, in these negotiations, the outlaw had the upper hand at the beginning but at the end lost the advantage to the state.

Various terms are loosely used to describe the negotiations: surrender, amnesty, treaty, all military in nature. The actual agreement appears to have been much more informal—it has been described as a "deal"—despite Phoolan's faith in the binding force of the written word.[26] The state most often negotiates with individuals precisely in the context of their criminality—when it seeks the approver's testimony, offers a plea bargain,[27] or negotiates with terrorists over hostages or ransoms. These are always fraught, contradictory, and contingent situations, though not lacking established procedural guidelines. The state's detractors would argue that (a) ideally it should not be "negotiating" with criminals in the first place, and (b) arguably it is not bound by its agreement with them once it has done so. The state (when not operating in secrecy) counters these objections by offering arguments about clemency, strategy, expediency, or "public interest" (as it may do under Section 321 of the Criminal Procedure Code). As a matter of expediency it is called on to honor such agreements in order to establish trust, though clearly it has some license in their observance. Phoolan was granted most of her demands; but her stay in jail extended well beyond the eight years she had stipulated, her family's fortunes were precarious, and she had to resort frequently to the services of her lawyer, the media, and her "contacts" and to staging scenes and riots in prison to get her demands accommodated.

The actual nature of Phoolan's judicial status continued to be that of a parolee on bail. The validity of the government's "deal" with her was constantly in doubt, as a matter of legality, expediency, and public opinion. Though it was reported that the Uttar Pradesh government had "dropped charges" against her at the behest of the Samajwadi party chief minister, Mulayam Singh, she still had fifty-five cases pending against her (for some of which, like the possession of arms, she had been tried, convicted, and had already served out a term while awaiting trial). In 1997 a warrant was issued against her in connection with the Behmai massacre (in which she was charged with twenty-two killings), and she went into hiding to avoid arrest. Mulayam Singh, by then Union defense minister, intervened to ask the Uttar Pradesh government to move a Special Leave Petition before the Supreme Court challenging the Allahabad High Court order that had issued the warrant for her arrest. Legally, no "amnesty" may be offered to a person charged with criminal offenses: she would have to stand trial, unless the government chose to withdraw charges. Or, following a trial and sentencing, there could be a presidential pardon. The validity and duration of Phoolan's freedom was a suspended question during her lifetime.[28]

Both legal and political issues were at stake in this complicated matter. Legally, the government did not have a free hand in dropping charges: it had to seek the court's permission to do so, and this might not always be forthcoming as a matter of course.[29] Politically, it had to balance the claims of the victims' rights (whose cause might be picked up by opposition political parties) and also judge the overall popular climate of feeling for or against the accused. This meant that

Phoolan's "freedom" was conditional, subject to the concerns—and whims—of a government in power (a situation that is contingent in a particularly acute way given that she was a figure in opposition politics).

The issues that emerged from this encounter were both large and small. The larger issue was that of the politics of civil violence, including dacoity, on which I have based the argument of this chapter. All forms of people's violent opposition—whether as organized crime, rioting, or insurgency—place the state in crisis. While among conservative sections it provokes questions about the state's responsibility for creating situations of lawlessness or for failing to restore the law, it also radically reopens the issue of the state's rights as the sole repository of the legitimate use of force to preserve law and order or punish. Even as crises authorize and consolidate such force, they question an authority that is grounded in it. If the state's "legitimate" use of force is open to question, its widespread *illegitimate* uses of it— through recourse to counterinsurgency tactics, "encounter" killings, police brutality, torture, other human rights abuses, corruption, the deployment of informers and spies, propaganda—make its constitutionality even more suspect, so that the state that seeks to preserve its liberal democratic credentials resorts to strenuous denial of such excesses.[30] At other times it seeks constitutional means to legitimize its excesses by declaring states of "emergency," suspending civil rights and laws of evidence and habeas corpus in order to contain opposition. Phoolan emerged at and created precisely such a point of crisis, challenging both the constitutional "pretension" of the Indian state and its force monopoly. Upendra Baxi, activist lawyer and legal theorist, holds that Phoolan's exploits demonstrated the citizen self-enforcement of constitutional rights and values "in ways that even the best genres of Euroamerican theorizing barely glimpse"[31] (personal communication).

The matter of the surrender brings us closer to the heart of the problem of the constitutionality of the state. What does it mean that the state is not constitutively, that is, constantly and at all times and equally, "legal" but is given to responding to contingent and imperative circumstances within a framework of legality—by taking on board "exceptional" considerations in securing outcomes? When rules of functioning are kept in abeyance the tension between the possible loss of discipline, authority, and principle on the one hand and the envisaged gains of flexibility and conflict resolution on the other provides insights into the pragmatics of rule.[32] More crucially, it is when a government offers to suspend hostilities that we become aware of the hostilities it unremittingly pursues through a continuing state of civil war with/within society.[33] Phoolan's surrender brought to visibility this normative Hobbesian nature of the state as a state of nature, as well as the conventions (not necessarily the laws) that regulate "lawful" citizenship.

The state intended the surrender to look like a way of bringing the outlaw in from the cold. It would reclaim *her* from the state of nature and reenter her into "society" by bestowing on her new (appropriately gendered) social identity, citizenship, livelihood, social function. The surrender had to be scripted as a public event in order that Phoolan could be *produced* to the public eye, brought out of the hiding that was the condition of her outlaw existence, and made visible as a citizen "like anyone else." (Momentarily only, for she had to be immediately consigned to hiding again in jail—where, however, the regime of surveillance would take over to maintain her as "visible" subject.) The politics of Phoolan as embodied (female) figure for the state was a matter of recasting her as newly minted subject, with all the appropriate social attributes of the lawful citizen. Her disempowerment had to be ritually enacted through the laying down of arms, the gestures of abjection, and her very *appearance*—in both senses of the word.

The rule-of-law state had to produce a *spectacular* surrender also as a public relations exercise (the "political gimmick"): it had to overcome criticism and gain points for ending the career of Phoolan and her gang by producing the "reformed" subject of its endeavors to capture and convert her. For the actual event the script had to be improvised to some extent (since surrenders are not everyday events). As happens in many such state-sponsored events, chaos reigned, there was confusion and unruly crowd behavior, and the police were anxious not only about protocol but about the safety of all the participants, the members of the gang and the vips present.[34]

Phoolan was groomed for her role, provided crisp khakis to wear, coached in protocol, and the props were provided (pictures of Gandhi and the goddess Durga to whom she would give up her arms). Surrender had to be coded as a performative: "I surrender." But

Phoolan also turned it into a performance. She too resorted to the public forum as an opportunity to (re-) present herself, undoubtedly helped in this by the event's confused, improvised script. Both parties sought to upstage the other, but there was no doubt that the crowd of some seven thousand, including the media, was there to see Phoolan. Sen reports Phoolan's "theatrical humility" before the chief minister, garlanding him, bowing to him, and laying her arms at his feet (215). This was also—not incidentally—the first and the last time Phoolan would be publicly seen in the khaki police uniform and red bandanna she wore as an outlaw (afterward she appeared only in the sari). A journalistic description of her at the surrender typically remarked on her "short, snub-nosed figure in a dirty, ill-fitting khaki uniform," a "boyish figure in a headband who looked more like a youthful *pahari chowkidar* than the Anarkali of legend" (Thakur 1995, 69). This androgynous cross-dressed figure was subversive in the performative sense that Judith Butler describes: "The structure of impersonation reveals one of the key fabricating mechanisms through which the social construction of gender takes place . . . drag fully subverts the distinction between inner and outer psychic space and effectively mocks both the expressive model of gender and the notion of a true gender identity" (1990, 136–37).[35] Though her appearance in outlaw guise was sanctioned, indeed required, by the surrender script, Phoolan's enactment of the cameo role of the female outlaw as androgynous armed figure has remained as the indelible image of her myth. To her disappointment she was given no speaking role, but she faced the crowd momentarily, arms upraised with her rifle held aloft. This was the image that came to represent her.

I end this chapter about Phoolan Devi's surrender with a moral—actually two (different) morals—in lieu of a conclusion.

One: Phoolan sought out the nation-space—its structures of state, police, judiciary, public figures, and the media—to negotiate freedom and justice for herself. This observation does not undermine the indictment of constitutional democracy in India that has been the thrust of this chapter and served as the sustained focus of the book as a whole—the indictment of vote politics, police criminality and terrorism, the dubious legalism of "negotiations," and the state's "production" of the outlaw. (I use "production" in all the senses of the word: responsibility for the conditions of civil unrest, the governmental construction of the name and category of criminality, and the public display of Phoolan at the surrender.) But it was nevertheless the state's resources that offered the route to Phoolan's escape from her village and community, from her local reputation, the local feuds, her immutable social status there[36]—to the abstract entitlements of nation-state citizenship as guarantor of justice, and to larger and different opportunities.[37] Law and the rights of citizenship, deeply, even constitutively, flawed though they may be as structures of egalitarianism and justice, are nevertheless an *option* available to those who have been traditionally denied them under conditions of long-standing oppression. It is an option that may be and has been exercised under varied circumstances, and not one that we would want to do without. Gayatri Spivak concedes that "citizenship" is "indeed the symbolic circuit of the mobilizing of subalternity into hegemony" (1999b, 309). The perspective of the subaltern reminds us that the critique of the "nation-state," as such, must also be located in the context of specific histories and viewed in relation to alternative (local, community) structures of regulation and rule. Pranab Bardhan has pointed out that, as community structures and local justice collapse, and local overlords' traditional patronage functions shrink in the modern postcolonial state, the people make appeals to "supra-local authorities for conflict resolution, arbitration and protection" (1997, 190). Phoolan's career describes one such trajectory, circuitously, via outlawry.

Two: Phoolan ensured her own and her family's safety, secured employment for her brother and brother-in-law, and some assurance for her livelihood through her negotiations. But it is not her exceptional "luck" that I wish to convey so much as the ironic moral of her story. For what she secured was survival, that is, escape from the death penalty, and the means of livelihood. We must see this not as something she managed to get despite being an outlaw but rather as something *to get which* she had to become an outlaw. As a reflection on citizenship and the inequalities of access to its privileges for the poor dalit woman in India, hers is a powerful and ironic parable.

Postscript

Phoolan Devi was murdered on July 25, 2001, shot by unknown assailants outside her official New Delhi residence. I have not recast any part of this chapter, written and sent to press before this date, in light of her death in this manner. It does not significantly alter the chapter's argument, which is based on accounts of an earlier period of her life. All the same this fact does of course add to the powerful irony of her life story. I would particularly not wish any simplistic "moral" about "justice" to usurp the morals with which I concluded. The nature of her violent death is a commentary as much on the lax security maintained by the Indian police as on the piety of truisms such as "those who live by the sword die by the sword."

Notes

Preface

1 An early article that I co-wrote, "Shahbano," was received by U.S. academic feminism as an instance of feminist "theorizing" of the "political" (the title of Butler and Scott's 1992 volume, in which it was reprinted). Writing about Shahbano in the wake of the passage of the Muslim Women's (Protection in Divorce) Act 1986, we had located female legal subjectivity as the theoretical problem at the heart of our analysis (Pathak and Sunder Rajan 1989).

1 Introduction

1 Several essays in *Recasting Women* describe these processes. See Sangari and Vaid 1989. Also see Tanika Sarkar 1996.

2 According to the Human Development Report released in June 2000, India ranks 128th on the Human Development index in the report's ranking of 174 countries. The index is based on three categories: health and mortality, education, and standard of living. The report commends the participation of Indian women in local politics as a result of 33 percent reservation of seats for them in panchayats (local councils) but notes that much still needs to be done to overcome social prejudice, especially in the area of schooling. The literacy rate for women is only 39 percent (against overall literacy of 52 percent), which is further lowered in the case of Scheduled Castes and Tribes to 18 percent.

3 Following the CSWI report, the government sponsored a report on women in the unorganized sector, headed by Ela Bhatt, which resulted in the Shram Shakti report of 1988. The National Perspective Plan for Women (1988–2000) followed. The National Commission for Women was set up in 1992. The government has recently formulated a National Policy for the Empowerment

of Women (2001), which incorporates many of the demands and objectives and deploys many of the assumptions of the women's movement over the past three decades.

4   While it is important not to collapse the feminist demands for equality and justice for women into the state's and international agencies' arguments for promoting women's welfare and "empowerment"—the former in the interests of women and in the language of entitlements, the latter primarily as instrumental to an agenda of national development—at the same time, to overlook the continuities and convergences between the two discourses or the possible cumulative effects of their impact would mark a loss for feminist analysis and strategic endeavors.

5   Nationalism and citizenship are distinguished by Yuval-Davis and Werbner in terms of their different temporalizing tendencies. While nationalism looks to the past, privileges "origin and culture," valorizes shared myths, and fosters deep passions, citizenship of the nation-state is a "thoroughly modern invention," "jural, cerebral, procedural," geared "towards the future, to common destinies" (1999, 2–3).

6   Niraja Gopal Jayal writes that "the uniqueness of historical trajectories [of each nation] encourages us to look beyond the purely formal attributes of the state to its cultural and symbolic specificities" (1999, 11). She suggests that, for instance, "the separation between the public and the private spheres, which is a theoretical requirement to speak of the state in the Western context, is inadequate to interpret the non-Western experience," so that we are called upon to study it in terms of "cultural processes, symbols, and rituals" (ibid.).

7   On the idea of nationalist thought as a "derivative discourse" see Chatterjee 1986. On the "illegitimacy of nationalism," as such, but with particular reference to colonial India, see Nandy 1994. "Catachresis" is used by Gayatri Spivak to describe those "regulative political concepts"—"nationhood, constitutionality, citizenship, democracy, socialism, even culturalism"—that are derived from imperialism. Though strictly they have no "historically adequate referent in postcolonial space," Spivak would maintain that they are "urgent" political claims (Spivak 1990, 794). For a defense of democracy in postcolonial nations, see Amartya Sen's *Development as Freedom* (1999), especially chapter 6.

8   Thus, broadly, India has moved through anticolonial, Nehruvian, and Hindutva-inspired nationalisms, the historical connections and differences among which are worth pursuing. The many regional and secessionist movements in the country have also posited subnationalisms.

9   Myron Weiner, writing about the large-scale neglect of Indian children by the state, notes with wonderment that the constitution, laws, government documents, and official policy nevertheless resound with commitment to their well-being and universal education. Quoting Upendra Baxi, he concludes that in India, "law has a symbolic value of setting norms, but there is little concern with law as a means of inducing compliance" (1991, 204). Laws on social issues are, he observes, "statements of intentions, and the words used in the legisla-

tion are a kind of modern talisman intended to bring results by the magical power of the words themselves. The legislation demonstrates that one is committed to all that is modern and progressive, and if the laws are not enforced the fault lies not with the legislators or bureaucrats but with a society that is not responsive to the law's injunction" (205).

10 To clarify the politics of this left-liberal alliance: if at this historical juncture the left supports a broadly liberal position on the state, it is less in the context of communitarian claims than in opposition to the regime of an economic liberalization that seeks to "roll back the state" on behalf of the free play of the market and divert it from its earlier socialist agendas and welfare commitments.

11 The classic statement about women's liberation as the "longest revolution" is, of course, Juliet Mitchell's. As she envisages it, it involves nothing less than the "long passage from Nature to culture," which is "the definition of history and society" (1966/84, 54).

12 MacKinnon's objections to these two hegemonic and influential positions are expressed in symmetrical terms: "Applied to women, liberalism has supported state intervention on behalf of women as abstract persons with abstract rights, without scrutinizing the content of these notions in gendered terms. Marxism applied to women is always on the edge of counseling abdication of the state as an arena altogether—and with it those women whom the state does not ignore or who are, as yet, in no position to ignore it. Feminism has so far accepted these constraints upon its alternatives: either the state, as primary tool of women's betterment and status transformation, without analysis (hence strategy) for it as male; or civil society, which for women has more closely resembled a state of nature. The state, and with it the law, has been either omnipotent or impotent: everything or nothing" (1983, 643).

13 Like other feminist academic critiques in the '70s and '80s, feminist political theorists initially focused on the trivialization and subordination of women, and often the active misogyny, in the work of the major (male) political philosophers of the Western tradition, Aristotle, Locke, Hobbes, Rousseau, Hegel, Mill, Rawls. See especially Okin 1979, Lloyd 1984, Coole 1988.

14 See Coole 1988, 253. Coole reviews early British Marxist-feminist positions in chapter 10. See also Barrett 1980, 231–37.

15 "Strategic essentialism" is the phrase made famous by Spivak (1987, 202–11). It is to be viewed, I think, less as a "weak theoretical compromise," as Satya Mohanty dubs it (1998, 232), than as a specifically deconstructive move performed within a constrained situation.

16 Women are not a "minority" in the same sense as other minorities, not only in the numerical sense but also in their "situation." As Susan Wolf points out: "While the predominant demand for recognition in multicultural contexts is the demand to have one's culture and one's cultural identity recognized as such. . . , the question of whether and how significantly and with what meaning one wants to be recognized as a woman is itself a matter of deep contention." This is because "there is not a clear, or a clearly desirable, separate cultural

heritage by which to redefine and reinterpret what it is to have an identity as a woman" (1994, 76).

17 This is cited in Lama-Rewal 2001, 1436. She also cites Kaka Kalekar, in the National Backward Classes Commission report of 1953, in which he concedes that women are also a "backward class"—but "since they do not form a separate community," it is hard to list them among the other backward classes for purposes of administrative affirmative action (1437).

18 The most notable proponent of the first kind of position is Carol Smart (1989); for a detailed consideration of feminist debates on the issue in the West, which ends with unambiguous support for feminist rights struggles, see Kiss 1997.

19 Hall (like Paul Gilroy) is responding to Raymond Williams's position: that the state's initiatives are only reflections of ruling-class interests (a classical Marxist position), and that "cultural" nationalism—a form of belonging to the "organic community"—is a more profoundly real identity than the state-secured formal, legal citizenship that black migrants obtain (a position deriving from Williams's romanticism) (Williams 1983, 195; all cited in Bennett 1998, 26).

20 Women's exclusion from citizenship, Yuval-Davis and Werbner suggest, following Pateman, "was an intrinsic feature of their naturalisation as embodiments of the private, the familial and the emotional." They mark this as an inaugural moment—and "one of the great paradoxes"—of modernity. It was following the French Revolution that women "lost their civil, economic, and political role in the emergent public sphere and were relegated to the familial, private sphere" (1999, 6).

21 On this, see Okin 1979. She points out that in the U.S. Constitution, "person" did not automatically include women until 1971, when the U.S. Supreme Court held a sex-based classification to be unconstitutional (248). Until 1968, women were also excluded from jury service, long considered one of the basic rights and obligations of citizenship (261).

22 In 1980 women's groups all over the country mobilized around the case of Mathura, a young woman raped in custody by police in Maharashtra state. Four prominent lawyers had written a joint open letter protesting the judgment in this case, which provided the impetus for this unprecedented coming together of different women's groups around the issue. They demanded a retrial of the case and major reforms in rape laws.

23 These included, in the '80s, reformed laws against dowry, rape, prenatal diagnostic techniques, domestic violence, primarily "bride-burning," as well as the following: the Immoral Traffic (Prevention) Act, the Indecent Representation of Women Act (1986), and the Commission of Sati (Prevention) Act (1988). See Agnes 1997. A Domestic Violence Prevention Bill has also been proposed.

24 Naila Kabeer has usefully traced the emergence of women as a constituency in development discourse and policy, with varying emphases, from the 1970s to the 1990s (1995).

25 Amartya Sen's insistence that "women . . . [are] active agents of change: the dynamic promoters of social transformations that can alter the lives of *both*

women and men" (1999, 189) has been influential. See, especially, chapter 8. See also Dreze and Sen 1995, especially chapter 7.

26 According to Ela Bhatt, "women are better managers and assets are safer in their hands." When 800 families changed land ownership to women's names, "not an inch of that land [was] sold." Further, "when a woman earns, she spends 90 per cent of it on the family, but men spend only 40 per cent." Reported in Singh 1996. See also 1999.

27 There is a largely culturalist explanation advanced by Yuval-Davis and Werbner to specify "Southern" women's participation in social and political life: that they "often command enormous women-specific cultural capital of a kind not readily available to their Western bourgeois counterparts" (1999, 8). Werbner argues that in postcolonial nations "women's active citizenship often starts from pre-established cultural domains of female power and rightful ownership or responsibility. . . . they can exercise their rightful claims *vis-à-vis* male members of their families while sustaining viable female cultural worlds. They can also draw upon indigenous traditions of cultural resistance and a strong sense of family and community" (26–27). Such romantic perceptions about "Third World women" seem to have been fostered by their substantial presence at the Beijing conference and by the solidarity and vigor with which they represented their views there. True, (all) women's forms of protest begin with what they have, but it is reductive to attribute protest itself to indigenous cultural spaces and forms. And there are equally, if not more, powerful cultural (as well as authoritarian/military/political) forces that inhibit protest in these parts of the world.

28 By "Indian feminism"—though the word "feminism" itself may be used with some caution because of its "alien" provenance—I refer loosely to a phenomenon that is recognizable as a political and intellectual force in the nation (though of course by no means clearly defined, unitary, or overwhelmingly influential), committed to combating gender discrimination and oppression in the social, economic, political, and cultural spheres. Women's organizations (of different persuasions) in policy institutions and smaller autonomous groups and within other social movements, institutional women's studies, academic research, theory and criticism, literary, art, film and theater endeavors have all been informed by a transformative feminist agenda. The fact of women's own initiatives, leadership, participation in contemporary Indian feminism is a feature that must (loosely) distinguish this phenomenon from the earlier as well as present-day concern for the "reform" of women's status, usually led by male political leaders or social reformers.

29 Indian feminists have begun to systematically analyze the reasons for this hiatus in activism only recently, attributing it variously to complacency, nationalist self-abnegation, optimism in the state, short-sightedness, and the liberal faith of prominent women activists in the Nehruvian promises of the early years. See, especially, Banerjee 1998, WS 6–7; Buch 1998, WS 20. Vina Mazumdar (1999) has written a candid and revelatory first-person account of the

evolution of the women's movement from the early years of independence into the second phase, evoking the "exhilaration" of the initial feeling that "the movement had achieved its objective" with the independence of the nation (343), and the subsequent disillusionment in those promises.

30 The issues around which women mobilized in this period included rape, dowry, dowry-deaths, price rise, contraception. See Gandhi and Shah 1991. On the CSWI report's insights and impact, see Mazumdar 1999.

31 For an overview of the women's movement's trends, issues, debates, and personalities in the '90s, see the informative article in *India Today* by Sengupta and Friese (1995).

32 See, especially, Tharu and Niranjana 1999; N. Menon 1996.

33 This is made explicit in Nivedita Menon's review (1999 b) of a collection of essays prepared in honor of Lotika Sarkar.

34 The opposition to obscenity laws has been forcefully articulated by Madhu Kishwar and Ruth Vanita (1986). Lotika Sarkar, a feminist legal scholar, opposed transferring the onus of proof to the accused in all cases of rape when it was proposed in 1981, arguing: "Do you want to hand over such power to the government, just after we have come out of Emergency? Don't you realise that such power could be used to stifle all dissent?" (reported in Mazumdar 1999). The National Commission of Women in its report "Rape: A Legal Study" (2000) opposed the death penalty for rape on the grounds that the rate of conviction, already as low as 4 percent, was likely to decrease further given such an irrevocable penalty (see "NCW Study Not for Death Penalty in Rape Cases," *The Hindu,* 4 April 2000, 4). See also Ramanathan 1998, and Sharma 1998, on the dangers of allowing the death penalty, written in response to Home Minister L. K. Advani's proposal advocating this measure.

35 The most extended consideration of law and women's struggles for social change in India is to be found in Ratna Kapur and Brenda Cossman's book *Subversive Sites* (1996). On the specific question of legal equality, see their essay "On Women, Equality and the Constitution" (1993).

36 There is currently much interest, though not as yet clarity, on the potential of transnational alliances. These alliances are created for the most part at international forums, and examples include the solidarity forged between a dalit women's NGO and black women at the Beijing conference, noted in Mencher (1999, 2085–86). International forums and alliances are achieved by other means as well: networking among NGO's, increasingly referred to as constituting an "international civil society"; the influence of international human rights organizations and the United Nations in getting universal human rights norms accepted; the success of organizations like SEWA in getting recognition of home-based workers via the ILO, in 1996, bypassing national legislation (the ILO Convention has force of law) (Bhatt 1999, 37). These are examples that still need to be consolidated into a theory, politics, organized praxis, and proper evaluation.

37 In 1992 Bhanwari Devi, a sathin active in fighting the prevalent child-marriage customs in her village, was raped by upper-caste men as a warning against

interference in local customs. The police first refused to register the case (leading to a delay in the medical examination), and the Sessions Court judgment subsequently acquitted the accused on the grounds that upper-caste men would not rape a lower-caste woman under the circumstances described. A long legal struggle by Bhanwari, helped by women's groups, led to the overturning of the judgment in the higher court.

38 Joan Mencher suggests that NGOs too should not be asking "the people to be responsible for those activities which should rightly be the responsibility of the government" (1999, 2086).

2 The "Ameena Case"

I am grateful to all those who responded so valuably to earlier versions of this chapter, in text and speech: Judith Plotz, whose lifelong interest in the child as subject, vast scholarship in Romantic childhood, and unremitting interest in my work led me to the subject of this chapter in the first place; Suvir Kaul, for editorial inputs for the version that appeared in *Oxford Literary Review;* Lee Schlesinger, for the disagreements and challenges expressed at my presentation at the University of Michigan; Arjun Appadurai, for posing questions about the construction of "childhood," at the South Asia forum at the University of Chicago; Cora Kaplan and Bruce Robbins, for inviting me to present the paper at Rutgers University and pursuing its arguments with an authority and skill that left me far behind; Paroma Roy, for her comments as respondent at the University of California, Berkeley presentation, especially for drawing upon "Shahbano" for comparison; Gayatri Spivak, for inviting me to present the paper at Columbia University's Gender Studies forum and there responding to the paper with her usual erudition and enthusiasm.

1 For a more comprehensive discussion of the controversy over a Uniform Civil Code, see chapter 5, "Women Between Community and State."

2 For the foregoing account I have availed of reports appearing in several English-language newspapers and weekly papers: *The Times of India, Tribune, The Indian Express, The Hindu, The Hindustan Times, The Telegraph, The Sunday Observer.* I have not indicated specific sources where there were no bylines given, or where all the newspapers only carried similar reports of events.

3 For more extended discussion of the Shahbano case, see Pathak and Sunder Rajan 1989, 558–82.

4 One reviewer of *Night of the New Moon* compares Jung's Ameena to an Eliza Doolittle: see Kazmi (1993).

5 Many of these details are reported in Sheriff 1993b.

6 The account forms part of a survey called "Where Are They Now?" and covers victims of other national scandals: the Bhagalpur blinded; the poor tribal girl, Banita, who was sold off for Rs 40; Maya Tyagi, whose rape led to a long trial and conviction of her police rapists; and Rajiv Goswami, a student leader who attempted self-immolation in the anti-Mandal agitations. See Mitta 1995.

7 I borrow the word "sightings" from Jennifer Wicke (1988), who uses it to

describe the "discovery" of wolf-children. Following the discovery of Kamala, the "wild" child, found in a wolf's den outside Midnapore in 1920, there were a spate of such reports of wild children, she points out. "Sightings of wild/wolf children are always *motivated*," Wicke argues, observing that they "generally occur in clusters when wild children themselves address some ideological gap or turbulence" (117; emphasis added). In the manner of such occurrences Ameena's sensational "rescue" was no sooner reported than a rash of similar or identical stories began to appear in the press, of Muslim child brides or little Muslim camel-drivers being sold to Arabs. During the time that the Ameena case occupied the national attention—almost a year—other cases of a similar nature came in for periodic media attention. Rukhshana Begum had been stopped by Bombay police at the airport on her way to Abu Dhabi with a forty-four-year-old Arab on 4 August 1991, just before the Ameena episode, though the incident came to light only after it; fifteen-year-old Fatima was rescued from a forty-five-year-old Afghan in June the following year. There was an unconfirmed report that another young "bride" had been allowed to leave the country with a forty-eight-year-old Saudi: it was alleged that there was a "racket in girl-running" at the Delhi airport and that "the police were involved in it." In the same month, police stopped several small boys at the Delhi airport and discovered that they had been sold to middlemen who were taking them to Dubai to ride in camel races. This incident also created a furor in Parliament and the press. In December 1993 the "rescue" by New Delhi police of a sixteen-year-old Muslim girl, Kaneez, from a thirty-five-year-old Saudi Arabian national was widely publicized. There is no doubt, as Wicke suggests, that it is an "increased sensitivity" to their "possible finding" that produces the "actual examples"; but more intriguing still is the mode of accommodation of the episodes within a given "ideological spectrum." Kamala's incorporation within the historical moment of incipient Indian nationalism, a beleaguered cultural imperialism, and the development of U.S. behavioral psychology in the 1920s (113–27) corresponds to the fraught years between the Shahbano and Ayodhya crises, as I have suggested.

8   Pathak and Sunder Rajan 1989, 563–65.

9   A poem by Sunanda Swarup, called "Ameena," expresses this sentiment of anticlimax as follows: "Sold off as a child bride/To an aged Arab-/Accidental rescue/to an inane existence-/miraculous, mere ink for the reams" (1997).

10 See also Tavleen Singh (1994). Singh criticizes the Muslim weekly *Radiance* for its justification of Muslim child marriage on the grounds that it is preferable to premarital sex: "This does not help the image of Islam." Singh's scolding is, of course, also symptomatic of the self-righteousness of the English-language press about its "secular" credentials.

11 This does not continue to be the case. It is important to note historical changes in the English-language press with regard to its secular progressiveness. The English press, during and since the Mandal and Ayodhya crises, ceased toeing an undifferentiated "secular" line; on the contrary, some of the most influential

ideologues of the anti-Mandal and pro-Hindutva positions are now identified with English-language publications.

12 A study of coverage of women's issues in the press in 1993 revealed that crimes against women or sensational incidents "are the favoured topics of most newspapers" (56.15 percent of all such stories), and "there is almost never any follow up." See Prasad 1993.

13 For an argument that traces historical changes in the English media's position on feminism, see Maitrayee Chaudhuri, who points out that in the '70s and '80s "there was an overt stated position of consensus and agreement that gender equality was desirable on the agenda of both the national movement and the state," which has now given way to a populist "hostility" (2000, 263–64). Earlier reforms, like the Mathura rape case, and even Shahbano, were greatly aided by press campaigns, as Usha Ramanathan urged me to remember. Not only is that so, but some of the best, most responsible, and politically engaged writing on women's issues continues to appear in the national newspapers, under the bylines of journalists like Kalpana Sharma, Seema Mustafa, Mrinal Pande, and others.

14 Shahbano's husband, in contrast, as representative of Indian Muslim husbands, aroused the envious wrath of Hindutva men for having the legal right to marry four wives and to divorce by pronouncement of the triple *talaq,* unilateral verbal divorce.

15 See Pathak and Sunder Rajan (1989) for a theoretical elaboration of the concept of protection, especially 565–70.

16 See chapter 3, "Beyond the Hysterectomies Scandal," for a longer discussion of the Indian state's welfare provisions, and especially of the conditions prevalent in state-run custodial institutions.

17 Both Fatima and Kaneez, rescued brides similarly placed in Nari Niketans, were to express the wish to return to their husbands simply in order to be let out of these "homes." Fatima said, "I had been in that terrible place for three days. I was a little scared they would not send me back to Calcutta [her home]. . . . The thought of staying in Nari Niketan forever horrified me and I believed the only way out was to go to Kabul [with her husband]" (*Indian Express,* 28 June 1992). Eventually both were released to their parents.

18 It is not an appropriate response even in cases of infanticide, as I point out in chapter 6, "Children of the State?"

19 Follow-up reports on the Ameena affair suggest that the aftermath of the publicity has been difficult for the family. Ameena is blamed for having brought disrepute to the family and creating a host of difficulties, including the criminal case against her parents.

20 India adopted a National Policy on Children in 1974, according to which the nurture and solicitude of children is the responsibility of the state. In 1986 the Juvenile Justice Act was passed, in line with the United Nations' Declaration of the Rights of the Child (India was the first country to adopt it), but it has no specific law against child trafficking. This act has now been amended as the

Juvenile Justice (Care and Protection of Children) Act of 2000 and includes revised guidelines on adoption. Adoption is regulated by a Central Adoption Resource Agency. There are too few social workers to keep tabs on destitute children, and, usually, if they are brought before a juvenile welfare board at all, it is because the police have rounded them up. According to figures I have been able to glean there are about 450 day care centers and about 60 institutions for the care of "street children."

21 The judgment was reported in detail in the *Times of India,* 13 March 1992.

22 For an eloquent and theoretically complex discussion of the female "object of property" see Patricia J. Williams, "On Being the Object of Property," in Williams 1991, 216–38.

23 What "Ameena," like "Shahbano" earlier, refuses in this instance is representation in terms of the unitary, homogeneous citizen-subject. As Chantal Mouffe puts it, "the social agent is [instead] constituted by an ensemble of 'subject positions' that can never be totally fixed in a closed system of differences, constructed by a diversity of discourses among which there is no necessary relation, but a constant movement of overdetermination and displacement. The 'identity' of such a multiple and contradictory subject is therefore always contingent and precarious, temporarily fixed at the intersection of those subject positions and dependent on specific forms of identification" (1992, 372).

24 Jacqui Alexander identifies "the ideological manipulation of the terrain of consent" as an important area for consideration (1991, 150; see also 141–42).

25 Brinda Karat of the JMS had demanded a drive by the state to get other evidence in the case against the Saudi. "But," she commented, "the inadequate inquiry had left the entire burden of proof on this young girl's shoulders. Clearly it was too much for her. This is the key point in the case" (*Times of India,* 18 November 1992).

26 The Ameena case in these respects offers a contrast to the notorious Phulmani case in 1890, which had led to the campaign for raising the age of consent from ten to twelve. Phulmani, a child wife, died as a result of brutal intercourse; her husband was exonerated of the charge of culpable homicide, and the evidence of the women in her family was dismissed. See T. Sarkar 1996, 225–29.

27 I pose this question in a review essay of the landmark volume *Social Reform, Sexuality, and the State,* edited by Patricia Uberoi, as follows: "Have we reached the end of 'social reform,' as such, in India (particularly in a climate where 'reform' is a term attached to the economic regime of liberalization)? How do we regard moves such as Mandal in the context of electoral politics, when it is the political party rather than the state that proposes large-scale social engineering? What is the efficacy of the 'new social movements'—the activism of oppressed groups themselves? Why reform, instead of revolution, as the means of national historical transformation? How are other contemporary women's issues—work, political representation, legal identity—linked to the question of female sexuality?" (1998, 128).

28 Not only did other communities, lower-caste Hindus, and tribal communities

in general have a higher marriage age for girls, they also permitted widow remarriage, the prohibition of which was a factor in the concern over upper-caste Hindu child marriages.

29 "Every fifth Hindu female was a widow," as a result of early marriage, according to the Census of 1891, and since Hindu widows' remarriage was not permitted by custom, the problem of regulating their sexuality was invoked to advocate a later age of marriage. See Nair 1996a, 166–67.

30 I have also drawn on other sources for this account: Kalpagam 1992, and Heimsath 1961.

31 Madhu Kishwar, journalist and feminist activist, in a mediawatch program on television, pointed out the distortions and inaccuracies of the Kaneez story that appeared in several newspaper reports (*Newswatch,* Doordarshan, 3 January 1994). Kaneez's point of view was subsequently carried in *Hindustan Times* (6 January 1994): she said she was "shocked at the way her name and photograph were splashed all over the country." The police, too, distorted her story, she claimed. Vir Sanghvi has argued that the Kaneez story was communalized in a way that Ameena escaped (1994, 8–9).

32 The bride's right to annul the marriage after reaching puberty is an ostensible safeguard against "coercion." In Hindu custom the "safeguard" is that the wedding itself is supposed to be only a form of betrothal, actual cohabitation beginning only after puberty is reached. In both situations, however, breaches in custom are frequent.

33 The discrepancy between the two measures of female "maturity," puberty being reached far earlier than the legal age of eighteen, leads to piquant and potentially disturbing legal decisions, as another recent controversy highlights. The case of Sashikala, an unmarried sixteen-year-old pregnant girl whose father sought medical termination of her pregnancy, was ruled on by the Madras High Court on 2 December 1993. In what has come to be termed a "landmark judgement," the court held that "a minor girl has the right to bear children." While the father held that the girl was both "legally and otherwise too young to take the decision to bear the child," the public prosecutor argued that "in the Indian Constitution there was no distinction between 'minor' and 'major' in so far as fundamental rights were concerned." The fundamental right in question was the "right to privacy" (under which she claimed the right to bear the child). The court agreed with the argument and also quoted English and U.S. laws on the rights of minors; the case laws held that "in the case of a mature and understanding minor the opinion of the parent or guardian was not relevant." Since the girl was "confident of facing life after the delivery of the child," her decision would be respected. It was clear, in this instance, that the judge was motivated by pro-life sentiments. Thus it is not only legal but also a matter of "right" for a girl to bear children at an age when it would be illegal for her to marry. (*Hindustan Times,* 3 December 1992.)

34 I would suggest that the postcolonial state, in this respect, is *both* external to the people (in its modernizing project) *and* internal to society (in its solicitude for

custom), defining a certain conjuncture in the concept of government in Foucault's sense (Foucault 1991, 91).

35 Only seven of the fifteen major states show a higher average marriage age of over eighteen. The most backward states in this respect are Madhya Pradesh, Rajasthan, Andhra Pradesh, and Bihar (Rustagi 2000, 4281).

36 These had been among the proposals announced by the Andhra Pradesh Wakf board minister, Mohammed Ali Shabbir, following the Ameena case. In Muslim marriages, he suggested that the *kazi* (priest) demand a birth certificate in the case of marriage with a foreign national, and also that the Wakf maintain a record of such weddings. The proposals were met with overwhelming scorn in the community (Sheriff 1993a).

37 For example, in 1997 there was a news report about the marriage of another Hyderabad Muslim girl, Massarath, who by the age of fourteen had been married off by her father to three Arabs within two months. Her mother, Shaheda Begum, finally reported the matter to the police, helped by feminist activist lawyers and social workers (Shanker 1997).

38 The bigamy rate among Muslims (Muslim men may marry up to four wives) is actually lower than among Hindus. Muslims form 11.35 percent of the country's population.

39 She told the reporter: "Do you know that the state social worker asked me, 'why do you beget so many children?' My husband said I should have thrown out the woman. What problem is that of hers? We don't need her permission, do we, to have children?" (Sheriff 1993b).

40 In an article published in 2000, "Politics of Childhood: Perspectives from the South," Vasanthi Raman has addressed specifically the United Nations Convention on the Rights of the Child (CRC), formulated in the wake of the International Year of the Child in 1979, and in the context of the structural adjustment programs with which it is contemporaneous.

41 Asad offers the example of compulsory identity cards, which, in Britain, are being viewed "as a threat to the freedom of individual subjects (i.e., *citizens*)," while, in contrast, in the other EU member-states they are regarded as "a necessary means for providing collective objects (i.e., *populations*) with equal and efficient welfare" (2000; emphasis in original).

42 The significance of naming the "girl child" in the developmental discourse of the region and the nation-state was emphasized by Razia Ismael of Women's Coalition on the occasion of the final anniversary of the SAARC Girl Child Decade (1990–2000), 8 December 2000, thus: " . . . the recognition of the girl child was not a small feat. . . . When it [the Girl Child Decade] was declared, SAARC become the first regional body to have made such a commitment, and the SAARC nations earned UN and international attention and approbation for their vision. The SAARC Decade has remained the only one of its kind." (SAARC is the acronym for South Asian Association for Regional Co-Operation, consisting of the seven nations in the subcontinent: India, Pakistan, Bangladesh, Sri Lanka, Nepal, Bhutan, and Maldives). Ismael elaborates on the rationale for

such a categorization: "The decade is about proportionate attention. The Indian population is a young one. People under 20 account for 47.6 percent of it. People under 15 are very numerous within this percentage, as are people under ten. India has the world's largest population of under-fives. The female population shows the same pattern, even though females do not add up to half our people. If we are investing in measures for the advancement of our female citizens (and I am advisedly using this term instead of 'women' to help us discern and understand), we must recognize that nearly half of them are children. . . . Should these [resources] not be very specific to the different needs of each of the many age clusters within the 0–18 age range? That is where the girl child lives, in the range between surviving foeticide and exercising her franchise as a voter. . . . Gender disaggregation of data is something we are constantly reminded to ensure. Age disaggregation of gender information is something we are not reminded to ensure, but should ensure. But if we do not measure either our ideas or our actions by these two vital markers, the girl child's prospects remain bleak." The UN Conference on Women in Beijing (1995) for the first time included the concerns of the girl child specifically in every section of its Platform of Action, and added the girl child's neglect as a new critical issue. The Secretary-General, Gertrude Mongella, pointed out: "Discrimination does not start at age 18 when most societies grant majority to the girl and consider her an adult woman."

43   This must serve as the defense for the many ways in which this chapter departs from the earlier published version of my discussion of the Ameena case.

3 Beyond the Hysterectomies Scandal

I am grateful for the responses I received from the participants (and especially from Ritu Menon, as respondent) at the conference on Violence against Women and Ideologies of Victimization, organized by the Social Science Research Council, New York, and International Center for Ethnic Studies, Colombo, in Colombo in March 1996, where I originally presented this material. Subsequent respondents at other forums, especially Karin Cope at McGill University, Montreal; Kalpana Seshadri-Crooks at the Center for Literary and Cultural Studies at Harvard; Chungmoo Choi and Gabriela Schwab at the Critical Theory Seminar at the University of California, Irvine; and participants in the Violence and the Limits of Justice Forum at New York University, made me revise and extend my thinking in challenging and difficult directions: I thank them all. Finally, my gratitude to Aalochana and Voluntary Health Association of India for providing material on file.

1   A report about the proposed operations first appeared in *Indian Express,* dated 4 February 1994. I have relied on the subsequent coverage in the English national dailies—*The Hindu, Indian Express, Times of India, Hindustan Times, The Telegraph, The Pioneer, Deccan Herald*—and the report by Nagmani Rao and Sarita Pungaliya, based on discussions with a cross-section of people in Pune, which

appeared in *Economic and Political Weekly* in March 1994. I have also had the benefit of access to a number of activist groups' reports: Action for the Rights of the Child; Stree Kuti, Shramjivika, Forum against Oppression of Women, Lokashahi hakk Sanghatana, and volunteers ("Butchers in the Guise of Saviours"); Paryay (c/o Aalochana); Research Centre for Women's Studies, SNDT Women's University; National Addiction Research Centre ("Hysterectomy and Mentally Retarded Women: Issues and Debates"); and the writ petition filed by Anant Phadke and others against the state of Maharashtra. These, and press reports, draw freely on each other. The coverage in the English-language press was extensive as well as exceptionally in-depth, and the activist reports provide invaluable background and research information. For the bare account of the facts of the case, on which the reports are fairly unanimous, I have not indicated specific borrowings. In subsequent discussion I do.

2 Dr. Seth said he had operated on sixteen patients the previous year in association with the Rotary Club of Bombay. See the *Hindustan Times,* 9 February 1994.

3 I have relied on Malhotra 1986, 86–93. The preamble affirms the resolve to secure justice, liberty, equality, and fraternity for all citizens; the Fundamental Rights guarantee equality and freedom of speech, expression, and assembly; Articles 23 to 30 are provisions against forced labor, child labor, and traffic in human beings, and for equal educational opportunity and protection of minorities. Various articles of the Directive Principles of State Policy (30 to 51, occurring in Part IV) explicitly commit the nation to the "welfare of the people" and to a "social order" that ensures social, economic, and political justice.

4 The literature on disability issues in India is a meager one. I have relied greatly on and benefited from Barbara Harriss-White's invaluable work in this area and am grateful to her and S. Subramanian for allowing me to read her article before its publication.

5 Lakshmi Iyer (1994) writes that the Maharashtra government "hinted at the incapabilities" of the state-run institution to provide specialized care to the handicapped, quoting the secretary of the Maharashtra Women and Child Welfare Ministry. In Maharashtra the majority of the institutions are already run by NGOs.

6 By way of grants, the government pays the NGO 100 percent of staff salaries, rent, etc. and 66 percent of all other expenditures but has few supervisory powers or control. See "Butchers in the Guise of Saviours" n.d., 9.

7 On healthcare issues in particular, see Ghosh 1996, 441–42. Ghosh quotes data taken from the Sample Registration Bulletin of January 1995 that reveals that, while infant mortality rates declined by 5.6 percent in the years 1987–90, the decline of IMR between 1990 and 1993 was only 2.6 percent (1991 being the year of the onset of structural adjustment programs in India).

8 Regarding the expansion of markets, Krishna Kumar argues that the "sustained official push for achievement of mass literacy has come at a time when the Indian economy is being speedily 'opened up' for penetration by the world

capitalist system" and sees functional literacy as serving the purpose, in this context, only of propagating advertisements and pulp literature (1993, 2727, 2730).

9 On the connections between reform and middle-class sensibilities in the context of Western societies, see Garland 1990. Reform movements in Victorian England, and especially the novels of Charles Dickens, provide a powerful illustration of the contradictions of middle-class self-interest and philanthropy in effecting changes in areas like crime, sanitation, public health, and housing, and in the conditions of factories, poorhouses, orphanages, schools, homes for "fallen women," and other public institutions.

10 I allude to what is a widespread perception about certain essentialized "civilizational" aspects of the Indian polity: an indifference to the plight of others, a fatalistic acceptance of one's own and others' misfortune, and an entrenched belief in hierarchies of age, caste, and gender.

11 The genre of scandal—its structure and operation specifically in the postcolony, and the nature and dimension of disclosure—calls for more detailed examination, one that lies beyond the scope of this chapter. Note, however, that "scandalous" reports never come to us as entirely new: there is a sense in which they have circulated for a long time in the subterranean streams of rumor, or have been a kind of popular suspicion or half-knowledge. The force of disclosure lies in the strength rumors may gather and in the publicity (even, the publication: cf. the 1838 definition in the OED) that they receive. In the case of "closed" government institutions where access is closely guarded and official information is of dubious value, there is a sense in which the scandal would consist precisely in there being no scandal, i.e., in the repression of public knowledge of a state of affairs for a long period.

12 Disability is of course not a homogeneous category: it has to be differentiated according to kind, degree, temporality, causes, kinds of attached social stigma, availability of cure or aid, etc. See Harriss-White 1999, 136.

13 Dr. Pandya, cited by Iyer 1994.

14 See the remarks made by Vandana Khullar, Director, WCHD, Maharashtra: "... the Government is always an easy target for levelling accusations at" (1994). Also see Dr. B. Ramamurthy: "We seem to be going the U.S. way in holding meaningless agitations out of which nothing good can come" (reported by Bhagat 1994).

15 Some of these are listed in "Butchers in the Guise of Saviours," 4–5, and include Mother Teresa's order's Asha Daan, in Bombay.

16 The prevention-of-pregnancy argument that the director of the Department of Women, Child, and Handicapped Development had advanced was withdrawn following accusations from protesters that the government was "rapist friendly," though the "expert" medical discourse kept it in view as a major reason for sterilization, the prevention of menstruation being (medically) viewed as a trivial reason for a major surgical intervention. The reality, however, is that women in custodial institutions, and in particular mentally retarded

women, are extremely vulnerable to sexual abuse, as the Calcutta case made clear (see note 18 below). But such an admission would obviously have been, as it had already proved, more damaging than exculpatory in this instance.

17 Ahalya Rangnekar (who had sought the stay on the operations), retracted: "On grounds of compassion and human dignity, these surgeries are okay. Our quarrel is over the manner in which the Rotary Club went about organizing it. We are against mass hysterectomy." Sharada Sathe of Stree Sanghatana expressed similar views. Both quoted in Iyer 1994.

18 This immunity leads to abuses of much greater violence than those caused simply by neglect. Women as well as juveniles in custody are routinely subjected to sexual harassment by their keepers, by other inmates, or by outsiders in connivance with their supervisors. A report on the pregnancy of a mentally retarded sixteen-year old girl in Calcutta, which appeared shortly after the Shirur case, revealed that there were few officials and caretakers on the premises of the home for destitute women in Uttarpara where she had been lodged (the superintendent was "highly irregular in her duties" and other employees were absent). The husband of an employee of the home was therefore able to regularly let in "miscreants" during the afternoons, when the other inmates were at school. The discovery of the girl's pregnancy led to a complaint to the police, and all the "Class IV employees . . . were issued show cause notices." See *The Telegraph,* 2 March 1994. Another recent report on the escape of twelve boys from a state remand home for juvenile delinquents in Ramnagar, near Benares, disclosed that they were frequently forced to "sexually gratify some of the officials." In response to this situation and to the sexual harassment of three women employees at the home, the boys went on a rampage, began a hunger strike, and demanded an enquiry. See the *Indian Express,* 9 January 1996.

19 For a recent report on state juvenile homes, see Dutta Gupta 1996. Stories of sexual abuse also figure in a newsmagazine's report on juvenile homes (Bhattacharya 1995). The *Times of India* published on 5 March 1996 a report of an eleven-year-old boy in a Delhi remand home beaten to death by an older inmate. It turned out, on investigation, that such abuse is routine in the institution, the caretakers permitting and even encouraging various brutalities.

20 In the Agra Protective Home case, however, it was a letter written by a member of the Board, Dr. R. S. Sodhi, to the *Indian Express,* in April 1981, describing the appalling conditions he had found on visits to the home, that served as the basis for the writ petition initiated by two lawyers on behalf of the rights of the inmates to rehabilitation and compensation. See Murlidhar 1999, 294.

21 See Murlidhar (1999) for a graphic account of the conditions prevalent at the Agra Protective Home.

22 The document prepared by seven women's organizations in India for the UN Conference for Women in Beijing in 1995 (Joint Women's Program's Report, "Women: Towards Beijing") begins the chapter on "Institutionalisation and Change" with the warning that an exclusive preoccupation with institutional *malfunctioning* and, following from this, with proposals for its reform, is

likely to make us overlook the "normative structure" of the institution and fail to subject it to interrogation (67).

23 The differences between the two schools of thought and other theories of social control are discussed in the introduction to *Social Control and the State* by Stanley Cohen and Andrew Scull (1983). See also Michael Ignatieff, "State, Civil Society, and Total Institutions: A Critique of Recent Social Histories of Punishment," in ibid.

24 David Garland observes that though the techniques and principles of the institution's development in the context of early European capitalism are "transferable and may be operated elsewhere and under different regimes," they do have a "special and interesting relationship to the development of democracy in the West, summed up in the aphorism that 'the "Enlightenment" which discovered the liberties, also invented the disciplines.'" (1990, 146–47).

25 Some examples of recent work, specifically related to institutions of medicine: essays in Macleod and Lewis 1988; Arnold 1993; Kakar 1996. Kakar points out that in the case of leprosy, colonial administrators did not have views very different from or more progressive than those of native people and maintained the same belief in segregation of leprosy patients.

26 Usha Ramanathan's article "Women, Law, and Institutionalisation" (1996) is an invaluable contribution to such an understanding. My rewriting of the following section of this chapter draws on her insights.

27 The Terrorist and Disruptive Activities (TADA) Act, which lapsed on 23 May 1995, is now succeeded by the Criminal Law Amendment Bill and the Prevention of Terrorism Act (POTA), which have similar provisions. From the inception of TADA in 1985 to June 1994, there were 76,036 arrests (National Human Rights Commission). On TADA see *Black Law, White Lies,* report of the People's Union for Democratic Rights (PUDR), 1995.

28 Menstruating women in many communities in India are traditionally required to be set apart from other members of the family—an ostracism that links contemporary solutions for the "problem" with traditional religio-political-medical ritual practices.

29 The passage of The Persons with Disabilities (Equal Opportunities, Protection of Rights, and Full Participation) Act of 1995 has filled some of the lacunae but still does not address issues such as guardianship and legal capacity as they affect the mentally disabled (Autism Network 1998, 11).

30 Since the legal status of persons with mental disability is not clear, legal activists have suggested that "some test cases could be filed in different courts in the country in order to persuade the courts to interpret the existing statutes in consonance with the fundamental rights of persons with mental disability." The results of these test cases would then help to "identify areas for legislative change" (Autism Network 1998:11)

31 The comparison is with the family as guardian. But as activists argued, the state's guardianship is different from the family's—the latter could be more unequivocally considered to have the interests of their daughters/sisters at

heart. The family's decisions were also influenced by the greater difficulties they experienced in the care and protection of handicapped family members. The state could not use the same excuse.

32 Dhanda has been involved in advocacy for the rights of the mentally disabled (about which more later). Part of the brief relates to the question of their capacities: "Law assumes that persons either have 'no capacity' or have 'full capacity.' A mean that considers the capabilities of persons with mental disabilities will have to be found." At the same time, "it must be recognised that there will be a small group of very severely disabled persons who will require care and support throughout their lives. They have a right to this care and support which it is the responsibility of the state to provide" (Autism Network 1998, 11).

33 In support of this supposition, Barbara Harriss-White shows that disability is correlated to poverty, caste, and gender. "In countries with mass poverty," she argues, it is not only the case that disability leads to poverty but also "that poverty causes disability" due to factors like malnutrition, lack of healthcare, and proneness to accidents and other risks. She cites a study by A. Sen that shows the links between mental retardation and poverty and caste factors. While sex ratios may show a general "female advantage," disabled women are actually "severely socially disadvantaged." In the case of mental retardation, "the sex ratio . . . in the population at large, at 1,650, is anti-male, but among mentally retarded schoolchildren it is 1900." Since the difference is attributable to factors like the low enrollment of girls in school and increased female-child mortality, Harriss-White concludes that "female advantage may thus be translated into female disadvantage by gender socialisation" (Harriss-White 1999, 139–40).

34 The opinions of the medical community are widely canvassed by Rasheeda Bhagat 1994.

35 Dr. Suresh Deshpande, president of the Indian Medical Association, Pune. Quoted in Sattar 1994.

36 I refer, in particular, to the use of Medline, Popline, and other global databases for this research by the National Addiction Research Centre (NARC) of India.

37 See Jacob 1994. Jacob specifies that in South Africa, "the Abortion and Sterilisation Act of 1975 authorises sterilisation for severely retarded women provided the procedure is performed in a state hospital, certified by two medical practitioners and the parent or guardian gives informed consent." In Britain the patient would first have to be made a ward of the court, and a court order then obtained for the sterilization.

38 See, e.g., Sridhar 1994. Sridhar cites some of the guidelines provided by the committee on bioethics of the American Academy of Pediatrics.

39 A recent public-interest advertisement on behalf of Tamana, a voluntary organization for the mentally impaired, is motivated by the same purpose of stressing their human identity: "They dream like we dream, they hope like we hope, they try like we try . . . the only difference is that they have to strive a lot harder

than we do." It carries a picture of a student of the Tamana school, identifies him by name ("Vipin"), and describes him in glowing terms as a "responsible and friendly" young man. (This advertisement was created by Akshara Advertising and appeared in the *Indian Express*, 9 January 1996.) This strategic pleading must be construed as a response to what, clearly, is perceived as the tendency in the public mind to dehumanize difference.

40 Bhagat bases these accounts on an interview with S. Vidyakar, director of a voluntary organization, Udavum Karangal, in Madras.

41 *Umbartha* (Threshhold) (also appeared in Hindi with the title *Subah*), dir. Jabbar Patel, Marathi/135 minutes/color/1982; *Damini,* dir. Raj Kumar Santoshi, Hindi/140 minutes/color/1993.

42 See Sunder Rajan 1993, especially the chapter "The Name of the Husband."

43 Karnad is primarily a playwright and himself a director of alternative cinema who occasionally acts in films and television in dignified and sympathetic roles.

44 Other similar letters may be found in the columns of the *Times of India,* 4 March 1994.

45 See the chapter "Real and Imagined Women" in Sunder Rajan 1993.

46 *Asian Age* (28 June 1994) reported that a writ petition was also filed by the director of the National Addiction Research Centre, Gabriel Britto. The Lawyers Collective, a collective of activist lawyers, also filed a case against the Maharashtra government. A decision is still pending on this matter.

47 All the legal experts I have cited are agreed that any transformative effect PIL may have is largely dependent on the vision and predilections of the judges concerned, especially since its success demands "extraordinary energies and legal imagination" on their part (Ramanathan 1996, 217–18). Judgments of the courts in PIL cases that illustrate conservative nonaction or merely bureaucratic solutions or transferrence of responsibility are detailed by all of them.

48 The objectives of the workshop were defined as follows: "to equip participants with basic knowledge on the legal status and capacity of persons with mental disability; to devise suitable legal measures to protect the interests of mentally disabled persons; to develop a paralegal support group to assist mentally disabled persons and their families themselves on issues pertaining to rights, guardianship, legal capacity; [clarify] the position of the mentally disabled with regard to contracts, marital capacity, criminal responsibility, etc.; to develop an informed core group that, through knowledge of existing laws and their inadequacies, can work for an appropriate alternative and build pressure for better legislation" (Autism Network 1998, 11).

49 Jan Madhyam, for instance, is a UN-supported NGO, and many of the support organizations are foreign NGOs.

50 The locus classicus here is the conversation between Foucault and Deleuze on the role of the intellectual in mass struggles—which is precisely to abdicate any role. The object, according to Deleuze, "is to establish conditions where the prisoners themselves would be able to speak." They, the masses, Foucault asserts, "know far better than [the intellectual] and certainly they say it very

well" (1977, 207). Gayatri Spivak's retort to this position criticizes their "un-questioned valorization of the oppressed as subject" and, more seriously, their reification of the "concrete experience" of the institutionalized ("prisoners, soldiers, schoolchildren") (1999b, 255–56). This leads to her famous discussion of the question of representation in its two differentiated senses, "representation within the state and the political economy, on the one hand, and within the theory of the Subject, on the other" (ibid., 257).

51 Any optimism about such a trajectory—exposure → investigation → public interest litigation → court intervention—would receive a severe check from the example of the notorious Agra Protective Home case. This institution housed both sex workers and mentally retarded women. S. Murlidhar (1999, 291–320) has traced the progress of this case from 1981 to 1997, from the first intervention by two concerned lawyers as a PIL, to the Supreme Court's closure via the "curtain order" handing over of the case to the National Human Rights Commission. In those sixteen years of close monitoring and despite repeated interventions, no appreciable improvement in the legal status of those in its custody or in the material conditions of the home was visible. Another notorious instance, of course, is the failure of the victims of the Bhopal gas tragedy to as yet receive their compensations or proper medical treatment, despite the worldwide publicity that activists have generated for their plight.

4 The Prostitution Question(s)

My grateful thanks to Ratna Kapur for her active help in every stage of the writing of the earlier version of this chapter, from the loan of material at the start to editorial suggestions for revision at the end. Anne McClintock offered stimulating comments as respondent to my talk at the University of Pennsylvania's Gender Studies forum, in October 1995 and shared her own work with me: my warm appreciation. Participants at the Centre for Feminist Legal Research (CFLR) workshop "Hustling for Rights" in August 1997 (at which the earlier published version served as resource material) provided invaluable and expert insights on a range of issues, from which I have benefited. Many thanks also to Prabha Kotiswaran for sharing her research on sex work in India with me.

1 In addition to the PITA, Prabha Kotiswaran notes, there are many other laws that, in fact, are called on to regulate prostitution "more than the ITPA itself." (This act is identified by the acronyms PITA and ITPA, which are used interchangeably.) These include, she explains, the Indian Penal Code of 1860, which has provisions against trafficking and slavery of children (2001, 167).

2 This is a point made most famously by Gayle Rubin (1975).

3 For a fuller discussion of the relationship between "prostitutes" and "other women," see Baldwin 1992, especially 47, 48, 81, 97.

4 The feminist legal theorist Mary Joe Frug has identified three strategies by which legal discourse constructs the meaning of the female body and the implication they have for prostitution laws. The first is the "terrorization" of

the female body, by means of provisions that "inadequately protect women against physical abuse which encourage women to seek refuge against insecurity"; the second is its "maternalization," by means of "provisions that reward women for singularly assuming responsibilities after childbirth and with those that penalize conduct—such as sexuality or labor market work—that conflicts with mothering"; and the third is its "sexualization" by means of "provisions that penalize individual sexual conduct, such as rules against commercial sex . . . or . . . homosexuality and also through rules that legitimate and support institutions . . . that eroticize the female body" (1992, 1048–59).

5 This is a point made persuasively by Sleightholme and Sinha in their book on the contemporary Calcutta sex trade, *Guilty Without Trial* (1996). The number of HIV cases among those screened is 7.79 per thousand, less than the numbers to be found in the general population. Nevertheless, HIV-related funds "pour in," and a "new interest" in the sex trade is visible, giving sex workers a "new bargaining power" (xiii), as well as a new role as social workers disseminating knowledge about safe sex.

6 Kathleen Barry, at the forefront of the abolition movement, titled her famous 1979 book on prostitution *Female Sexual Slavery*.

7 See Aiyar 1989. Aiyar quotes statistics drawn from a Shreemathi Nathibai Damodar Thackersey (SNDT) University–sponsored study of Bombay for the years 1980–84 to show that though all "captured" brothelkeepers and procurers were released on bail in this period, and only two were convicted, there was a "cent per cent conviction of prostitutes." Prostitutes also received harsher penalties than pimps or brothelkeepers. Clients are never arrested. Bombay police received Rs 100,000 from bribes.

8 One study of Delhi police (conducted by Dr. J. Mohanta of the Institute of Criminology and Forensic Sciences) showed that they had no knowledge of the altered definition of prostitution under the amended 1986 act, and that, consequently, there has been no drop in the number of arrests of prostitutes and pimps even after its enactment. See Ahmed 1993.

9 "Cathy," one of the participants in the Canadian conference, puts it like this: "The way the laws have been written so far, it's legal to be a prostitute. It's just illegal to do absolutely anything else around it. Everything around it is illegal. It's exactly as though the government is saying to us, 'Here, you can buy a new car. You can drive this car anywhere you want to. Take it anywhere, anytime. But you can't turn on the ignition'" (Bell 1987, 91).

10 In this discussion I use the terms "radical" and "liberal" feminists to describe two broadly differentiated approaches toward sexuality issues in feminism, including prostitution, following Baldwin 1992 and Frug 1992.

11 For extended description and discussion, see Fernand-Laurent 1985; also see UNESCO Report on the International Meeting of Experts on the Social and Cultural Causes of Prostitution and Strategies for the Struggle against the Procuring and the Sexual Exploitation of Women 1986: Kathleen Barry et al. 1984, especially 64–72; Mitter 1986.

12 Many of the additions and changes in this chapter from the earlier published

version (in Kapur 1996) have been made necessary by these developments and the feminist politics and literature they have generated.

13 On the notorious case of the Agra Protective Home, see Murlidhar 1999, and as it relates to PITA, especially 315–17.

14 This workshop, titled "Hustling for Rights: The Legal Regulation and Representation of the Sex Trade in South Asia," was organized by the Centre for Feminist Legal Research, New Delhi, 16–18 August 1997, in New Delhi. The participants represented a wide range of disciplines, organizations, and views.

15 The entire controversy over the Contagious Diseases Acts, leading to their repeal, is discussed in Walkowitz 1980. See also Jeffreys 1987. Walkowitz points to the "ironies" of the Victorian situation: "In their defense of prostitutes, feminist repealers were still limited by their own class bias and their continued adherence to a separate-sphere ideology that stressed women's purity, moral supremacy, and domestic virtues" (7).

16 For a popular journalistic perception of the differences, see the report by Bachi Karkaria on the International AIDS Conference in Yokohama in August 1994. Focusing on the presence and speech of Cheryl Overs, leader of the International Sex Workers' Project Network, at the conference, Karkaria writes with admiration of the liberated, independent, and authority-defying politics that this prostitute-activist from Australia represented. Specifically, Karkaria contrasts Overs's refusal of victim identity with the Indian socialworker Priti Patkar's "heart-tugging descriptions of conditions in Indian brothels." But ultimately she cannot see any affinity between "this articulate forty-something woman" and "the ghoulish, painted masks of Kamathipura": "Cheryl Overs may advocate a unionised Utopia, but in Bombay's claustrophobic cages, it will be a long time before dearness allowances are given on the cost of dying index" (Karkaria 1994).

17 See, on this, Chapkis 1997, 13–30.

18 If the mainstream women's movement is taken as representative of "Indian feminism," as such, then it must be acknowledged that sexuality questions have been marginal to its agenda. As John and Nair admit, it is chiefly questions of violence (rape, assault, and harassment) or health and reproductive matters that have figured under the head of sexuality issues (1998, 9–10). Indifference, discomfort, impatience, or outright hostility has been expressed toward, for instance, the politics of alternative sexualities. The National Conferences on Women's Movements (held periodically since 1980) included a separate workshop theme on "sexuality" for the first time in 1994. Prostitution was not discussed at any length; the focus was on "accepting lesbian sexuality," though on this issue too there were dissenting voices among the participants. Ruth Vanita has criticized Indian women's groups for this "reluctance to question gender and sexuality categories" and concludes: "Their self-characterization as 'women's movements' and dropping the word 'liberation' is not fortuitous. Today many people outside of women's movements are far more advanced in thinking through and enacting liberatory modes of life, relationship and com-

munity" (1999, 534). Prostitute rights have, therefore, not formed a significant part of the politics of the women's movement in India until recently, when the pressures of the conjuncture that I have broadly outlined brought the issue to prominence. (Examples of the new turn are the workshop on prostitution organized by the National Commission of Women in 1996, at which sex workers from all over the country participated and spoke; the NCW also organized the conference to discuss reform of the PITA in 1997 to which I have alluded.) The issue of prostitute rights and of prostitutes as workers remains, nevertheless, a contested one in the Indian women's movement. The initiative to rethink and reformulate strategies of reform and activism has come mainly from feminist legal activists in Bangalore and Delhi.

In Taiwan pro-prostitution feminists similarly place themselves within a broadly sexual liberation politics, as against "gender politics" as such. The position of "state feminism" in Taiwan is, however, more explicitly hostile to prostitute activism than is the case in India. Taiwanese "state feminism" has a nationalist and reformist cast and privileges middle-class, "respectable" housewives as agents of political change (Ho 2000; Ding 2000).

19 I have identified Lillian Robinson as the source of these observations in this coauthored book given that chapter 8, "Sexual Theory and its Discontents," from which I mainly draw, is identified in the preface as Robinson's work.

20 *India Cabaret,* 1985, is a documentary film that won several international film awards. Nair does not explicitly identify the cabaret dancers as prostitutes, but the connections between the two professions exist, and the argument of Nair's film is extendable to cover the case of prostitution.

21 See, for instance, the report of the conference on sex workers in Calcutta in 1998 by Meena Menon in *The Hindu,* 14 June 1998.

22 Cf. Bishop and Robinson 1998 for a similar comparison between North American and Thai prostitute groups (235–44).

23 This workshop, "Hustling for Rights: The Legal Regulation and Representation of the Sex Trade in South Asia" (at which I was a participant), has been referred to earlier. Some participants held that the pleasure/desire angle of prostitution did not figure enough in our discussions, that women in prostitution loved talking about their bodies, that Annie Sprinkle's work was important in addressing questions of sexual pleasure rather than only the politics of sexuality. The opposition to this position was equally forceful and was not limited to the argument about a "different" "South Asian" context.

24 This broad alliance among postmodern positions, pro-prostitute activism, and "sex radical" feminist politics would appear to hold in Taiwan too, with even clearer markers. Pro-prostitution feminists in Taiwan are accused, says Naifei Ding, of "postmodern performance" or "'posturing' politics" (also elsewhere termed an "identity" politics) by their opponents in the women's movement (2000, 305). Josephine Chuen-Juei Ho, writing from within the camp of "sex radical"/pro-prostitute feminists in Taiwan, views sex workers' empowerment at least significantly as a matter of the "discursive manoeuvres"—the ways of

dressing, speech, and behavior—adopted by "betel-nut beauties" in Taiwan (2000, 288–91).

25 Prostitute speech is not, of course, univocal. And the problem of assuming a transparency of speech is also widely acknowledged. Neither of these is a reason to write out prostitute voices from our accounts, but only a caution about how we read them. Methodologically, scholarship in this area has recourse to surveys and questionnaires, ethnographies and participant observation, documentary and journalistic investigation, interviews and access to direct first-person prostitute writings/speeches/videos etc. as a way of soliciting prostitute voices.

26 On the question of agency in the context of the sati-debate, my "Subject of Sati" is relevant. See Sunder Rajan 1993.

27 An interesting and unusual example of rehabilitation is the first registered cooperative for sex workers in the country, set up in Sonagachi, West Bengal. "The prostitutes' efforts to get their co-operative registered received support from doctors and social workers. . . . The co-operative will provide loans at low rates of interest . . . start self-employment schemes for sex-workers above the age of forty [and] run a store which will sell condoms at subsidised rates to sex-workers to prevent AIDS." See Abdi 1995.

28 See, for an argument about the limits of the transformative possibilities that prostitute collectives can achieve, O'Connell-Davidson 1998; see also Jenness 1993, cited in Kotiswaran 2001, 227.

29 Some groups have expressed serious dissatisfaction with NGOs working with women in prostitution, accusing them of representing their own interests and not those of the women they were working with and for. One sex worker at the 1998 sex workers' conference in Calcutta said: "We do not need NGOs to speak on our behalf, they are a big problem." See M. Menon 1998.

30 Its chief exponent is Lars Ericsson (1980).

31 Baldwin's essay (1992) cites opposed accounts of prostitute experiences. Some prostitutes explain that "the first time they felt powerful was the first time they turned a trick" (96). Another described her initiation as rape by a group of men, "It went on and on and there was no point to it" (53).

32 Mary Joe Frug writes about the sex worker Judy Edelstein: "the discomfort she experienced because she sexually responded to her customer during an act of prostitution [was because] her orgasm in those circumstances broke down a distinction she sought to maintain between her work and the sexual pleasure she obtained from her non-work-related sexual activity" (1992, 1053). Frug's source is Edelstein 1987. Ruth Colker takes up Frug on this point, arguing that since Edelstein had identified herself as lesbian (as well as Jewish and feminist), her discomfort, rather than being a "work/nonwork discomfort," could have been a "heterosexual/lesbian discomfort" (1992, 1088).

33 This critique of bourgeois marriage is most forcefully articulated by Frederick Engels in *The Origin of the Family, Private Property, and the State* (1884/1968, 493 ff). Prostitution "follows mankind in civilisation as a dark shadow upon the fam-

ily," writes Engels, quoting Lewis Henry Morgan, the American anthropologist. The comparison of marriage with prostitution, only legalized, was made by Mary Wollstonecraft earlier, in 1790, and by many feminist writers since then. See Pateman 1988, 190.

34 In 1995 the media coverage of the British actor Hugh Grant's liaison with a prostitute disclosed a widespread feeling that "paying for sex is for the desperate, the sad losers who live in sexless relationships or who are simply alone." The *Guardian* report observed, "It comes as a shock to learn that a charming, suave Hollwood God should have to resort to this and it throws up some unsettling clues as to the real reasons why men visit prostitutes." Cited in Sharma 1995.

35 The first Calcutta sex workers' conference in 1997 made this its theme: "Sex work is real work, we demand workers' rights" (M. Menon 1998).

36 Karkaria quotes Cheryl Overs's observations: "Every industry has the potential to create nuisance, exploit workers, be a health hazard. . . . But elsewhere, the mechanisms to control these are in place. There are now-taken-for-granted rules which prevent people from going bareheaded on a construction site or coal miners form working in the pits for 18 hours. Just extend these safeguards to the sex industry, and all the cliched charges against it will disappear" (1994).

37 Pateman takes on Marx's observation that "prostitution is only a *specific* expression of the *general* prostitution of the labourer." She comments on the "irony" that " 'the worker' is masculine—yet his degradation is symbolized by a female emblem, and patriarchal capitalism is pictured as a system of universal prostitution" (1988, 201).

38 Sibyl Schwarzenbach, for instance, recasts commercial sex as "sexual therapy . . . [i.e.] a therapeutic process which frees sexual gratification and erotic desire from their present fascination with domination and subservience." Admittedly, the proposal, as Schwarzenbach preemptively concedes, can seem like yet another ingenious rationalization of the old argument of male sexual need. (Pateman points out that it has been used by contractarians: 192). But it has several merits: one, that it links a client's recourse to a prostitute's services (or sex with a "surrogate partner") to situations of clearly defined therapeutic need, not a "universal" urge; it thereby proposes a specificity of purpose for commercial sex; it indicates the skills that the prostitute possesses, or would need to develop, for "emotional and sexual" therapy, so that the value of her work may be acknowledged; and, finally, it defines the function of commercial (therapeutic) sex as a response to the broader situation of sexual violence and unequal gender relations in society (1990–91, 124).

39 Books based on such research discussed by Robinson include Horigard and Finstad's Norwegian study, *Backstreets* (1992), and Walker and Ehrlich's interviews with Thai bar girls, *"Hello My Big Honey!"* (1992).

40 Examples are, of course, numerous. One of the most famous in Indian journalism is the story of Kamla, a poor woman who was "bought and sold three times in a week" in 1981 at a guest house in Shivpuri, Madhya Pradesh. Three journal-

ists from the *Indian Express* bought her for Rs 2,500 the third time and ran her story prominently in the newspaper. The editor took up her case in the Supreme Court, which ordered her to be placed in a Nari Niketan in Delhi. But Kamla disappeared and has never been heard of again. Her story was adapted into a play by the Marathi playwright Vijay Tendulkar and subsequently filmed. See Upendra Baxi 1999. In 1997 Ruchira Gupta, a BBC reporter, made a documentary about the trafficking in Nepali child prostitutes, *The Selling of Innocents,* which won an Emmy award in the Best Investigative Journalism category. Gupta's film follows these young girls from rural Nepal into the brothels of Bombay's Kamathipura and is uncompromising in its depiction of violence, force, greed, corruption, and disease. The politics of such representation is, of course, always a problematic one: Baxi, for instance, objects to the "commodification" of Kamla in "avant-garde" film and theater. A more recent collection of photographs and essays, *Fallen Angels: The Sex Workers of South Asia,* ed. John Frederick and Thomas L. Kelly (2001), has been similarly accused of sensationalism and voyeurism.

41   I have referred to other courtesan accounts by Oldenberg, Srinivasan, etc. For an account of the changes in the traditional systems of prostitution that took place under colonial administration in India, see Janaki Nair 1996b; see also Chatterjee 1993 and Dang 1993.

42   What *both* modes of representation commonly do is render the subjectivity of the prostitute merely symbolic, though for different purposes: even in a story (of the first kind) as powerful as Mahasweta Devi's "Douloti the Bountiful," the tragedy of the life of the exploited, exiled, diseased tribal girl, Douloti, is used to indict a system of bonded labor, and the tragedy of her death to ironize the pieties of nationalism (Mahasweta Devi 1995).

5 *Women Between Community and State*

Earlier versions of this chapter were presented at various forums. It was originally presented as a paper at a conference on gendered communities at Tel Aviv University, in March 1998, and subsequently at the Modern Language Association Convention in San Francisco in December 1998, and at the South Asia seminar of the George Washington University in April 1999. I wish to thank here, particularly, Billie Melman, Bruce Robbins, and Aamir Mufti, and Alf Hiltebeitel and Judith Plotz for inviting me to these forums, and I am grateful to audiences at all of them for their questions and comments. Ann Pelligrini made valuable editorial responses to the version that appeared in the special issue of *Social Text* that she coedited with Janet Jacobson. Niraja Gopal Jayal, Rachel Reidner, and Priya Gopal offered immensely valuable suggestions which have helped me think through the most difficult parts of the argument. Its limitations reflect, of course, the limitations of my endeavors alone.

1   In 1985 the Supreme Court of India ruled in favor of Shahbano, a seventy-two-year-old Muslim woman, in a case of maintenance in divorce. It was awarded to

her, as was customary, under Section 125 of the Criminal Procedure Code. The husband and the Muslim Personal Law Board, however, protested that this was contrary to Muslim personal law under which no maintenance was payable beyond a stipulated period (*iddat*). In response to Muslim sentiment on the issue, the government, under Rajiv Gandhi, passed the Muslim Women (Protection of Rights on Divorce) Bill in 1986, removing Muslim women from the ambit of Section 125's provision for maintenance to destitute women. There was a nationwide controversy over both the Supreme Court judgment and the new legislation. The Hindu right protested that the ruling party was seeking to "appease" the Muslim community.

2 Achin Vanaik points out that Hindutva parties have made no effort to formulate a gender-just UCC despite the BJP's electoral promises, "because their going about this job would definitely alienate the Hindu male bastion and the Brahmanical base of the party. Indeed, comprehensive and genuine gender just laws will trigger an uproar from the overwhelming majority of men, be they Sikh, Hindu, Muslim or Christian" (1998).

3 There is a large body of feminist writing on the struggles of women in the Arab world against religious fundamentalism, and specifically personal-law structures, among them Kandiyoti 1991 and Badran 1994. Badran 1998 has recently described the feminist efforts in Yemen to protest the imposition of a reactionary personal status law in 1997.

4 Many of these essays have been conveniently brought together in Rajeev Bhargava's edited volume *Secularism and Its Critics* (1998). See, in this volume, T. N. Madan, "Secularism in Its Place"; Ashis Nandy, "The Politics of Secularism and the Recovery of Religious Toleration"; Partha Chatterjee, "Secularism and Tolerance"; Akeel Bilgrami, "Secularism, Nationalism, and Modernity." Also in line with Nandy's position, see Kakar 1996 and Fox 1996. For a critique of Madan, Nandy, and M. N. Srinivasan, see also Tharamangalam 1995.

5 Some examples are Rajeev Bhargava, "What Is Secularism For?" in Bhargava 1998, above, and Bharucha 1998.

6 Exceptions among left intellectuals, those who have supported feminist positions on the UCC, are Gautam Navlakha, author of "Women's Rights: Walking the Tightrope" (1996) and a member of the Working Group on Women's Rights that prepared the statement "Reversing the Option: Civil Codes and Personal Laws" (1996); Achin Vanaik (1997); and Praful Bidwai (1995). While the first two toe the orthodox left line in supporting a UCC, Bidwai comes out in favor of leaving personal-law reform to religious communities to effect internally. Clearly there is room within a broad left-feminist alliance for negotiating questions of gender like the UCC.

7 An exception is Niraja Gopal Jayal, who incisively (and extensively) explores the contradiction of gender in her analysis of secularism and democratic government, using the Shahbano issue as the case in point. See chapter 3, "The Secular State," of her book (1999).

8 On this see, especially, Parasher 1992. This book has been invaluable in initiat-

ing the recent feminist work in India around the UCC question and in providing access to and information about a complicated constitutional, historical, and legal-political issue. See, on this, especially 241.

9 This is spelled out in the proposal prepared by the Working Group on Women's Rights in 1996, which appeared in *Economic and Political Weekly*.

10 The position of AIDWA is outlined by Gautam Navlakha in "Women's Rights" (1996, 1180–83).

11 There is by now a substantial body of feminist legal studies and political analyses in India, including and going beyond the UCC. Book-length studies include Parasher's (1992); Agnes, *State, Gender, and the Rhetoric of Law Reform* (1995); Ratna Kapur and Brenda Cossman, *Subversive Sites: Feminist Engagements with Law in India* (1996); Maitreyee Mukhopadhyay, *Legally Dispossessed: Gender, Identity, and the Process of Law* (1998). Important anthologies are Zoya Hassan's *Forging Identities: Gender, Communities, and the State in India* (1994), and Kamla Bhasin, Ritu Menon, and Nighat Said Khan, eds. *Against All Odds: Essays on Women, Religion, and Development from India and Pakistan* (1994). In addition there have been numerous articles in newspapers and periodicals by feminist lawyers (Indira Jaising, Vasudha Dhagamwar, Geeta Ramaseshan, Usha Ramanathan), pamphlets issued by women's groups and research centers, and articles in the feminist journal *Manushi*, edited by Madhu Kishwar, on these issues. Not all are equally critical of law and feminist legal-reform struggles: for example, Kapur and Crossman conclude that the law is a significant site of struggle, and Parasher recognizes its limitations but cautions against "inappropriate expectations" about what it can achieve (1992, 30).

12 For a defense of feminist struggles for equality, see Parasher 1992, especially 26–36.

13 See, for instance, Freitag 1996. Valsan Thampu (1998) has remarked on the culturally heterogeneous character of the Indian Christian community, for instance: "There is little in common between a Tamil Christian and his Punjabi or Gujarati counterpart." Yet, under the new threat to their minority identity, they "are transcending the denominational, caste and culture barriers and rediscovering their common destiny."

14 Ram's book-length study of the Mukkuvar women is titled *Mukkuvar Women: Gender, Hegemony, and Capitalist Transformation in a South Indian Fishing Village* (1991).

15 For example, Chowdhary 1994.

16 See the introduction to this book for such a discussion.

17 I have discussed the questions posed by the conceptual and empirical category of "women" more extensively in the introduction to this book.

18 The relevant literature would consist of Hegel 1967, Gramsci 1971, Habermas 1989, and Taylor 1990, usefully surveyed in Cohen and Arato 1992 and Chandhoke 1995.

19 On this see, especially, Pateman 1989, 182.

20 Thus Susanne Rudolph points to the different contexts of "highly unequal

societies in the grip of radical change" and the conditions of "social revolution" that obtain in the countries of the south, which challenge both the northern conceptions of the nature of associations and their "benign readings" of its links to social capital and cooperation. Social revolution in India, she suggests, takes place "both within and on the margins of the constitutional framework" (2000, 1764–65). Sandra Freitag analyzes the "differences" of civil society in India as it emerges from colonial rule and the construction of communities. In post-Independence India, communal movements, deploying cultural terms relating to religion, language, ethnicity, caste, and region resemble and usurp the space of a civil society (1996, 219–23, 228–34). In Partha Chatterjee's view, too, the colonial state produced only a civil society of subjects, not citizens, so that the colonized "construct their national identities within a different narrative, that of community" (1994, 236). In a later work, he has argued that the conditions for a proper civil society formation do not exist in post-Independence India either. Community formation takes, rather, the form of *political society,* the difference being that in a civil society people have active citizenship rights—lacking these, they negotiate with the state and its agencies for resources for livelihood and survival as a "political" community (1998a, 281). Sanjay Kumar holds that the dispossessed in India who are engaged in "direct struggles against the state" for their rights are not organized as a civil society or mediated by its institutions and therefore must not be confused with a normative civil society "associated with liberal polity in which sections with social power participate" (2000, 2779).

21 Pradeep Chibber, however, finds associational tendencies lacking in India (associations, according to his definition, being those organizations that formally mobilize people as voters around political issues), so that he discovers in India the anomaly of a "democracy without association" (1999). The question of whether communities based on cultural identities (primordial or voluntary) can constitute a civil society remains disputed among those arguing the case of India (see note 18, above). Neera Chandoke emphatically denies that "particularist loyalties such as religion, caste, tribe, ethnicity, linguistic affiliations" can vitalize the public sphere—rather they "threaten to demolish" it. They constitute, therefore, a "counter-civil society" and belong more properly to the sphere of the private where, following Habermas, she holds that identity formation must take place (1995, 241–51). Chandhoke's remains a normative view of civil society, and she is uncomfortably aware that in India religious mobilization overwhelms the appeal and influence of civil society (245). I will follow her, nevertheless, in excluding religious and other identitarian mobilization and communitarian practices from my working definition of an implicitly secular civil society in India.

22 The "new visibility" of women in the 1990s has been discussed in Tharu and Niranjana 1999. They view the phenomenon, however, exclusively in terms of a co-optation and deflection of feminist initiatives and as "a crisis of democracy and secularism in our times" (495).

23   See my introduction for a discussion of the post-Independence Indian state's repression of women's contribution as workers—which stands particularly in contrast to a radical (and until recently forgotten) 1939 document, the report of the National Planning Committee's report on Women's Role in Planned Economy (WRPE). This report emphasized women's rights in the economy, since "entry into the production sphere was seen as the key to resolving the unequal status of women" (Chaudhuri 1996, 213). The report was buried and its position ignored in subsequent years.

24   On this, see Kabeer 1995; John 1999; Sen 1999. Sen has been particularly influential in pushing for women's empowerment as a developmental strategy. See also Dreze and Sen 1995.

25   A recent instance of such election-motivated concern for women voters: the chief minister of Andhra Pradesh, N. Chandrababu Naidu, addressed a series of meetings of District Women's Committees and Mothers Committees in the north coastal region as a launch to his election campaign in June 2001. Naidu made a pitch about his government's welfare measures for women, including the significant representation of women in elected bodies. He praised women as being "100 times better than men if given a fair chance" and asked for their "participation as well as cooperation" in electing leaders. Naidu freely promised "any amount" for the welfare of women. "Naidu Rings the Campaign Bell at Regional Women's Meet," *Times of India,* 13 June 2001.

26   His examples are women's organizations like SEWA (Self-Employed Women's Association) in India and credit and cooperative organizations in India and Bangladesh.

27   The point will be clearer if we distinguish livelihood struggles from *identitarian* ones. Women's prominence in the latter kinds of movements, such as the militant Hindutva and anti-Mandal protests, is a recent and unexpected phenomenon—arguably, even an aberrant one. It is primarily middle-class women with a perceived stake in religious and caste hegemony who are active in these movements. See Tharu and Niranjana 1999, 494–525.

28   For a documentation of the extent and range of women's work in the unorganized sector, their dismal conditions of work and demands for benefits and other guarantees to them, see the landmark report *Shram Shakti* (Government of India, 1988).

29   Naila Kabeer has discussed SEWA's working in chapter 9, "Empowerment from Below" (1995). See also Bhatt 1998. On peasant women's organizations, see Omvedt 1994. On women teachers in Delhi Universitys' Teachers' Association, see Sunder Rajan et al. 1986, "Women Teachers and the DUTA Strike."

30   These counterarguments were advanced by several penetrating readers and critics of earlier versions of this paper, Niraja Gopal Jayal, Judith Plotz, Rachel Reidner, and Ann Pelligrini. I am grateful to all of them for engaging so generously with my argument and for helping me to draw the limits of its validity.

31   As I warn in chapter 6 ("Children of the State?"), when arguments about women's "worth" are used to counter femicidal practices, we are in danger of implicitly supporting "worth" as a measure of the right to live itself.

32 I am not arguing for the kind of civic republicanism that regards citizenship as a matter of obligations as well as rights, insisting especially on the citizen's obligation to work. But radical democratic feminists in the West have been urging women's active participation in the public sphere as a way of asserting their rights and promoting their interests. Ruth Lister describes this as a concept of citizenship as "agency" (1997, chapter 1, "What Is Citizenship?"). My argument about women's work and women-as-workers may be regarded as an outline of the *preconditions* for such full and active participation.

6 Children of the State?

Earlier versions of this chapter were presented at invited lectures: originally at Rice University, Houston, in February 1999; then as the Doris Stevens Memorial Lecture at Haverford College in April 1999; as the Barbara Stoller Miller Annual Lecture at Columbia University in April 2000; and at the George Washington University South Asia seminar, also in April 2000. To all those who were present and responded to its arguments in the audience, I am, as always, indebted. I especially wish to thank Betty Joseph at Rice University and Gayatri Spivak at Columbia University for their comments as respondents. My grateful thanks, too, to Madhavi Kale for inviting me to Bryn Mawr–Haverford College and to Val Daniels for the invitation to Columbia University. Above all, I acknowledge here the work of V. Padma ("Mangai") and Ravindran in the area of female infanticide, and the generous and inspirational guidance they gave me in the form of materials and discussion. Mary John, Anuja Agarwal, Hoon Song, and Chloe Silverman read earlier drafts and gave me the benefit of their special areas of scholarship and interest in this subject, for which I am profoundly grateful. If I have failed to reproduce the acuity of their observations or display the breadth of their scholarship in the resulting revision, the limitation is entirely mine.

1   Miller's book was first published by Cornell University Press in 1981. The Indian reissue of 1997 has a new postscript and is the one referred to in this chapter.

2   See, for example, Dreze and Sen 1995, 143–45. Dreze and Sen argue that excess juvenile female mortality lies in "age groups beyond that of female infanticide" (i.e., beyond the first month of birth) and is attributable rather to overall neglect (144). Alaka Basu does not discuss female infanticide, but she refuses to attribute sex differentials in mortality to sex-selective abortions at the wider or national level (1992, 189). Leela Visaria denies significance to the differences in sex ratio, as well as to sex-selection procedures as having any appreciable impact on them (1994, cited in Miller 1997, 210). Sabu George and Ranbir S. Dahiya arrive at a figure of 1.2 million "missing girls" in India in the decade 1981–1991, less than 1 percent of all female births at present—but the trend (in female feticide) that they predict is one of increase and expansion (1998, 2196). For a contrary view, see Sudha and Irudaya Rajan 1998 and Agnihotri 1996, 3369. According to some analysts, the decline in sex ratios visible in the 1991

census despite the increase in life expectancy of females is hard to explain except as underenumeration of females in recent censuses. The alternative— "large scale surplus emigration of females over males," or "a sudden drop in the percentage of female births to male births," both in the millions, couldn't have gone unnoticed. See Srinivasan 1997. At present it is disaggregated, district-level, and age-specific sex ratios that most unambiguously establish the existence of large-scale female infanticide. Though the 2001 census appears to show an improvement in the overall sex ratio (from 927 to 933), the under-six ratio has declined from 976 in 1961 to 927 in 2001.

3   Section 102 f the IPC (Indian Penal Code) defines infanticide as murder. Other provisions of the IPC also punish neglect, abandonment, and ill-treatment of children.

4   Recently there have been attempts by activists in the medical profession and women's groups and UNICEF in India to appeal to religious heads to issue specific edicts against female feticide and infanticide, in the belief that this prohibition would have a significant impact on discouraging the practice.

5   Writers of fiction have conjured up vivid scenarios of demographic nightmares in such a situation, for example, Amin Maalouf, *The First Century after Beatrice* (1993), discussed in Harriss-White 1999. Viji Srinivasan includes a piece of fiction as a preface to her field studies about female infanticide in Salem district. In this story, sex-selective killings have come full circle: the scarcity of girls created by their systematic killing has led to an acute shortage that in this terrible future is countered by male infanticide; and meanwhile women as virgins, wives, and widows are subjected to rigid patriarchal controls (Venkatachalam and Srinivasan 1993, 7–15). The story is untitled.

6   An editorial, "Jack or Jill?," in the British medical journal *The Lancet* (20 March 1993: 727–28), offers an argument along these lines. For a critique of "the economic logic of 'rational man'," see Arora 1996, 420–24, especially 421.

7   Dreze and Sen explain that variables that relate to the *general* level of development often amplify the gender bias in child survival (1998, 161). R. Venkatachalam and Viji Srinivasan also relate the success of the small family norm to development and link the former to more intense son-preference (1993, 55).

8   See, for instance, the discussion led by Nivedita Menon (1998a, PE 2 and ff.).

9   In the debates on abortion in the United States, the comparison between feticide and infanticide is routine. See, for instance, the argument offered by Robert Card: that the "liberal" position on abortion (in this instance, that held by Mary Anne Warren) is compatible with the "moral acceptability of infanticide," since the criteria of "personhood" denied to the fetus could also apply to the neonate (2000, 340–51). Note, however, that this debate is conducted not in the specific context of sex selection but of abortion, and that infanticide is not an actual social phenomenon but figures only as a conceptual possibility.

10 See Menon 1996. There is a substantial volume of other discussion on the issue of sex-determination technologies in India, including Arora 1996 and George and Dahiya 1998 (see n. 2). The campaign of the Forum Against Sex Determi-

nation and Sex Selection also generated a number of articles; see Ravindran 1993. For a more general feminist philosophical discussion, see Holmes and Hoskins 1987, 15–29.

11 This argument is central to Padmanabhan 1993. See also Kumar 1983b.

12 On this, see especially Kumar 1983a, 61–64.

13 Cf. Toni Morrison, *Beloved* (1988). Morrison's protagonist Sethe, the slave-mother haunted by the infant child she has killed, offers this poignant logic for her killing: "I'll explain to her, even though I don't have to. How if I hadn't killed her she would have died and that is something I could not bear to happen to her" (200).

14 Mary Anne Warren (2000) responds to Robert Card (see note 9, above) by stressing, similarly, the significance of *birth* in distinguishing the late fetus from the neonate: though both might fulfill similar criteria of personhood (like sentience), "birth is morally significant because, once the infant is physically separate from the mother, its life can be protected through the attribution of legal personhood without simultaneously endangering her life and, in effect, her legal personhood" (358). She also mentions the (better) alternatives to the killing of infants that are available in most advanced societies today, such as contraception, abortion, adoption (356–57).

15 The mother's conflict and her resolution to resist the pressure to kill the child is powerfully represented in the poet Gaddar's song "Nindu Amassenade" (On a Moonless Night). See note 47 for details.

16 Venkatachalam and Srinivasan record a number of informal conversations with village women. Largely, it seems, because of the rapport they managed to establish with them, the women candidly admitted to killing their girl babies, spelling out the methods they used and the pressures they were under to do so (including those from district nurses offering to do scans and abortions in order to meet government family planning targets) (1993, chapter 3). Elisabeth Bumiller, an American journalist, also persuaded four couples in the field she visited to speak to her in a similar vein about the infants they killed (1990, chapter 5).

17 Robert Deliege does not report female infanticide in his study village, Valghira Manickam, and reports that aversion to girls is unusual there (1997, 237). But the more recent report by Chunkath and Athreya notes an "alarming" change in scheduled caste communities, including paraiyars and pallaars, who are veering toward the practice (1997, WS 27–28).

18 In this instance the contrast with colonial official discourse—with its moral denunciations of the practice, the confident imperial stereotypes of the people who practiced it, the alternating despair and determination about its eradication—could not be greater.

19 See, for example, Hrdy 1996 and Haraway 1991.

20 I am grateful to Chloe Silverman for alerting me to the discourses of sociobiology in this area and engaging the distinction between them and cultural discourses.

21 For Agamben as well as Foucault the historical event that had to be read as rule rather than exception in this manner was the Holocaust.

22 I am indebted to Hoon Song's formulations on Agamben's project, both in his own work (Song, unpublished) and in his personal communications with me, for the foregoing discussion.

23 The discovery of (the persistence of) female infanticide in contemporary India was a journalistic coup. A 1986 story in the English newsmagazine *India Today,* "Born to Die," by S. H. Venkataramani, reported large-scale killings of girl children in Salem district in Tamilnadu. This story, together with an earlier report in the Tamil magazine *Junior Vikatan* in 1985, caused a public outcry loud enough to alert the Tamilnadu government and provoke it into announcing measures to "save" girl children. Some years later *India Today* published a story on Rajasthan, reporting that some districts in the state had not received a single *barat* in decades, which suggests that female infanticide continues to be practiced in these places. The BBC current affairs program "Let Her Die" followed in 1993.

24 The Indian government makes similar periodic gestures of concern about girl children: 1990 was designated the SAARC Year of the Girl Child, and the 1990s the decade of the Girl Child; other state governments have announced incentive schemes for girls; in 1997 the prime minister of India announced in his Independence Day speech (India's fiftieth anniversary of Independence) that every girl child would be given Rs 500 at her birth.

25 For detailed examination of income levels and caste composition of the sample population of their study, see Venkatachalam and Srinivasan 1993.

26 Other forms of incentive have been suggested: Dharma Kumar, for example, suggests special pensions for couples who do not have sons. She also recommends preference in jobs for single women (1983b, 1076). The Jayalalitha government in fact reserved all primary-school teaching positions for women (George 2001).

27 In a recent interview, Sabu George, one of the earliest activists in the area and among those who first "documented the existence of female infanticide in the face of widespread belief that it didn't exist in Tamilnadu," looked back on Jayalalitha's cradle baby scheme, and pronounced: "It was a fraud. The babies were kept in the government hospitals, but 90 to 95 per cent of them died. The scheme itself is flawed. How many women will come to a public place to give up their children?" (2001).

28 Contemporary scholarship on the subject includes Pakrasi 1970; Panigrahi 1972; Kasturi 1994, 169–93; Viswanath 1996 and 1998, 1104–12; Singha 1998, 130–36.

29 Panigrahi, in particular, constantly praises British colonial efforts in this direction.

30 For example, the BBC current affairs program "Let Her Die" (1993), on female feticide and infanticide in different parts of India, called forth a predictable range of Indian governmental responses: shame, denial, indignation, concern. The documentary film offering an exposé of life in India to the Western gaze, relying on a diagnosis based on civilizational otherness, is of course a familiar

genre in the Western media. (For a perceptive discussion of this television program, see Natarajan 1997, 11–12.) More recently, the *Wall Street Journal* carried a lengthy article on female infanticide in Bihar state on page 1. See Jordan 2000.

31　The Tamilnadu government was not only quicker to respond to the reports about female infanticide than northern states, especially Rajasthan and Bihar, where the practice is also widespread, it has been fortunate as well in having some dedicated government functionaries who have been able to initiate programs of social change in areas like literacy, labor, untouchability, and health. It was also the government health departments that documented the prevalence and extent of female infant deaths by recording them at district Primary Health Centres. And as Sabu George concedes, Chief Minister Jayalalitha did make it possible for donors to give money to NGOs. Hence there is more active NGO intervention in Tamilnadu than in the northern states, as well as "more knowledge about what is happening in this state" (George 2001). In Bihar, voluntary groups follow a different strategy of mobilizing midwives (who are traditionally called on to kill female infants) as agents of change.

32　Such a conclusion appears most clearly and unequivocally in the statement of M. Jeeva of SIRD (Society for Integrated Rural Development), in Venkataramani 1986, 31. But see also Venkatachalam and Srinivasan 1993, Negi 1997, Natarajan 1997, Mangai 1998, and the activists they cite for similar diagnoses. In its address to the issue of female infanticide, the activist play *Pacha Mannu* (Green Earth) deals in large part with the dowry and female ritual-expenditure problem.

33　Goody and Tambiah (1973) is a major anthropological resource. On dowry in India, with special reference to caste, see Srinivas 1984 and Rajaraman 1983. The Indian feminist debate includes Kishwar 1986, 2–13; 1988, 10–13; 1989, 2–9. A number of feminists wrote opposing Kishwar's position: see, especially, Palriwala 1989.

34　Here too I am indebted to Hoon Song for pushing me to articulate a position distinct from Agamben's on the dialectic of subjectivity and objective "power," or as he put it, "structure and sentiment."

35　Indira Rajaraman held in an early article (1983) that dowry would disappear with the rise in female contribution to family income, a prediction that has not proved entirely correct. The rational calculus of dowry requires that it have a "purely compensatory character" for the "lifetime subsistence cost of a woman." Dowry and bride-price would operate by the same logic of costs of maintenance vis-à-vis the combined value of the economic contribution she makes plus the value of the child-rearing and household tasks performed by her. Whereas dowry is uniform in the unorganized sector for this reason, in the organized sector "dowry is the result of a bidding process where potential grooms are *bid for* by aspirant families." If the expenses incurred on the wedding ceremony and rituals and on gifts were reduced, then dowry's amount would be identical to that of bride-price (275–79).

36　There is a widespread belief in the fatalism of Hindus, which is contradicted by the active, even aggressive, intervention in this "fixing."

37   See also the explanation advanced in the Status of Women report (Government of India 1975) that the spread of dowry is linked to the decline of women in the labor force since the 1911 census, which Miller would seem to endorse.

38   The National Sample Surveys have responded to pressures by women's groups by including women's unpaid work in different areas in their surveys and in the computations of the national economy.

39   Sabu George, for instance, stresses the need for "aggressive gender justice," especially property rights for women, action against bigamy, and enforcement of the law against sex-determination to prevent female feticide. He is pessimistic, however, about the impact of women's literacy, which causes a male backlash in the form of increased male violence against them. Also, he believes it is "not empowering": "women get into credit self-help groups, but they use the funds for foeticide and ostentatious weddings" (2001).

40   A revealing legal case involving the "worth of a daughter" was decided in 1983: the order issued by a motor accidents claim tribunal on the claim for compensation made by the parents of a nineteen-year-old college student, Madhu Bala Mittal, who died in a road accident, pronounced that "there is no evidence to show that the applicants suffered any pecuniary loss due to the death of their daughter. . . . She was not earning anything. She must rather be a liability for the applicants (parents). So because of her burden, the parents cannot be said to have suffered any pecuniary loss and as such no general damages can, in my opinion, be allowed to them due to the death of their daughter." (The parents had sought Rs 1 lakh in compensation and Rs 4,000 to 5,000 for medical expenses incurred during their daughter's four-day hospital stay.) The High Court on appeal did not significantly reverse the tribunal judgment. Finally, however, the Supreme Court in 1995 condemned the earlier ruling as "shocking," "insensitive to human feelings," "perverse," and prejudiced. On the grounds of constitutional equality of sexes and nondiscrimination the court awarded the parents the compensation and medical expenses they had sought. See Bhatnagar 1995.

41   Elisabeth Bumiller describes the difficulties of her journalistic attempts to investigate infanticide in Tamilnadu because of the sensitivity of the subject. The Kallar community had burned copies of the 1986 *India Today* issue that carried the report about the incidence of female infanticide in the community (1990, 105).

42   Mangai also mentions Freireian ideology and Boalian techniques as animating the structure of the play. Its declared aim, she writes, is to call forth "change, not action" (1998, WS-72).

43   The taking of any individual life can only be the singular and limit instance that will be surrounded and decided by its own conditions. The debates around euthanasia, suicide, abortion, and killing in self-defense are clearly not resolvable by any simple fiat against the taking of life. I have no wish to reduce their complexities by advocating an absolutist position.

44   Rorty therefore privileges literature over philosophy as a means of broadening

our sympathies and making possible imaginative identification with "other" people (192).

45 For a feminist critique of Rorty's politics ("complacency," "bourgeois liberalism"), as opposed to the radical potential of his postmodern pragmatic philosophy, see Fraser 1989, 5–6; and chapter 5.

46 The only feature film that has so far dealt with the issue, *Karuthamma* (Tamil, dir. Bharatiraja, 1994), uses the popular idiom of melodrama in depicting the travails of rural women's poverty and distress, though with some powerful effects (also discussed in Natarajan 1997, 24–26). Viji Srinivasan's and Venkatachalam's 1993 monograph (portions of which also appeared under Srinivasan's byline in *Frontline,* 9 October 1992: 82–84) also expresses horror and sorrow at the plight of the countryside, the poverty and destitution of the women, the oppressive patriarchal values of the region, etc. (in contrast to the objective tenor of most government reports), though in terms that are clichéd and sometimes histrionic. I mention these examples to suggest that an idiom of affect is beginning to take shape in support of bringing about a change of heart.

47 Gaddar's song, "Nindu Amassenade" (On a Moonless Night), was translated and glossed for me by D. Venkat Rao. My grateful thanks to him.

48 For some recent discussions of the uses of literature, other than Rorty, see Nussbaum 1995; Kleinman et al. 1997, especially on this topic, David B. Morris, "Voice, Genre, and Moral Community" in this volume; and Spelman 1997, 128–43.

49 Among these are the story of Abraham and Isaac in the Old Testament; Aeschylus's *Agamemnon;* George Eliot's *Adam Bede* (1859); Toni Morrison's *Beloved* (1988).

50 On "Experience and semiotics," see chapter 6 of Teresa de Lauretis's *Alice Doesn't* (1984).

7 Outlaw Woman

An earlier version of this chapter was presented as a lecture in the Gender and Change lecture series at the Institute of Research for Women at Rutgers University in February 1998: I am grateful to Marianne DeKoven for inviting me, and to everyone who contributed suggestions, comments, and questions at this forum. Thanks also to audiences at New York University, Oberlin College, University of Michigan, Ann Arbor, the Forum for Contemporary Theory workshop at Maharaja Sayajirao University, Baroda, Tulane University, New Orleans, and cscs (Center for the Study of Culture and Society), Bangalore, where I presented it subsequently. Upendra Baxi offered extensive and incisive criticism in writing following the presentation at NYU, as did Steven Pierce after the lecture at Tulane: my heartfelt thanks to them.

1 The visual "scene," as David Richards describes it, in a different context, "contracts the ... historical imagination into a moment so that it may be visualized." It appeals to a "unity of vision," "gathering together ... traces into an iconic

resolution," and thus covers over the "fractures of the historical moment" (2001, 411).

2   For an explanation of "supplement" in this sense, see Derrida: "But the supplement supplements. It adds only to replace. It intervenes or insinuates itself *in-the-place-of;* if it fills, it is as if one fills a void. If it represents and makes an image, it is by the anterior default of a presence. Compensating . . . and vicarious, the supplement is an adjunct, a subaltern instance which *takes-(the)-place*" (1976, 145).

3   See, for instance, Hansen (1988) for the representation of Phoolan as a "Virangana," or militant female in the Hindu goddess tradition; for the latter, the title of the "autobiography" produced by the French publishing house Laffont, *I, Phoolan Devi,* consciously echoing the celebrated Guatemalan testimonio *I, Rigoberta Menchu,* and market phenomena like those cited by Mala Sen, e.g., T-shirts imprinted with Phoolan's name (as one of a list of "Wild Women"), available in London's Brixton market (Sen 1993, 245).

4   Usha Ramanathan has suggested to me that the women's movement is not free of the social prejudices of the middle class, and hence Phoolan's criminality was a serious obstacle to feminist championship of her cause. I am also grateful to Ramanathan for reminding me that the arguments over the controversial representation of Phoolan's multiple rapes in the film *Bandit Queen* included the feminist position (Mala Sen's, among others) that it was acceptable in the interests of the "larger" cause of feminism (especially given that rape has been an important point of mobilization for the Indian women's movement) (personal communication). Other Indian feminists have raised the accusation of a "Brahminical" mainstream women's movement that is silent on caste issues and insisted that "dalit women speak differently" (Guru 1995; Anupama Rao 1999, 205–09).

5   I have not found any significant recent work on dacoity in the Chambal region. Most of the extant work was produced in the wake of the surrenders inspired by the Sarvodaya movement led by Jayprakrash Narayan in the 1970s, or earlier by Vinoba Bhave. A good account of dacoity in the '70s, based on first-hand journalistic reporting, is Bhaduri 1972.

6   This fact is sometimes sensationally exaggerated to represent Indian politics *tout court* especially in the Western media. For example, John F. Burns, reporting the 1998 Indian elections in the *New York Times,* invoked, predictably, "the land of Mohandas K. Gandhi, the apostle of nonviolence" to underscore the irony of this perception (1998).

7   From Sleeman's experience the police learn that an elusive dacoit may be flushed out by taking his family hostage and using them as bait!

8   Henry Sleeman was also the first to create and deploy the "approver" as an "extra-legal" source of information to catch thugs. Shahid Amin points out that Woodruffe and Ameer Ali's "classic Indian handbook of evidence," which set out how the approver's testimony is to be interpreted, was in its fourteenth edition in 1981 (1995, 74–75).

9   Radhika Singha's work on colonial "rule of law" (1993) provides brilliant insights into the complicated terrain of the thuggee campaign and the ways in which its leader, Henry Sleeman, sought special dispensation for its prosecution, deploying primarily a rhetoric of "abolition" and reform, while actually contending with the colonial office's efforts at the time to more stringently define the provisions of the penal code.

10 See, on this, Guha 1983 and 1988.

11 Thus Phoolan Devi since her release explicitly recast her dacoit exploits as caste politics. An interesting development in the Veerappan saga following his kidnapping of the popular Kannada film star Raajkumar is that he made demands on behalf of the activist/terrorist group, the Tamil Liberation Army.

12 Baxi cites figures that show that between 1979 and 1981, 7,879 Indians were killed in anti-dacoity operations through police "encounters." The "majority" of those killed were "innocent citizens, mainly lower-caste Hindus, who could not be proved to have any complicity with 'dacoit' depredation." No action was taken to punish the guilty police or compensate the innocent victims (1994, 62).

13 I base this account on Bhaduri (1972, 165–73, and appendix II, 190–98).

14 Even as early as 1960, K. F. Rustomjee, the Madhya Pradesh Inspector-General of police, had issued a statement protesting the surrenders instigated by the Vinoba Mission. He complained about the "blow to the morale of the force," the "confusion of values" engendered by glorifying criminals, and the "easy" and "temporary" solution provided by engineering surrenders (cited in Bhaduri 1972, 185–88). Upendra Baxi has commented on the state's "power to act outside the law" as one that "can be used for good causes as well as for bad causes." The surrenders of dacoits in the '60s and '70s ("the most important and sadly neglected sphere of Indian criminology") was a good cause but was handled with a typical disregard for legality: "The Vinoba mission had no basis in law, and in effect violated several provisions of the Penal Code and other laws. . . . Neither the government nor Parliament thought of providing statutory basis for the Vinoba operation in Chambal. Instead, the law was suspended by agreement among the government and party leadership" (1982, 25).

15 This touches on another significant aspect of the surrenders, the gaze of the Western world, represented as it most often has been in India by the BBC's cameras; what would the world think of this peculiarly, not to say peculiar, Indian way of doing things on the national scene?

16 Vinoba Bhave chided the government for "too much concern with its prestige on the vain question as to whom the dacoits in the state have surrendered" (Bhaduri 1972, 172–73).

17 In a long interview with Minoo Masani in the *Illustrated Weekly of India* (11 June 1972), he expressed bewilderment at the government's "inhibitions" about the surrenders he had inspired.

18 In 1995 some ninety former dacoits met at a "mahapanchayat" convened by the Mahatma Gandhi Seva Ashram and the Gandhi Peace Foundation to formulate their demands for proper rehabilitation and other facilities by the gov-

ernment. The state chief minister, Digvijay Singh, was quick to respond to them, in recognition of their electoral support. Many former dacoits expressed their continued loyalty to Arjun Singh. Phoolan was excluded from this gathering of predominantly Thakur men (Saxena 1995, 76–77).

19 See, for example, the report in the *Times of India* at the time of her surrender (dated 13 February 1983), which facilely offers this as fact, not as possible interpretation: "Hatred for the Thakurs turned her into a dacoit."

20 A politics circulates around Phoolan's image. While negotiating the surrender, she resisted being photographed despite Chaturvedi's repeated requests, for the obvious reason that a dacoit always resists it: a "wanted" poster with her picture on it would be dangerous for her. Her actual appearance at the surrender, as I will argue, was therefore invested with a great deal of significance. The celebrity status that came after her release, the release of the film, and her entry into politics made her image significant in different ways that are familiar to our media age; her objections to the film had to do in large part with the ways in which her sexuality was represented, and indeed with its representation itself.

21 Usha Ramanathan has suggested to me that journalistic access to Phoolan in jail may have been sought in the hope that she would implicate herself and her companions even as she explained her actions. Thus the sympathy for her as "wronged woman" by no means supplanted the media's righteousness in viewing her as a "criminal" brought to justice.

22 In India (as perhaps elsewhere too) female criminality shows a rising trend. Upendra Baxi cites the figures for 1971–1981 during which there was a "phenomenal" increase in female criminality, of 78.56 percent (1994, 73). A recent study by Anju Bajpai and P. K. Bajpai (2000) quotes from data available from the National Crime Records Bureau to show that the trend has continued. Women committed 3.4 percent of the total penal crimes in 1991, rising to 4.7 percent in 1996.

23 In Mexico during the years 1857–67, the female bandit "La Carambada" is reputed to have dressed in male clothes and to have waved a pistol in one hand while baring a breast with the other. " 'Look who has looted you,' she crowed, in a frontal assault on machismo" (Vanderwood 1987, 17).

24 The other terms that Phoolan recalled for Mala Sen are: housing and land to cultivate after release, free education for the children of the gang members, arms licenses, the right to remain silent about sources of arms and ammunitions and about the people who had helped them, no police remand, no handcuffing, decent treatment in jail (1993, 213).

25 The Veerappan crisis during September–November 2000 provided a close contemporary look at the ways of government. The Karnataka government deployed a special task force to capture Veerappan and also sought the Center's assistance with more forces (the National Security Guard). Television reports were filled with shots of the police and military and their equipment spread over the forest areas of Veerappan's operations. In response to journalists' queries about whether his government would bring pressure on the outlaw to

surrender, the chief minister replied that "the thought did not occur to him," but in the same breath offered, "However, he would like to study the pattern that emerged when the dacoits of the Chambal valley surrendered" (*The Hindu,* 24 November 2000).

26 There is a politics of (il)literacy here. Phoolan insisted on assurances being given to her on government stationery and had her own demands put down in writing. It appears that she did get a written agreement, which she claimed was taken away from her at the time she was taken to jail (Kamini Jaiswal, personal communication).

27 Plea bargaining is not a legal procedure available in the Indian judicial system.

28 If she had been successfully tried and sentenced to more than six years in prison, she would have been ineligible to continue as Member of Parliament. Convicted criminals' rights of participatory citizenship are curtailed (in the United States felons stand on the threshold of loss of citizenship, losing forever the right to vote).

29 In the Veerappan hostage crises in 2000, the Supreme Court in a significant judgment refused to let the governments of Karnataka and Tamilnadu release the détenues they held under the Terrorists and Disruptive Activities (Prevention) Act/National Security Act in response to Veerappan's demands, squashing the state High Court's orders. The three-judge bench of the Supreme Court indicted the governance that had led to such a situation.

30 It may also justify the use of such force as "an aspect of development, here conceived in terms of the reason of state, as reinforcing national unity and integration" (Baxi 1994, 56). Baxi identifies a range of "actors and arenas" of the state/regime whose "criminal conduct" is given "virtual immunity." Thus the state privileges criminality in the use of repressive force against secessionist and revolutionary groups and dacoits and overlooks or is complicitous with violence against lower-castes and women (58–59).

31 Baxi criticizes the Indian state thus: "The Indian state has tenuous hold on its own proclamation of legality; it combines, variously, the 'inlaw' and 'outlaw' (as it were) elements; the state as a network of ethnoclientism and jamani relationships order contrasted with the constitutional state embodying the Weberian rational legal tradition." I am grateful to Professor Baxi for his comments, offered at the presentation of an earlier version of this paper at New York University in April 1999. Compare Gramsci's comments about postwar Italy in 1919: "The Constitution—that juridical fiction of the impartial and superior sovereignty of the law, voted in by the representatives of the people—was, in reality, the beginning of the dictatorship of the propertied classes, their 'legal' conquest of the supreme power of the State" (1994, 88).

32 Thus, for example, the term "amnesty" is also used to describe dropping charges against tax offenders who voluntarily disclose their tax arrears. Baxi describes noncognizance of offenses as "an important strategy for law enforcement, crime prevention and treatment of offenders," but "only when crimes are cognized, arrest and investigations made." But many such instances of non-

cognizance, nonimplementation, or nonprosecution are self-serving (1994, 80–81).

33 Gramsci: "The concept of the sovereignty of the law is based on . . . social instability and lack of cohesion. . . . It is an anti-social concept, because it envisages the 'citizen' as being locked in an eternal war with the State. It regards human beings as the perpetual and implacable enemies of the State, which is the living, the elastic form of society—which means that it regards human beings as enemies of themselves. The Constitution is a codification of disorder and anti-human chaos" (1994, 88).

34 Consider the funeral of Mother Teresa analogously: here too the Indian state produced an inappropriate ceremony—a military funeral for a missionary of charity—with many embarrassing gaffes and missed cues. Though it had no precedent and could therefore only cobble together elements from different rituals, secular and religious, clearly the state was reluctant to lose the opportunity to stage a spectacle for national and international audiences via satellite television.

35 True, Phoolan was not a deliberately iconcoclastic cross-dresser; wearing a uniform as a dacoit and member of a (male) gang was merely practical. For instance, she rebuts the representation of the seminude bathing scene in the film by offering a reasonable explanation: "I was angry about the bathing scene. I never wore a saree, I wore a police uniform. The leaders go to bathe four by four—two watch. You have to be *hoshiar* (alert). Many have died like this. I never bathed without my blouse and lungi. If they had asked me I would have told the truth" (interview by Jain 1994, 92). But her displacement of sexuality and sexy representations by considerations of harsh necessity is equally a subversion of femininity. For a discussion of another female outlaw figure, the Palestinian "terrorist" Leila Khaled, and the politics of appearance circulating similarly around her recognition, beauty, and sexuality, see Mohan 1998/99, especially 74–78. Mohan also speaks of the "unveiled Arab woman, whose disguise is her unveiling" (75), a paradox that applies to Phoolan's emergence from hiding into a public visibility that startles (and disappoints) spectators.

36 Her experiences with the police in the locality were harrowing. In subsequent interviews and talks she repeatedly condemned police criminality, and her family received a favorable judgment in their property dispute only when it was moved from the panchayat to the higher court in the state capital.

37 Beyond the nation-state, Phoolan had access also to international forums of support. (A British Labour MP even nominated her for the Nobel prize!) Mala Sen, arguing against the ban on the screening of *Bandit Queen* that Phoolan demanded, pointed out that "the film would have made her an international figure and no government would have wanted to put her back in jail" (interview by Shrabani Basu 1994, 74). As Spivak warns, subaltern empowerment may be "manipulated to legitimize globalization" (1999b, 310). This is the unavoidable aporia of such situations.

References

Abdi, S. N. M. 1995. "Red-light Co-op Gets the Green Signal." *Times of India,* 25 June: 25.

Afzal-Khan, Fawzia. 2000. "Street Theatre in Pakistani Punjab: The Case of Ajoka, Lok Rehs, and the (So-Called) Woman Question." In *The Pre-Occupation of Postcolonial Studies,* edited by Fawzia Afzal-Khan and Kalpana Seshadri-Crooks. Durham: Duke University Press.

Agamben, Giorgio. 1998. *Homo Sacer: Sovereign Power and Bare Life,* translated by Daniel Heller-Roazen. Stanford: Stanford University Press.

Agarwal, Bina. 2000. *The "Family" in Public Policy: Fallacious Assumptions and Gender Implications.* New Delhi: National Council of Applied Economic Research.

Agnes, Flavia. 1994. "Women's Movement Within a Secular Framework: Redefining the Agenda." *Economic and Political Weekly,* 7 May: 1123–28.

——. 1995. *State, Gender, and the Rhetoric of Law Reform.* Bombay: SNDT Women's University.

——. 1996. "The Hidden Agenda Beneath the Rhetoric of Women's Rights." In *The Nation, The State, and Indian Identity,* edited by Madhushree Dutta, Flavia Agnes, and Neera Adarkar. Calcutta: Samya.

——. 1997. "Protecting Women Against Violence?: Review of a Decade of Legislation, 1980–89." In *State and Politics in India,* edited by Partha Chatterjee. Delhi: Oxford University Press. (First published in *Economic and Political Weekly,* 25 April 1992.)

Agnihotri, Indu, and Rajni Palriwala. 1993. "Tradition, the Family, and the State: Politics of the Contemporary Women's Movement." Mimeograph. Centre for Contemporary Studies, Nehru Memorial Museum and Library, New Delhi.

Agnihotri, Satish. 1995. "Missing Females: A Disaggregated Analysis." *Economic and Political Weekly,* 19 August: 2074–84.

——. 1996. "Juvenile Sex Ratios in India: A Disaggregated Analysis." *Economic and Political Weekly,* 28 December: 3369.

Ahmed, Syed Zubair. 1993. "Redefining Prostitution." *Times of India,* 27 January.

Aiyar, Shahnaz Anklesaria. 1989. "Raw Deal to Prostitutes." *Indian Express,* 14 January.

Akhileswari, R. 1999. "Of 'humanitarian deeds' and a fast buck!" *Deccan Herald,* 1 April.

Alexander, M. Jacqui. 1991. "Redrafting Morality: The Postcolonial State and the Sexual Offences Bill of Trinidad and Tobago." In *Third World Women and the Politics of Feminism,* edited by Chandra Talpade Mohanty, Ann Russo, and Lourdes Torres. Bloomington: Indiana University Press.

Amin, Shahid. 1995. *Event, Metaphor, Memory: Chauri Chaura, 1922–92.* Delhi: Oxford University Press.

Anthias, Floya, and Nira Yuval-Davis, eds. 1989. *Women-Nation-State.* London: Macmillan.

Anveshi Law Committee. 1997. "Is Gender Justice Only a Legal Issue? Political Stakes in UCC Debate." *Economic and Political Weekly,* 1 March: 453–58.

Arendt, Hannah. 1982. *Lectures on Kant's Political Philosophy.* Chicago: University of Chicago Press.

Arnold, David. 1993. *Colonizing the Body: State Medicine and Epidemic Disease in Nineteenth-Century India.* Berkeley: University of California Press.

Arora, Dolly. 1996. "The Victimising Discourse: Sex Determination Technology and Policy." *Economic and Political Weekly,* 17 February: 420–24.

Asad, Talal. 2000. "What Do Human Rights Do? An Anthropological Enquiry." *Theory and Event* 4, no. 4 (December). Available online at muse.jhu.edu/journals/theory_and_event/v004/4.4asad.html.

Athreya, Venkatesh, and Sheela Rani Chunkath. 2000. "Tackling Female Infanticide: Social Mobilisation in Dharmapuri, 1997–99." *Economic and Political Weekly,* 2 December: 4345–48.

Atwood, Margaret. 1986. *Handmaid's Tale.* London: Jonathan Cape.

Autism Network. 1998. Legal Advocacy Workshops. *NETWORK* 5, 1.

Badran, Margot, ed. 1994. *Feminists, Islam, and the Nation; Gender and the Making of Modern Egypt.* Princeton: Princeton University Press.

——. 1998. "Unifying Women: Feminist Pasts and Presents in Yemen." *Gender and History* 10, no. 3: 498–518.

Bagchi, Jashodara, ed. 1995. *Indian Women: Myth and Reality.* Hyderabad: Sangam Books.

Bajpai, Anju and P. K. Bajpai. 2000. *Female Criminality in India.* Delhi: Rawat.

Baldwin, Margaret. 1992. "Split at the Root: Prostitution and Feminist Discourses of Law Reform." *Yale Journal of Law and Feminism* 5: 47–120.

Balibar, Etienne. 1991. *Masses, Classes, Ideas: Studies on Politics and Philosophy Before and after Marx.* New York: Routledge.

——. 1995. "Ambiguous Universality." *differences: A Journal of Feminist Cultural Studies* 7, no. 1: 165–87.

Banerjee, Nirmala. 1998. "Whatever Happened to the Dreams of Modernity? The Nehruvian Era and Woman's Position." *Economic and Political Weekly,* 25 April: WS 2–7.

Bardhan, Pranab. 1997. "The State Against Society: The Great Divide in Indian Social Science Discourse." In *Nationalism, Democracy, and Development: State and Politics in India,* edited by Sugata Bose and Ayesha Jalal. Delhi: Oxford University Press.

Barrett, Michele, and Anne Phillips, eds. 1992. *Destabilising Theory: Contemporary Debates.* Cambridge: Polity Press.

Barrett, Michele. 1980. *Women's Oppression Today.* London: Verso.

Barry, Kathleen, Charlotte Bunch, and Shirley Castley, eds. 1984. *International Feminism: Networking Against Female Sexual Slavery.* New York: The International Women's Tribune Centre. Report of workshop held in Rotterdam in 1983.

Barry, Kathleen. 1979. *Female Sexual Slavery.* Englewood Cliffs: Prentice-Hall.

——. 1995. *The Prostitution of Sexuality.* New York: New York University Press.

Basu, Alaka Malwade. 1992. *Culture, the Status of Women, and Demographic Behaviour Illustrated with the Case of India.* Oxford: Clarendon Press.

Basu, Kaushik, and Sanjay Subrahmanyam, eds. 1996. *Unravelling the Nation: Sectarian Conflict and India's Secular Identity.* New Delhi: Penguin.

Basu, Shrabani. 1994. "She Changes her Mind Everyday." (Interview with Mala Sen). *Sunday,* 20–26 November: 70–74.

Bauman, Zygmunt. 1989. *Modernity and Holocaust.* Cambridge: Polity Press.

Baxi, Upendra. 1982. *The Crisis of the Indian Legal System.* New Delhi: Vikas.

——. 1988. "Taking Suffering Seriously." In *Law and Poverty,* edited by Upendra Baxi. Bombay: Tripathi.

——. 1994. *Mambrino's Helmet: Human Rights for a Changing World.* New Delhi: Har-Anand Publications.

——. 1999. "From Human Rights to the Right To Be a Woman." In *Engendering Law: Essays in Honour of Lotika Sarkar,* edited by Amita Dhanda and Archana Parasher. Lucknow: Eastern Book Company.

Beauvoir, Simone de. 1974. *The Second Sex,* translated and edited by H. M. Parshley. New York: Vintage Books. (First published in French in 1949.)

Bell, Laurie, ed. 1987. *Good Girls, Bad Girls: Feminists and Sex Trade Workers Face to Face.* Toronto: Seal Press.

Bell, Shannon. 1994. *Reading, Writing, and Rewriting the Prostitute Body.* Bloomington: Indiana University Press.

Benhabib, Seyla. 1992. *Situating the Self: Gender, Community, and Postmodernism in Contemporary Ethics.* Cambridge: Polity Press.

Bennett, Tony. 1998. *Culture: A Reformer's Science.* London: Sage.

Besant, Annie. 1987. "The Legislation of Female Slavery in England." In *The Sexuality Debates,* edited by Sheila Jeffreys. New York: Routlege and Kegan Paul.

Bhabha, Homi. 1994. *The Location of Culture.* London: Routledge.

Bhaduri, Taroon Coomar. 1972. *Chambal: The Valley of Terror.* Delhi: Vikas.

Bhagat, Rasheeda. 1994. "Agony in the Asylum." *Indian Express,* 20 February.

References   281

Bhargava, Rajeev, ed. 1998. *Secularism and Its Critics.* Delhi: Oxford University Press.

Bharucha, Rustom. 1998. "The Shifting Sites of Secularism: Cultural Politics and Activism in India Today." *Economic and Political Weekly,* 24 January: 167–80.

Bhasin, Kamla, Ritu Menon, and Nighat Said Khan, eds. 1994. *Against All Odds: Essays on Women, Religion, and Development from India and Pakistan.* New Delhi: Kali for Women.

Bhatnagar, Rakesh. 1995. "Fixing the Worth of a Daughter." *Times of India,* 4 September.

Bhatt, Ela R. 1998. " 'Doosri Azadi': SEWA's Perspectives on Early Years of Independence." *Economic and Political Weekly,* 25 April: WS 25–27.

——. 1999. "Towards the Second Freedom." In *From Independence Towards Freedom: Indian Women Since 1947,* edited by Bharati Ray and Aparna Basu. Delhi: Oxford University Press.

Bhattacharya, Lopamudra. 1995. "Home Sickness." *Sunday,* November 26–December 2.

Bidwai, Praful. 1995. "Revamping Personal Laws: Reform, Yes; Common Code, No." *Times of India,* 17 August.

Bilgrami, Akeel. 1998. "Secularism, Nationalism, and Modernity." In *Secularism and Its Critics,* edited by Rajeev Bhargava. Delhi: Oxford University Press.

Bishop, Ryan, and Lillian S. Robinson. 1998. *Night Market: Sexual Cultures and the Thai Economic Miracle.* New York: Routledge.

Bose, Sugata, and Ayesha Jalal, eds. 1997. *Nationalism, Democracy, and Development: State and Politics in India.* Delhi: Oxford University Press.

——. 1997. "Nationalism, Democracy, and Development." In *Nationalism, Democracy, and Development: State and Politics in India,* edited by Sugata Bose and Ayesha Jalal. Delhi: Oxford University Press.

Brown, Wendy. 1995. *States of Injury: Power and Freedom in Late Modernity.* Princeton: Princeton University Press.

Brownmiller, Susan. 1976. *Against Our Will: Men, Women, and Rape.* New York: Simon and Schuster.

Bryson, Valerie. 1999. *Feminist Debates: Issues of Theory and Political Practice.* London: Macmillan.

Buch, Nirmala. 1998. "State Welfare Policy and Women, 1950–1975." *Economic and Political Weekly,* 25 April: WS 18–20.

Bumiller, Elisabeth. 1990. *May You Be the Mother of a Thousand Sons.* New York: Random House.

Burns, John F. 1998. "In India, Criminals Take to the Campaign Trail." *New York Times,* 26 February.

"Butchers in the Guise of Saviours." (No date noted, but probably 1994.) Report prepared by Stree Kuti, Shramjivika, Forum against Oppression of Women, Lokashahi hakk Sanghatana, and volunteer parents and social workers.

Butler, Judith, and Joan Scott, eds. 1992. *Feminists Theorize the Political.* New York: Routledge.

Butler, Judith. 1990. *Gender Trouble: Feminism and the Subversion of Identity.* New York: Routledge.

Card, Robert. 2000. "Infanticide and the Liberal View on Abortion." *Bioethics* 14, no. 4: 340–51.

Centre for Feminist Legal Reform (CFLR). 1997. Memorandum on Law Reform of Sex Work/Prostitution in India, Working Draft. Presented at the CFLR seminar "Hustling for Rights: The Legal Regulation and Representation of the Sex Trade in South Asia," 16–18 August, New Delhi.

Chancer, Lynn Sharon. 1993. "Prostitution, Feminist Theory, and Ambivalence: Notes from the Sociological Underground." *Social Text* 37 (winter): 143–72.

Chandhoke, Neera. 1995. *State and Civil Society: Explorations in Political Theory.* New Delhi: Sage.

Chapkis, Wendy. 1997. *Live Sex Acts: Women Performing Erotic Labour.* London: Cassell.

Chatterjee, Partha. 1986. *Nationalist Thought and the Colonial World: A Derivative Discourse?* Delhi: Oxford University Press.

———. 1994. *The Nation and Its Fragments: Colonial and Postcolonial Histories.* Delhi: Oxford University Press.

———. 1998a. "Community in the East." *Economic and Political Weekly,* 7 February: 277–82.

———. 1998b. "Secularism and Tolerance." In *Secularism and Its Critics,* edited by Rajeev Bhargava. Delhi: Oxford University Press.

———. 2000. "Democracy and the Violence of the State: A Political Negotiation of Death." Lecture delivered at the Centre for the Study of Developing Societies, New Delhi.

Chatterjee, Ratnabali. 1993. "Prostitution in Nineteenth-Century Bengal: Construction of Class and Gender." *Social Scientist* 21, nos. 9–11 (September–November): 159–72.

Chaudhuri, Maitrayee. 1996. "Citizens, Workers, and Emblems of Culture: An Analysis of the First Plan Document on Women." In *Social Reform, Sexuality, and the State,* edited by Patricia Uberoi. New Delhi: Sage.

———. 2000. " 'Feminism' in Print Media." *Indian Journal of Gender Studies* 7, no. 2 (July–December): 263–88.

Chhachi, Amrita. 1994. "Identity Politics, Secularism, and Women: A South Asian Perspective." In *Forging Identities: Gender, Communities, and the State in India,* edited by Zoya Hassan. New Delhi: Kali for Women.

Chhachi, Amrita, Farida Khan, Gautam Navlakha, Kumkum Sangari, Neeraj Malik, Ritu Menon, Tanika Sarkar, Uma Chakravarty, Urvashi Butalia, Zoya Hasan. 1998. "UCC and Women's Movement." *Economic and Political Weekly,* 28 February: 487–88.

Chibber, Pradeep. 1999. *Democracy Without Associations: Transformation of the Party System and Social Cleavages in India.* Ann Arbor: University of Michigan Press.

Chowdhary, Prem. 1994. *The Veiled Women: Shifting Gender Equations in Rural Haryana, 1880–1990.* Delhi: Oxford University Press.

Chunkath, Sheila Rani, and V. B. Athreya. 1997. "Female Infanticide in Tamil Nadu: Some Evidence." *Economic and Political Weekly,* 26 April: WS 21–28.

Cohen, Jean L., and Andrew Arato. 1992. *Civil Society and Political Theory.* Cambridge: MIT Press.

Cohen, Stanley, and Andrew Scull, eds. 1983. *Social Control and the State: Historical and Comparative Essays.* Oxford: Martin Roberton.

Colker, Ruth. 1992. "The Example of Lesbians: A Posthumous Reply to Professor Mary Joe Frug." *Harvard Law Review* 105: 1084–95.

Connolly, William. 1991. *Identity/Difference: Democratic Negotiations of Political Paradox.* Ithaca: Cornell University Press.

Coole, Diane. 1988. *Women in Political Theory: From Ancient Misogyny to Contemporary Feminism.* Sussex: Wheatsheaf Books.

Corea, Gena, Jalna Hanman, and Renate Duelli-Klein, eds. 1987. *Man-made Woman: How New Reproductive Technologies Affect Women.* Bloomington: Indiana University Press.

Corrigan, Philip, and Derek Sayer. 1985. *The Great Arch: English State Formation as Cultural Revolution.* Oxford: Basil Blackwell.

D'Cunha, Jean. 1992. "Prostitution Laws—Ideological Dimensions and Enforcement Practices." *Economic and Political Weekly,* 25 April: WS 34–44.

Dang, Kokila. 1993. "Prostitutes, Patrons, and the State: Nineteenth-Century Awadh." *Social Scientist* 21, nos. 9–11 (September–November): 173–96.

Das, Veena. 1995. *Critical Events: An Anthropological Perspective on Contemporary India.* Delhi: Oxford University Press.

De Lauretis, Teresa. 1984. *Alice Doesn't: Feminism, Semiotics, Cinema.* Bloomington: Indiana University Press.

Deliege, Robert. 1997. *The World of the "Untouchables": The Paraiyars of Tamil Nadu.* Delhi: Oxford University Press.

Derrida, Jacques. 1976. *Of Grammatology,* translated by Gayatri Chakravorty Spivak. Baltimore: Johns Hopkins University Press.

——. 1987. *Glas.* Translated by J. Leavey and R. Rand. Lincoln: University of Nebraska Press.

Devi, Mahasweta. 1995. "Douloti the Bountiful." In *Imaginary Maps,* translated by Gayatri Chakravorty Spivak. New York: Routledge.

——. 1995. *Imaginary Maps,* translated by Gayatri Chakravorty Spivak. New York: Routledge.

Dey, J. 1996. "Prostitutes Oppose Khairnar's Rescue Bid." *Indian Express,* 13 January.

Dhagamwar, Vasudha. 1997. "Tale of Ameena, Chhotu, and Countless Other Children." In Dhagamwar, *Criminal Justice or Chaos?* New Delhi: Har-Anand Publications.

——. 2000. Letter in the "Opinion" section. *The Hindu,* 16 September.

Dhanda, Amita, and Archana Parashar, eds. 1999. *Engendering Law: Essays in Honour of Lotika Sarkar.* Lucknow: Eastern Book Company.

Dhanda, Amita. 1995. "Law, Psychiatry, and Human Rights." *Seminar* 430 (June): 22–25.

Dhanda, Meena. 2000. "Representation for Women: Should Feminists Support Quotas?" *Economic and Political Weekly,* 12 August: 2969–76.

Dhareshwar, Vivek. 1993. "Caste and the Secular Self." *Journal of Arts and Ideas* 25–26 (December): 115–26.

Ding, Naifei. 2000. "Prostitutes, Parasites, and the House of State Feminism." *Inter-Asia Cultural Studies* 1, no. 2 (August): 283–300.

Dow, Unity. 1998. "Birth registration: The 'First' Right." In *The Progress of Nations.* New York: UNICEF.

Dreze, Jean, and Amartya Sen. 1995. *India: Economic Development and Social Opportunity.* Delhi: Oxford University Press.

Dreze, Jean. 1997. Government Grants and the Girl Child. *Times of India,* 29 September.

Dutta Gupta, Reeta. 1996. "Juvenile Homes Are Like Jails." *Times of India,* 11 January.

Dutta, Madhushree, Flavia Agnes, and Neera Adarkar, eds. 1996. *The Nation, The State, and Indian Identity.* Calcutta: Samya.

Edelstein, Judy. 1987. "In the Massage Parlor." In *Sex Work: Writings by Women in the Sex Industry,* edited by Frederique Delacoste and Priscilla Alexander. Pittsburgh: Cleis Press.

Engels, Frederick. 1968. *The Origin of the Family, Private Property, and the State.* In Karl Marx and Frederick Engels, *Selected Works* (in one volume). Moscow: Progress Publishers. (Engels's essay originally published in 1884.)

Enloe, Cynthia. 1992. *Let the Good Times Roll: Prostitution and the U.S. Military in Asia.* New York: Free Press.

Ericsson, Lars. 1980. "Charges Against Prostitution: An Attempt at a Philosophical Assessment." *Ethics* 90: 335–66.

Fernand-Laurent, Jean. 1985. *Activities for the Advancement of Women: Equality, Development, and Peace.* New York: United Nations.

Foucault, Michel. 1977. *Language, Counter-Memory, Practice: Selected Essays and Interviews.* Translated by Donald Bouchard and Sherry Simon. Ithaca: Cornell University Press.

——. 1980. *The History of Sexuality,* Volume I. Translated by Robert Hurley. London: Allen Lane.

——. 1991. "Governmentality." In *The Foucault Effect: Studies in Governmentality,* edited by Graham Burchell, Colin Gordon, and Peter Miller. Chicago: University of Chicago Press.

Fox, Richard G. 1996. "Communalism and Modernity." In *Making India Hindu: Religion, Community, and the Politics of Democracy in India,* edited by David Ludden. Delhi: Oxford University Press.

Fox-Genovese, Elizabeth. 1988. *Within the Plantation Household.* Chapel Hill: University of North Carolina Press.

——. 1991. *Feminism Without Illusions: A Critique of Individualism.* Chapel Hill: University of North Carolina Press.

Franzway, Suzanne, Dianne Court, and R. W. Connell. 1989. *Staking a Claim: Feminism, Bureaucracy, and the State.* Sydney: Allen and Unwin.

Fraser, Nancy. 1989. *Unruly Practices: Power, Discourse, and Gender in Contemporary Social Theory.* Minneapolis: University of Minnesota Press.

——. 1993. "Beyond the Master-Subject Model: Reflections on Carole Pateman's *Sexual Contract.*" *Social Text 37* (Winter): 173–82.

——. 1997. *Justice Interruptus: Critical Reflections on the "Postsocialist" Condition.* London: Routledge.

Frederick, John, and Thomas L. Kelly, eds. 2001. *Fallen Angels: The Sex Workers of South Asia,* Delhi: Roli Books.

Freitag, Sandra B. 1996. "Contesting in Public: Colonial Legacies and Contemporary Communalism." In *Making India Hindu: Religion, Community, and the Politics of Democracy in India,* edited by David Ludden. Delhi: Oxford University Press.

Frug, Mary Joe. 1992. "A Postmodern Feminist Legal Manifesto." *Harvard Law Review* 105: 1045–75.

Gandhi, Nandita, and Nandita Shah. 1991. *The Issues at Stake: Theory and Practice in the Contemporary Women's Movement in India.* New Delhi: Kali for Women.

Gangoli, Geetanjali. 1998. "Prostitution, Legalisation, and Decriminalisation." *Economic and Political Weekly,* 7 March: 504–5.

Garland, David. 1990. *Punishment and Modern Society: A Study in Social Theory.* Oxford; Clarendon Press.

George, Sabu, and Ranbir S. Dahiya. 1998. "Female Foeticide in Rural Haryana." *Economic and Political Weekly,* 8 August: 2191–98.

George, Sabu, Rajaratnam Abel, and B. D. Miller. 1992. "Female Infanticide in Rural South India." *Economic and Political Weekly,* 30 May: 1153–56.

George, Sabu. 2001. "Little Girl Lost. Interview with Vidya Subramaniam." *Times of India,* 30 August.

Ghose, Sanjoy. 1997. "Development and Nationalism: An NGO Perspective." *Times of India,* 5 December.

Ghosh, Arun. 1996. "Health Care and Globalisation: Case for a Selective Approach." *Economic and Political Weekly,* 24 February: 441–42.

Gilbert, Paul. 1994. *Terrorism, Security, and Nationality: An Introductory Study in Applied Political Philosophy.* New York: Routledge.

Goody, J., and S. J. Tambiah, eds. 1973. *Bridewealth and Dowry.* Cambridge: Cambridge University Press.

Government of India. 1975. *Towards Equality.* Report of the Committee on the Status of Women in India. New Delhi: Ministry of Educaiton and Social Welfare, Department of Social Welfare.

——. 1988. *Shram Shakti.* Report of the National Commission on Self-Employed Women and Women in the Informal Sector, Department of Women and Child Development, New Delhi.

Gramsci, Antonio. 1971. *Selections from the Prison Notebooks,* edited and translated by Quention Hoare and Geoffrey Nowell Smith. New York: International Publishers.

——. 1994. *Pre-Prison Writings,* edited by Richard Bellamy and translated by Virginia Cox. Cambridge: Cambridge University Press.

Guha, Ranajit. 1983. *Elementary Aspects of Peasant Insurgency in Colonial India.* Delhi: Oxford University Press.

——. 1988. "The Prose of Counter-Insurgency." In *Selected Subaltern Studies,* edited by Ranajit Guha and Gayatri Chakravorty Spivak. New York: Oxford University Press.

Guru, Gopal. 1995. "Dalit Women Talk Differently." *Economic and Political Weekly*, 14 October: 2548–49.

Habermas, Jürgen. 1989. *The Structural Transformation of the Public Sphere: An Enquiry into a Category of Bourgeois Society.* Translated by Thomas Burger. London: Polity Press.

Haksar, Nandita. 1999. "Human Rights Lawyering: A Feminist Perspective." In *Engendering Law: Essays in Honour of Lotika Sarkar*, edited by Amita Dhanda and Archana Parashar. Lucknow: Eastern Book Company.

Hale, Sondra. 1997. *Gender Politics in the Sudan: Islamism, Socialism, and the State.* Boulder: Westview Press.

Hall, Stuart. 1993. "Culture, Community, Nation." *Cultural Studies* 7, no. 3 (October): 349–63.

Hansen, Kathryn. 1988. "The *Virangana* in North Indian History, Myth, and Popular Culture." *Economic and Political Weekly*, 30 April: WS 25–33.

Haraway, Donna. 1991. "The Contest for Primate Nature: Daughters of Man-the-Hunter in the Field." In Haraway, *Simians, Cyborgs, and Women: The Reinvention of Nature.* New York: Routledge.

Harriss-White, Barbara. 1999. "Gender-Cleansing: The Paradox of Development and Deteriorating Female Life Chances in Tamilnadu." In *Signposts: Gender Issues in Post-Independence India*, edited by Rajeswari Sunder Rajan. Delhi: Kali for Women.

——. 1999b. "Onto a Loser: Disability in India." In *Illfare in India: Essays on India's Special Sector in Honour of S. Guhan*, edited by S. Subramanian and Barbara Harriss-White. New Delhi: Sage.

Hassan, Zoya, ed. 1994. *Forging Identities: Gender, Communities, and the State in India.* New Delhi: Kali for Women.

Hay, Douglas. 1975. Preface. In *Albion's Fatal Tree: Crime and Society in Eighteenth-Century England*, edited by Douglas Hay, Peter Linebaugh, and Edward Thompson. New York: Pantheon Books.

Haynes, Douglas, and Gyan Prakash, eds. 1992. *Contesting Power: Resistance and Everyday Social Relations in South Asia.* Delhi: Oxford University Press.

Hegel, G. W. F. 1967. *Philosophy of Right.* Translated by T. M. Knox. London: Oxford University Press.

Heimsath, Charles H. 1961. *Indian Nationalism and Hindu Social Reform.* Princeton: Princeton University Press.

Heng, Geraldine. 1997. " 'A Great Way to Fly': Nationalism, the State, and the Varieties of Third-World Feminism." In *Feminist Genealogies, Colonial Legacies, and Democratic Futures*, edited by Chandra Talpade Mohanty and M. Jacqui Alexander. New York: Routledge.

Ho, Josephine Chuen-Juei. 2000. "Self-Empowerment and Professionalism: Conversations with Taiwanese Sex Workers." *Inter-Asia Cultural Studies* 1, no. 2 (August): 283–300.

Hobsbawm, Eric. 1965. *Primitive Rebels: Studies in Archaic Forms of Social Movements in the Nineteenth and Twentieth Centuries.* New York: Norton. (First published in 1959.)

——. 1981. *Bandits.* New York: Pantheon Books. (First published in 1969.)

Holmes, Helen B., and Betty B. Hoskins. 1987. "Prenatal and Preconception Sex

Choice Technologies: A Path to Femicide?" In *Man-Made Woman: How New Reproductive Technologies Affect Women,* edited by Gena Corea, Jalna Hanman, and Renate Duelli-Klein. Bloomington: Indiana University Press.

Horigard, Cecilie, and Liv Finstad. 1992. *Backstreets: Prostitution, Money, and Love.* Translated by Katherine Hanson, Nancy Sipes, and Barbara Wilson. University Park: Pennsylvania State University Press. (Originally published in 1986.)

Hossain, Rokeya Sakhawat. 1988. *Sultana's Dream.* Edited and translated by Roushan Jahan and Hanna Papanek. New York: Feminist Press. (First published in 1905.)

Hrdy, Sarah Blaffer. 1996. "Fitness Tradeoffs in the History of Delegated Mothering with Special Reference to Wet-Nursing, Abandonment, and Infanticide." In *Human Nature: A Critical Reader,* edited by Laura Betzig. New York: Oxford University Press.

Human Development Report. 2000. New York: United Nations Publications; also New Delhi: Oxford University Press.

Igntieff, Michael. 1983. "State, Civil Society, and Total Institutions: A Critique of Recent Social Histories of Punishment." In *Social Control and the State: Historical and Comparative Essays,* edited by Stanley Cohen and Andrew Scull. Oxford: Martin Robertson.

Irigaray, Luce. 1985. *This Sex Which Is Not One.* Translated by Catherine Porter and Carolyne Burke. Ithaca: Cornell University Press.

Ismael, Razia. 2000. "The Girl Child: India's Forgotten Priority, a Policy Consultation at the Close of the SAARC Decade." Lecture delivered at SAARC Girl Child Day celebration, India International Centre, New Delhi.

Iyer, Lakshmi. 1994. "Pune Operations: Some Ethical Questions." *Hindustan Times,* 14 February.

Jacob, Nitya. 1994. "Ethics of Hysterectomy for the Retarded." *Pioneer,* 23 February.

Jain, Kalpana. 1994. "The Mindless Matter." *Times of India,* 20 February.

Jain, Madhu. 1994. "The Truth on Trial." (Includes interview with Phoolan Devi.) *India Today,* 15 October: 92–94.

Jayal, Niraja Gopal. 1999. *Democracy and the State: Welfare, Secularism, and Development in Contemporary India.* Delhi: Oxford University Press.

Jeffery, Patricia, and Amrita Basu, eds. 1999. *Resisting the Sacred and the Secular: Women's Activism and Politicized Religion in South Asia.* New Delhi: Kali for Women.

Jeffery, Patricia. 1999. "Agency, Activism, Agendas." In *Resisting the Sacred and the Secular: Women's Activism and Politicized Religion in South Asia,* edited by Patricia Jeffery and Amrita Basu. New Delhi: Kali for Women.

Jeffreys, Sheila, ed. 1987. *The Sexuality Debates.* New York: Routledge and Kegan Paul.

Jenness, Valerie. 1993. *Making It Work: The Prostitutes' Rights Movement in Perspective.* New York: Aldinede Gruyter.

John, Mary E. 1999. "Gender, Development, and the Women's Movement: Problems for a History of the Present." In *Signposts: Gender Issues in Post-Independence India,"* edited by Rajeswari Sunder Rajan. New Delhi: Kali for Women.

John, Mary E., and Janaki Nair, eds. 1998. *A Question of Silence? The Sexual Economies of Modern India.* New Delhi: Kali for Women.

Joint Women's Program. 1995. "Women: Towards Beijing." *Lokayan Bulletin* 12, nos. 1–2 (July–October): 67–73.

Jordan, Miriam. 2000. "Brief Lives: Among Poor Villagers, Female Infanticide Still Flourishes in India." *Wall Street Journal,* 9 May: 1.

Jung, Anees. 1993. "The Lost Honour of Ameena Begum." In *Night of the New Moon.* New Delhi: Penguin. Originally published in *Times of India,* 19 July 1992.

Kabeer, Naila. 1995. *Reversed Realities: Gender Hierarchies in Development Thought.* New Delhi: Kali for Women.

Kakar, Sanjiv. 1996. "Medical Developments and Patient Unrest in the Leprosy Asylum, 1860–1940." *Social Scientist* 24, nos. 4–6 (April–June): 62–81.

Kakar, Sudhir. 1996. "The Construction of a New Hindu Identity." In *Unravelling the Nation: Sectarian Conflict and India's Secular Identity,* edited by Kaushik Basu and Sanjay Subrahmanyam. New Delhi: Penguin.

Kalpagam, U. 1992. "Colonising Power and Colonised Bodies." *Indian Journal of Social Sciences* 5, no. 1 (January–March): 61–80.

Kandiyoti, Deniz, ed. 1991. *Women, Islam, and the State.* Philadelphia: Temple University Press.

Kannabiran, Kalpana. 2001. "Empowering Women." *The Hindu,* 26 August.

Kaplan, Cora. 1986. *Sea Changes.* London: Verso.

Kapur, Ratna, ed. 1996. *Feminist Terrains in Legal Domains: Interdisciplinary Essays on Women and Law in India.* New Delhi: Kali for Women.

Kapur, Ratna, and Brenda Cossman. 1993a. "Communalising Gender/Engendering Community: Women, Legal Discourse, and Saffron Agenda." *Economic and Political Weekly,* 24 April: WS 35–44.

———. 1993b. "On Women, Equality, and the Constitution: Through the Looking Glass of Feminism." Special Issue on Feminism and Law. *National Law School Journal* 1: 1–61.

———. 1996. *Subversive Sites: Feminist Engagements with Law in India.* New Delhi: Sage.

Karkaria, Bachi J. 1994. "Sex Workers of the World, Unionise." *Times of India,* 21 August.

Karlekar, Malavika. 1998. "Domestic Violence." *Economic and Political Weekly,* 4 July: 1741–51.

Kasturi, Malavika. 1994. "Law and Crime in India: British Policy and the Female Infanticide Act of 1870." *Indian Journal of Gender Studies* 1, no. 2: 169–93.

Kaviraj, Sudipta. 1992. "The Imaginary Institution of India." In *Subaltern Studies 7,* edited by Partha Chatterjee and Gyan Pandey. Delhi: Oxford University Press.

Kazmi, Nikhat. 1993. "Behind the Begum's *Burqa.*" *Times of India,* 19 September.

Kempadoo, Kamla, and Jo Doezema, eds. 1999. *Global Sex Workers.* London: Routledge.

Kher, Aparna. 2000. "Dreams Die Young." *Pioneer,* 25 January.

Khullar, Vandana. 1994. "A Move to Help These Girls Live with Dignity." *Indian Express,* 14 February.

Kim, Elaine H., and Chungmoo Choi, eds. 1998. *Dangerous Women: Gender and Korean Nationalism.* New York: Routledge.

Kishwar, Madhu, and Ruth Vanita. 1986. "Using Women as a Pretext for Repression." *Manushi: A Journal about Women and Society* 37, no. 2 (November–December): 2–8.

Kishwar, Madhu. 1986. "Dowry—To Ensure Her Happiness or Disinherit Her?" *Manushi: A Journal about Women and Society* 34 (May–June): 2–13.

———. 1988. "Rethinking Dowry Boycott." *Manushi: A Journal About Women and Society* 48 (September–October): 10–13.

———. 1989. "Towards More Just Norms for Marriage: Continuing the Dowry Debate." *Manushi: A Journal About Women and Society* 53 (July–August): 2–9.

———. 1994. "Codified Hindu Law: Myth and Reality." *Economic and Political Weekly*, 8 May: 2145–67.

Kiss, Elizabeth. 1997. "Alchemy or Fool's Gold? Assessing Feminist Doubts about Rights." In *Reconstructing Political Theory: Feminist Perspectives*, edited by Mary Lyndon Shanley and Uma Narayan. Cambridge: Polity Press.

Kleinman, Arthur, Veena Das, and Margaret M. Lock. 1997. *Social Suffering*. Berkeley: University of California Press.

Kosambi, Meera. 1991. "Girl Brides and Socio-Legal Change: Age of Consent Bill (1891) Controversy." *Economic and Political Weekly*, 30 August: 1857–68.

Kotiswaran, Prabha. 2001. "Preparing for Civil Disobedience: Indian Sex Workers and the Law." *Boston College Third World Journal* 21, no. 2, (spring): 161–242.

Krishna Iyer, V. R. 1980. *Justice and Beyond*. New Delhi: Deep and Deep.

Krishnakumar, Asha. 1992. "Beyond Symptoms: Will the Government's Measures Help?" *Frontline*, 4 December: 105.

Krishnaraj, Maitreyi, ed. 1995. *Remaking Society for Women: Visions—Past and Present*. New Delhi: Indian Association of Women's Studies.

———. 1998. "Women and the Public Domain: Critical Issues for Women Studies." *Economic and Political Weekly*, 21 February: 391–95.

Kshirsagar, Alka. 1994. "No Method in the Madness." *Times of India*, 20 February.

Kuhn, Annette, and Anna Wolpe, eds. 1978. *Feminism and Materialism*. London: Routledge and Kegan Paul.

Kulkarni, Mangesh. 1996. "Action Groups and the State." *Seminar* 496 (October): 43–47.

Kumar, Dharma. 1983a. "Amniocentesis Again." *Economic and Political Weekly*, 11 June: 1075–76.

———. 1983b. "Male Utopias or Nightmares?" *Economic and Political Weekly*, 15 January: 61–64.

Kumar, Krishna. 1993. "Market Economy and Mass Literacy." *Economic and Political Weekly*, 11 December: 2727–34.

Kumar, Sanjay. 2000. "Civil Society in Society." *Economic and Political Weekly*, 29 July: 2776–79.

Lama-Rewal, Stephanie Tawa. 2001. "Fluctuating, Ambivalent Legitimacy of Gender as a Political Category." *Economic and Political Weekly*, 28 April: WS 1435–40.

Linebaugh, Peter. 1992. *The London Hanged: Crime and Civil Society in the Eighteenth Century*. Cambridge: Cambridge University Press.

Lister, Ruth. 1997. *Citizenship: Feminist Perspectives.* London: Macmillan.

Lloyd, Genevieve. 1984. *The Man of Reason: "Male" and "Female" in Western Philosophy.* London: Methuen.

Ludden, David, ed. 1996. *Making India Hindu: Religion, Community, and the Politics of Democracy in India.* Delhi: Oxford University Press.

Maalouf, Amin. 1993. *The First Century After Beatrice.* Translated by Dorothy Blair. London: Quartet Books.

MacKinnon, Catharine A. 1983. "Feminism, Marxism, Method, and the State: Toward Feminist Jurisprudence." *Signs: Journal of Women in Culture and Society* 8, no. 11: 635–58.

Macleod, Roy, and Milton Lewis, eds. 1988. *Imperial Health in British India, 1857–1900.* London: Routledge.

Madan, T. N. 1998. "Secularism in Its Place." In *Secularism and Its Critics,* edited by Rajeev Bhargava. Delhi: Oxford University Press.

Malhotra, Vinay Kumar. 1986. *Welfare State and Supreme Court in India.* New Delhi: Deep and Deep.

Mana. 1998. "Thottil Kuzhandaigal Thittam Enna Aachhu?" [Whatever Happened to the Cradle-Babies Scheme?] *Kumudam,* 21 May: 16–23.

Mangai, A. 1998. "Cultural Intervention Through Theatre: Case Study of a Play on Female Infanticide/Foeticide." *Economic and Political Weekly,* 31 October: WS 70–72.

Marshall, T. H. 1950. *Citizenship and Social Class.* Cambridge: Cambridge University Press.

Mazumdar, Vina. 1994. *Amniocentesis and Sex Selection.* Occasional paper. New Delhi: Centre for Women's Development Studies.

——. 1999. "Political Ideology of the Women's Movement's Engagement with Law." In *Engendering Law,* edited by Amita Dhanda and Archana Parasher. Lucknow: Eastern Press.

McClintock, Anne. 1993. "Sex Workers and Sex Work: Introduction." *Social Text* 37 (winter): 1–10.

McIntosh, Mary. 1978. "The State and the Oppression of Women." In *Feminism and Materialism,* edited by Annette Kuhn and Anna Wolpe. London: Routledge and Kegan Paul.

Mencher, Joan. 1999. "NGOs: Are They a Force for Change?" *Economic and Political Weekly,* 24 July: 2081–86.

Menon, Meena. 1998. "Legitimising Prostitution." *The Hindu,* 14 June.

Menon, Nivedita. 1996. "The impossibility of 'justice': Female foeticide and feminist discourse on abortion." In *Social Reform, Sexuality, and the State,* edited by Patricia Uberoi. New Delhi: Sage.

——. 1998a. "Rights: Rethinking Theory and Practice." *Economic and Political Weekly,* 31 January: PE 2.

——. 1998b. "State/Gender/Community: Ctizenship in Contemporary India." *Economic and Political Weekly,* 31 January: PE 3–10.

——, ed. 1999a. *Gender and Politics in India.* New Delhi: Oxford University Press.

——. 1999b. Review of *Engendering Justice. Seminar* 483 (November): 65–67.

Menon, Ritu, and Kamla Bhasin. 1998. *Borders and Boundaries: Women in India's Partition.* New Delhi: Kali for Women.

Menon, Ritu. 1999. "Reproducing the Legitimate Community: Secularity, Sexuality, and the State in Postpartition India." In *Resisting the Sacred and the Secular: Women's Activism and Politicized Religion in South Asia,* edited by Patricia Jeffery and Amrita Basu. New Delhi: Kali for Women.

Mernissi, Fatima. 1999. *Women and Islam.* Oxford: Basil Blackwell.

Miller, Barbara D. 1987. Female Infanticide. *Seminar* 331: 18–21.

——. 1997. *The Endangered Sex: Neglect of Female Children in Rural North India.* Delhi: Oxford University Press. (First published by Cornell University Press in 1981.)

Minow, Martha. 1992. "Incomplete Correspondence: An Unsent Letter to Mary Joe Frug." *Harvard Law Review* 105: 1096–105.

Mitchell, Juliet. 1984. *The Longest Revolution: On Feminism, Literature, and Psychoanalysis.* New York: Pantheon Books. (First published in 1966.)

Mitta, Manoj. 1995. "Where Are They Now: Ameena." *India Today,* 31 December: 157–59.

Mitter, Swasti. 1986. *Common Fate, Common Bond: Women in the Global Economy.* London: Pluto Press.

Mohan, Rajeswari. 1998/99. "Loving Palestine: Nationalist Activism and Feminist Agency in Leila Khaled's Subversive Bodily Acts." *Interventions* 1, no. 1: 52–80.

Mohanty, Chandra Talpade, and M. Jacqui Alexander, eds. 1997. *Feminist Genealogies, Colonial Legacies, and Democratic Futures.* New York: Routledge.

Mohanty, Chandra Talpade, Ann Russo, and Lourdes Torres, eds. 1991. *Third World Women and the Politics of Feminism.* Bloomington: Indiana University Press.

Mohanty, Satya. 1998. *Literary Theory and the Claims of History: Postmodernism, Objectivity, Multicultural Politics.* Delhi: Oxford University Press.

Monks, Judith. 1999. " 'It Works Both Ways': Belonging and Social Participation Among Women with Disabilities." In *Women, Citizenship, and Difference,* edited by Nira Yuval-Davis and Prina Werbner. London: Zed Books.

Morris, David B. 1997. "Voice, Genre, and Moral Community." In *Social Suffering,* edited by Arthur Kleinman, Veena Das, and Margaret M. Lock. Berkeley: University of California Press.

Morrison, Toni. 1998. *Beloved.* New York: Knopf.

Mouffe, Chantal. 1992. "Feminism, Citizenship, and Radical Democratic Politics." In *Feminists Theorize the Political,* edited by Judith Butler and Joan Scott. London: Routledge.

——. 1993. *The Return of the Political.* London: Verso.

Mukherjee, Mukul. 1999. "Women and Work in India: A Collage from Five Decades of Independence." In *From Independence Towards Freedom: Indian Women Since 1947,* edited by Bharati Ray and Aparna Basu. Delhi: Oxford University Press.

Mukhopadhyay, Maitreyee. 1998. *Legally Dispossessed: Gender, Identity, and the Process of Law.* Calcutta: Stree.

Mukhopadhyay, Swapna, ed. 1998. *In the Name of Justice: Women and Law in Society.* New Delhi: Manohar.

Murlidhar, S. 1999. "The Case of the Agra Protective Home." In *Engendering Law: Essays in Honour of Lotika Sarkar,* edited by Amita Dhanda and Archana Parasher. Lucknow: Eastern Book Company.

Nair, Janaki. 1996a. "Prohibited Marriage: State Protection and the Child Wife." In *Social Reform, Sexuality, and the State,* edited by Patricia Uberoi. New Delhi: Sage.

———. 1996b. "The *Devadasi,* Dharma, and the State." In *Feminist Terrains in Legal Domains: Interdisciplinary Essays on Women and Law in India,* edited by Ratna Kapur. New Delhi: Kali for Women.

Nair, Mira. 1986–87. "*India Cabaret:* Reflections and Reactions." *Discourse* 8 (fall-winter): 58–72.

Nandy, Ashis. 1994. *The Illegitimacy of Nationalism: Rabindranath Tagore and the Politics of Self.* Delhi: Oxford University Press.

———. 1998. "The Politics of Secularism and the Recovery of Religious Toleration." In *Secularism and Its Critics,* edited by Rajeev Bhargava. Delhi: Oxford University Press.

Narayan, Uma. 1997. "Towards a Feminist Vision of Citizenship: Rethinking the Implications of Dignity, Political Participation, and Nationality." In *Reconstructing Political Theory: Feminist Perspectives,* edited by Mary Lyndon Shanley and Uma Narayan. Cambridge: Polity Press.

Natarajan, Sarada. 1997. *Watering the Neighbour's Plant: Media Perspectives on Female Infanticide in Tamilnadu.* Monograph 6. Chennai: M. S. Swaminathan Research Foundation.

Navlakha, Gautam. 1996. "Women's Rights: Walking the Tightrope." *Economic and Political Weekly,* 24 February: 454–55.

Nead, Lynda. 1988. *Myths of Sexuality: Representations of Women in Victorian Fiction.* Oxford: Basil Blackwell.

Negi, Elizabeth Francina. 1997. *Death by "Social Causes."* Monograph 5. Chennai: M. S. Swaminathan Research Foundation.

Niranjana, Tejaswini, P. Sudhir, and Vivek Dhareshwar, eds. 1993. *Interrogating Modernity: Culture and Colonialism in India.* Calcutta: Seagull.

Nussbaum, Martha. 1995. *Poetic Justice: The Literary Imagination and Public Life.* Boston: Beacon Press.

O'Connell-Davidson, Julia. 1998. *Prostitution, Power, and Freedom.* Cambridge: Polity Press.

Okin, Susan Moller. 1979. *Women in Western Political Thought.* Princeton: Princeton University Press.

Oldenberg, Veena. 1992. "Lifestyle as Resistance: The Case of the Courtesans of Lucknow." In *Contesting Power: Resistance and Everyday Social Relations in South Asia,* edited by Douglas Haynes and Gyan Prakash. Delhi: Oxford University Press.

Omvedt, Gail. 1994. *Reinventing Revolution: New Social Movements and the Socialist Tradition in India.* New York: M. E. Sharpe.

O'Neill. Maggie. 2001. *Prostitution and Feminism: Towards a Politics of Feeling.* Cambridge: Polity Press.

Padmanabhan, Manjula. 1993. "Outlawing Sex-Determination No Solution." *Pioneer,* 22 September.

——. 1996. "The Stain." In Padmanabhan, *Hot Death, Cold Soup.* New Delhi: Kali for Women.

Pakrasi, Kanti B. 1970. *Female Infanticide in India.* Calcutta: Temple Press.

Palriwala, Rajni. 1989. "Reaffirming the Anti-dowry Struggle." *Economic and Political Weekly,* 29 April: 942–44.

Panigrahi, Lalita. 1972. *British Social Policy and Female Infanticide in India.* New Delhi: Munshiram Manoharlal.

Parasher, Archana. 1992. *Women and Family Law Reform in India: Uniform Civil Code and Gender Equality.* New Delhi: Sage.

Parker, Andrew, Mary Russo, Doris Sommer, and Patricia Yaeger, eds. 1992. *Nationalisms and Sexualities.* New York: Routledge.

Pateman, Carol. 1988. *The Sexual Contract.* Cambridge: Polity Press.

——. 1989. *The Disorder of Women: Democracy, Feminism, and Political Theory.* Cambridge: Polity Press.

Pathak, Zakia, and Rajeswari Sunder Rajan. 1989. " 'Shahbano.' " *Signs: Journal of Women in Culture and Society* 14, no. 3 (spring): 558–82.

People's Union for Democratic Rights (PUDR). 1995. *Black Law, White Lies.* New Delhi.

Pheterson, Gail, ed. 1989. *A Vindication of the Rights of Whores.* Seattle: Seal Press.

——. 1993. "The Whore Stigma: Female Dishonor and Male Unworthiness." *Social Text* 37 (Winter): 39–64.

Philipose, Pamela. 2000. "A Paddy Grain in the Mouth of an Infant." *Indian Express,* 4 October.

Phillips, Anne. 1991. *Engendering Democracy.* Cambridge: Polity Press.

——. 1993. *Democracy and Difference.* Cambridge: Polity Press.

Phoolan Devi, with Marie-Therese Cuny and Paul Rambali. 1996. *I, Phoolan Devi: The Autobiography of India's Bandit Queen.* London: Warner Books. (First published by Little, Brown and Company.)

Poovey, Mary. 1992. "The Abortion Question and the Death of Man." In *Feminists Theorize the Political,* edited by Judith Butler and Joan Scott. London: Routledge.

Prasad, Nandini. 1993. *A Pressing Matter: Women in Media.* Delhi: Friedrich Ebert Stiftung.

Pringle, Rosemary, and Sophie Watson. 1992. " 'Women's Interests' and the Post-Structuralist State." In *Destabilising Theory: Contemporary Debates,* edited by Michele Barrett and Anne Phillips. Cambridge: Polity Press.

Rai, Shirin M., and Geraldine Lievesley, eds. 1996. *Women and the State: International Perspectives.* London: Taylor and Francis.

Rajaraman, Indira. 1983. "Economics of Bride-Price and Dowry." *Economic and Political Weekly,* 8 February: 275–9.

Ram, Kalpana. 1991. *Mukkuvar Women: Gender, Hegemony, and Capitalist Transformation in a South Indian Fishing Village.* Sydney: Allen and Unwin.

——. 1996. "Rationalism, Cultural Nationalism, and the Reform of Body Politics: Minority Intellectuals in the Tamil Catholic Community." In *Social Reform, Sexuality, and the State,* edited by Patrica Uberoi. New Delhi: Sage.

Ramachandran, Sujata. 1999. "Of Boundaries and Border Crossings: Undocumented Bangladeshi 'Infiltrators' and the Hegemony of Hindu Nationalism in India." *Interventions* 1, no. 2: 235–53.

Raman, Vasanthi. 2000. "Politics of Childhood: Perspectives from the South." *Economic and Political Weekly*, 11 November: 4055–64.

Ramanathan, Usha. 1996. "Women, Law, and Institutionalisation: A Manifestation of State Power." *Indian Journal of Gender Studies* 3, no. 2 (July–December): 199–224.

——. 1998. "Only a Safety Valve." *The Hindu*, 22 November.

Ramaseshan, Geetha. 1994. "What About Their Rights?" *The Hindu*, 16 April.

Rao, Anupama. 1999. "Understanding Sirasgaon: Notes Towards Conceptualising the Role of Law, Caste, and Gender in a Case of 'Modernity.'" In *Signposts: Gender Issues in Post-Independence India*, edited by Rajeswari Sunder Rajan. New Delhi: Kali for Women.

Rao, Nagmani, and Sarita Pungaliya. 1994. "Human Concern or Convenience? Debate on Hysterectomies of Mentally Handicapped." *Economic and Political Weekly*, 12 March: 601–2.

Ravindran, R. P. 1993. "The Campaign Against Sex Determination Tests." In *The Struggle Against Violence*, edited by Chaya Datar. Calcutta: Stree.

Rawls, John. 1971. *Theory of Justice*. Cambridge: Harvard University Press.

Ray, Bharati, and Aparna Basu, eds. 1999. *From Independence Towards Freedom: Indian Women Since 1947*. Delhi: Oxford University Press.

Reiter, Rayna, ed. 1975. *Toward an Anthropology of Women*. New York: Monthly Review Press.

Richards, David. 2001. "Staging the Word: The Spectacle of the Text in African Literature." *Interventions* 3, no. 3: 405–18.

Rorty, Richard. 1989. *Contingency, Irony, and Solidarity*. Cambridge: Cambridge University Press.

Rubin, Gayle. 1975. "The Traffic in Women: Notes on the 'Political Economy' of Sex." In *Toward an Anthropology of Women*, edited by Rayna Reiter. New York: Monthly Review Press.

Rudolph, Susanne H. 2000. "Civil Society and the Realm of Freedom." *Economic and Political Weekly*, 13 May: 1762–69.

Rustagi, Preet. 2000. "Identifying Gender Backward Districts Using Selected Indicators." *Economic and Political Weekly*, 25 November: 4276–86.

Saheli. 1995. "Development for Whom: A Critique of Women's Development Programmes." (Report prepared by Saheli Women's Group.) New Delhi: Saheli Women's Resource Centre.

Sahgal, Priya, and Sarita Rani. 1993. "Brides for Sale." *Sunday*, 19–25 December: 36–42.

Sangari, Kumkum, and Sudesh Vaid, eds. 1989. *Recasting Women: Essays in Colonial History*. New Delhi: Kali for Women.

Sangari, Kumkum. 1995. "Politics of Diversity: Religious Communities and Multiple Patriarchies." *Economic and Political Weekly*, 23 December: 3287–310; 30 December: 3381–89.

Sanghvi, Vir. 1994. "More Than a Kiss." *Sunday*, 16–22 January: 8–9.

Sarita, Rani. 1993. "More Surprised than Sorry." *Sunday,* 9–15 December: 42.

Sarkar, Sumit. 1996. "Indian Nationalism and the Politics of Hindutva." In *Making India Hindu: Religion, Community, and the Politics of Democracy in India,* edited by David Ludden. Delhi: Oxford University Press.

Sarkar, Tanika. 1996. "Colonial Lawmaking and Lives/Deaths of Indian Women: Different Readings of Law and Community." In *Feminist Terrains in Legal Domains: Interdisciplinary Essays on Women and Law in India,* edited by Ratna Kapur. New Delhi: Kali for Women.

Sattar, Arshia. 1994. "The Blood of Others." *Times of India Sunday Review,* 20 February.

Saxena, Deshdeep. 1995. "Voices from Chambal." *Sunday,* 30 April–6 May: 76–77.

Saxena, Sadhna. 2000. "Looking at Literacy." *Seminar* 493 (September): 30–34.

Scheper-Hughes, Nancy. 1987. "Culture, Scarcity, and Maternal Thinking: Mother Love and Child Death in Northeast Brazil." In *Child-Survival: Anthropological Perspectives on the Treatment and Maltreatment of Children,* edited by Scheper-Hughes. Dordecht: D. Reidel Publishing Co.

——, ed. 1987. *Child-Survival: Anthropological Perspectives on the Treatment and Maltreatment of Children.* Dordecht: D. Reidel Publishing Co.

Schwarzenbach, Sibyl. 1990–1991. "Contractarians and Feminists Debate Prostitution." *Review of Law and Social Change* 18: 103–30.

Scott, Joan. 1996. *Only Paradoxes to Offer: French Feminists and the Rights of Man.* Cambridge: Harvard University Press.

——. 1997. "'La Querelle des Femmes' in the Late Twentieth Century." *New Left Review,* no. 226 (November–December): 3–19.

Sen, A. K. 1987. "Africa and India: What Do We Have to Learn from Each Other?" WIDER (World Institute for Development Economics Research) discussion paper no. 19.

Sen, Amartya. 1997. "On Interpreting India's Past." In *Nationalism, Democracy, and Development: State and Politics in India,* edited by Sugata Bose and Ayesha Jalal. Delhi: Oxford University Press.

——. 1999. *Development as Freedom.* Oxford: Oxford University Press.

Sen, Mala. 1993. *India's Bandit Queen: The True Story of Phoolan Devi.* (Revised, updated version). New Delhi: HarperCollins. (First published London: Harvill, 1991.)

Sengupta, Arnab Neil, and Kai Friese. 1995. "A Lobby of their Own." *India Today,* 15 February: 174–85.

Shah, A. M., B. S. Baviskar, and E. A. Ramaswamy, eds. 1996. *Social Structure and Change,* vol. 2. New Delhi: Sage.

Shanker, M. S. 1997. "Massarath, 14, Married Three Arabs Within Two Months." http://www.rediff.com/news/jul/02pros.htm.

Shanley, Mary Lyndon, and Uma Narayan, eds. 1997. *Reconstructing Political Theory: Feminist Perspectives.* Cambridge: Polity Press.

Sharma, Kalpana. 1995. "Britain's Magnificent Obssession." *The Hindu,* 16 July.

——. 1998. "Inadequate Laws." *The Hindu,* 22 November.

Sheriff, Shameem Akhtar. 1993a. "Few Takers for Curbs on Marriages." *Times of India,* 21 December.

——. 1993b. "Ameena's Mother Spews Venom." *Times of India,* 23 December.

Singh, Gurmukh. 1996. "Women Need Equal Opportunities, Not Reservations." *Times of India,* 25 October.

Singh, Shankar, and Nikhil Dey. 1994. "Child Marriage, Government, and NGOs." *Economic and Political Weekly,* 28 May: 1377–379.

Singh, Tavleen. 1994. "Muslims Need to Stop Resurrecting the Past." *Indian Express,* 6 February.

Singha, Radhika. 1993. " 'Providential' Circumstances: The Thuggee Campaign of the 1830s and Legal Innovation." *Modern Asian Studies* 27, no. 1: 83–146.

——. 1998. *A Despotism of Law: Crime and Justice in Early Colonial India.* Delhi: Oxford University Press.

Sleightholme, Carolyn, and Indrani Sinha. 1996. *Guilty Without Trial: Women in the Sex Trade in Calcutta.* Calcutta: Stree.

Smart, Carol. 1989. *Feminism and the Power of Law.* New York: Routledge.

Song, Hoon. Unpublished paper. " 'We Kill Pigeons, Not Babies': The 'Ambivalent' Biopolitics of Whiteness."

Spelman, Elizabeth V. 1997. "The Heady Political Life of Compassion." In *Reconstructing Political Theory: Feminist Perspectives,* edited by Mary Lyndon Shanley and Uma Narayan. Cambridge: Polity Press.

Spivak, Gayatri Chakravorty. 1987. *In Other Worlds: Essays in Cultural Politics.* London: Methuen.

——. 1990. "The Making of Americans, the Teaching of English, and the Future of Culture Studies." *New Literary History* 21, no. 4 (autumn): 781–98.

——. 1999a. Letter to the editor. *The New Republic,* 19 April: 43.

——. 1999b. *A Critique of Postcolonial Reason: Toward a History of the Vanishing Present.* Cambridge: Harvard University Press.

Squires, Judith. 1999. *Gender in Political Theory.* Cambridge: Polity Press.

Sridhar, G. R. 1994. "A Beginning Must Be Made." *The Hindu,* 20 March.

Srinivas, M. N. 1984. *Some Reflections on Dowry.* Delhi: Oxford University Press.

Srinivasan, Amrit. 1985. "Reform and Revival: The Devadasi and Her Dance." *Economic and Political Weekly,* 2 November: 1869–76.

Srinivasan, K. 1997. "Sex Ratios in India: What They Hide and What They Reveal." In *India's Demographic Transition: A Reassessment,* edited by S. Irudaya Rajan. New Delhi: MD Publications.

Stevens, Jacqueline. 1997. "On the Marriage Question." In *Women Transforming Politics: An Alternative Reader,* edited by Cathy J. Cohen, Kathleen B. Jones, and Joan C. Tronto. New York: New York University Press.

Subramanian, S., and Barbara Harriss-White, eds. 1999. *Illfare in India: Essays on India's Special Sector in Honour of S. Guhan.* New Delhi: Sage.

Sudha, S., and S. Irudaya Rajan. 1998. *Intensifying Masculinity of Sex Ratios in India: New Evidence, 1981–99.* Working Paper no. 288. Thiruvanthapuram: Centre for Development Studies.

Sunder Rajan, Rajeswari, Rashmi Bhatnagar, Nalini Natarajan, and Nira Mira Gupta. 1986. "Women Teachers and the DUTA Strike." *Manushi: A Journal about Women and Society* 6, no. 4: 27–33.

Sunder Rajan, Rajeswari. 1993. *Real and Imagined Women: Gender, Culture, and Postcolonialism.* London: Routledge.

———. 1998. Review essay. *Contributions to Indian Sociology* 32, no. 1: 123–28.

———, ed. 1999. *Signposts: Gender Issues in Post-Independence India.* New Delhi: Kali for Women.

Suresh, V., and D. Nagasila. 1995. "In Public Interest." *Seminar* 430 (June): 37–41.

Swarup, Sunanda. 1999. "Ameena." http://www.indiaworld.co.in/open/rec/poetry/march8–99women1.html.

Taylor, Charles. 1990. "Modes of Civil Society." *Public Culture* 3, no. 1: 102–19.

Thakur, Punam. 1995. "Bandit Screen." *Sunday,* 26 March–1 April: 68–76.

Thampu, Valsan. 1998. "Christians Unite Under Attack." *The Pioneer,* 5 December.

Tharamangalam, Joseph. 1995. "Indian Social Scientists and Critique of Secularism." *Economic and Political Weekly,* 4 March: 457–61.

Tharu, Susie, and Tejaswini Niranjana. 1999. "Problems for a Contemporary Theory of Gender." In *Gender and Politics in India,* edited by Nivedita Menon. New Delhi: Oxford University Press. Reprinted from *Subaltern Studies* 9, ed. Shahid Amin and Dipesh Chakrabarty. Delhi: Oxford University Press, 1998.

Tharu, Susie. 1995. "Slow Pan Left: Feminism and the Problematic of 'Rights.'" In *Indian Women: Myth and Reality,* edited by Jashodara Bagchi. Hyderabad: Sangam Books.

Tooley, Michael. 1983. *Abortion and Infanticide.* Oxford: Clarendon Press.

UNESCO. 1986. Report on the International Meeting of Experts on the Social and Cultural Causes of Prostitution and Strategies for the Struggle Against the Procuring and the Sexual Exploitation of Women.

Vaasanthi. 1995. "Salem: The Killing Goes On." *India Today,* 30 September: 83.

Vanaik, Achin. 1997. *Communalism Contested: Religion, Modernity, and Secularization.* New Delhi: Vistaar.

———. 1998. "The BJP's Manifesto." *The Hindu,* 2 March.

Vanderwood, Paul J. 1987. "Nineteenth-Century Mexico's Profiteering Bandits." In *Bandidos: The Varieties of Latin American Banditry,* edited by Richard W. Slatta. New York: Greenwood Press.

Vanita, Ruth. 1999. "Thinking Beyond Gender in India." In *Gender and Politics in India,* edited by Nivedita Menon. New Delhi: Oxford University Press.

Venkatachalam, R., and Viji Srinivasan. 1993. *Female Infanticide.* New Delhi: Har-Anand Publications.

Venkataramani, S. H. 1986. "Born to Die." *India Today,* 15 June: 26–33.

Visaria, Leela. 1994. "Deficit of Women, Son Preference and Demographic Transition in India." Paper presented at the Symposium on Issues Related to Sex Preferences for Children in the Rapidly Changing Demographic Dynamics in Asia, Seoul. November.

Viswanath, L. S. 1996. "Female Infanticide and the Position of Women in India." In *Social Structure and Change,* vol. 2, edited by A. M. Shah, B. S. Baviskar, and E. A. Ramaswamy. New Delhi: Sage.

———. 1998. "Efforts of Colonial State to Suppress Female Infanticide: Use of

Sacred Texts, Generation of Knowledge." *Economic and Political Weekly*, 9 May: 1104–12.

Walker, Dave, and Richard S. Ehrlich, eds. 1992. *"Hello My Big Honey!": Love Letters to Bangkok Bar Girls and Their Revealing Interviews.* Bangkok: Dragon Dance.

Walkowitz, Judith. 1980. *Prostitution and Victorian Society: Women, Class, and the State.* New York: Cambridge University Press.

Warren, Mary Anne. 1997. *Moral Status: Obligations to Persons and Other Living Things.* Oxford: Clarendon Press.

——. 2000. "The Moral Difference Between Infanticide and Abortion: A Response to Robert Card." *Bioethics* 14, no. 4: 352–59.

Weiner, Myron. 1991. *The Child and the State in India.* Princeton: Princeton University Press.

Whitehead, Judy. 1996. "Modernising the Motherhood Archetype: Public Health Models and the Child Marriage Restraint Act of 1929." In *Social Reform, Sexuality, and the State,* edited by Patricia Uberoi. New Delhi: Sage.

Wicke, Jennifer. 1988. "Koko's Necklace: The Wild Child as Subject." *Critical Quarterly* 30, no. 1 (spring): 113–27.

Williams, Patricia. 1991. *The Alchemy of Race and Rights.* Cambridge: Harvard University Press.

Williams, Raymond. 1983. *Towards 2000.* London: Chatto and Windus.

Wolf, Susan. "Comment." In *Multiculturalism: Examining the Politics of Recognition,* edited by Amy Gutmann. Princeton: Princeton University Press.

Working Group on Women's Rights. 1996. "Reversing the Option: Civil Codes and Personal Laws." *Economic and Political Weekly,* 18 May: 1180–83.

Yuval-Davis, Nira, and Prina Werbner, eds. 1999. *Women, Citizenship, and Difference.* London: Zed Books.

Yuval-Davis, Nira. 1997. *Gender and Nation.* London: Sage.

Zutshi, Somnath. 1993. "Women, Nation, and the Outsider in Contemporary Hindi Cinema." In *Interrogating Modernity: Culture and Colonialism in India,* edited by Tejaswini Niranjana, P. Sudhir, and Vivek Dhareshwar. Calcutta: Seagull.

Index

Bandit Queen: myth of, 213–14, 225–26, 228, 274 n.3

Bandit Queen, 213, 214, 225

Banditry. *See* Dacoits/dacoity

Banerjee, Nirmala: on women's work, 27

Bardhan, Pranab: on communities and the state, 234; on state-versus-community debate, 154–55

Barry, Kathleen: on prostitution, 128, 133, 137, 145, 257 n.6

Baxi, Upendra: on amnesty, 277–78 n.32; on development and crime, 221; on female criminality, 276 n.22; on Indian state, 277 nn.30 and 31; on Kamla, 262 n.40; on law in India, 238 n.9; on Phoolan Devi, 231; on public-interest litigation, 109–10; on state's use of force, 277 n.30

Beauvoir, Simone de; on women's rights, 18

Bedi, Kiran, 228

Behmai massacre, 230. *See also* Devi, Phoolan

Beijing Conference. *See* United Nations Conference on Women (Beijing)

Bell, Shannon: on prostitution, 128–29, 139

Besant, Annie: on Contagious Diseases Act, 120. *See also* Law(s)

Bhabha, Homi: on infanticide, 189; on nation and people, 30

Bharatiya Janata Party (BJP), xi, 148, 263 n.2

Bhatt, Ela: on women in the unorganized sector, 237 n.3, 241 n.26. *See also* Self-Employed Women's Association; Shram Shakti report

Bhave, Vinoba, 222–23, 274 n.5, 275 n.16

Bhopal gas tragedy, 111, 256 n.51

Bilgrami, Akeel: on secularism, 155

Brown, Wendy: on modalities of state power, 9–10

Brownmiller, Susan: on prostitution, 135

Buch, Nirmala: on women's work, 27

Bumiller, Elisabeth: on female infanticide, 269 n.16, 272 n.41

Bureaucracy, xi, 5, 73, 219

Butler, Josephine: opposition to Contagious Diseases Bill, 128. *See also* Law(s)

Butler, Judith: on cross-dressing, 233; and feminist theory, 8, 30

Capitalism, 6, 9, 10, 20, 136, 138, 141, 145, 146, 153, 218, 253 n.24, 261 n.37; capitalist production, 138–39

Centre for Feminist Legal Research (CFLR), 125–26, 131, 259 n.23

Chancer, Lynn Sharon: on prostitution, 146

Chandhoke, Neera: on civil society, 265 n.21

Chatterjee, Partha: on civil society in India, 265 n.20; on communitarianism, 159; on governmentality, 155; on nationalism, 238 n.7; on the nation-state, 30, 160

Chaturvedi, Rajendra, 222, 227–28

Chaudhuri, Maitrayee: on media and feminism, 245 n.13

Chibber, Pradeep: on "democracy without association" in India, 265 n.21

Child Marriage Restraint Act (CMRA), 44, 45, 46, 49, 59, 60, 62, 63–66

Chunkath, S. R.: on female infanticide in Tamilnadu, 179–81, 201–2, 208. *See also* Athreya, Venkatesh

Cinema. *See* Film

Citizen(s), 25, 41, 45, 123, 136, 147, 167; agency of, 170; Ameena as, 55; Phoolan Devi as, 228, 231–32, 234; production of, xi, 6; prostitutes as, 123, 126; as victims, 74–81, 113

Citizenship, 17–23, 24, 37, 42, 147, 224;

Development (Third World) (*cont.*) ticide and, 184–85, 191, 192, 195; NGOs and, 31, 34; women and, 27–28, 35, 170, 240 n.24, 240–41 n.25, 266 n.24

Devi, Bhanwari, 34, 67, 242–43 n.37

Devi, Mahasweta: "Douloti the Bountiful," 19, 20, 262 n.42

Devi, Phoolan, 6, 37; as dacoit, 222, 224, 227; life of, 213–14; murder of, 234–35; Indian feminism's relationship to, 215–17, 225–26, 228; surrender of, 221, 224, 227, 228–29, 231–33

Dey, Nikhil: on child marriage, 68. *See also* Singh, Shankar

Dhagamwar, Vasudha: on Child Marriage Restraint Act, 65–66, 67. *See also* Law(s); Marriage

Dhanda, Amita: on rights of the mentally disabled, 93–94, 110, 254 n.32

Dhanda, Meena: on identity of "women," 13–14

Dhareshwar, Vivek: on secularism, 53–54

Difference(s), 4, 15, 16, 34, 80, 97, 159, 161, 167, 171; cultural, 223

Disabilities, 75, 81, 251 n.12; Persons with Disabilities (Equal Opportunities, Protection of Rights, and Full Participation) Act, 253 nn.29 and 30

Discipline, 6, 89, 90

Dow, Unity: on children's rights, 66–67

Dowry, 29, 32, 37, 66, 67, 68, 100, 192, 196, 197, 203–6, 208, 219, 271 nn.33 and 35, 272 n.37

Dreze, Jean: on incentive schemes, 197; on sex ratios, 267 n.2, 268 n.7; on women and development, 241 n.25, 266 n.24. *See also* Sen, Amartya

Durga (goddess), 225, 232

Education, 19, 29, 34, 52, 58, 63, 66, 67, 78, 80, 93, 104, 110, 126, 160, 183, 219

Elections, 5, 17, 19, 214, 274 n.6

Emergency, 24, 26, 31, 77, 109, 215, 231

Engels, Friedrich: on marriage, 260–61 n.33

Enlightenment, 154, 156

Equality, x, xi, 4, 5, 14, 16, 17, 18, 21, 25, 80, 107, 159, 166, 171, 215, 242 n.35

Family, 2, 10, 27, 36, 47, 52, 56–57, 58, 59, 60, 61, 64, 65, 69, 72, 74, 83, 88–89, 90, 91, 94, 96, 97–106, 118, 148, 162, 163, 165–66, 168, 171, 182, 184–85, 186, 187, 188–89, 196, 197, 200, 204, 205, 210, 215, 234; planning, 26, 34, 64, 189. *See also* Community; Marriage

Female infanticide, 7, 37, 100, 103, 177–211, 213, 268 n.9. *See also* Femicide; Feticide

Female Infanticide Act, 199

Femicide, 203, 204, 210. *See also* Female infanticide; Feticide

Feminism, ix, x, xi; and child marriage, 65–68; critique of citizenship, 17–23; critique of family, 99–102, 106; critique of institutions, 87–91; and dowry, 207; and female infanticide, 185–90; Indian, 30–36, 241 n.28 (*see also* Women's movement [in India]); and "other women," 106–9, 112–13; and Phoolan Devi, 214–17; and prostitution question, 117–19, 120, 124–27, 127–46; radical and liberal, 123–24, 257 n.10; and sexuality, 258–59 n.18; and state, 8–12, 259 n.18; and UCC, 150, 156–62, 173; and "women," 12–16, 17–18, 167. *See also* Prostitution; Uniform Civil Code (UCC)

Feticide, 178, 183, 185, 186–87, 189, 202, 205

Film, 102–6, 129, 130, 143, 144, 212, 213, 214, 225, 255 n.43

State (*cont.*)
Citizenship; Government; Law(s);
Nation; Police
Sterilization, 73, 77, 81, 82, 84, 90, 92,
93, 94, 95, 96, 107, 196, 213, 254
n.37. *See also* Hysterectomy
Stevens, Jacqueline: on the state, 2, 10
St. James, Margo: on sex work, 120,
127, 128, 135, 137
Subalternity, 234. *See also* Spivak,
Gayatri
Subject(s), 37, 53, 58, 59, 63, 70, 71, 83,
117, 145, 164, 173, 205, 216, 224,
232; national, 147, 169; subject-
positions, 49, 50, 58
Subjecthood, 97, 162
Subjectification, 50, 51, 75, 87, 90, 91
Subjectivities, 22, 25, 29–30, 36, 61, 64,
82, 94, 130, 145, 208
Sunder Rajan, Rajeswari: on Indira
Gandhi, 216; *Real and Imagined
Women,* xii, 14; on Shahbano, 164 (*see
also* Pathak, Zakia)
Supreme Court, 25, 55, 110, 229, 230.
See also Courts

Television, 43, 128, 201, 215, 247 n.31,
255 n.43. *See also* Media
Terrorism, 220–21, 233; Prevention of
Terrorism Act (POTA), 253 n.27; Ter-
rorist and Disruptive Activities Pre-
vention Act (TADA), 253 n.27
Tharu, Susie: on "new visibility of
women," 265 n.22. *See also* Niranjana,
Tejaswini
Theater, 29, 63, 192, 201, 202, 262 n.40.
See also Performance/performativity
Thuggee, 219–20, 274 n.8, 275 n.9. *See
also* Dacoits/dacoity
Tilak, Bal Gangadhar: opposition to
the Age of Consent Bill, 62
Tradition, 7, 12, 25, 65, 82, 108, 157,
160, 182, 199, 205, 218–19
Transactions, nature of, x, 4, 24, 29

Travancore Christian Succession Act,
25
Tuker, Francis: on Henry Sleeman, 219

Umbartha, 106, 255 n.41. *See also* Patel,
Jabbar
Uniform Civil Code (UCC), ix, 16, 37,
46, 147–73, 263 n.6; positions on,
148–51, 156–62
United Nations (UN), 3, 79, 80, 121, 124
United Nations Children's Fund
(UNICEF), 66
United Nations Conference on Women
(Beijing), 111, 241 n.27, 249 n.42,
252 n.22
United Nations Convention for the
Suppression of the Traffic in Persons
and the Exploitation of the Prostitu-
tion of Others (1949), 122
United Nations Convention on the
Rights of the Child, 248 n.40

Vanita, Ruth: on obscenity laws, 242
n.34 (*see also* Kishwar, Madhu); on
women's movement in India, 258–59
n.18
Veerappan (sandalwood smuggler),
219, 275 n.11, 276–77 n.25, 277 n.29
Venkataramani, S. H.: on female infanticide, 189–90, 192, 270 n.23
Victim(s), 74, 79–81, 94, 110, 112, 113,
117, 125, 127–32, 144, 145, 216, 230;
victimhood, 80; victimization, 9, 79,
100, 132
Vidyasagar, Ishwar Chandra: on abolition of child marriage, 62
Violence, x, xii, 9, 11, 25, 26, 29, 32, 34,
79, 89, 99, 113, 120, 125, 132, 133,
135, 137, 164, 165, 179, 183, 195,
207, 220; civil, 231; communal, 154;
domestic, 158; female infanticide
and, 185–90; patriarchy and, 185,
193; sexual, 261 n.38; against
women, 183, 185–88

Rajeswari Sunder Rajan is Reader in English and Fellow
of Wolfson College, University of Oxford. She is the
author of *Real and Imagined Women: Gender, Culture, and
Postcolonialism* and the editor of *Signposts: Gender Issues in
Post-Independence India.*

Library of Congress Cataloging-in-Publication Data
Sunder Rajan, Rajeswari.
The scandal of the state : women, law, citizenship in
postcolonial India / Rajeswari Sunder Rajan.
p. cm. — (Next wave)
Includes bibliographical references and index.
ISBN 0-8223-3035-0 (cloth : alk. paper)
ISBN 0-8223-3048-2 (pbk. : alk. paper)
1. Women—Legal status, laws, etc.—India. 2. Women—
Government policy—India. 3. Women's rights—India.
4. Citizenship—India. I. Title. II. Series.
KNS516.R35 2003   305.42′0954—dc21   2002013284